D1527585

ENTREPRENEURIAL STATES

A VOLUME IN THE SERIES

CORNELL STUDIES IN POLITICAL ECONOMY

edited by Peter J. Katzenstein

A list of titles in this series is available at www.cornellpress.cornell.edu

Entrepreneurial

States REFORMING CORPORATE

GOVERNANCE IN FRANCE, JAPAN, AND KOREA

Yves Tiberghien

Cornell University Press ITHACA AND LONDON

First published 2007 by Cornell University Press

Printed in the United States of America

Library of Congress Cataloging-in-Publication Data

Tiberghien, Yves.
    Entrepreneurial states : reforming corporate governance in France, Japan, and Korea /
Yves Tiberghien.
        p. cm.—(Cornell studies in political economy)
    Includes bibliographical references and index.
    ISBN 978-0-8014-4593-4 (cloth : alk. paper)
    1. Corporate reorganizations—Political aspects—France.   2. Corporate reorganiza-
tions—Political aspects—Japan.   3. Corporate reorganizations—Political aspects—Korea
(South)   4. Corporate governance—Political aspects—France.   5. Corporate governance—
Political aspects—Japan.   6. Corporate governance—Political aspects—Korea (South)
7. Capital movements—Government policy—France.   8. Capital movements—Government
policy—Japan.   9. Capital movements—Government policy—Korea (South)   I. Title.
II. Series.
    HD2856.T53 2007
    338.6—dc22
2007011004

Cornell University Press strives to use environmentally responsible
suppliers and materials to the fullest extent possible in the publishing
of its books. Such materials include vegetable-based, low-VOC
inks and acid-free papers that are recycled, totally chlorine-free, or
partly composed of nonwood fibers. For further information, visit
our website at www.cornellpress.cornell.edu.

Cloth printing   10 9 8 7 6 5 4 3 2 1

For Daniel Okimoto

Contents

Tables and Figures

Tables

Figures

Preface and Acknowledgments

When do governments choose to pursue reforms that promise uncertain and long-term benefits, yet assure short-term costs? When do they get away with them? How do political leaders evaluate their chances of getting away with them? These questions lie at the core of the corporate restructuring dilemma, particularly in the stakeholder economies of Asia and Europe.

In a narrow sense, corporate restructuring refers to steps taken by firms to improve their profitability. These steps include layoffs, factory closures, disinvestment from less profitable units, mergers and acquisitions, and the introduction of new management methods. Since competition is the essence of capitalist economies, firms are constantly reassessing their asset and liability structures and making such adjustments. When many firms make similar adjustments at the same time, they aggregate into a visible economic phenomenon, be it at the national or global level. The 1970s and early 1980s saw a wave of such adjustments sweeping across most developed countries.

In the 1990s, however, corporate restructuring came to represent a deeper process of change. In a broad sense, corporate restructuring is a fundamental transition in the internal organization of firms and in the relations between firms and other social and economic actors. When fully carried out by many firms and encouraged by national policy, it aggregates into a structural transformation of the social and economic institutions of the post–World War II system. It largely amounts to a transformation of the corporate governance structure.

Corporate restructuring is a highly political process (see Gourevitch and Shinn 2005). At one stroke, it affects power relations within the firm, the social and political pact embedded in the postwar system, and ultimately the competitiveness of nations. Governments have the power to slow or accelerate the process and to shape its direction through myriad policy instruments. Conversely, political leaders are held responsible for layoffs and social dislocation, and also for any national competitiveness or welfare loss incurred through a slowing of the process. Measures taken by governments to facilitate corporate restructuring, both the removal of obstacles and the adoption of new inducements, are the focus of this book.

Since the early 1990s, a transformation in the global financial environment has made the corporate restructuring dilemma more salient. Financial deregulation in all developed economies and technological change have led to the rise of global equity and bond markets. For large competitive firms, these markets offer a cheaper source of capital than do traditional domestic banks. For governments, tapping into these global equity markets, in addition to attracting the more traditional foreign direct investments (FDI), brings the promise of cheaper capital, higher firm competitiveness, and greater national welfare.

In this book, I introduce a novel interpretation of global capital flows, namely, the concept of a *golden bargain*. De facto, global investors offer domestic politicians a deal whereby abundant and cheap capital flows come in exchange for corporate reforms that guarantee the rights of minority shareholders and a high return on investment through the facilitation of corporate restructuring. This bargain may also be seen as a Faustian pact or devil's bargain, given the far-reaching social and political consequences involved. The concept here represents merely an empirical set of incentives, not a positive outcome.

Global equity flows are a conditional displacement. While policy actors cannot ignore the new global forces, a range of policy options is available to them. They can take the full menu of recipes offered by global investors (and formalized by the Organisation for Economic Co-Operation and Development, OECD), refuse most of it, or pick only parts of the menu and add new ones. This book underscores the variety of choices in the face of this new challenge and the differentiation of pathways within hitherto stable clusters.

I focus on the differences among three countries, France, Japan, and South Korea, long seen as relatively similar in their political economic structures—bank-centered stakeholder systems with significant state involvement and some degree of labor stability (Katzenstein 1985; Krasner 1977; Wade 1990; World Bank 1993; Zysman 1983). It concentrates on the following puzzles:

- What explains the variation in national responses to the golden bargain, even among relatively similar economies?

- Why is France willing to implement some deep changes in its postwar structure without changing its discourse, whereas Japan is willing to change its discourse without deeply affecting its actual structure?
- And why can Korea amplify the external signals and sweep aside both its longstanding discourse and structure?

In response, I argue that the variation in degrees of political autonomy available to political entrepreneurs within national institutions and party systems explains the variation in reform outcomes. The variation in opportunities for effective bureaucratic delegation within national institutions also plays a role. French political entrepreneurs in key positions such as prime minister or finance minister have been able to rely on the high degree of executive control over the legislative agenda granted in the constitution, high degrees of autonomy within political parties and coalitions, and a high capacity for bureaucratic delegation. By contrast, Japanese political entrepreneurs in similar power situations have faced high institutional and party constraints, especially due to the internal rules and power plays of the Liberal Democratic Party (LDP). Only some limited windows of opportunity for reform have appeared, owing to short-term party alignments and creative institution-building. As for Korea, political entrepreneurs have been able to ride on the nearly limitless political autonomy of the president's early term years and on malleable institutions and parties.

Thus the variation among these countries does not primarily originate in differences in interest group coalitions or voter preferences, or even in the variety of economic shocks that affected them during the 1990s and early 2000s. Rather, the ability of political entrepreneurs to tip the political balance toward one coalition over another determines the type of national responses to the golden bargain. When a global shift divides interest group coalitions and when governments face complex cross-pressures, opportunities exist for political entrepreneurs to craft new bargains. In situations where opposite coalitions are finely balanced, the outcome depends on how leaders tip the stalemate one way or the other. Political entrepreneurs thrive on the fertile ground of uncertainty and interest group fragmentation. Such individuals grasp the existence of arbitrage opportunities between a suboptimal present and a potential future. Their main contribution consists of devising a politically feasible pathway toward institutional change. They balance inducements with coercion. They enlarge an existing coalition through manipulation of the political agenda and craft political compromises that link unrelated issues.

The degree of strategic political autonomy available to such entrepreneurs within the party system and the degree of bureaucratic delegation available to political leaders determine their ability to succeed. National systems, therefore, conserve a high degree of choice in their chosen path of adaptation to global inducements. The mediation of global signals is political and entrepreneurial. The transformation of national social contracts ultimately depends on the individual gambles of political entrepreneurs and on the wiggle room provided to them by party and government institutions.

Corporate reforms are a case of modernization from above. In the face of the usual stalemate between opponents and proponents of reforms, state leaders act as crucial catalysts. In addition, while elite bureaucrats tend to be on the side of reform and want to play a major role in the process, the central actors are political leaders: heads of governments, party leaders, and finance ministers. This book is, therefore, consistent with the varieties of capitalism (VOC) approach in so far as it emphasizes continued national diversity (Hall and Soskice 2001, 49). But unlike the VOC approach it argues that political and state institutions play a large and active role in crafting this renewed diversity. In addition, small strategic decisions taken by political actors may aggregate into significant irreversible change in key institutions, independent of linkages with other institutional components. Hybridization is occurring as a result of these political actions.

The bulk of the data in this book consists of over 170 interviews with politicians, bureaucrats, labor officials, business managers, and economic analysts; archival documents (government documents, position papers, and analyses by economic and social actors); and secondary quantitative data collected in fieldwork in all three countries between 1999 and 2002. Most written sources used in this study are primary sources in the local language, except for Korea, where the sources are in English.

The remainder of the book is organized in five chapters. Chapter 2 provides systematic comparative data on the three countries. It runs through each step of the argument and offers compelling aggregate evidence linking the variation of outcomes to the variations in degrees of political autonomy.

Chapters 3 to 5 present analytical narratives of the reform processes in France, Japan, and Korea, respectively. Through careful inductive process tracing, the chapters expose the causal mechanisms present in each country. Each chapter analyzes the capital flow constraint, the degree of strategic political autonomy, and the politics of key restructuring reforms. Chapter 3 argues that France represents the purest case of a highly strategic political economy and rapid, albeit invisible, reforms. It also underlines the political bargains made by Prime Minister Jospin and Finance Minister Strauss-Kahn and the long-term implications of the reform process.

In contrast, chapter 4 turns to the slower and more limited reform outcomes in Japan and links them to the restricted autonomy of political leaders under most circumstances. The chapter explores the role of political entrepreneurs, such as Hashimoto Ryūtarō, Yosano Kaoru, Obuchi Keizō, and Koizumi Junichirō, and the limited windows during which reforms have proceeded. It identifies one institutional innovation in Japan: the Industrial Competitiveness Council. This council, chaired by Prime Minister Obuchi, operated between March 1999 and January 2001. It became the political tool through which political reformers initiated a number of corporate reforms and overcame their institutional obstacles.

Chapter 5 focuses on reforms in Korea since 1997, and contrasts the drastic change of that period with the mostly failed attempts of the 1993–97 period. This contrast reveals the determining role played by President Kim Dae-Jung under conditions of high political autonomy after December 1997. The Korean experience with the so-called Big Deal also shows how structural reforms can take an unexpected and deviant path as a consequence of strong executive control over the legislative agenda.

Chapter 6 brings the argument to the firm level. It offers a political interpretation of recent variations in the restructuring of the automobile industry. The chapter analyzes the impact of political entrepreneurs and of their degree of autonomy on this process. It contrasts the role of the French state in bringing about the transformation of Renault with that of the Korean state in precipitating the reorganization of their automobile industry (Daewoo Motors), as well as with the politics of Nissan's path-breaking restructuring in Japan. The final chapter looks at how the conclusions I have reached can potentially be applied to Germany, the EU, China, and other countries. The chapter also analyzes the long-term costs and implications of "invisible" reforms from above in corporate restructuring.

This is a book about corporate restructuring, structural reforms, and financial globalization. At a deeper level, it is a book about the degrees of control that people have over the large forces that shape the rules and trends of the global economy. It is a book about prosperity, justice, and democracy. The movement toward or away from these higher goals is often distilled through micro-level rules and institutions. But the sum total of these micro-level changes defines where society and humanity are going.

In this quest to understand the roots of government actions in response to financial globalization, I have been blessed with the help and support of many individuals. In the first instance, I thank Daniel Okimoto, who inspired this research program and opened many doors along the way. Through his amazing life, scholarship, and teaching, Dan offered me a role model to follow. Dan's generosity with his time and care are rare treasures for his students. One such memorable moment was a long discussion with Dan in Kyoto's Maruyama Park, a discussion that was no doubt inspired by delicious sushi, pickled vegetables, and miso-spinach. I dedicate this book to him, in admiration for his extraordinary humanity.

Jean Oi provided me with tremendous insights in comparative Asian political economy and with unwavering help at every step along the way. Her energy and enthusiasm were perpetual sources of inspiration. Jean's research on "local state corporatism" provided me with important insights on the interactions between market and state. My research with Jean on the reform of state-owned enterprises (SOEs) in China was influential in pointing me toward corporate structural reforms. Judith Goldstein's research on the democratic implications of World Trade Organization agreements has also been a powerful source of inspiration for this book. Judy's spirited feedback has been invaluable in this work. Stephen Krasner shaped the construction of this book through long discussions on the rigor of comparative research. He steered me through the vast literature on global capital flows, a literature that has been growing at exponential speed. He repeatedly pointed out the unexamined assumptions of many studies on globalization and gave me a good dose of healthy skepticism.

Andrew Walder's comments at a critical time and his ability to restate my words were a great source of improvement. Dave Abernethy was a wonderful teacher of comparative politics and a mentor throughout my years at Stanford. His teaching and his high personal standards are permanent sources of inspiration for me. Condoleezza Rice took hours of her busy schedule as provost to repeatedly explore with me the interactions between globalization and domestic politics and inspired me to do comparative research on these issues. She pointed out that structural reforms of European states in the 1990s amounted to the undoing of postwar institutions. Chip Blacker's focus on the integration of theory and policy at the highest level has been a great source of stimulation. I was fascinated by our discussions on the growing relevance of globalization in public policy. Philippe Schmitter was a valuable source of insights on European politics and the comparative method throughout my years at Stanford. This book also owes a lot to the lengthy exchanges and comradeship with my fellow explorers of Japanese political economy at Stanford: Jennifer Amyx, Takenaka Harukata, Maria Toyoda, and Toya Tetsuro. Jennifer and I have discussed issues related to this book during dozens of meetings over the years. Her support and mentorship have carried me further than I could have gone on my own.

Through countless exchanges at various conferences and panels, Peter Gourevitch has played a tremendous role in the genesis of this book. As we argued about the role of the state and whether the French nation or the French state came first, or about the origins of Belon oysters, I was able to hone the argument in novel ways. Peter's work with James Shinn on the politics of corporate governance has been a great source of intellectual stimulation and inspiration. Peter's feedback on various drafts and presentations led me to several epiphanies.

Several scholars generously gave their time in reading early drafts of this manuscript and in providing wonderful thoughts and advice. Jerry Cohen helped me improve the structure of the book with his thorough comments on the interactions between capital flows and domestic politics. Ronald Dore gave me full comments as well and provided a source of inspiration throughout the work. Kim Byung-Kook spent hours discussing the draft and his advice, notably on the Korean case, was pathbreaking. Frank Langdon read the full manuscript and provided me with an insightful and prescient multi-page review. Greg Noble read several drafts and gave me incredibly pointed, useful, and caring advice. Christian Sautter's long letter and countless follow-up discussions were critical in improving the French chapter. Steven Vogel's full review of the early draft was particularly detailed and helpful. I also thank Kent Calder, John Campbell, Helen Callaghan, Phil Cerny, Jennifer Chan, Jerry Cohen, Ronald Dore, Martin Hoepner, Nicolas Jabko, Sara Konoe, Frank Langdon, Peter Lorentzen, Robert Madsen, Mark Manger, Egon Matzner, Angel O'Mahony, Mo Jongryn, Hugh Patrick, T. J. Pempel, Ulrike Schaede, James Shinn, Leonard Schoppa, Yu Uchiyama, Nicolas Véron, and Mark Zacher for invaluable comments on early drafts.

During my time at the Harvard Academy for International and Area Studies, Jorge Dominguez and James Clem organized an author's conference. The comments and insights received through a day of intense exchanges have allowed me to push this book to a new level. I am particularly grateful for ideas and feedback from the discussants of the conference: Suzanne Berger, Frank Dobbin, Peter Hall, and Richard Samuels. Peter Hall additionally graciously took much time to discuss my book and help me explore interactions with his pathbreaking work on the varieties of capitalism. He provided much inspiration during my time at Harvard. I also received invaluable comments from Rawi Abdelal, Daniel Aldrich, Kentaro Fukumoto, Nahomi Ichino, Stanislav Markus, Andrew Martin, Kyoko Sato, and Sherrill Stroschein. Intense discussions with Jorge Dominguez at the Harvard Academy also played a great role in the final development of this book. David Soskice kindly shared an entire flight between Paris and Seoul to explore applications of the VOC ideal types to the troublesome cases of France, Korea, and even Japan. These long discussions above the empty frozen land of Siberia, accompanied by good wine and unmatchable British humor, left me a much wiser man.

This book also owes a lot to Peter Katzenstein's and Roger Haydon's dedication and utmost professionalism. As well, I am extremely grateful to the wonderful and thorough comments from two anonymous reviewers.

Many colleagues and scholars provided me with invaluable ideas, insights, or data. I am particularly grateful to the following intellectual companions: Christina Ahmadjian, Masahiko Aoki, Jean-Marie Bouissou, Robert Boyer, Max Cameron, John Cioffi, Pepper Culpepper, Gerald Curtis, Larry Diamond, Barry Eichengreen, Margarita Esteves-Abe, Shin Fujihara, Erica Gould, Michel Goyer, Bill Grimes, Stephan Haggard, Sebastian Heilmann,

Higashi Daisaku, Sunshine Hillygus, Hiwatari Nobuhiro, Kurt Huebner, Imai Kenichi, Inoguchi Takashi, Alan Jacobs, Richard Johnston, Jung Joo-Youn, Kasuya Yuko, Kohno Masaru, Phil Lim, Chao-Chi Lin, Julia Lynch, Pierre Martin, Masuyama Mikitaka, Matsui Tomoyo, Claude Meyer, Miura Mari, Miyajima Hideaki, Nakano Koichi, Ben Nyblade, Alicia Ogawa, Otake Hideo, Susan Pharr, Richard Price, Fritz Scharpf, Song Jiyeoun, Wolfgang Streeck, and Cornelia Woll.

I presented earlier drafts of this work at various conferences and universities, and greatly benefited from the feedback received there. Among others, my exploration of the links between Japanese and Korean politics was aided by an early presentation in Kobayashi Yoshiaki's graduate workshop at Keio University in November 1999. Senior bureaucrats at the Japanese Ministry of Finance (MOF) kindly provided feedback during an early presentation of this research at the ministry in April 2000. Helpful comments from fellow participants of the International Dissertation Research Fellowship workshop organized by the Social Science Research Council (SSRC) in Amsterdam in October 2000 have also enriched this dissertation. I thank Ron Kasimir and Laura Hein for their great insights. I presented an early draft of this research at the SSRC Japan Studies Dissertation Workshop and received excellent comments, in particular from Barbara Brooks, Christian Brunelli, Paul Dunscomb, David Howell, Abby Margolis, David Obermiller, Mary-Alice Pickert, and Robert Uriu. I also thank the participants of the A/PARC project on the Japanese economic crisis for their invaluable comments during symposia in November 1999, January 2001, and August 2001, particularly Jennifer Amyx, David Brady, Robert Madsen, Isabela Mares, Ron McKinnon, Muramatsu Michio, Hugh Patrick, Noguchi Yukio, Adam Posen, Harry Rowen, Kay Shimizu, Takenaka Harukata, and Maria Toyoda. I am also grateful for valuable comments received at presentations at the annual congresses of the American Political Science Association, the International Studies Association, the Association for Asian Studies, and the Council for European Studies; as well as during presentations at the Reischauer Institute (Harvard), the Max Planck Institute (Cologne), the Institut de Sciences Politiques, the École des Hautes Études en Sciences Sociales, Tokyo University, Korea University, and the University of Pennsylvania.

At the University of British Columbia (UBC), wonderful students in my seminars on international political economy have been a continual source of inspiration, ideas, and puzzles (often unbeknownst to them). I express my thanks to, among others, Aron Ballard, Elena Feditchkina, Matt Gillis, Guo Li, Higashi Daisaku, Jessica Li, Mark Manger, Omukai Asako, Marko Papic, Lisa Rickmers, Tamura Atsuko, Cornelio Thiessen, Michael Thomson, and Mike Weisbart.

So many individuals extended a helping hand during my fieldwork in Japan, Korea, and France. In Tokyo, I am particularly grateful to Nishimura Yoshimasa, Okubo Yoshio, Kawakami Yosuke, Takimoto Toyomi, and Ryusuke Nakayama for arranging my affiliation with the Institute of Fiscal and Monetary Policy at the MOF and for smoothing my path there throughout my research. I am extremely grateful to Kobayashi Yoshiaki for arranging my affiliation with Keio University and for welcoming me to his graduate seminar on Japanese politics. Minister Yosano Kaoru provided me with support and access to important advisers. Shiozaki Yasuhisa offered great insights and helped me contact other Diet members. I am also indebted to Nakagawa Katsuhiro and Isayama Takeshi for providing me with frank analyses of policy processes and for opening countless doors in the Ministry of International Trade and Industry and other places. Tanaka Seiwa and Yoshida Yasuhiko opened many more doors and provided me with strong support and friendship. Nakano Koichi and Miura Mari generously gave their time to discuss my research and to explore possible avenues. I address special thanks to Scott Callon, Robert Feldman, Nakahara Hirohiko, and Masaki Yoshihisa for their help and advice. Countless other senior bureaucrats, politicians, labor union leaders, business leaders, and others, have been remarkably generous with their time and have made this work possible. I am unable to acknowledge them personally in light of their desire to remain anonymous.

In Korea, I am especially grateful to Minister and Professor Han Sung-Joo of Korea University, who kindly arranged my affiliation with the Institute for International Relations and great supported my research. I am also greatly indebted to Kim Byung-Kook of Korea University for opening more doors and mentoring me through my Korean journey. I acknowledge the invaluable help received from Dr. Suh Sang-Mok in helping me gain entrance to the Korean Parliament. Lim Soo-Taek made my research in Korea possible through his kind chaperoning and occasional translation of Korean discussions into Japanese. Park Jin-Hyung introduced me to Korean politics and life, and offered great insights. Christy Lee provided me with invaluable information and support. Other senior politicians, bureaucrats, business leaders, and labor leaders who wish to remain anonymous have given me great support.

In France, I am greatly indebted to Minister and Professor Christian Sautter for his deep trust and extraordinary mentorship. Minister Sautter wrote dozens of letters to key French leaders on my behalf and made my research in France possible. Nicolas Véron generously shared his time, insights on the hot politics of accounting, and great tips on key actors. My old friend Bertrand Badré has also been a tremendous supporter of my research, and I owe much to him. Nicolas Jabko led me to new intellectual avenues and to countless sources of further information. Vincent Tiberj has supported me throughout my research in France and chaperoned me through the halls of Sciences-Po. I also thank Michel Albert, Robert Boyer, Pierre Jacquet, Paul Jobin, Ethan Kapstein, Jacques Mistral, Nezu Risaburo, Benoit Rengade, Jacques Tierny, and Jean-Philippe Touffut, as well as countless others who wish to remain anonymous, for making my research so multifaceted.

I benefited from wonderful research assistantship during the writing of this book and am particularly grateful to Mark Manger for his staunch support at many crucial moments. I thank Lee Hyunji, Elisabeth St-Jean, Atsuko Tamura, and Sean Starrs. Fieldwork in Japan was generously supported by the Japan Foundation. Research in Korea and France was assisted by a fellowship from the International Dissertation Research Fellowships Program of the SSRC with funds provided by the Andrew W. Mellon Foundation. The initial write-up was further supported by the Institute of International Studies at Stanford (Littlefield Fellowship) and by the Mustard Seed Foundation (Harvey Fellowship). Additional research was funded by the Peter Wall Institute, the Center for Japanese Research, the Institute for European Studies, and the Department of Political Science at UBC. The final research and write-up of the book were supported by a general fellowship from the Harvard Academy for International and Area Studies at Harvard University in 2004–06.

Several sections of this book were adapted from previously published work and it is with gratitude that I acknowledge the publishers' permission to reprint them here. Parts of chapters 4 and 5 draw on my article "State Mediation of Global Financial Forces: Different Paths of Structural Reforms in Japan and South Korea," *Journal of East Asian Studies* 2, no. 2 (2002):103–41 (permission granted by the East Asia Institute, Seoul, Korea); and the chapter "Policy-Making in the Era of Financial Globalization: The Battle for Japanese Corporate Reforms, 1996–2002," in *From Crisis to Opportunity: Financial Globalization and East Asian Capitalism*, ed. Jongryn Mo and Daniel I. Okimoto (Stanford, CA.: The Walter H. Shorenstein Asia-Pacific Research Center, Stanford University, 2006) (permission granted by Shorenstein A/PARC). Chapter 5 briefly draws from my article "Navigating the Path of Least Resistance: Financial Deregulation and the Origins of the Japanese Crisis." *Journal of East Asian Studies* 5, no. 3 (2005):427–64 (permission granted by Lynne Rienner Publishers).

I express my gratitude to special friends who have kept up with me and been wonderful friends through this long project: Dominique Pustoc'h and Patricia Drouglazet, Shannon and Jim Campbell, Patrick Labelle, Rebecca Hardin, Beth Baiter, Nakano Koichi, Benoit Rengade, Ono Kenji, Aymeric de Salvert, Jeanette Lee-Oderman, Jean-François Sabouret, Jérôme and Corine Henry, Paul Jobin and Jenyu Peng, Guy Thiébaud, Cécile Doan and Thierry Louzier, Yuichi Goto, Inoue Keiko, Sharon and Andrew Rand,

Susan Schonfeld, and Riina Toya. At UBC, I am grateful for the friendship of and support from Barbara Arneil, Bruce Baum, Karen Bakker, Philippe Lebillon, Josephine Calazan, Ken Carty, Pete Chamberlain, Tim Cheek, Julian Dierkes, Ken Foster, Stefan Gaenzle, Sima Godfrey, Laura Janara, Brian Job, Paul Marantz, Dianne Newell, Petula Mueller, Rob Stoddard, Dory Urbano, John Wood, Mark Zacher, and many others.

Finally, I thank my family for crucial (if sometimes unwilling) companionship in this journey. I owe much to my parents for instilling both a dedication to peace and justice and international curiosity in my heart. My daughter, Claire, has had a huge role in this book. Her birth coincided with the beginning of the project in 1999, and she has shared it every step of the way. At two months old, she began trekking through the Stanford library in a baby carrier. At four months old, she was in Paris, laying foundations for the French field research. At six months old, she began her Japanese life, experiencing the advanced childcare system of Japan and keeping me out of the joys and dangers of Kasumigaseki's bureaucratic life by requiring early mad dashes back to the "*hoiku* mama." At twelve months old, she proved qualified to join in struggling through planes, subways, and trains, and attending some interviews in Paris. Thus began her traveling life: attending several conferences and expressing her deep disapproval when she was not invited. Claire grew up with this book at Stanford, UBC, and Harvard in a kind of sibling rivalry. Her strong claims for priority attention kept me sane and allowed this book to slowly mature like a French wine. I also thank my son Paul, a latecomer to the project. As early as two years old, he took it upon himself to help with the book. He figured that systematically flipping through the pages of every book in the huge piles next to my desk would help finish the book faster and get him more playtime. His moral support, numerous hugs, and regular wishes of "*bon courage*, papa" were much appreciated. Last, but not least, I thank Jennifer for the shared journey of life and academia, invaluable advice, and patience. This book owes tremendously to Jennifer's kind feedback, sharp mind, and creative spirit.

This page would not be complete without a mention of the beautiful ridges and ocean vistas of Galiano island (British Columbia), which provided me with the space and inspiration necessary for the final revisions.

ENTREPRENEURIAL STATES

1

Political Entrepreneurs and the Corporate Restructuring Dilemma

Corporate restructuring involves high political risks in stakeholder or co-ordinated economies.[1] These systems integrate a complementary set of industrial organizational features (large groups, cross-shareholdings), stable employment practices, bank-centered corporate finance, and welfare corporatism that set them apart from the more liberal systems in the United States and the United Kingdom. The liberal Anglo-Saxon systems contained radically different practices, in particular, direct financing through capital markets, dispersed corporate ownership, and more flexible labor markets. The contrast is one between stakeholder capitalism and investor capitalism (Dore 2000).

Corporate restructuring in its far-reaching manifestation affects key pieces of these systems. Most important, it weakens the political compact between the core socio-economic constituencies and the state. Therefore, engaging with large-scale corporate restructuring may appear paradoxical and costly in stakeholder economies given the complex interdependence between institutions of capitalist systems revealed in varieties of capitalism and regulation theory (Amable, Barré, and Boyer 1997; Boyer 2004; Hall and Gingerich 2004; Hall and Soskice 2001; Vogel 2006).

The dilemma for firms and policymakers is how to enable a smoother process of creative destruction and effect a higher degree of capital allocation, while preserving key linkages that lie at the core of the national com-

---

1. Stakeholder economies have also been defined as "non-liberal," or "coordinated-market economies." See Berger and Dore (1996); Hall and Soskice (2001); Schmidt (2002); Streeck and Yamamura (2001); Yamamura and Streeck (2003).

parative advantage. Firm organization, labor management, cross-firm networks, main bank relations, and interactions with the government all form a coordinated whole that linked firms to other actors and provided the basis for Japanese economic competitiveness. Can key components of the system, such as corporate governance, be overhauled without jettisoning other components, such as labor policy and in-company training? In recent work on Germany, Hall and Gingerich (2004) argued that a coordinated market economy (CME), which abandoned some of the strategic institutional complementarities through partial reforms of components of the mix, could end up at the bottom of the U-shape efficiency curve. Unless an economy transforms completely from a CME to a liberal market economy (LME), prospects of success are grim.

In addition, long-term economic institutions are buttressed by norms and beliefs that have come to shape the behavior of economic actors (Aoki 2001; Milhaupt 2001). Changing rules without affecting such norms and beliefs can lead to a dysfunctional and decoupled outcome. A smooth process must be partially driven by change in the focalizing norms of participating actors, although such a process starts with a stage of institutional crisis (Aoki 2001).

The Core of Post–World War II Stakeholder Systems: The Social Contract

At the core of stakeholder systems lies a political bargain involving all social actors and the state as guarantor. The so-called social contract refers to a set of formal regulations and informal norms that ensures both economic competitiveness and social stability (lifetime employment, stable industrial relations, and a stable financial system). This postwar social contract is often called the compromise of embedded liberalism (Ruggie 1982).

This modern social contract has roots in both the Great Depression and World War II. The Great Depression of the 1930s shattered the nineteenth-century belief in self-regulating markets.[2] The postwar economic system was built around one key priority: preventing another Great Depression or at least limiting its social and political impact. At a global level, the decision was made to encourage free trade while building a stable exchange rate regime and controlling capital flows (Helleiner 1994; Ruggie 1982). At the national level, governments in Japan and Western Europe chose to organize their domestic socio-economic systems around a stable social contract.

2. See, for example, Carr (1939); Eichengreen (1996); Helleiner (1994); Kindleberger (1986); Polanyi (1944).

Over decades, both widespread public support and a dense network of vested interest groups served to solidify this compromise.

In Japan, the social contract has roots that reach as far back as the late Meiji period. As demonstrated by Samuels (2003b, 88), Shibusawa Eiichi, the "father of Japanese capitalism," saw the mission of entrepreneurs as guarantors of the social order in addition to profit maximizers. Unlike in the United States, capitalists should embed samurai values and concern for society in their approach to business. In 1919 the government of Hara Kei brought the state into the social contract arena for the sake of political order by putting a statist social policy and distributional politics in place (100), yet the Hara government pointedly excluded labor from participating in this emerging social order, a choice reconfirmed by postwar leaders.[3] The core components of the Japanese social contract (such as lifetime employment) fell into place in the late 1920s and early 1930s under a compromise that Samuels calls "corporate paternalism" (126). The state spread practices of "warm-hearted" social relations within firms initially developed by corporate pioneer Mutō Sanji. This emerging state-corporate compromise aimed to keep social change under control and prevent social dislocation. The Great Depression beginning in 1929 led to further consolidation (Sakakibara 1993, 1997). Industrial policy, perfected during wartime mobilization by the Ministry of International Trade and Industry (MITI), completed the institutional organization of capitalism, although its true effectiveness remains a point of debate, at least in some sectors (Callon 1995; Miwa and Ramseyer 2002, 2006; Okimoto 1989). On the welfare side of the equation, recent scholarship has shown that Japan gradually developed a far-reaching system and that "welfare policy helped to mobilize public backing for the developmental state" (Kasza 2006, 178).

It is important to note, however, that the Japanese social contract always remained more limited than its European counterpart. First, it targeted select articulated interests and systematically excluded large social groups such as women, temporary workers, workers in small and medium corporations, and minorities (*burakumin*). These groups provided flexibility. Lifetime employment only concerned long-term employees in large firms, possibly a third of the labor force. Even long-term contractual linkages between manufacturers and suppliers (*keiretsu*) may have been less significant than often described (Miwa and Ramseyer 2001, 2006).

In 1945 Europe, the social contract served as the new cornerstone for deeply shattered nations attempting to rebuild viable political systems (Rhodes and Mény 1998; Rosanvallon 1995). It was the source of a new patriotism and a bulwark against potential Communist revolutions. After the collapse of the legitimacy of political regimes in France and Germany, social

---

3. See Pempel and Tsunekawa (1979).

activism was necessary for nation-building. In Rousseau's tradition, it offered the paternal protection of the state as the only guarantor of the public good and individual freedom. Building upon work done by Thomas Hobbes and John Locke, Rousseau (1762) defined the social contract as a pact between individuals and the community, whereby the individual sacrificed physical autonomy, but gained the freedom to act rationally and live a truly human life. The post-1945 reincarnation of this pact saw individuals acquiesce to the continuation of conservative regimes (giving up ideas of revolution) and high taxation in exchange for social protection and social stability. By the 1980s, the concept of the social contract came to encompass not just the welfare state systems developed in Europe and Japan, but also the interdependent institutions of industrial relations and labor, including stable employment.

Government promotion of corporate restructuring amounts to a major paradigm shift in stakeholder economies. In essence, the state is undoing the social and economic regulations built in the wake of the Great Depression of the 1930s and is involved in a second "Great Transformation" (Polanyi 1944).

Corporate Restructuring and the J-Curve Dilemma

When politicians engage in reforms that promote corporate restructuring, they start riding a political J-curve where they don't control the depth of the initial drop, nor the timing and speed of the recovery. This is because of the conjunction of a *timing inconsistency* and a *responsibility inconsistency*. During the initiation phase of reforms, political reformers must bring flexibility to entrenched institutions and face the prospect of objective social costs (such as unemployment) and opposition by vested interests.[4] It is only after a few years that the benefits of a more flexible industrial structure may become visible in the form of accrued capital inflows, firm profitability, higher growth, and higher employment. Reformers must have the ability and willingness to wait for this turnaround of political fortunes. In addition, while the short-term costs are clear, the timing and extent of long-term benefits are less so. Much of that uncertainty is related to the indirect nature of corporate governance reforms and other measures targeting restructuring. Such measures affect firm incentives, but represent only one of the many inputs that shape firm behavior. The realization of the benefits of corporate governance reforms ultimately depends on the actions of firms and investors,

---

4. See Olson's (1982) third hypothesis: "Members of small groups have disproportionate organizational power for collective action."

over which the government has little control. In the end, benefits and costs may not even be evenly distributed.

The dilemma of responsibility inconsistency is also clear, if we consider the inducement of corporate restructuring as the effort to provide a public good (growth and long-term employment) in the face of a partial collective action problem (Frohlich, Oppenheimer, and Young 1971; Olson 1965). In the face of new financial and technological forces, most individuals would be better off in the long term with significant institutional change. However, moving toward the new equilibrium involves cooperation among key groups, all of which must accept significant short-term costs. Each group is better off if it can shift most of the burden to other groups, and all groups fear the defection of any other group during the process. The result is stalemate and the absence of reforms. In this context, the government takes steps to solve the collective action dilemma by directing reforms from above, in the name of the public good. In doing so, however, it runs the risk of becoming responsible for the costs or success of reforms in the eyes of social and economic actors, even though the benefits of the reform process depends on the actions of these other actors.

The corporate restructuring dilemma can be summarized this way: Can political reformers survive and diffuse political costs long enough for the benefits to kick in? Can they provide strong enough signals to convince investors to bring in abundant capital, while reassuring voters long enough for tangible benefits to become visible?

The risks and uncertainty involved immediately raise the following questions: Why would governments engage in such a process? What will affect the choices of different countries in the face of the corporate restructuring dilemma?

National Policy Choices in Response to the Corporate Restructuring Dilemma

In the context of intensifying global competition and new incentives from global investors, governments face mounting costs for inaction on the corporate restructuring dilemma. Yet, as they consider the menu of reforms favored by financial investors, national governments can put together different combinations. As they explore options in this new environment, politicians must decide between two kinds of tradeoffs.

The first decision relates to the choice of policy instruments and the ensuing intensity of corporate restructuring. Governments can choose to increase the level of access by financial investors to corporate governance, an arena hitherto dominated by management and labor. Passing measures to facilitate the efficient movement of capital within the economy would also be consistent with such an intent. Governments can do so by improving the flow of accounting and financial information (transparency reforms), improving minority shareholder protection, and improving the ability of minority shareholders to participate and vote in shareholder meetings. Governments can also pass framework regulatory reforms that facilitate the efficient movement of capital within groups and between industrial sectors. Such reforms include bankruptcy reforms, support for enterprise creation, tax incentives for the undoing of cross-shareholdings (lower capital gains taxes), and legal tools that facilitate mergers and acquisitions (stock swaps, holding structures, etc.) or divestment. However, in some national settings, these reforms may have limited effects on firm restructuring or economic efficiency. Indeed, oligopolistic networks or tight labor–management relationships may be strong enough to block the signals of such reforms. In such cases, governments can choose to target the distribution of power within the firm through corporate governance reforms, takeover reforms, or far-reaching labor reforms.

This first decision has far-reaching political consequences. By taking active steps on access and capital efficiency, governments may have some impact on corporate restructuring and meet the demands of global investors while preserving the support of certain important interest groups. The process may also create important imbalances. Alternatively, political leaders may go further and spread the costs equally among labor and management. This may alienate both groups, but also offset one group's loss by the other's concomitant loss.

The second tradeoff facing governments concerns the degree to which change should be brought upon firms and sectors. A limited approach creates new options for management, labor, and investors to interact in more efficient ways in only some firms or sectors. This increases the diversity of legal forms and types of behavior allowed to firms, mixing old and new. It leads to a funnel outcome at the firm level. A more systematic approach uses across-the-board regulations, bank management rules, and direct state leadership to bring about change across sectors and firms. This approach is more coercive, more political, and involves higher stakes. It may lead to a corridor-like outcome at the firm level: most firms are forced to move and the economy mutates as a whole.

The Outcome: Variation across Three Countries

The three countries analyzed in this book reveal a wide range of responses to these global incentives. Despite relatively similar structures of political economy, their reform processes differ in content, intensity, and reach. Table 1.1 summarizes the choices made by countries, regarding the contents of reforms and relative outcomes.

Table 1.1. Typology of responses to the corporate restructuring dilemma

	Reform approach	
Reform focus	Options/Incentives	General regulations
Access	1. Diversification *Japan*	2. Reinforcement *France*
Power	3. Market *OECD—EU Commission*	4. Transformation *Korea*

The first type of response to new global incentives is a reform pathway focusing only on increasing access. Improving access means partial structural reforms, with limited or no action on labor rights, financial management, and takeovers (market for corporate control). When states choose to move forward on access through enabling reforms[5] that increase options and incentives for firms, without demanding mandatory change, the outcome is one of diversification of the industrial structure (no. 1 in table). This *market-tolerant* pathway opens up new opportunities for firm innovation and market mechanisms, without forcing such change on reluctant firms. This is, by and large, the pathway chosen by Japan. As firms face new possibilities in terms of corporate governance structures (board types), tools for reorganization (holding company options, legal tools for splitting or merging firms), or funding sources, the capitalist model tends to bifurcate and fragment. The growing confrontation between traditionalist Toyota and reformist Nissan in Japan is a case in point.

States can also prioritize access reforms by demanding mandatory change across firms or creating strong signals to push such change forward (no. 2). In this case, the sum of new framework regulations and direct impulses through privatization, state-sponsored mergers and acquisitions, or bank-led restructuring can create strong incentives for most firms to change and restructure. This *market-enhancing* approach fits the French reform path and leads to an outcome of reinforcement through reforms. In this case, the high degree of state impulse can make the outcome both unstable (transitional stage) and socially volatile.

A third possibility consists in pushing for a broader spectrum of reforms, while limiting the degree of coercion (no. 3). This *market-conforming* (liberal) path fits most closely with OECD recommendations and the liberalization program of the European Commission. In this category, states go beyond access-type reforms and also enact labor reforms, corporate governance reforms, and takeover reforms that have a direct impact on the balance of power within the firm. At the same time, the role of the state is

5. I am indebted to the excellent analysis by Milhaupt (2004) for the term "enabling reforms."

limited to providing new possibilities and incentives, leaving the actual restructuring process to market mechanisms and corporate innovation. Beyond accounting and transparency reforms, the role of the state is enabling change, not fostering it. Interestingly, few states beyond the European Union agenda fall in this box.

Lastly, states can adhere to the broad reform agenda recommended by the OECD and the International Monetary Fund (IMF), but decide to take it upon themselves to shape the restructuring pathway, without letting markets and firms be in the driver's seat (no. 4). This *market-bending* pathway of systemic restructuring, chosen by Korea (and to some extent, by China) enables the state to reorganize the balance of power within its political economy and within firms, while encouraging corporate restructuring and reaping the fruits of the golden bargain. Table 1.2 offers a full battery of scorecards, contrasting the contents of the reforms pursued by France, Japan, and Korea. The items in bold are the areas of non-reform. There are more non-reform areas in Japan than in France and Korea.

While all three countries have engaged in active reform plans on transparency, accounting, foreign direct investment promotion, and minority shareholder protection, the key differences among them relate to reforms that directly affect the balance of power within firms (labor, privatization, and takeover reforms). Japan has clearly chosen not to take such steps, while Korea has attempted to use all available tools to force deep change. France stands in between, with some potentially power-affecting change through privatization, but has mostly chosen not to touch the power relations between management and labor, nor to force management to bow to shareholders. Instead, France has sought to reinforce managers by giving them tools to increase capital efficiency and meet some of the demands of investors.

Common External Incentive: The Golden Bargain

Global capital flows are not an automatic straitjacket that forces states to submit to rules set by blind markets. They are not an overwhelming flood that breaks the national institutions, which have been built slowly over the centuries. Rather, the correct image is that of a golden bargain (or a pact with the devil). In exchange for corporate and structural reforms, global investors offer abundant equity inflows and the promise of a lower capital cost and increased competitiveness. National politicians have the choice of entering into this golden Faustian pact or turning it down. The bargain itself may be attractive, yet may also bring about disruptive social consequences (Dore 1999, 2000). The key issue is how politicians respond to this novel bargain, rather than the flows of capital themselves. The deal between global

Table 1.2. Scorecards with respect to restructuring, 1990–2002*

Dimensions	France (Reinforcement)	Japan (Diversification)	Korea (Transformation)
Accounting reforms/ transparency	YES (delegated to EU)	YES	YES
Minority shareholder protection/voice	YES NRE bill, 2001	YES (partial)	YES
FDI liberalization (inflows, equal treatment)	YES, through EU (with a few exceptions)	YES (gradual)	YES
New managerial incentives (stock options, merit pay)	YES (partial 1997, stop 2000)	YES	YES
Tools for financial reorganization (spin-offs, stock issuance, capital gains tax, holding companies.)	Limited (mostly done in 1980s and delegated to EU)	YES (all)	YES
Bankruptcy reforms	Not relevant	YES	YES
Support for new enterprise creation (SMEs)	**NO-Limited**	**Limited**	YES
Banking reforms (lending criteria)	Not relevant (done in 1980s)	**Partial (except SMEs)**	YES (massive, leading to bankruptcies)
Anti-trust—oligopoly busting	Delegated to EU	**NO (limited FTC strength)**	YES (anti-*chaebol* actions)
Shareholder-focused management of SOEs	YES	**NO (limited attempts)**	YES
Labor flexibility (layoffs, temps)	**NEGATIVE (tightening of layoff conditions)**	**NO (limited openings on temps)**	YES
Takeovers—market for corporate control	YES through EU (2004–06) But backlash	**NO (very limited)**	YES But partial backlash

*For detailed information on the types of reforms followed in each country, please refer to table 2.5.

investors and national politicians involves the risk of short-term disruptions, as reforms go against the interests of entrenched domestic groups, but also the potential promise of high political returns in the long run.

I focus on one major type of capital flow: equity flows. While the effects of foreign trade and FDI are relatively well recognized, the impact of the rise in equity portfolio flows is less perfectly understood. I argue that the surge in global portfolio flows represents a major external force that affected most developed economies in the mid-1990s.

Equity portfolio flows refer to foreign investment in domestic stock markets. Unlike FDI, portfolio investments do not result in controlling stakes in domestic companies. Generally, the cutoff between portfolio investment and FDI is 10 percent ownership (Kogut and Macpherson 2003, 185).

Portfolio investors are spread over many domestic companies and represent a much greater force for institutional change than direct investors. As OECD countries liberalized financial flows starting in the mid-1980s and as large pension funds in the United States and the United Kingdom turned to portfolio diversification strategies in the 1990s, portfolio flows increased exponentially, reaching trigger levels for change in a large number of countries. Chapter 2 provides comparative data across OECD countries.

What is the origin of the explosion of capital flows in the 1980s and 1990s? Clearly, this was not a spontaneous economic phenomenon. Both the creation of a global financial market and the massive inflows and outflows for each individual country were the result of active political decisions. The key events that led to a departure from the Bretton Woods system of capital control and currency stability included the creation of the British- and U.S.-supported Euromarket in London in the 1960s, U.S. decisions to abandon the fixed parity system in 1971 and to abolish capital controls in 1974, and the British decision to follow suit in 1979.[6] Both also initiated domestic financial deregulation. This, in turn, created a competitive dynamic that led most advanced industrialized countries to deregulate their capital controls in the 1980s and early 1990s (Goodman and Pauly 1993).

Among the three countries explored in this book, Japan moved first with gradual financial deregulation (capital account and domestic finance) after 1984, following a path of least resistance between global pressures and domestic interest group coalitions (Tiberghien 2005b). France embraced both domestic financial deregulation (1984–90) and open capital flows (1990) as part of a vision to continue the modernization of France (Abdelal 2007). The framework decisions were also deeply embedded in a pact with Germany and within a strategy laid out by the European Commission over the acceleration of EU integration (Jabko 1999). As for Korea, the key decisions were made by the Kim Young Sam administration (1992–97), under the active prodding of the U.S. Treasury, as part of a grand national strategy to modernize and globalize (Jung and Kim 1999; S. Kim 2000; Moon and Mo 1999; Oh 1999; Stiglitz 2002). However, financial deregulation was only partly achieved in 1997; the process was completed during the IMF-sponsored reforms of 1997–98.

Faustian Pact or Golden Bargain?

What are the incentives for both global investors and domestic politicians to engage in the golden bargain? Global investors are seeking lower risk

---

6. For a great review of these decisions, see Helleiner (1994), Rajan and Zingales (2004), and Strange (1998).

and higher return. Lower risk entails high transparency in the financial situations of national firms and protection of minority shareholder rights (corporate governance regulations). Higher return entails a flexible industrial structure in which corporate restructuring can occur without insurmountable obstacles when the profitability of the firm decreases. Investors invest in individual firms and make risk-return evaluations at the firm level, yet they also care about state regulations and policies. Indeed, turning firms toward shareholder-friendly corporate governance one at a time may lead to the formation of a cluster of firms with good corporate governance practices. But it may take a considerable period of time until such a cluster is large enough to affect the rest of the economy—the "tipping point" in Kogut and Macpherson's (2003, 202) terminology. Purely market-enforced change may be limited. State regulations are a more efficient means of lowering risk and tilting managers toward a higher sensitivity to the interests of minority shareholders.

In addition, global investors care about the efficiency of capital allocation and the removal of obstacles to the efficient process of corporate restructuring. Again, state actions may make a big difference in inciting firms to increase their return on equity (ROE). State actions may have several types of beneficial impacts for foreign investors. The state can remove legal and institutional impediments and establish the legal and regulatory infrastructure required for efficient corporate restructuring. The state can also act as a catalyst in the restructuring process, through signaling or through direct incentives, thus offering political cover for corporations and initiating a bandwagon effect.[7] The state may also be directly involved in forcing restructuring when existing corporate cartels block all market signals (as in the case of Korean *chaebols* (large, family-controlled, and diversified conglomerates that have come to dominate the Korean economy) since 1997).

If investors need the arm of the state, it is less clear why politicians would be responsive to the interests of global investors. Global investors do not vote and do not belong to the circle of politically influential interest groups. Their voice is diffuse and fragmented. Why would politicians take on the golden bargain and engage in corporate reforms? The golden bargain offers two main advantages for politicians in a competitive situation: it can solve major problems and can offer a long-term opportunity to create a modern reputation and foster growth and employment. Because the golden bargain holds the promise of inflows of equity capital, it can help political leaders who have to deal with financial and banking crises, or privatization

---

7. A clear manifestation of such a demand by external actors, albeit by a global bond rating agency, can be seen in Fitch's report about Japan's bad loan management in the fall of 2001. The report argued that a major weakness in the banks' approach stemmed from "a reluctance to get ahead of government and public sentiment toward restructuring and redundancy" (Sinclair 2005, 90).

programs. In 1999, for example, Japan's prime minister, Obuchi Keizō, faced a banking crisis and a lending crunch. The conjunction of high levels of non-performing loans in banks and the importance of unrealized capital gains from equity holdings for bank lending made the government highly sensitive to the level of the stock market. Given that foreign investors were the main source of inflows into the stock market at a time when domestic firms and banks were trying to unwind cross-shareholding, the health of the stock market and of bank capital adequacy ratios came to depend on global investors.[8]

Likewise, in the wake of the December 1997 financial crisis, the Korean government desperately needed to reduce the debt leverage of large Korean conglomerates. The easiest and cheapest way to do so was to entice these companies to issue shares on the stock market and increase their equity financing in a context of abundant inflows into the stock market. The inflows would come from global investors. For European countries such as France, Portugal, and Spain, the attractiveness of the golden bargain arises from their commitment to large privatization programs in the 1990s. In a context of limited national inflows into the stock market and the absence of U.S.-style pension funds, these countries saw foreign equity flows as a great and cheap opportunity to sustain successful privatization programs. At the same time, the process allowed these governments to finance part of their budget deficits through the revenues of privatization sales (courtesy of global investors).

Second, the golden bargain can offer individual politicians the opportunity to be seen as modernists who are more interested in long-term competitiveness and growth than in the protection of vested interest groups. Although such politicians know that, initially, public opinion rarely supports structural reforms that have the explicit aim of increasing capital efficiency at the short-term cost of accelerated corporate restructuring, they bet that opinion will shift over the medium term. This is particularly true in countries with rapidly aging populations where long-term savers may carry more and more weight. In other countries, pension reforms with the aim of enabling capitalization systems may also lead to a larger pool of voters concerned about ROE and capital allocation.

Finally, politicians learn through experience. By the early 2000s, politicians in most developed countries had experienced cases in which dissatisfied global investors were instrumental in a stock market crash (at the firm or national level) and in which the public came to blame the government for it. Japan experienced the positive side of the golden bargain in 1999

---

8. It is worth noting that the Japanese government around that time also became sensitive to a second external input, namely the downgrading decisions made by bond rating agencies. See Sinclair (2005).

when net equity inflows reached ¥11.2 trillion (about US$110 billion), sustaining a major rebound in the stock price level (40 percent increase). In turn, as Mori Yoshirō took over as prime minister in the spring of 2000 and slowed structural reforms, a significant foreign outflow corresponded to a major drop in the stock market. The press and opinion polls blamed the Mori government for this. The same thing happened in 2002 when foreign investors lost faith in the reform process initiated by Prime Minister Junichirō Koizumi.

The contrast between France and Germany offers a clear picture of the impact of different responses to the golden bargain. France was more forthcoming about corporate governance reforms and the promotion of corporate restructuring than Germany, especially in the period between 1997 and 2002, the main focus of political analysis in chapters 3, 4, and 5. As a result, France received a larger share of equity inflows than Germany during this period, despite its much smaller economy. In 1997, Germany still had a significantly greater total stock market capitalization than France ($825 billion versus $674 billion) (World Bank 2005), while both had similar levels of total foreign equity ($187 billion versus $209 billion) (International Monetary Fund 2005a). Five years later, France had leapt ahead of Germany, with a total market capitalization of $967 billion, while Germany stagnated at $686 billion. A key difference was the much greater foreign presence in France ($339 billion) than in Germany ($212 billion). Between the end of 1997 and the end of 2002, the French stock index (CAC 40) weathered the global stock market crash well by holding up to the same level (+2 percent overall), while the German index (DAX 30) lost 32 percent.

In sum, the rise of global portfolio equity is best seen as a common stimulus affecting most OECD countries at around the same time—in the mid-1990s—and leading to different political responses. It is similar to Lindblom's depiction of an "all-pervasive constraint" of business and markets on government authority (Lindblom 1977, 178). Although the actual level of capital inflows differs from country to country, the opportunity presented by the golden bargain is a common one. Most major economies (G10 countries), with the exception of Canada and Italy, settled to similar levels of foreign penetration, between 20 percent and 35 percent, by the early 2000s.

Political Entrepreneurs as Tipping Mechanisms

The golden bargain presents a new matrix of incentives and costs for nonadaptation to all countries. Yet, as in Gourevitch's (1977; 1986) consideration of global economic shocks in earlier periods, countries have choices.

The international system is rarely coercive. Rather, the distribution of power and domestic institutions within each system mediate the external signal and shape each country's response.

The intrusion of global investors onto the domestic political economy brings about a realignment in positions. It increases the power of investors in most stakeholder economies in their traditional confrontation with managers and labor (Gourevitch and Shinn 2005). In addition, given the differential exposure of firms to global capital, the golden bargain splits the position of managers into a minority pro-reform position and a majority pro–status quo position. A similar pattern takes place within the labor movement. The entry of global investors also gives rise to uncertainty; uncertainty creates room for political action.

Transforming a deeply entrenched social contract is not a simple process, even when investors can count on the support of some firms and labor leaders. In most countries, a ring of interest groups and bureaucracies has crystallized around the postwar institutions. They are ready to fight in defense of a system that has long been successful. Voters also tend to be on the side of the social contract since it has generated job stability and a sense of shared community. Institutional change transforms the distribution of benefits within a society as well as the pecking order of winners and losers.

How can a political system move from one set of well-protected institutions to a new, partially reformed set, when there is no clear coalition alignment? To elucidate this political transition and understand how various systems react differently to the same external displacement, it is crucial to open the black box of policymaking and come down to the level of individual actors.

Financial globalization is the common context for all developed countries in the late 1990s. What is disputed is the significance of this new global context for the survival of distinct national capitalist models. Does financial globalization force convergence around norms and structures of industrial organization and corporate governance? Or can states control it in their pursuit of distinct and socially acceptable outcomes? Does globalization force systemic convergence or can it sustain multiple durable outcomes?

Predominant concepts of national responses to globalization tend to cluster around three poles. One pole represents theorists of convergence and diffusion.[9] According to these theorists, the external forces may be structural (Andrews 1994) or purely normative, but states react to such forces by adopting globally efficient or globally legitimate institutions. Change is mostly externally driven. However, recent empirical studies have tended to

---

9. Crouch and Streeck 1997; Dore 2000; Keohane and Milner 1996; Rajan and Zingales 2004; Strange 1998; Yamamura and Streeck 2003.

emphasize the limits of such convergence on the ground and the important interactive effects taking place on the domestic level.[10]

A second pole emphasizes the linkages between global changes and domestic interest groups (Frieden and Rogowski 1996; Frieden 1991). International economic forces favor certain interest groups over others and the empowered groups lobby politicians to deliver institutional reforms directly or by threatening exit. Meanwhile, threatened groups lobby politicians to thwart reforms and demand compensation for external disruptions. The reform outcome hangs on the balance of power between these two coalitions (Gourevitch and Shinn 2005).[11] Variants of such approaches focus on the role of political parties and partisan politics, but mostly in terms of underlying societal interests (Garrett 1998a, b). A key example is Roe's (2002) focus on "political and social predicates." For Roe, political requirements and the search for social peace shape corporate governance. The left-right axis predicts ownership concentration and regulations favoring shareholder interests. Strong social democratic politics in most European countries lead to less diffuse ownership and to weak minority shareholder protections (49–61). The political game may also allow unusual alliances between societal groups, such as shareholders and labor (Cioffi and Höpner 2004; Gourevitch and Shinn 2005; Höpner 2003). Indeed, center-left parties may seek improved investor protection and ownership-manager separation as a means to improve employee welfare.

Finally, a third pole emphasizes institutions as critical in shaping reform outcomes. The VOC approach emphasizes a set of interlocking and interdependent institutions in CMEs spanning industrial relations, welfare, and finance. These institutions have arisen over time as responses to coordination problems within national economies and are resistant to change (Hall and Soskice 2001). On the issue of corporate governance, several prominent theories emphasize the crucial role of domestic legal systems. For la Porta et al., differences in legal systems are the prime variable: civil law systems tend to lead to poor shareholder protection (1997, 1998). Thus, "French civil law countries have both the weakest investor protections and the least developed capital markets" (1997, 1131).

The regime type and the electoral system may also be crucial in aggregating national preferences. A prominent hypothesis infers that proportional electoral systems are more likely to lead to a more stable status quo and limited change (Gourevitch and Shinn 2005; Lijphart 1984, 1999;

10. Amable 2003; Berger and Dore 1996; Gourevitch and Shinn 2005; Guillén 2001; Howell 2003; Kitschelt and Streeck 2004.

11. Gourevitch and Shinn (2005) find that interest group coalitions (various arrangements between labor, managers, and owners) are the primary explanation for various types of corporate governance systems.

Pagano and Volpin 2004). Systems with multiple veto points are less prone to far-reaching reforms (Tsebelis 1995, 2002). Another key institutional source of variation can be found in the structure and belief system of the state. The response to globalization takes different shapes according to a country's enshrined norms and national bureaucratic structures (Vogel 1996). Institutional approaches to national reform pathways in a global context all tend to typologize countries in clusters according to enduring features.

This book builds on these three theories but breaks new ground in specifying the microlevel mechanism through which reform paths are crafted. It emphasizes the centrality of political leaders under specific conditions. When coalitions are evenly balanced, political leaders play an essential role in breaking the stalemate. In turn, legislative, electoral, and party institutions determine the ability of political leaders to tilt the reform outcome one way or the other.

Uncertainty, Fragmentation, and Institutional Crisis

When conflicting cross-pressures exert pressure on a political economic system, there exist multiple potential equilibria. Leaders matter in choosing pathways among these competing pressures. The intrusion of the golden bargain presents novel opportunities, but also reveals a displacement in the global environment. This displacement exposes a new potential misalignment between the dominant forces of the global economy and the domestic economy. Societies can choose to live with this misalignment or to reduce the gap. If they do not take action, they may expect that the gap will grow and that national competitiveness and growth will be affected.

The existence of misalignment between dominant global currents and the domestic system—or the mere belief of such a misalignment—puts the survival of domestic arrangements into question. The government may initiate change at any point to reduce the gap, but the timing is unknown to most economic and social actors. The impact of possible reforms is also unknown. The cost of living with the domestic-external mismatch is unknown as well. Facing this new uncertainty, politically influential groups will react differently. As shown by Downs, uncertainty divides voters (1957, 82–83) and, one may add, affects the cohesiveness of social and political groups. The bonds are loosened. Uncertainty offers opportunities for "persuaders," particularly interest group leaders and parties, to provide new facts and reduce uncertainty (83).

The other immediate consequence of the displacement induced by the golden bargain is to introduce a gap between economic and socio-political logic. Institutions such as the social contract or the relationship-based capitalism analyzed by Dore (1983) were sustainable because they were at once socially effective and economically efficient. In most systems, many national economists quickly rise in support of the golden bargain and the OECD proposals.[12] Increasing the efficiency of capital allocation, supporting the capitalist process of "creative destruction," and reducing the cost of corporate capital make great economic sense. In a replay of Polanyi's nineteenth-century process, however, this economic logic goes against the logic of social and political stability. Facing the uncertainty offered by the golden bargain, political leaders need to balance economic gains and social risks. So do interest groups.

This rise of uncertainty and the growing decoupling of economic and social logic lead to an institutional crisis. Most actors realize that domestic institutions are no longer optimal, even though the path toward change is not obvious. In this situation, North's and Aoki's work on institutions and institutional change is particularly illuminating. North argues that institutions serve to reduce uncertainty and transaction costs. At the same time, institutions are "created to serve the interests of those with the bargaining power to devise new rules" (North 1990, 16). In his limited analysis of institutional change, North states that changes in relative prices lead key actors to renegotiate contracts and incrementally change rules (86). Aoki's work integrates the role of cognitive aspects of institutions. He starts out by defining an institution as the equilibrium outcome of a game or, more specifically, as a "self-sustaining system of shared beliefs" (Aoki 2001, 10). This allows for a new approach to institutional change. According to Aoki, environmental and internal changes can trigger an institutional crisis in the cognitive sense: "the shared beliefs regarding the ways in which a game is played may begin to be questioned, and the agents may be driven to reexamine their own choice rules based on new information not embodied in existing institutions" (18). Aoki defines a general cognitive disequilibrium as a situation in which a "gap between aspiration and achievement occurs in a critical mass" (240). Examples of factors that could trigger such a general disequilibrium include technological innovation, external shocks, or a change in the distribution of assets and power among key actors.

Aoki identifies an interactive mechanism between triggers of change and accumulation of internal tensions: "External shocks alone may not be sufficient to trigger institutional change. Without the accumulation of the seeds of change, agents may adapt their subjective game models only marginally . . ." (240). The disequilibrium phase entails a period of competition in which different actors generate novel ideas. In turn, a new institution may emerge that is more consistent with the internal state of the domain (242).

The institutional mismatch created by the new situation of the golden bargain matches Aoki's definition of a cognitive disequilibrium. The very

---

12. See Dore's excellent analysis of these new voices in late 1990s Japan (1999, 2000).

knowledge of the mismatch between domestic institutions and the global environment among key domestic actors creates uncertainty, and this uncertainty triggers a process of readjustment among interest groups. Does this readjustment lead to institutional change?

Coalition Logjam and Political Resistance

In a stakeholder capitalist system, corporate restructuring and reforms affect the core of the postwar social contract. By reintroducing flexibility and inducing change in the long-stable system of industrial relations, corporate reforms tend to run directly against the interests of labor. At the same time, because they shift the balance of power between shareholders and management and challenge the long-guaranteed sovereignty of managers, corporate reforms also run into opposition by management.

Furthermore, when large corporations engage in restructuring, the second-tier suppliers, distributors, and associated companies suffer even more. This leads to upheaval in certain regional areas, bringing determined opposition by all affected members of parliament. For good measure, in most stakeholder systems, some associated ministries, such as the ministry of labor, or the ministry of construction, or even the ministry of justice, are bound to oppose drastic change. These various opposition centers amount to a vast and powerful coalition of labor, organized management, traditional politicians, and selected ministries. This coalition can rely on appeals to a public that is chiefly concerned about unemployment and on the whole supportive of the system that guaranteed success for decades.

At the same time, however, these pro–status quo interest groups are fragmented. Subgroups of corporate managers who are directly exposed to global finance and individual entrepreneurs speak up for reforms. In some cases, leaders support reforms because they have long been excluded from the cozy networks of the current system. So do some labor leaders—not necessarily followed by their base. These more independent actors function as social entrepreneurs and may seek a realignment of interest groups with a view to the future.[13] Nevertheless, these future-oriented entrepreneurs remain a minority and do not control key interest groups at the time of the displacement.

The pro-reform coalition also includes selected private investors, who support global investors, and elite cross-sectoral ministries. Investors have the most to gain in corporate reforms, since such reforms aim at improving the return on equity in industry. Private domestic investors have the same interests as global investors. Elite bureaucrats who have a stake in the overall long-term competitiveness or sanity of industry support corporate

---

13. For a classic analysis of interest group entrepreneurs, see Moe (1980), particularly 36–39.

reforms because they are directly related to a better allocation of capital in the economy. In addition, they support corporate reforms because in a post-deregulation, post-industrial policy world, corporate reforms offer the state a chance to regain a significant role. Finally, urban voters have a stake in reforms that may lead to economic revival and better long-term opportunities, although this group is diffuse and not highly motivated.

Overall, while the pro-reform coalition possesses significant force, it is more than offset by the pro–status quo coalition. Because the social contract arrangement is a mutually beneficial situation for a large set of interest groups, these groups are bound together in defense of the status quo. Therefore, the process of realignment in societal coalitions—presented as essential to shifts in corporate governance systems by Gourevitch and Shinn (2005)—is unlikely to occur "naturally."

As a result of this lineup of societal forces, political forces are also initially aligned in defense of the status quo. Members of parliament with significant support from either labor, organized management, or small and medium-sized enterprises stand in opposition to structural reforms. Political parties on the Right and the Left remain organized around clientelist links to core interest groups and are unable to embrace structural change. In the case of Japan, Pempel (1999a) finds that this high degree of political resistance to structural reforms goes a long way in explaining institutional resilience in the face of external stimuli. Similarly, Kitschelt finds that the party systems in Germany and Japan "operated more as fetters than as catalysts for reforms" (Kitschelt 2003, 334).

Thus, while the external impetus of equity capital changes the behavior of some economic actors and fragments the interest group structure, it is not sufficient to induce a shift in broad societal coalitions and institutional change. The interest group structure and the party system remain tilted toward preserving the status quo.

Political Entrepreneurs as the Source of Institutional Innovation

The missing link in the political analysis of structural reforms in response to global signals is the role of political entrepreneurs. In this book, I build on existing work on political entrepreneurs (Downs 1957; Geddes 1994; Kingdon 1984; Moe 1980), yet link their role to the mediation of new global forces and unpack the key determinants for their effectiveness.

Who are political entrepreneurs and what do they do? Kingdon defined policy entrepreneurs as "people willing to invest their resources in return for future policies they favor" (1984, 204). They are individuals with both short-term capital and a long-term goals. They have the ability to influence others and to shift the positions of voters or of societal groups, when uncertainty creates doubt over multiple pathways. Kingdon also emphasizes the role of entrepreneurs in bringing problems to the top of the political agenda, presenting proposals, and coupling problems with solutions. Thus, political entrepreneurs may not be just persuaders in a context of uncertainty, but also active opportunity seekers who put together proposals and deals that serve to meet the needs of key groups.

Political entrepreneurs are individuals endowed with specific knowledge of and information about the golden bargain and a particular situation that makes them likely to have a role in gaining support from their audience. Typically, they are ambitious young politicians with a need to create a reputation that may carry them to power in the long run. They bet on reform, given their own assets as well as their own evaluations of the gap between the current system and the global system. They spot opportunities for arbitrage and attempt to realize latent gains through leadership.

What motivates political entrepreneurs? Fundamentally, political entrepreneurs act the way they do because they anticipate that taking on the cause of reform will improve their political position in the long-term. Self-interest can be seen as a key motivation for the actions of political entrepreneurs, even though it is usually reinforced by a vision of national modernization and community service. In a competitive political environment, emerging new political leaders seek novel issues to build a visible reputation on and to persuade voters that they are the most qualified candidates. An emerging leader needs to spot an opportunity for arbitrage under situations of uncertainty and offer a clear solution, betting that he or she may gain power if he or she successfully spurs institutional change. Taking on the golden bargain offers such an emerging leader the opportunity to pass for a "modernist" and to tap new resources. Such political entrepreneurs tend to have a higher discount ratio of short-term costs and a lower discount ratio of future benefits. That is, they are either safer and more impervious to short-term political costs (and interest group wrath) than their colleagues, or their risk-taking character and long-term ambition leads them to value long-term political benefits more than other politicians. Or both. In Japan, they almost always are second-generation or safe-seat politicians with high-flying ambitions. Or they tend to be extraordinarily ambitious individuals who are willing to bet the house on the ultimate goal of becoming prime minister.

Political entrepreneurs may act from different political positions. Three main avenues of political entrepreneurship can be identified: the golden avenue, where the prime minister or the president acts as the critical political entrepreneur; the cabinet minister or coalition partner route; and the Young Turk route. In the golden avenue, the political entrepreneur manages to obtain the position of prime minister on the back of a bet on reform or through other bargaining mechanisms. Although constrained by party, coalition, and voters, the political entrepreneur is then able to directly use the tools of power to work for institutional change and reap the benefits from global investors. In the cabinet minister route, either a key ally of the prime minister in the main party or a leader from a junior coalition party is the key entrepreneurial actor.[14] These middle level leaders negotiate their political support in exchange for reform coverage. In some cases, when acute political competition or a weak majority increases the leverage of the opposition, political entrepreneurship can even originate with the leadership of an opposition party.[15]

In the Young Turk route, the political entrepreneur remains locked on the second rung of power and pushes his agenda from below. Should the entrepreneur gather a significant following and pose an important threat to powerful elders, however, the prime minister or political leader is likely to co-opt the entrepreneur and give him a chance to pursue institutional change from a ministerial position. As early as 1915, Michels (1962, 179–80) described this classic mechanism in the following terms: "The older leaders always endeavor to harness to their own chariot the forces of those new movements which have not yet found powerful leaders, so as to obviate from the first all competition and all possibility of the formation of new and vigorous intellectual currents." Within parties, Michels observed that leaders tend to close ranks in order to preserve their oligarchy over the party rank and file. Thus, a political entrepreneur is often able to lead the charge of structural reform from a secondary position. Being in the prime ministerial seat is not a sine qua non condition.

In their effort to enlarge the pro-reform coalition, political entrepreneurs resort to three main tools: persuasion, manipulation, and delegation. Persuasion is the art of influencing key groups by providing clear visions and roadmaps.[16] It can operate at a rational level, when leaders make use of direct tools of power, such as the threat of dissolving parliament. Power may also allow political entrepreneurs to induce recalcitrant members of their group with side payments and support on other issue areas. Persuasion can also operate at the level of beliefs or world views (Sabel 1982, 14–22). Leaders may craft a powerful long-term vision and initiate a reordering in trust relationships and a transformation of identities, what Sabel calls "deliberation" in his work on constitutional orders (1997, 170).

14. A key example can be found in the disproportionate impact of a very small party, Sakigake, and of its leader, Takemura Masayoshi in 1994–96 (Curtis 2002, 10; Kusano 1999). I am also grateful to comments received from Sara Konoe on this issue.

15. A key example is provided by the role played by the opposition Democratic Party (DPJ) during the financial Diet of fall 1998 in Japan. Due to the loss of a majority in the Upper House, the prime minister was compelled to incorporate some policy elements championed by Young Turks within the DPJ.

16. For well-known rationalist definitions of persuasion, see Downs (1957) in the electoral arena, or Neustadt (1980) on the use of persuasion by presidents. Zaller's (1991) pathbreaking work analyzed the process of mass persuasion of voters through media.

Political leaders also resort to manipulation, or the art of changing the material conditions of the world so as to shift its direction. The art of manipulation by political entrepreneurs consists in tying the targeted corporate reforms to other types of reforms in an effort to divide the coalitional majority lined up against corporate reforms. Political leaders may also redefine a component of reforms in a novel direction so as to sow uncertainty in the midst of reform opponents. Societal and party coalitions can be manipulated and divided, so as to engineer support for institutional change.[17] In addition, manipulation can also operate at the level of world views and culture.

In many cases, however, persuasion and manipulation only get political entrepreneurs part of the way toward institutional change. The other tool that political leaders can count on is delegation to the state bureaucracy.[18] For political entrepreneurs, bureaucratic delegation offers great advantages. In systems where an elite cross-sectoral bureaucracy exists (as in France, Japan, and Korea),[19] it may offer the services of an elite think tank and act as a booster for reforms. By delegating the crafting of particular reforms to such an elite bureaucracy, political entrepreneurs may be able to deflect the blame of painful reforms in the short-term onto the bureaucrats. This artifact may also decrease the visibility of reforms among the public at the most difficult time and lead to discreet invisible reforms.

17. For a rationalist account of manipulation of agendas or social choices, see Riker (1982; 1986, 142–43). Riker's findings conform to Michels' (1962, 168) earlier empirical observations that in the battle between oligarchic leaders and the masses, leaders are often victorious if they act together. The sources of their superiority lie in their asymmetric knowledge and control of the agenda and rules.

18. Regarding the lively debate concerning the dangers of capture embedded in the relationship between politicians and bureaucrats, see Aberbach, Rockman, and Putnam (1981); Carpenter (2001); Cowhey and McCubbins (1995); Curtis (2002); Downs (1966); Epstein and O'Halloran (1999); Huber and Shipan (2002); Inoguchi (1989); McCubbins and Noble (1995); Shonfield (1965); Suleiman (1984); Tiberghien (2002a). This book, however, accepts the insights of agency theory, which shows that delegation does not mean loss of control. Political entrepreneurs have both the tools and motivation to monitor their agents in the crafting of reforms.

19. It is important to note that this elite bureaucracy is only a small part of the entire bureaucracy. The elite bureaucracy is a small corps historically joined by the best and brightest of each generation and is responsible for setting the overall economic strategy. In France, it is part of the Ministry of Industry, Economy, and Finance, but mostly located in the Trésor (Treasury, a sub-part of the ministry). In Japan, it has historically been divided between the Ministry of Finance (MOF) and the Ministry for International Trade and Industry (MITI, now called METI or Ministry for Economy, Trade, and Industry). Socialization sets this elite bureaucratic corps apart from the rest of the bureaucracy and from bureaucracies in other systems. In most state-led systems, members of the elite corps are trained in a single and ultra-competitive institution (ENA in France, the faculty of law of Tokyo University in Japan), where they enter at a very young age. The training includes strong identity-formation as the national elite and a strong message of service to the nation.

The Threat of Voter Backlash

Although the argument emphasizes the role of leaders in situations of uncertainty and fragmentation and downplays the voice of voters in setting the course for reform, voters may yet have the last word. As shown in 2002 in the French presidential elections or in 2005 in the French referendum on the EU, voters may suddenly become relevant and call off the game played by political leaders. Political leaders may thus obtain enough slack through manipulation, delegation, and institutional slack, but this slack is temporary. Political entrepreneurs remain aware of this latent medium-term threat and bet that they can succeed in demonstrating tangible benefits before a backlash occurs.

Structural Determinants of Reform Entrepreneurship

What are the sources of freedom and constraints that determine the action of political entrepreneurs? Where do they get their slack? Because political entrepreneurs promote reforms that go beyond the position of their own party and aim at reshaping the status quo within their party, their ability to act depends on political space available to them within their party, coalition, and legislature. Political autonomy is to political entrepreneurs what oxygen is to living beings. Under tight constraints and strict rules, political entrepreneurs are bottled up and unable to push reforms forward. Persuasion and manipulation operate within institutional constraints.

National political systems vary in their receptiveness to political entrepreneurs. Some empower government leaders with sizeable advantages over legislative parties, enabling them to take bold steps and push their base in new directions. Other political systems entangle leaders in complex rules and ensure that multiple veto points exist in the system, so as to limit the chance of leaders straying beyond a broad-based consensus. Although legislative and constitutional rules play a significant part in delineating degrees of political autonomy for political entrepreneurs, the most important differentiating feature is found in the party system. Depending on the number and strength of parties and intra-party rules within the ruling party, a Westminster-style parliamentary system may or may not leave great political autonomy for political entrepreneurs. In addition, political entrepreneurs may gain autonomy through delegation to an elite cross-sectoral bureaucratic corps, when such a corps exists.

Strategic Political Autonomy: Breaking Loose from Parties and Coalitions

Kingdon (1984) used the concept of "policy windows" to indicate propitious conditions for political action. In this book, I advance strategic political autonomy (SPA) as the key concept that best measures the degree of political slack available to political entrepreneurs in interaction with key support groups.

Strategic political autonomy is defined as the political space available to empowered political entrepreneurs in their relations to party, coalition, and legislature. This builds upon Kitschelt's (1994) concept of leadership autonomy and expands it beyond European Socialist parties and beyond the relations of party leaders with their party. Kitschelt's pathbreaking work on European social democracy underlines the crucial role of internal party organization in the evolution of electoral strategies. In Kitschelt's analysis, however, the focus is on parties and their ability to react to systemic change. In this book, I reverse the focus from parties to political leaders and enlarge it beyond the parties' internal structure.

As a measure of the political space available to empowered political entrepreneurs (prime ministers, ministers, or cabinet members in particular), strategic political autonomy centers on three sets of relations: between government leaders and the party, between government leaders and coalition partners, and between government leaders and the legislature.

However, a certain degree of autonomy from voters is also necessary for political leaders to move forward with structural reforms. In the short-term, uncertainty, asymmetric information, and inattentive citizens may indeed give political space to government leaders (Bartels 1996; Kuklinkski et al. 2001; Lau and Redlawsky 2001; Zaller 1992). Ultimately, however, voters may make up for their limited information through heuristics (the use of simplifying cues and proxies, such as party labels) and fuller information (Lupia and McCubbins 1998; Lupia, McCubbins, and Popkin 2000; Popkin 1991; Sniderman, Brody, and Tetlock 1991). They may also be responsive to new information provided during political campaigns (Lodge, Steenbergen, and Brau 1995). Political entrepreneurs gamble that they can ride the J-curve of reforms and show benefits by the time voters become more attentive or informed.

I define strategic political autonomy as the combination of four components. The first one, *autonomy within the party*, refers to the ability of the leader to override party preferences and to stray from established party positions. In a parliamentary system the most essential characteristic for reform effectiveness relates to the legitimacy and power of the majority party leadership over the rank-and-file members. If the leadership is directly elected by the party membership at large, rather than chosen by a smaller group (such as the caucus of party MPs), its legitimacy will be enhanced. If the leadership controls party purses and appointments, its leadership is likewise enhanced. Conversely, cooptation by a group of senior party members within an oligopolistic party structure (as in the case of the factionalized LDP in Japan) does not bequeath a high degree of autonomy. By their very fragmented nature such oligopolistic parties offer interest groups multiple points of entry and opportunities for competitive bidding. Factional parties create intense intra-party competition and include—at all times— credible alternative leaders. These parties tend to demand intense consultation and co-decisions from the party leader and to keep that leader on a short leash. In a presidential system, reform effectiveness hinges on a strong president with agenda-setting powers and a weak or fragmented party system (as in Korea between 1997 and 2000).

The second component is the *degree of leadership security*. This refers to the breadth of support in the initial selection and the length of the leadership term. A party leader elected with a large margin of victory in a vote by grassroots militants is more secure than a leader chosen by a few faction leaders. In Japan, LDP leader Mori Yoshirō was selected by a secret meeting of five faction leaders in April 2000 and remained beholden to these leaders. By early 2001, when some of these leaders asked him to resign, his time was up. His margin of security within the party remained limited throughout his tenure. By contrast, Koizumi Junichirō was selected through a general vote of all party militants in combination with a vote of members of parliament and became assured of a certain amount of political time. This leadership security was reinforced by favorable opinion polls. In addition, leadership security is strengthened by political time in office. Political time for party leaders is a function of two clocks. The prime mechanism is the routinization of leadership selection. If leaders must run for re-election every two or three years and are limited to two mandates (as with the LDP in Japan), they have less political space than those who are free to call selection conferences at a time of their choosing (as with the Socialist Party in France until 2006). In addition, the longer the electoral time between national elections, the greater the political autonomy. Non-concurrent elections for two chambers of parliament or between president and parliament reduce political autonomy. Political autonomy is highest in the honeymoon phase of a new government.

The third component is the *degree of autonomy within ruling coalitions* (when relevant). When a government relies on a ruling coalition, autonomy and security within the party are not sufficient. Political entrepreneurs must also gain autonomy from their ruling partners. This happens when the party of the political entrepreneur wields a high degree of control over its coalition partners. Balanced coalitions are more likely to result in complex processes of coordination and co-decision, processes that reduce the political space available to political entrepreneurs.

The fourth and final component of political autonomy is an institutional one: the *degree of control over the legislative agenda*. Empowered political entrepreneurs in the executive branch must have the ability to win battles over their own party's opposition in parliament. The existence of constitutional or legislative rules that give direct leverage to the cabinet over the legislature is conducive to higher degrees of political entrepreneurship. Such rules allow the cabinet to set the day-to-day agenda or control the amendment process. On the other hand, when rules bestow wide autonomy to the legislature in setting the legislative agenda or amendments, they encourage the creation of veto points or counterpowers in the legislature. Legislative leaders gain the ability to stand up to executive leaders and extract compromises, especially when the party rules do not impose strict hierarchical control. In addition, legislative rules or norms may give opposition leaders a role in setting the legislative agenda and further dilute the political space of political entrepreneurs.[20]

Strategic Bureaucratic Delegation: Avoiding Obstacles and Blame

Bureaucratic delegation is a key tool used by political entrepreneurs to outflank opponents. Political entrepreneurs can resort more effectively to bureaucratic delegation when they have a suitable partner. The ideal bureaucratic partner for the delegation of structural reforms is a unified elite cross-sectoral economic bureaucracy. Such a strong and unified entity offers both the capacity for action and clear opportunity for control by political leaders. By contrast, a divided or fragmented bureaucracy offers multiple avenues for penetration by interest groups and is difficult for the executive leadership to control. In a battle against traditional interest groups and party militants, an elite bureaucratic corps offers allies, rather than rivals, to political entrepreneurs. When unified under a hierarchical (monopolistic) structure, the bureaucratic leadership stands to gain by siding with a reform-oriented executive leadership. By writing the rules and reorganizing industry, the elite bureaucracy may gain in power and future opportunities. Conversely, a unified elite bureaucracy is more easily monitored by the political leadership than a fragmented one.[21] In the case of countries like France, the coordination between elite economic bureaucrats and political leaders is further facilitated by the close-knit social, educational, and class links that exist among them. Senior bureaucrats from

20. See, for example, Mochizuki (1982). On the legislative process and legislative agenda control, a large body of work exists both within American politics and comparative politics (Cox, Masuyama, and Mathew 2000; Cox 1987; Cox and McCubbins 1993, 2005; Huber 1996; McCubbins and Noble 1995; McCubbins and Sullivan 1987).

21. This approach builds upon recent work by Huber and McCarty (2004, 481). They argue that "low bureaucratic capacity diminishes incentives for bureaucrats to comply with legislation, making it more difficult for politicians to induce bureaucrats to take actions that politicians desire." In other words, politicians are more likely to successfully monitor senior bureaucrats when the bureaucracy has a high capacity and is unified. In turn, when such conditions are fulfilled, delegation from political leaders to bureaucrats is more likely to succeed and to lead to bureaucratic behavior that fits the goals of empowered political entrepreneurs.

the Treasury and political leaders are almost all graduates of the same elite school, the *Ecole Nationale d'Administration* (ENA), which trains a mere two hundred to three hundred students per year.

As in the relationships between political leaders and political parties, political control over elite bureaucrats is most endangered when the elite bureaucracy is fragmented into competing factions (bureaucratic oligarchy). A fragmented elite bureaucracy generates competing reform visions and piecemeal reforms. Various bureaucratic actors develop different positions with respect to reforms and entrench these positions as a way to differentiate themselves from other actors. This situation offers possibilities for political leaders opposed to reforms to exploit this competition. The political entrepreneur loses the ability to effectively delegate to elite bureaucrats.

In addition to the existence of an elite cross-sectoral bureaucracy without sectional interests and a high degree of unity within this elite bureaucracy, international institutions may augment the capacity for successful delegation by empowered political entrepreneurs. International institutions that include some degree of sovereignty transfer and where the national leadership has some degree of control are likely to facilitate the domestic process of structural reforms. In situations of strong linkages with an international institution, political leaders can indeed delegate the creation of unpopular structural reforms to the international sphere, either directly or through national elite bureaucrats.[22] International institutions serve as Trojan horses for domestic leaders. They enable domestic leaders to let reform blueprints boomerang back to the national sphere. The ideal case for this mechanism to work includes two main features: overall national support for some transfer of sovereignty to a given international organization but a large degree of control by the national bureaucracy over the details of agreement.

Methodology and Case Selection

This book relies upon the comparative method in three similar countries: France, Japan, and Korea. The comparative analysis of these three cases reveals the salience of domestic institutional variables in crafting three distinct pathways. At the same time, cross-temporal comparisons within each case between reform periods and non-reform periods allow for change in the degree of strategic autonomy of the political leadership and its impact on reform outcomes. To perform such inter-temporal comparisons and to tease out causality within the processes followed by each case, the book

---

22. A prime example is that of the European Union, particularly for issues that fall under the prerogatives of the Competition Directorate in the European Commission.

relies upon the process-tracing methodology. Namely, as a country moves from the initial state to a reformed state, I have attempted to identify all key political steps (proposals, hearings, electoral platforms, cabinet decisions, and parliamentary proceedings) and all key actors involved in the process at each step. Through this approach, the actual political genesis becomes visible. The core causal line can be teased out of the complexity and noise. The actual role of political entrepreneurs and their degrees of autonomy can be appraised at different periods.

Traditionally, France, Japan, and Korea have been considered as alternatives to the mainstream free market systems of the United States and the United Kingdom. These alternative systems have been sometimes labeled as "state-led economies," "dirigiste states," or "developmental states."[23] All three countries followed an "alternative" capitalist model, however, and were permeated by similar beliefs of "exceptionalism,"[24] beliefs that fed upon a strong sense of nationalism. All three states used the ultimate tool of credit control (Zysman 1983). All three gave paramount importance to industrial development and economic competitiveness. The French (and Korean) state(s) sponsored the emergence of "national champions" and channeled scarce resources to them. Japan relied on an active industrial policy for the emergence of certain priority industries (albeit only in certain sectors, as shown by Okimoto 1989).

These systems have been seen in the past as the strongest alternative to the liberal model. Given the central presence of the state in these economies, structural reforms are expected to be tougher to pursue there. This is especially true as these reforms target the very factors seen as the sources of national comparative advantage. These three nations can therefore be considered as a set of independent countries with initially similar systems, a good set for the study of differences and variations.[25]

The principal focus of this study is the post-financial deregulation period between 1995 and 2002. This marks an era of open capital flows in all countries when states lost the tools of credit control and foreign exchange control and had fewer direct means of intervening in the industrial structure.[26] The mid- to late-1990s also correspond to a relatively homogeneous worldwide

23. A large literature exists on the statist model (Cohen 1992; Johnson 1982; Katzenstein 1985; Krasner 1977, 1984; Loriaux et al. 1997; Otake and Naoto 1999; Sautter 1996; Zysman 1983).

24. For example, see Otake (1999) on the analysis of exceptionalism in his comparative study of the French and Japanese political processes.

25. J.S. Mill's Method of Difference.

26. Financial liberalization had a major impact on the state-business relationship, particularly in Korea. Woo-Cummings (1997) argues that financial liberalization led to the growing reliance of conglomerates on equity markets for their financing and their decreasing need of the state.

wave of corporate restructuring. Unlike the first wave of restructuring that occurred in the late 1970s and 1980s,[27] the developments of the 1990s appear to have been driven by financial forces (return on equity concerns, global trends of mergers and acquisitions, and changes in corporate governance).[28] All three countries underwent major change in the period from 1995 to 2000, and their divergence also became clear.

27. See Uriu (1996), Smith (1998), and Cohen (1989) for excellent studies of the politics of restructuring in the 1980s in Japan, Spain, and France.

28. These trends have been analyzed in a growing number of publications. For example, Lemasle and Tixier (2000) and the Bank of Japan (Takahashi 2000; Takahashi and Tsuyoshi 2000).

2

A Story of Change and Divergence

What explains the variation in national responses to the golden bargain, even among relatively similar economies? Why have Korea and France been able to go further in reforming their economic structure than Japan?

The degrees of strategic political autonomy and options for effective bureaucratic delegation define the reform capacity of political entrepreneurs as they mediate the incentives of the golden bargain. In this chapter, I systematically analyze the components of this argument and present aggregate comparative data on all three countries that clearly demonstrates the linkage between political autonomy and reform outcome. In particular, I provide overall data to measure the intensity of the golden bargain, the degrees of political autonomy and bureaucratic delegation, as well as reform outcomes, before analyzing the relation between these variables.

The primary focus is on the period from 1995 to 2002. Indeed, 1995 can be seen as a cutoff point when the golden bargain becomes visible in most stakeholder systems. Indeed, by 1995, most OECD countries had opened their capital accounts and largely deregulated finance (with some limitations in Korea) and the flood of equity capital was becoming visible across the globe. Although the visible jumps in the foreign penetration of domestic stock markets varied somewhat (1995–97 in France, 1998–2000 in Korea, and 1999 in Japan), the global presence of the golden bargain can be traced back to about 1995. I therefore analyze the immediate response of relatively similarly economic systems to this new external stimulus.

Common External Impulse: The Revolution of Global Portfolio Flows

What is the actual magnitude of global equity flows, and do they affect Japan, France, and Korea similarly? Cross-border capital flows as a whole took off after 1985. In particular, cross-border transactions in bonds and equities, as a percentage of GDP, skyrocketed among G7 countries. Starting in the 2–5 percent range in 1975, they reached 100 percent of GDP by the late 1990s in all but Japan—at 91 percent, due to an enduring cyclical depression of its financial markets. They further increased to the 300–500 percent range by 2003 in most countries. Figure 2.1 summarizes the evolution of total portfolio flows (equity and bonds) in five of the seven major developed economies.

The explosion in portfolio flows as a percentage of GDP is visible in all five advanced economies included in figure 2.1 beginning in the early 1980s. Yet a great acceleration takes place after 1995, particularly in all

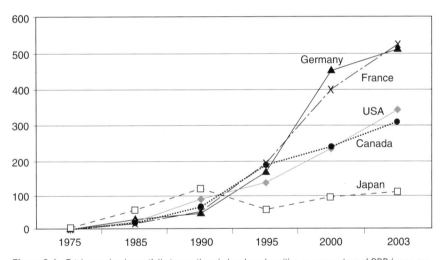

Figure 2.1. Total cross-border portfolio transactions in bonds and equities as a percentage of GDP (gross purchases and sales of securities between residents and nonresidents) among five key countries
   Source: Table VI.5, Bank of International Settlements (BIS), 69th Annual Report, available on the BIS web site at www.bis.org/publ/ar99e.htm. Updates for 2000 and 2003 from BIS Monetary and Economic department, May 2006. The data originates from central banks and national statistics.
   Notes:
   • Unfortunately, data for other countries, such as the UK or Korea, is not included in the BIS report. The UK, in particular, discontinued the reporting of gross capital flows in the early 1990s.
   • The year 1990 was the year of the summit and the subsequent burst of the stock bubble in Japan. It was an anomaly.
   • For France in 1975, the data was not available. To retain the integrity of the graph, the average of the other four countries (3) has been used here, instead of a distorting 0.

three European economies considered in the Bank of International Settlements (BIS) sample. Initially, the bulk of the portfolio flows consists of bond flows. Equity flows take off after 1995 and their rate of growth after that date is greater than that of bond flows. Again, the flows are greatest in France and Germany (as well as in Canada).

Equity inflows are one of the most rapidly growing components of global capital flows. Equity flows are primarily driven by U.S. and, to a lesser degree, British pension funds and other institutional investors. During the 1990s, as the sums managed by British and U.S. funds grew, these investors sought to diversify their portfolios and increase their overseas investments. Between 1990 and 1998 alone, U.S. investments in foreign shares grew from $197.3 million to $1.4 trillion (Ahmadjian and Robbins 2002, 4). As of 2000, the assets managed by U.S. and UK institutional investors represented 70 percent of global institutional assets. While all other institutional investors kept their share of investment in equity at below 10 percent, U.S. and British investors placed 65 percent and 15 percent, respectively, of their assets in equity (Gourevitch and Shinn 2005, 207).

Within OECD countries (where the bulk of equity inflows and outflows are concentrated), the cumulated stock of equity flows has surged sevenfold over the last twelve years, increasing from $800 billion in 1990 to $5.6 trillion in 2002 (despite the collapse of the stock bubble in 1990) (International Monetary Fund 2005a). As a proportion of stock market capitalization in OECD countries, the share of foreign equity more than doubled from 9.1 percent to 21.2 percent between 1990 and 2002.[1]

The national impact of this flood of global equity capital is uneven, although the global capital market shapes overall opportunity costs. Countries may be net global capital importers, but also net equity capital exporters (as in the United States). For example, although the United States is dependent on massive capital inflows to sustain its large balance of payment deficit, most of this capital consists of government bonds and foreign direct investment (FDI).[2] Conversely, Japan, a major capital exporter, finds itself in a resource-dependent situation on the equity side: equity liabilities of $308 billion and equity assets of $211 billion.

Table 2.1 presents data on foreign penetration of national stock markets in all OECD countries in 2002, using the IMF's *International Financial Statistics*. It confirms the existence of different clusters of countries with respect to equity capital inflows. Countries with low penetration (below 12 percent)

1. International Financial Statistics (IFS) for individual countries' equity liabilities (International Monetary Fund 2005a); World Development Indicators for stock market capitalization by country and for OECD totals (World Bank 2005); and the author's calculations.

2. On the equity side, the U.S. ledger at the end of 2002 shows foreign liabilities of $900 billion and total equity assets of $1.3 trillion (International Monetary Fund 2005b).

Table 2.1. Total portfolio equity investments in OECD countries (end 2002)*

Countries	Total equity liabilities (billions, 2002 US$)	Total stock market capitalization (billions, 2002 US$)	Total foreign equity/ stock market capitalization
Australia	$93	$381	24.5%
Austria	17	32	54.4
Belgium	21	128	16.4
Canada	**47**	**575**	**8.1**
Czech Republic	4	16	26.7
Denmark	23	77	29.8
Finland	89	139	64.2
France	**339**	**967**	**35.1**
Germany	**213**	**686**	**31.0**
Greece	8	69	12.3
Hungary	4	13	28.9
Iceland	0	6	1.6
Ireland	350	60	584.0
Italy	**30**	**477**	**6.2**
Japan	**340**	**2,126**	**16.0**
Korea, Rep.	77	249	30.9
Luxembourg	0	23	0.0
Mexico	43	103	41.5
Netherlands	262	401	65.3
New Zealand	6	22	26.1
Norway	0	67	0.0
Poland	4	29	15.3
Portugal	17	43	40.6
Slovak Republic	1	2	26.8
Spain	123	462	26.6
Sweden	54	177	30.5
Switzerland	315	554	56.9
Turkey	3	34	10.1
UK	**660**	**1,864**	**35.4**
USA	**1,261**	**11,052**	**11.4**
TOTAL OECD	$4,405	$20,833	21.1%

Source: IMF's International Financial Statistics for equity liability totals (available online at ifs.apdi.net/imf/about.asp) and World Bank's World Development Index for stock market capitalization data (available online at devdata.worldbank.org/dataonline.
*G7 countries are in bold.

include both the major exporter of equity capital (the United States), but also countries such as Canada and Italy that may still be less attractive to global capital or have significant obstacles. A second group of countries shows a moderate level with foreign shares between 12 and 24 percent. This group includes Japan, Poland, and Australia. Finally, some countries, mostly in northwestern Europe, have a high penetration of foreign equity capital. In particular, the Netherlands, the United Kingdom, France, Switzerland,

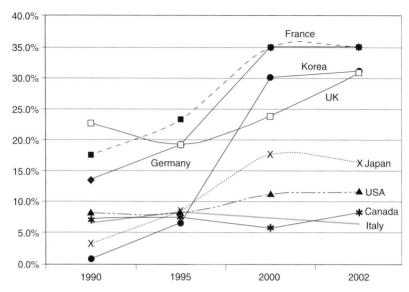

Figure 2.2. Total foreign equity liabilities as a percentage of total stock market capitalization in G7 countries plus Korea
Source: Same as table 2.1.

Germany, and Korea have levels above 30 percent, while Spain is in the up-per 20 percent range.[3] Figure 2.2 summarizes the trends for G7 countries and Korea, using the same IFS data.

It is important to note that equity flows and stock market capitalization can also follow cycles of exuberance and panic that are independent from the fundamentals studied in this book.[4] Thus, the global collapse of the technology stock bubble in 2000 led to an immediate steep drop in stock market capitalization and has affected global equity flows. Some countries, such as Germany, which has seen the collapse of its venture capital market, were hit harder than others.

Foreign penetration in the United States, Canada, and Italy remained stable and low during the 1990s. On the other hand, France, the United

3. The extremely high number for Ireland is explained by the large presence of mutual funds. Mutual funds present a reporting problem. Indeed, the balance-of-payment data used by the IMF includes (as equity investment) holdings in mutual funds. Most of them, however, are not included in the capitalization values of stock markets, as most mutual funds are open-ended and so do not trade. Luxembourg has the same problem, but its balance-of-payment in-formation is lumped together with Belgium in IMF data, creating unusual numbers for both countries.

4. On the issue of psychologically driven cycles in financial markets, see the seminal analy-sis by Kindleberger (2000).

Kingdom, Germany, and Korea all enjoyed a major jump in foreign penetration, from the 15 percent range in 1990 to 30–35 percent in 2002. The Korean jump is particularly noteworthy (from near 0 percent to 30 percent). Japan appears as a moderate case, experiencing a major jump from below 5 percent to 16 percent, but still below the European-Korean cluster. In 2003, however, preliminary data indicate a further jump above 20 percent. Thus, Japan is on its way to joining the highly globalized cluster.[5]

The development and global integration of equity markets lead to the growing "acceptance of common values and standards" among investors around the globe (Nestor and Thompson 2001). In other words, the growing integration of equity markets leads to a convergence of investor expectations toward the concept of shareholder value—or more concretely, a focus on return on equity. This convergence in investor behavior occurs because it is the norm accepted by the dominant world players, that is, U.S. (and UK) pension and mutual funds.[6] Concretely, dominant players in global equity markets, such as CalPERS, can be seen as pacesetters on issues like corporate governance. Once significantly present in a non-liberal system (such as France, Korea, or Japan), they tend to set the agenda of corporate governance reforms and to be followed by other investors, both international and domestic. The behavior of investors and domestic corporations evolve and the state is under pressure to facilitate the evolution by changing the legal framework. The difference between foreign investors and domestic mutual funds or financial investors has become blurred. Financial globalization increasingly means that the models used by investors around the world and their resulting behavior have become homogenized.

The transformative punch of global equity flows is accompanied by the development of international codes and norms. Several international financial organizations with an interest in the global financial system are involved in the process, particularly the BIS, the IMF, and the OECD.[7] With respect to the linkage between global portfolio flows and corporate governance reforms, the role of the OECD is particularly noteworthy. The OECD codification process started in 1998 with a mandate from the G7 countries. It is worth noting that the push from global equity investors is often

---

5. This highly aggregate data using IMF portfolio surveys or balance-of-payment data give figures very close to those reported by individual stock exchanges at the national level. According to such national data, by 2000, foreign ownership of the domestic stock market reached 35 percent in France, 30 percent in Korea, and 18.8 percent in Japan (as a percentage of market capitalization), numbers that closely match the IFS data.

6. Global financial markets are dominated by key players (almost all of them U.S. and British) and structured by regulations that mostly originate with the U.S. hegemon. In Simmons' (2001, 592) words, "Few other areas of international activity are so profoundly dominated by only one or two countries." As much as 85 percent of foreign transactions involve the U.S. dollar, and New York and London are the main centers for global finance.

7. See Gourevitch and Shinn (2005, 224–25) for a good discussion of this point.

reinforced by the independent actions of global bond rating agencies.[8] These two sets of actors carry similar sets of norms and values.

Mediating Variables: National Savings, Cross-Shareholdings, the Banking Crisis, Pensions, and Privatization

Will a large increase in equity inflows automatically lead to strong pressures for change and to structural reforms? No. Five economic variables mitigate the process, amplifying the external signals under certain conditions. These variables modulate the impact of foreign penetration in domestic equity markets. All five variables relate to the fluidity and salience of the stock market in the national setting. The first one is the level of domestic inflow into the stock market. If a large portion of national savings goes into the stock market, the resource dependence on foreign investors will be limited. On the other hand, if the bulk of national savings shuns the stock market, the impact of foreign investors will be leveraged. This is where the irony lies for capital-exporting countries such as Japan, Germany, and France. Although the pool of national savings is enormous, the national stock market remains starved for funds, as most national savings go into bank deposits, postal savings, or real estate. As of 1996, the share of national savings going into stocks is as low as 6 percent in Japan (Hoshi and Kashyap 2001, 243).

Second, the structure of the pension system plays a major role. When pensions are either set up as a generational transfer system or are managed conservatively with few investments in equity, the stock market is more dependent on foreign equity (France). Conversely, when the pension system is managed through capitalization and when a large proportion of these funds is invested in equity following the acceptance of portfolio diversification strategies, the stock market is structurally less dependent on foreign equity (United States).

Third, the fluidity of the stock market matters. If more than half of the shares remain in the hands of stable shareholders and are not traded on the stock market (as in Japan), then the actions of active traders (such as foreign investors) are leveraged and their influence is larger than the size of their absolute presence. Countries such as France, Japan, and Germany had levels of cross-shareholding as high as 40–55 percent of stock market capitalization until the mid-1990s, although these ratios have been falling since. By contrast, foreign institutional investors (especially mutual funds) have been more active in regularly trading shares. As a result, the share of foreign investors in total stock value may lead to a much higher ratio of actual

8. See Sinclair (2005).

share transactions. For example, the 18.3 percent share of foreign investors in the Tokyo stock market in 2001 translated into 50 percent of all stock transactions and a dominant impact on the process of share price formation.[9] Similarly in France in 2001, the 35 percent foreign share of capitalization translated into between 81 and 85 percent in each quarter in the years 1998 and 1999 (Grandjean 2000, 92).

Fourth, the presence of a banking crisis may accentuate the national sensitivity to foreign equity flows. The capital strength of national banks is an important variable that increases the salience of stock market levels for policymakers. Given that banks often hold large amounts of corporate shares and that up to 40 percent of unrealized capital gains are included in computations of capital amount, a strong drop in the stock market level has a powerful detrimental effect on banks' capital adequacy and on their ability to lend. This variable is particularly salient in Japan. When foreign equity investors pull out, as occurred in 1998 and 2000, and when the stock market declines sharply, bank capital shrinks and a credit crunch ensues. This raises political alarm bells.

Finally, a large ongoing program of privatization may make policymakers more sensitive to foreign equity inflows. Indeed, the success of privatization depends on the availability of excess capital, and foreign investors are often the crucial marginal element that can make or break a privatization program. This was particularly true in the case of France in the mid- and late 1990s.

By the turn of the millennium, for different reasons, various countries found themselves in a situation of external resource dependence with respect to equity capital. This is particularly true in France after 1995 and Japan after 1998.

Variations in Initial Situations and the Challenge of Comparison

In a comparative design based on similar cases (Mill's Method of Difference), it is necessary to ensure that unique national variables are sufficiently limited to keep unexplained variance to a minimum. Is it the case for Japan, France, and Korea?

At an aggregate level, despite extensive systemic similarities emphasized in the introduction, the three countries also exhibit significant differences. Some of the most important differences can be found in the political sphere. While Japan has a parliamentary system with a weak prime minister

---

9. See, in particular, the thorough analysis made by Shirota (2002) in his book on foreign investors in the Japanese stock market.

chosen by the National Diet and is often forced to rely on unstable coalitions (in the 1990s), Korea has a presidential system and France a semi-presidential system.[10] In addition, France has transferred some its sovereignty to the European Union, while Japan and Korea are heavily influenced by their military alliances with the United States. Regarding the role of the state in the economy, Okimoto has argued that the Japanese state, as a "network state," has been much less intrusive than the French state in terms of regulatory control, direct ownership of corporations, state revenues, and industrial planning (1989, 2, 24, 48). Similarly, Sautter has noted the difference between the state as a "catalyst" in Japan and the state as a "direct producer" in France (1996, 13). This is why the more recent literature on types of capitalist systems has ceased classifying Japan as a "statist" system altogether (Hall and Soskice 2001). One could also point out key differences in the role of labor: while national labor unions have a large impact on policymaking in France and Korea, the impact of labor is mainly at the firm level in Japan.

Furthermore, the three countries found themselves in different economic and political situations at the onset of the structural reform process. For example, the Korean financial crisis of late 1997 was a hugely important event. As a national liquidity crisis largely brought about by enormous conglomerates over-borrowing in short-term foreign currency loans and over-investing in long-term domestic investments, it was a unique event. In many ways, the Korean financial crisis is not even comparable with the Thai or Indonesian crisis because of the specific role of *chaebols* and the size and development level of the Korean economy (tenth biggest OECD country). As a crisis triggered by massive outflows of capital from foreign investors in emerging market funds, it is also different in nature from the exchange rate crisis suffered by France in 1982–83. Some analysts would further argue that the entire reform process that ensued in Korea was overwhelmingly determined by the scale of financial crisis and by the necessity to rely on IMF funds. That makes Korea unique in its experience and difficult to compare with Japan and France.

10. The term "semi-presidential regime" was coined by Duverger, although his inclusion of other countries in the category (Austria, Ireland, Portugal) is usually disputed by most other scholars (Avril 2001; Avril, Duverger, and Centre d'analyse comparative des systèmes politiques [France] 1986; Duverger 1968, 1978). The French system under the Fifth Republic is particularly hard to classify, given its two concurrent features: (1) A president elected through universal suffrage and granted strong specific competences; and (2) A prime minister and a government who report to the parliament and can be dismissed by it (although the prime minister is formally nominated by the president. In fact, France's institutions give its government an oscillating nature. When the parliamentary majority is in agreement with the president, the president has dominant powers. When the parliamentary majority is made up of parties that oppose the president, the power of the president is limited and the regime mostly resembles a parliamentary system.

True enough, but the argument of this book is that the crisis does not explain everything. It cannot explain the exact type and sequence of reforms. The Korean government did have a higher degree of freedom with regard to *chaebol* corporate reforms than is often assumed. The IMF did impose strict conditions in terms of interest rates and government spending, but the inclusion of *chaebol* reforms in the IMF agreement was made at the request of Korean negotiators (as shown in chapter 5). It was highly unusual for an IMF agreement to contain such provisions. There is therefore a sufficient degree of variance to be explained, even considering the specificity of the Korean financial crisis. This is what makes comparison possible.

Yet another unique Korean feature is its entrenched political regionalism, a feature that polarizes electoral battles on regional divides rather than policy issues. In particular, the two large southern provinces are in perpetual rivalry. The populous southeastern Kyongsang province has consistently dominated Korean politics since 1945, just as the Satsuma and Choshu domains dominated the political scene in Meiji Japan from 1869 until the 1910s. The Korean dictator Park Chung Hee, as well as his successors, Chun Doo Hwan, Roh Tae Woo, and Kim Young Sam all hailed from Kyongsang. The strongest national party (Grand National Party or Hanara, the conservative party) is based in Hanara and usually gains every single parliamentary seat there.[11] Meanwhile, the southwestern region of Cholla is Kim Dae Jung's home base. His party, the Millennium Democratic Party, gets most of its strength from Cholla. The only "neutral" political region is the capital city of Seoul, although even there, people vote according to allegiances to their ancestral region (as most Seoul residents are recent immigrants). Kim Dae Jung's support for anti-*chaebol* reforms is directly related to his Cholla region connection, which has been mostly bypassed by past national industrial policy and therefore is home to few *chaebols*.

However, this unique Korean future can easily be exaggerated. The capital city of Seoul is of rising importance as a swing region. More and more, it is holding the trump card in the battle between Cholla and Kyongsang. As young Seoul voters are losing their regional ties, they increasingly vote according to policy preferences. Such a sea change was visible in the 2002 elections that led Roh Moo Hyun to power. In addition, the regional divide cannot explain many of the precise economic reforms that have occurred in Korea since 1997. In some ways, it may have a positive role in the autonomy of political entrepreneurs, but only a limited one. Again, a large variance in the outcome remains to be explained despite this disrupting factor.

11. More precisely, intra-party politics within Hannara are themselves driven by the need to balance the northern part (Park Chung Hee's home base) with the southern part of Kyongsang (Kim Young Sam's home base, centered on Pusan), reflecting the merger of two formerly opposed parties in the late 1980s.

The French case also includes unique features that complicate the comparison process. Principally, the early structural reforms that took place in France in the 1980s—including financial deregulation (beginning in 1984), privatization (after 1986) and a commitment to European liberalization—happened *before* the financial globalization of the 1990s and followed a domestic sequence of events. The coming to power of the Left in 1981 after twenty-four frustrating years in the context of the second oil shock was an unusual event with unique consequences. In order to meet the high expectations of their overjoyed supporters, the coalition of unreformed communists and Socialists embarked upon an intense program of social welfare and demand stimulation. Because of supply-side constraints, the program led to massive imports and pressures on the franc. France became stuck between its commitment to quasi-fixed exchange rate parities with Germany and other European partners (as a member of the European Monetary System) and the balance-of-payment crisis generated by its domestic program. After very contentious political debates within the coalition, the French government decided not to bolt out of the European Monetary System for purely political reasons. In turn, this decision forced the government to make a 180-degree turn in its economic policy and to focus on supply-side reforms after 1983. In other words, France embarked upon the structural reform path earlier than it would have been expected to, as an unintended result of political events. Just as France stumbled across the *minitel* (a system that allowed data search and communication through screens and keyboards using phone lines in the 1980s) a decade before the Internet arrived around the world, it initiated a precursor program of structural reforms that complicates the analysis of reforms in the 1990s.

Two responses can be made to deal with this problem of French specificity. First, the impact of financial globalization actually came much earlier to France than to Japan and Korea due to early financial deregulation moves and a low level of domestic investments in the stock market. Second, the initial push for structural reforms in 1983 lost steam by the late 1980s. In fact, by the early 1990s, particularly under the Cresson government, there was a period of relative backlash. Then, in 1995 and particularly after 1997, reforms began again with a newfound impetus. These two elements leave a sufficiently large portion of the reform process to be explained, even after recognizing the importance of the domestic political events of 1981–83.

Finally, Japan has two important and unique domestic variables of its own. Japan is a much bigger economy than France and Korea and the yen is the second most significant global currency. More important, Japan's huge pool of savings, consistently large current account surplus, and accumulated reserves give it a level of autonomy unmatched by any other country.

In addition, the sequence of economic events between 1985 and 2000 is also relatively unique: a phenomenal financial bubble between 1985 and 1990,[12] followed by a protracted financial and economic crisis (except for a spike in 1995–96), albeit a crisis mitigated by the government's access to unlimited savings.

However, these two factors have a much stronger influence over the reform process in the period from 1985 to 1995. After 1995, they are in many ways neutralized. With rising government debt (reaching 160 percent of GDP in 2004), the cushion has reached its limits. Financial reserves bought Japan time and autonomy, but only up to a point. Although it is true that part of the over-capacity conundrum that has become a rationale for corporate restructuring has roots in the bubble years, Japan's economic system was reaching its limits after three decades of success. In fact, some of the structural weaknesses that demand structural reforms were spotted as early as 1985–86, notably in the Maekawa report (a well-remembered government report advocating structural change and deregulation in 1986). The bubble years delayed the need to tackle the issue of economic structural weaknesses, but did not create all of these weaknesses. The bubble event can be seen as a temporary interference and there remains much variance to be explained, particularly in the post-1995 reform process.

To sum up, the comparison between Japan, France, and Korea can only be partially controlled, given the weight of specific national variables in each case. Two strategies can be taken in the face of this dilemma. The first one consists of a limited direct comparison, focusing on the variance in outcome that is not explained by the national variables. This constitutes the approach of this chapter. The second strategy consists of applying a common model and studying the impact of common intervening variables in each national context separately. This second approach (parallel national longitudinal comparisons) holds the unique national variables constant and focuses on variations over time in each setting. This approach is used in chapters 3, 4, and 5.

Measuring Variations in Strategic Political Autonomy and Bureaucratic Delegation

I now turn to the analysis of causal factors and to measures of strategic autonomy and bureaucratic delegation enjoyed by political entrepreneurs.

As argued in chapter 1, political entrepreneurs are the principal actors in the process of corporate reforms. Once in the presence of the golden

---

12. For an excellent analysis of the Japanese financial system and the bubble, see Meyer (1996).

bargain, their ability to shift the status quo depends on the degree of political autonomy and on the degree of bureaucratic capacity available to them in their political system and party.

To measure political autonomy and bureaucratic delegation, two scores are developed, as shown in table 2.2. The table summarizes the aggregate data across the three countries over different political periods. A change of period is determined either by an election, a new cabinet, a new coalition, or a significant change within the party structure.

The table shows that, on balance, strategic political autonomy (SPA) is higher in Korea and France than in Japan. But in all three cases, one observes important fluctuations. The greatest variation is found in Japan, where party system, coalition structures, and party organization (for the Liberal Democratic Party, LDP) have been in flux since 1993. The highest scores were obtained by the Hashimoto (1996–98) and Obuchi (1998–2000) administrations, although the Koizumi cabinet after 2005 would also score high. Strategic bureaucratic delegation (SBD) shows less fluctuation within the three countries, although Japan has seen its score go down in the wake of tough administrative reform battles and bureaucratic fragmentation since 1994.

In Korea, the president has the national legitimacy and the agenda-setting power to proceed with reforms. In normal times, his domination of the majority party and the relative weak opposition parties ensure that there is only one veto player. However, if the opposition party controls the assembly, gridlock can occur. This situation happened once in the period from 1988–90, when the majority party led by Roh Tae Woo gained only 125 seats out of 299 total and found itself in the minority. For twenty months, the executive seemed adrift and unable to pass important bills (Oh 1999, 111). A solution only came in January 1990, with the merger of two opposition parties, led by Kim Young Sam and Kim Jong-Pil, with the government party. The potential gridlock situation in Korea is particularly intense because the 1987 constitution made the naming of the prime minister by the president conditional on confirmation by the assembly.[13] French-style *cohabitation* can thus occur with graver consequences, given the greater powers in the hands of the president. A weaker reform process can also occur when the president must rely on a coalition and when he has difficulty controlling it. This situation occurred following the parliamentary elections of 2000.

The case of France shows strong institutional features favoring executive leadership. Yet the political autonomy of reform entrepreneurs ebbs and flows according to the relationships between the president, the prime minister, and governing parties. The prime minister has strong legitimacy

---

13. See the discussion in Shugart and Carey (1992, 162).

Table 2.2. Degrees of strategic political autonomy and strategic bureaucratic delegation

	FR 95–97 Juppé	FR 97–99 Jospin1	FR 00–02 Jospin2	JP 94–96 Murayama	JP 96–98 Hashimoto	JP 98–00 Obuchi	JP 00–01 Mori	JP 01–02 Koizumi1	SK 97–00 KDJ1	SK 01–02 KDJ2
Strategic political economy[a]										
1. Autonomy within party[b]	1	1	0.5	0.5	0.5	1	0	0.5	1	0.5
2. Security of leadership[c]	0.5	1	0.5	0	0.5	0.5	0	1	1	1
3. Autonomy within coalition[d]	1	0.5	0	0	1	0.5	0.5	0.5	1	0
4. Legislative autonomy[e]	1	1	1	0	0.5	0.5	0	0	1	0
Total SPA	**3.5**	**3.5**	**2**	**0.5**	**2.5**	**2.5**	**0.5**	**2**	**4**	**1.5**
Strategic bureaucratic delegation[f]										
1. Cross-cutting bureaucracy	1	1	1	1	1	1	1	1	1	1
2. Unified elite bureaucracy	1	1	1	1	0.7	0.7	0.5	0.5	0.5	0.5
3. Secondary delegation (IO)	1	1	1	0	0	0	0	0	1	0
Total SBD	**3**	**3**	**3**	**2**	**1.7**	**1.7**	**1.5**	**1.5**	**2.5**	**1.5**

[a] Following the analysis of chapter 1, strategic political autonomy is the sum of four components and each is scored between 0 and 1.

[b] Autonomy within party refers to the degrees of freedom given to party leaders and is related to the hierarchical structure of the party. 0 refers to an oligarchic party structure where the leader does not control the party agenda and appointments. 1 refers to a hierarchic structure with direct leadership control. Under most circumstances, the leader of the French Socialist Party enjoys high autonomy (1), while the leader of Japan's LDP is constrained by the oligarchic power structure and the high degree of bureaucratization and structure within the party (0.5 to 0). The leadership autonomy falls to 0 when the leader stems from a minority faction and is under the control of other faction leaders (Mori Yoshirō in 2000–01).

[c] Leadership security is measured by the legitimacy of the selection process and the degree of control over duration in power. 0 refers to a low selection legitimacy and short timeframe. 1 refers to high legitimacy and long timeframe. In the table, the score varies from high (1) in the case of Korean presidents and Japanese prime ministers Hashimoto and Koizumi to medium (0.5) in the cases of Prime Minister Jospin in 1997–2002 (under cohabitation) or Japanese Prime Minister Obuchi, to low (0) in the cases of Japanese Prime Ministers Murayama and Mori (0).

[d] Autonomy within coalition is set to 1 when there is a single ruling party or when the prime minister has a high level of control over coalition partners (Prime Minister Jospin in France from 1997 until the municipal elections of March 2000). The index takes the value 0 when the prime minister is in a minority situation in parliament or must deal with a much larger coalition partner (Japan in 1994–95). The values takes 0.5 in other cases.

[e] Finally, the index of leadership autonomy relative to the legislature is estimated as a function of legislative rules. For example, the index takes the value of 1 in France in most situations owing to the constitutional empowerment of the cabinet relative to the legislative leadership in setting the legislative agenda and the flow of amendment. The value normally takes 0.5 in Japan, a Westminster-style parliamentary system where the legislative agenda is decentralized and set by a potentially autonomous parliamentary leadership. However, when the prime minister faces an upper house controlled by a different party or is in a minority situation within his own party (Koizumi Junichirō), the value falls to 0.

[f] The same approach is taken for strategic bureaucratic delegation. All three countries considered here have a cross-cutting elite bureaucracy and score 1 on that indicator. Germany, however, does not and would obtain a 0 on this variable. Next, the degree of fragmentation within the elite bureaucracy takes the value 1 when the elite ministries are unified and offer a higher potential for political control (France) and is set to 0 in cases of high elite bureaucratic fragmentation. The final indicator measures the degrees of second-level delegation to international organizations such as the European Union and the IMF.

stemming from his or her dual appointment by the assembly and the president. The constitution of 1958 also bestows upon the prime minister direct control over the daily agenda of the national assembly, ensuring that his or her *projets de loi* (law proposals) have primacy over the *propositions de loi* submitted by deputies. Only a constitutional reform from 1995 marginally diluted this power by reserving one day per month for the review of parliamentarian-led law proposals. Even then statistics show that government-led proposals outnumbered parliamentarian-led proposals by a ratio of 5 to 1 in the final list of laws passed.[14] In addition, the prime minister has the ability to cut short all parliamentary debate on a bill and to force an immediate vote. This famous Article 49.3 of the constitution has been likened to nuclear blackmail, but in effect gives tremendous power to the prime minister.

However, two features can weaken the political autonomy of the prime minister. First, when parliamentary elections lead to a parliament dominated by the party opposed to the president, a so-called period of *cohabitation* ensues. Fundamentally, the regime becomes a parliamentary regime with a strong cabinet arising out of the parliamentary majority. As in the United Kingdom, the first-past-the-post electoral system ensures strong majorities. However, the president holds important disruptive powers. On all issues touching upon foreign affairs and in particular the EU, the president retains a constitutional preeminence. Even on issues of economic policy, the government can complicate matters and raise the stakes by refusing to sign government decrees and ordinances, thus forcing the government to adopt the more dangerous parliamentary route. Mitterrand resorted to this option in April 1986 by refusing to sign the ordinances of privatization initiated by Prime Minister Chirac. Similarly, the president can obstruct government-led reforms as the constitutional chair of cabinet meetings. The prime minister can also be hampered in a reform attempt when he or she relies on a fractious coalition, particularly when his or her party is a decreasing power relative to coalition partners.

Finally, strategic political autonomy in Japan is essentially a matter of party leadership and party system. The Japanese constitution is remarkably short on the legislative process. Article 72 states that "the Prime Minister submits bills to the Diet" but does not give him or her power over the daily agenda of the Diet. In effect, the prime minister has very little control over the legislative agenda, which is left to the decision of each house. In practice, therefore, control over the legislative agenda lies with the leadership of the majority party (or parties). Between 1955 and 1993, the LDP held a

---

14. Quoted in *Documents d'Etudes* #1.12 of 1997, la Documentation Française: "La procedure legislative en France."

systematic majority in both houses of parliament, with some minor exceptions. This situation allowed the LDP to mediate the entire legislative process through its leadership. The LDP leadership mode was one of consensus among its top leaders, principally its four to six faction leaders and the five top party officials (party president, general secretary, chairman of the policy research council, chairman of the general council, and upper house party leader). This mode left room for backroom politics, or the decisive influence of shadow *shōguns*. The most famous of these shadow *shōguns* were Tanaka Kakuei, Takeshita Noboru, and Ozawa Ichirō. Government effectiveness in driving legislative change thus critically hinged upon the capacity of the LDP to nominate a leader or a leadership that could sustain sufficient legitimacy to drive change. This capacity has ebbed and flowed, but generally can be said to have collapsed in 1989 with a notorious share-for-favors scandal—the Recruit scandal. Once LDP one-party rule ended in 1993, an additional complication was added. Not only did an effective intraparty coordination and leadership nomination process become necessary, but also an effective coalition coordination mechanism. The lack of such mechanisms made Japan's regime after 1993 quite similar to France's Fourth Republic or to the Italian Republic, both of which had great difficulty handling crisis situations. The reform process in Japan after 1993 is thus closely tied to intra-LDP leadership questions and to problems of coalition coordination. During the years when the LDP regained a near majority and managed to nominate a legitimate leadership (1996–98 and 1998–2000), one should expect comparatively more reforms than during other years.

Leadership Security and Electoral Cycles

Leadership security is another aspect of strategic political autonomy. An important component of leadership security is the electoral time available to political entrepreneurs. This time is a function of both party leadership elections and national elections. Table 2.3 compares the situation in France, Japan, and Korea and shows how electoral time is shorter in Japan than in the other two countries, which explains why leadership security is also structurally lower in Japan.

In Japan, the sequence of lower house elections and upper house elections in effect throws the leadership mantle in the political field every 1.6 years. During the period of stable LDP leadership, this rapid cycle of elections did not matter as much, because the LDP dominance was rarely at stake. However, since 1989, the majority of the LDP or of LDP-led coalitions is razor-thin, and even a defeat in the less powerful upper house elections tends to topple the prime minister (as happened in 1989, 1995, 1998, and

Table 2.3. Effective electoral timeframes in France, Japan, and Korea in the 1990s

	Japan	France	Korea
Regime type	Parliamentary, bi-cameral	Semi-presidential, bi-cameral	Presidential, unicameral
Primary election cycle	• Lower house election: 4-year cycle (shorter cycles when no confidencemotion, 1993; or tactical dissolutions, 1996) • LH election years: 07/1986, 02/1990, 07/1993, 11/1996, 06/2000	• Presidential election: 7-year cycle until 2002, 5-year cycle after that • Election years: 1981, 1995, 2002, 2007	• Presidential election: 5-year cycle • Election years: 1987, 1992, 1997, 2002, 2007
Secondary election cycle	• Upper house election: 3-year cycle • UH election years: 1986, 1989, 1992, 1995, 1998, 2001 (all July)	• National Assembly elections: 5-year, but president can dissolve • Election years: 1986, 1988, 1993, 1997, 2002, 2007	• Parliamentary elections: 4 year • Election years: 1988, 1992, 1996, 2000, 2004, 2008
Staggered or not	Yes	Yes until 2002	Yes
Party leadership cycle	• LDP elections every 2 years	• In effect, quasi-infinite	• Parties are defined around key leaders
Effective electoral time frame	1990: 2 years 1992: 1 year 1993: 2 years 1995: 1 year 1996: 2 years 1998: 2 years 2000: 1 year	1986: 2 years 1988: 5 years 1993: 2 years 1995: 2 years 1997: 5 years	1987: 1 year 1988: 4 years 1992: 4 years 1996: 1 year 1997: 3 years 2000: 2 years
Average electoral time	1.6 years	3.2 years	2.5 years

preemptively in 2001). The net outcome is a very short political timeframe for most governments, a feature that reduces political autonomy and discourages political entrepreneurship. The longest electoral times during the 1990s were two years in 1996 (Hashimoto government) and two years in 1998 (Obuchi), although the latter was interrupted by Prime Minister Obuchi's untimely death in May 2000. The electoral time frame is further weakened by the short LDP leadership cycle (every two years) and by fragile and shifting coalitions since 1993.

Korea is next with a theoretical electoral time of only two and a half years, due to the staggered nature of presidential and parliamentary elections. In most cases, however, the parliamentary elections do not produce a legislature under strong unified opposition control and do not therefore question the integrity of the executive leadership (including the prime minister). So although the staggering of parliamentary elections potentially shortens the electoral cycle by half, in practice, most Korean presidents have had a full five years of relatively secure political time, ensuring their reform capacity.

As for France, both presidential elections and parliamentary elections usually result in a change in prime minister and government, because both have authority over the executive.[15] This dual line of authority shortens the real electoral lifetime the average government to 3.2 years in recent years. Strategic political autonomy is highest when the time available to a cabinet is longest (Jospin government).

Bureaucratic Fragmentation and Bureaucratic Delegation

The elite bureaucracy in Japan has always been at least bipolar, with a well-known rivalry between the Ministry of International Trade and Industry (MITI, METI after 2001) and the Ministry of Finance (MOF). While in MITI, the balance of power has tilted toward the internationalists from as early as the mid-1980s, the MOF remained heavily dominated by the two large domestic bureaus: the budget bureau and the tax bureau. The voice of the international bureau within the ministry was systematically muted by the power of other bureaus. Consequently, while MITI gradually developed a pro-deregulation, pro-structural reforms vision as early as 1993, MOF at first remained in favor of the status quo. It opposed many of the MITI-initiated reforms on the grounds that they would rely on fiscal incentives and would thus weaken the national fiscal position. Some of the opposition was also driven by a desire to uphold MOF's power against MITI's intrusions. MOF later converted to a reform vision where the reform engine was accelerated financial deregulation (the Big Bang), although MOF and MITI had intense turf and vision battles on this issue in 1996 (Amyx 2004; Toya and Amyx 2006). In turn, the battles between MITI and MOF complicated the actions of political reformers and made it almost impossible for political reformers to rely on both MITI and MOF in the process of delegation. This translated into a lower degree of control over the elite bureaucracy.

15. In reality, the parliamentary majority is the primary factor in naming the prime minister, because the prime minister is responsible to the assembly. However, since the president can dissolve the assembly soon after presidential elections and can then name a new prime minister if the new majority is favorable, the president also has a big say.

Interesting institutional change has been taking place in Japan since 1997. In response to separate scandals and crises, the Ministry of Finance has been hollowed out piece by piece. This process has given rise to a series of new actors within the elite economic bureaucracy, most of which have an institutional commitment to reform. The most important of the new actors has been the Financial Service Agency with jurisdiction over both financial supervision and financial planning as of 2001. In practice, its head since 2001 (beginning with Yanagisawa Hakuo, and including Takenaka Heizō) has been a strong pro-reform actor, although some of the previous ministers (Ochi, Kuze, Aizawa) were nominated to the position by the LDP to limit the reforming role of the new agency and were conservative anti-reform politicians. Another key actor on the political economic scene has been the Bank of Japan (BOJ). Wielding the weapon of its newfound monetary independence, the BOJ under its leader Hayami (1998–2004) has been linking monetary policy with the advancement of corporate reforms and other structural reforms. This behavior, however, has raised questions as to whether BOJ was overstepping its mandate. A third important actor after 2001 is the Minister for Economic and Fiscal Policy (without a real ministry, though).[16] Although its legal power may not be strong, it has the potential of being a strong pro-reform actor if a powerful leader is appointed as its leader. This was the case under the Koizumi government with well-known economist Takenaka Heizō as minister. The net result of this multiplication of elite bureaucratic actors is a more fragmented picture.

In contrast to that situation, the French and Korean situations reveal a relatively united bureaucratic front. In France, the elite economic bureaucracy has been organized into one single super ministry since the fusion of the Ministry of Finance and the Ministry of Industry in 1986.[17] The fusion was reinforced by the construction of a single, new, and lavish building for the entire economic bureaucracy, the so-called Bercy Fortress.[18] Most ministries moved into Bercy gradually after 1989, a move that was mostly completed in 1997. The Ministry of Industry moved from 101 rue de

16. I am indebted to Jennifer Amyx for this clarification and many other elements on the process of financial reforms since 1998.

17. The 1986 merger was initially temporary. The ministries split again after 1988 before being permanently merged in 1997.

18. The imposing Bercy fortress has its own heliport, its own pier on the river Seine, and its own brand-new automated subway line connecting it to the rest of the political world in Paris. In some ways, it is similar to the modern governmental campus in southern Seoul, also completed in the late 1980s. It certainly makes a striking contrast to the outdated and cramped buildings of the MOF and METI in Tokyo. The MOF building was actually built during World War II, at a time of great constraints on resources.

Grenelle to Bercy in 1997.[19] The unity of the super ministry is reinforced by its strong central functions. The center of power in the Ministry of Economy and Finance lies in the Ministerial Cabinet and in the Treasury, the unit that manages all assets and liabilities of the French state (including state-controlled enterprises such as Renault). Both the Ministerial Cabinet and the Treasury are heavily dominated by an elite from a small "corps," the Inspection des Finances.[20] Members of that elite group are all former graduates from the ENA who were in the top five of each graduating class. Their close interpersonal ties are notorious. The voice of the ministry in the political and economic process is increased by the fact that many "Finance Inspectors" move on to become key politicians (a famous case is former president Giscard d'Estaing) or CEOs of large corporations.[21] A second network, the Corps des Mines, has historically dominated the Ministry of Industry and many industrial corporations[22] until 1997 and a significant rivalry has existed between the two networks. After the 1997 merger, the Corps des Mines accepted its inferiority to the Inspection in the enlarged Bercy. At the same time, as is usually the case, the merger gradually changed the culture of the merged total, especially in the Trésor (Treasury) where the *mineurs* and more generally the *ingénieurs* (i.e. corps recruited from the *Polytechnique*) gained a lot of influence.[23]

The unity of thought and vision among top economic bureaucrats (and a few CEOs and politicians as well) is reinforced by intellectual clubs or think tanks that bring many of them together. A great case in point was the Fondation St-Simon, which between 1983 and 1999 had a large impact on the French bureaucratic conversion process and on the development of a class of reform entrepreneurs. One of its leading members was Roger Fauroux, CEO of the large Saint-Gobain industrial group, and a former finance inspector. Another key leader was Pierre Rosanvallon, a Social Democratic thinker and academic. The Fondation St-Simon has been described as "a mix between a US-type think tank and a French reflection club."[24] Bringing

19. I am grateful to Nicolas Véron for precise information on the Ministry of Industry, the ministry merger in France, and on elite networks.

20. For a great analysis, see Ottenheimer (2004).

21. The former business star Jean-Marie Messier, CEO of Vivendi and manager of Universal Studio in the United States is a case in point. Another famous case is Louis Schweitzer, the CEO of Renault until 2006.

22. While *inspecteurs* dominate financial services, at least the non-mutualized part (Pébereau at BNP Paribas, De Castries at AXA, Bouton at SocGen), *mineurs* are strong in manufacturing and energy (Desmarets at Total, Collomb at Lafarge, Folz at PSA, Beffa at Saint-Gobain, Kron at Alstom, Lauvergeon at Areva, Olivier at SAGEM-SNECMA, etc.).

23. Interview with Nicolas Véron, February 2005.

24. Quoted in *Le Monde Diplomatique*, September 1998: "Enquête sur la Fondation St-Simon: les architectes du social-libéralisme."

together some of the most influential intellectuals, bureaucrats, politicians, and industrial managers in France, it generated blueprints for reforms aimed at continuing the modernization of France. It has been compared to the elite group of technocrats and liberal thinkers that clustered around the banner of St-Simon during the period of Napoleon III (1850–70), an elite that spearheaded the French industrial takeoff in the nineteenth century.[25] Including leading political actors from both Left and Right, it became an architect of a French consensus for reform and a facilitator in the bureaucratic conversion. To sum up, there were many reinforcing features leading to unity among the elite bureaucracy and to a "unified" bureaucratic conversion process.

Furthermore, the strong French bureaucracy is itself embedded in French political culture and in deeply entrenched practices. In his path-breaking study of industrial policy in the age of railroads (late nineteenth century), Dobbin (1994, 95) shows that existing political culture and "rationalized social institutions" shaped the state-centered response to the growth of railroads. In turn, the crystallization of state-led industrial policy at the time of the railroads enshrined the paradigm of state coordination in French political economy.

Korea lies somewhat in the middle. To some extent, the elite economic bureaucratic structure mirrors that of Japan (until 1995). As in France and Japan, meritocracy is the dominant principle within the elite bureaucracy. As of 1989, nearly two-thirds of level III bureaucrats in the Ministry of Finance (and 47 percent of those in the Economic Planning Board) had graduated from a single elite school, Seoul National University (Kang 2002, 61). However, the Ministry of Commerce and Industry never had the same clout as MITI in Japan. Given that the Korean industrial structure was centered on giant *chaebol* conglomerates (similar to Japan's prewar *zaibatsu*), control of the *chaebols* lay principally with the banks, and thus with the Ministry of Finance and Economy (MOFE). The function of overall economic policy lies clearly with MOFE, unlike in Japan. Also in contrast to Japan, the Korean bureaucratic autonomy is much more limited. Given the strong power of the president over the bureaucracy, bureaucrats have less room for maneuver and for rivalry. The Korean executive has stronger top-down features than the Japanese executive.[26] In Korea, the key political confrontation is between the presidency and the *chaebols*. In that battle, the bureaucracy is essentially an instrument in the hands of the presidency.

---

25. *Libération*, 6 July 1999. "St Simon libéré."

26. For an excellent analysis of presidential control over the Korean bureaucracy, see Kang (2002).

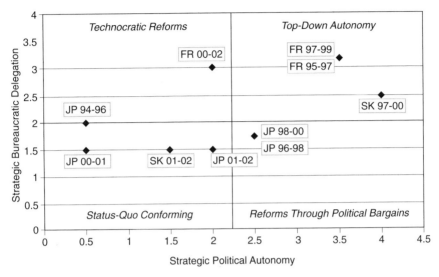

Figure 2.3. Typologies of regimes in terms of degrees of political autonomy and bureaucratic delegation in France, Japan, and Korea, 1995–2002
Source: Table 2.2 for data points.

Typology of Regimes and Political Space for Political Entrepreneurship

By comparing the two dimensions of political autonomy and bureaucratic delegation it is possible to place the various regimes in four quadrants (Figure 2.3).

Figure 2.3 identifies four situations with respect to the political space available to political entrepreneurs in pushing for corporate reforms. When their degree of political autonomy and possibilities for bureaucratic delegation are low, political entrepreneurs are held in check and reforms are limited. When political autonomy is high but bureaucratic delegation is low, political entrepreneurs are able to push reforms in a visible way through legislative bargains and side payments. This is the principal reform method in Japan. When political autonomy is low and bureaucratic delegation opportunities are high, political entrepreneurs may push reforms on one engine, that is, the indirect use of elite bureaucracies to devise technical and invisible reforms that push the status quo in the direction of the golden bargain. Finally, when both variables are high, political entrepreneurs have significant room to push reforms from above, both through a technocratic route and through open political bargains.

We now turn to the evaluation of the outcome of structural reforms, the dependent variable, before testing the relation between strategic political autonomy and reform intensity.

Where France, Japan, and Korea Stand: Indicators of Structural Reforms

How can one assess and measure the level of change in corporate structural reforms and their impact on corporate restructuring? How can the variation across cases be measured? The usual strategy consists of seeking comparable economic proxy data. To measure the output and intensity of structural corporate reforms, one might look at data on firm restructuring, firm-level change in corporate governance, changes in levels of cross-shareholding, or data on return on equity. However, economic outcomes at the firm level result from a myriad of economic, corporate, individual, and political factors. Changes in regulatory frameworks are only one type of change in this larger nexus.[27] In some settings, one can identify firm-level responses rapidly. In other settings, there are significant time lags and mitigating factors.[28] Ideally, an indicator of changes in the regulatory framework would provide a better evaluation for corporate reforms. At this stage, however, such indicators remain in their infancy. The OECD has been working on comparative indicators of corporate governance for several years but has not yet produced them, partly because of their high political sensitivity. This book introduces such an indicator of regulatory change, one based on the regulatory output within each country. The usefulness of this indicator stands out in light of potential fallback economic proxies. I address them in turn.

Economic proxy indicators of corporate reforms include assessments by international organizations such as the IMF and the OECD, and by global private actors, such as pension funds and financial firms. For example, one may consider data on decreasing cross-shareholding ties as evidence that firms are responding to significant state-level changes. Using private sector data compiled by Daiwa Research Institute, the OECD provides a measure of cross-shareholdings as a proportion of stock market capital-

27. Most studies of corporate governance reforms rely on aggregate firm level data developed by LaPorta et al (1997). For example, Gourevitch and Shinn (2005) use measures of ownership dispersion and a minority shareholder protections index as a proxy for corporate governance reforms (passed at the state level). The causal chain is sometimes long from political decisions to these proxy variables and political decisions may be a "junior partner" in the mix.

28. See Milhaupt and West (2004) for an excellent quantitative analysis of the economic impact of reforms in Japan's commercial code.

ization in Japan. The data show that the level was very high at around 40–45 percent throughout the 1980s (Japan's historical peak).[29] Then, the ratio began to slowly decline in 1990, to reach about 37 percent in 1997.[30] The evidence suggests a drastic acceleration of the trend in 2000 and beyond. In fact, the unwinding of cross-shareholdings was blamed as the key downward force on the stock market in late 2000 and early 2001, spurring Kamei Shizuka, the number three leader of the ruling LDP, to specifically blame banks and to urge them to stop unwinding cross-shareholdings. This situation contrasts with that of France, where the unwinding of cross-shareholding came much earlier in the 1990s and proceeded much faster. An OECD report estimated that inter-company holdings decreased from 59 percent to 20 percent of total market capitalization between 1993 and 1997 alone, as the stable shareholder cores put in place by the government at the time of privatization (the so-called *noyaux durs*) melted away (Nestor and Thompson 2001, 14). The crucial years were 1997 and 1998.

Other indicators of corporate restructuring include data on mergers and acquisitions (M&A). Data computed by Nikkō Shōken on the number of M&A deals in Japan show that M&A remained at the same level between 1989 and 1997 (at around 600 deals per year). The trend began to pick up in 1998 with 929 deals, continuing its rise in 1999 (1,160 deals) and 2000 (1,635 deals).[31] Such data suggest that restructuring began very late in Japan (1998) but has accelerated since 1998.

However, all these economic indicators remain at best loosely connected to institutional change originating in the political system. For example, Milhaupt and West (2004, 193) conclude their analysis of the rise of M&A activities in Japan with very prudent and tentative conclusions: "Merger activity in Japan has increased significantly in recent years, our sense, confirmed in discussions with practitioners, is that institutional reforms are a significant cause of the increase." Time lags are common. Some institutional reforms lead to little change on the ground, while others combine to lead to major changes at the firm level. Therefore, a safer way to measure the process of institutional change led by the state consists of moving upstream to an indicator of regulatory output. This is the strategy used in this book. Before measuring reforms, I divide them in three types.

29. In fact, the ratio is as high as 55 percent if life insurance is included.
30. OECD's corporate governance website at www.oecd.org.
31. Data on strategic M&A (*senryakuteki* M&A *tōkei*) computed by Nikkō Shōken. Nikkei Shinbun provides the 2000 data on 17 January 2001. Similar data compiled by Thomson Financial showed an increase from one hundred transactions on average in 1990–94, to 1,300 transactions in 1999 (in-in transactions only). Out-in transactions also jumped from fifty per year average 1990–94 to 227 in 1999 (Milhaupt and West 2004, 193).

A Typology of Corporate Structural Reforms

Although corporate restructuring is primarily a corporation-led process, the state has a great deal of influence over the process. Most of these reforms are technical, and invisible to the uninformed public; indeed, the International Monetary Fund is often better informed about them than voters. But the sum of these reforms has a large impact on the political and economic system and on employment and industrial organization. In the case of stakeholder economic systems, such reforms can be grouped into three types.

The first type refers to legal and regulatory reforms that tend to remove obstacles from the process of corporate restructuring. Such reforms constitute the orthodox type, a type of reform advocated by international organizations such as the OECD and the IMF. Most of them fall under the category of corporate governance reforms, hence the general OECD view that corporate restructuring is fundamentally a problem of corporate governance.[32] Corporate governance can be defined as the "structure of relationships and corresponding responsibilities among a core group consisting of shareholders, board members, and managers designed to best foster the competitive performance required to achieve the corporation's primary objective" (generating long-term economic profit).[33] Some wider definitions used in Japan and Germany often include workers among the core group, but not the OECD report. The structure of these relationships is heavily influenced by government regulations. Such relevant regulations include both direct regulations—company law—and indirect regulations that set the environment for these relationships—accounting standards, regulation of FDI, financial regulations, even some labor and social regulations.

The second type of corporate structural reforms refers to corporate reforms through finance. Often, states are involved in direct initiation of corporate restructuring through financial reforms. For example, the state may have the ability to directly control credit institutions. Because of a fi-

32. Interview conducted at the OECD headquarters in June 2000. The OECD argues that even in Korea, the problem of how to deal with the *chaebols* should be seen strictly as a corporate governance problem.

33. OECD definition. As acknowledged by the OECD, these relationships "are the result of government regulations, public perception and voluntary private initiatives." A key feature of these relationships is that they are problematic, fraught with information asymmetry and principal-agent dilemmas. That is why some definitions of corporate governance tend to emphasize these problems. The OECD analysis of French corporate governance in 1997 used the following definition: "the rules and practices whereby economic systems cope with the information and incentive problems inherent in the separation of ownership and control in large enterprises." (Organisation for Economic Co-operation and Development 1998).

nancial crisis, the state can end up nationalizing financial institutions.[34] Once banks have been nationalized, the state has a crucial influence over the credit flows to the corporate customers of these banks. A milder version of this process may occur when the state gains control over financial institutions through bank recapitalization with public funds without actually nationalizing them. This was the case in Japan in February 1999 when most major banks (fifteen of them) accepted a total of ¥7.45 trillion of taxpayer money (over $70 billion). These funds came with a conditionality clause. Banks were required to submit a restructuring plan that forced them, among others, to exert stronger supervision over their corporate clients.

The third type refers to direct state interventions in industrial reorganization that have a lasting effect. When the state has significant control over corporations, either through direct ownership, credit control, or regulations, it can direct the restructuring activity. Sometimes, the state can engage in direct industrial reorganization under the guise of guided privatization (for example, the establishment of stable cores of shareholders in France). Not surprisingly, this third path is highly suspicious in the eyes of international organizations such as the IMF and the OECD and constitutes an unorthodox reform path. Using these three types of reforms, I next develop an index to measure the intensity of reform.

An Indicator of Reform in the Corporate Regulatory Framework

The index developed here is a measure of change in the corporate regulatory framework based on the output of laws and major state decisions by type of reforms and across time. In this index, all laws that affect corporate restructuring are counted and given a measure of intensity (1 for a simple change, 2 for a major change, and 3 for a extremely important change). Major decisions by the state, such as a bailout package, or involvement in a major M&A, are also counted. Laws and political decisions are counted at the time of passage in parliament or issuance by government. Each reform is also given a sign. A positive sign refers to a law that facilitates corporate restructuring and is welcomed by global equity investors. It goes in the direction of the golden bargain. A negative sign is assigned to laws that go against the golden bargain and make corporate restructuring more difficult.

The details of reform pathways in each country are given in tables in the appendix of this book, but the aggregate results are summarized here in tables 2.4 and 2.5.

---

34. This is the case in Japan in 1998–99 with the Long-Term Credit Bank and the Nippon Credit Bank, and in Korea after 1998.

Table 2.4. Evaluating reforms: Changes in corporate regulatory frameworks in France, and Korea, 1995–2002

Overall data	France	Japan	Korea
Initial stage evaluator	10	2	0
Type I—indirect	13	13	16
Type II—through finance	0	2	16
Type III—direct	14	−1	23
Total	**27**	**14**	**55**
Time sequence	France	Japan	Korea
1995	−1	0	0
1996	1	2	0
1997	9	2	1
1998	5	2	31
1999	3	6	10
2000	3	−1	9
2001	4	−1	3
2002	3	4	1
Total	**27**	**14**	**55**

Notes:
- This table summarizes the results of detailed reform tracking in each country, the results of which are found in appendix tables A1, A2, A3a, and A3b.
- The index captures all significant legal changes or government intervention with respect to corporate restructuring, from the point of view of foreign investors (based on tracking of evaluations in analyst reports, publications such as the *Financial Times* and the *Economist*, and the daily reports from Morgan Stanley Dean Witter.
- The changes are captured at the time of passage in parliament (for laws) or at the time of decision for non-parliamentary government actions.
- A government move that facilitates corporate restructuring takes a positive value, while a move that hinders restructuring and reinforces the status quo takes a negative value.
- The great majority of reforms are coded as 1 (+1 or −1). Under a few circumstances, legal changes with a very significant impact and trickle-down consequences are coded as +2, or even +3 in a few cases.

Table 2.4 only measures the amount of regulatory change in the corporate framework. An immediate question relates to the different starting points of the countries considered. Although the different starting points are extremely hard to measure, a rough indicator is included in the table to signify that France has already gone through a significant process of corporate regulatory change since the mid-1980s.

As is apparent in the table, all three countries are going through institutional change, often more than is usually assumed (e.g. Japan). At the same time, the three countries have clearly pursued different strategies and moved at different speeds. While Korea has pursued an all-out and extremely intense campaign of *systemic change* concentrated in a mere three years, most other OECD countries have pursued selective reform paths. France has followed a pathway of *selective reinforcement*, whereby the state had led corporate reforms with two engines of regulatory reforms and state-led reorganization during privatization. This pathway has imposed a major evolution of corporate governance, enlivened the market of corporate control, and diffused new norms of management. At the same time, it has been accompanied and cushioned by a strengthening of labor rights (some obstacles on layoffs) and an increase in the responsibilities of the state in terms of public employment. Change has been concentrated in the industrial sector. It has partly excluded public sectors such as utilities or railways.[35]

In contrast, Japan has followed a *pathway of gradual diversification*: the state has acted as an enabler for change exclusively through the use of regulatory and indirect reforms, enlarging the possibilities offered to firms, while shying away from hard constraints. This has led to a multipolarization in the Japanese model as firms choose to respond differently to the new opportunities. Unlike Korea, there has been little change on the labor side. Table 2.5 offers a comparative analysis of change and non-change in the three main countries under study.

In contrast to the expectations raised by convergence theories, various countries tend to emphasize different reforms and tools. Some rely on mandatory reforms, others on facilitating or enabling reforms. While one might expect convergence to OECD-type regulatory frameworks, it is clear that countries like France and Korea rely on a high degree of direct state interventions to promote corporate change.

Countries such as France and Japan move faster on the capital side, while maintaining or even strengthening labor regulations. All countries accumulate significant political liabilities in the process of corporate reform, engaging in political bargains and side payments. The net picture of changes and non-changes presented in table 2.5 is one of a strong diversity of responses and new experimental pathways. Rather than converging to one pole of capitalism, capitalist systems may be fragmenting toward a multiplicity of hybrid forms. Formerly stable clusters of capitalist systems seem increasingly more diverse and fragmented.

Politically, tables 2.4 and 2.5 emphasize that change is not linear but explodes in particular years: 1997–98 for France, 1999 for Japan, and 1998–2000 for Korea. Periods of change are followed by periods of non-change. The aggregate tables also mask significant reverse reforms (negative index).

---

35. On sectoral limitations, see Schmidt (2002, 102).

Table 2.5. Analysis of change and non-change in the corporate regulatory framework in France, Japan, and Korea, 1997–2002

Initial stage Evaluator	France *Reinforcement*	Japan *Diversification*	Korea *Transformation*
Type I—indirect	• Stock options • Takeover law, support for EU takeover law • New Economic Regulations: competition, corporate governance, mergers • Employee savings plan (support of corporate stock) • Support of new enterprise creation, innovation • Gaz market deregulation (competition)	• Abolition of ban on holding corp. • Accounting • Bankruptcy Law • Commercial code reforms: spin-offs, swaps, voting, stock options, optional U.S.-style board • Special economic zones, special laws in FDI promotion	• Transparency: accounting, consolidation • Shareholder rights: voting, suit thresholds, external auditors, external directors, minority shareholder protection • Bankruptcy Law, then pre-packaged bankruptcy • Commercial Code: Corporate split system, M&A procedures, asset backed securities, debt-to-equity swaps • Prohibition of cross-debt guarantees (FSC)
Type II—through finance	None	• Banking regulation • Bank nationalization / recapitalization tied to restructuring • IRCJ: support for restructuring of clients	• Improvement of bank capital structure (FSC) • FSC-directed corporate workout programs, selection • Lending criteria
Type III—direct	• Massive program of privatization throughout period, active industrial reorganization • Management reform in state-owned companies • Support for Renault-Nissan takeover	• Industrial Revitalization Law • Daiei bailout (-)	• Big Deals (state-led group reorganization) • Debt-equity ratios set at 200% for top *chaebols* • State involvement in mergers, Daewoo's bankruptcy, Hyundai's break-up, takeover deals (Samsung Motors) • Privatization

(**Table 2.5**—*cont.*)

Initial Stage Evaluator	France *Reinforcement*	Japan *Diversification*	Korea *Transformation*
Non-change	• Entrenched labor rights, increase in obstacles to layoffs with 2001 social modernization law (anti-layoff law)	• Labor: obstacles to layoffs maintained, enlargement of part-time labor • Takeovers, M&A • Main bank system's endurance • Sectoral exclusion • Enabling reforms: firm-level fragmentation	• Enduring family control and insider system in some *chaebols*
Side-payments	• Work time reduction: 35-hour labor week (1999–2001) with same pay • Increase in public sector, public deficit	• Through public expenditures • Public deficit (7% GDP 2001–04), debt	• Labor: postponement of measures weakening labor unions to 2007 • Government promotion of 40-hour week (failed 2002)

Source: Personal evaluation based on data presented in appendix tables A1–A4.

Next, I turn to an aggregate study of the linkages between political autonomy and reform outcome.

Aggregate Comparative Results: Relations between Strategic Political Autonomy and Reform Outcome

Once the external incentive of the golden bargain is present (after 1997), to what degree can indicators of political space explain the reform outcome? Although the indices of political autonomy and reform intensity presented in this chapter are only rough ordinal estimates, they nonetheless lend themselves to a study of correlations. Figure 2.4 plots the two variables against each other. We focus here on the first indicator, strategic political autonomy (SPA), because it is the one determining reform intensity. Strategic bureaucratic delegation shapes the type of reform pursued and its process, two dimensions that are not captured by the index of reform intensity presented above. The graph begins in 1997 and runs through 2002 for all three countries. Each point represents one country year. The Y axis represents the value of the reform index that year. The X axis represents the value of SPA for each country year (based on table 2.2 above). Because table 2.2 gives data per government and not on annual basis, the value taken in the graph is pro-rated by month when a cabinet change took place that year. The graph excludes one outlier: SK98. With a reform index at 31 for the year 1998, Korea is clearly off the scale used above. This unusual result can be explained by the extraordinary booster of the financial crisis and the IMF package.

The figure confirms the high degree of correlation between the degree of strategic political autonomy and the index of reform intensity. The correlation coefficient for these seventeen data points comes to 0.81.[36] Among the interesting findings contained in the figure, we observe that all countries experience significant variation, but that Japan varies within a smaller spectrum. While Korea and France tend to cover the full spectrum of both SPA and reform intensity, Japan remains within the left-hand half of the figure. This is due to institutional constraints, as well as structural party constraints, which tend to limit the political space available to political entrepreneurs at all times. We also find that Japan's reform index tends to underperform France and Korea in all years but 1999. This may be due to a delayed sensitivity to the signals of the golden bargain in the early years (1997, 1998) and to a particular state of leadership flux and vacuum in 2000 and 2001. Under Koizumi after 2002, Japan has moved to higher levels.

36. It is important to note certain caveats. The seventeen data points naturally constitute a small N. Furthermore, SPA levels may not be fully independent within country clusters. Nonetheless, the correlation is significant.

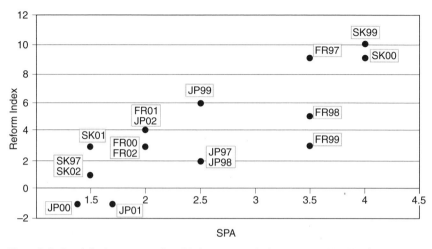

Figure 2.4. Correlation between strategic political autonomy and reform outcome 1997–2002 (minus one outlier, SK98)

Sources: Table 2.2 for strategic political autonomy and table 2.4 for reform index

The graph also reveals a few outlying cases and remaining puzzles. Japan in 1999 under Obuchi outperforms France and Korea at equivalent levels of SPA. This cannot be explained by the degree of SPA alone. As shown in chapter 4, Obuchi ends up milking his somewhat limited political autonomy to the fullest, partly through effective delegation, and partly through institutional innovation (which acts as a booster). Further, some time lags may affect the relationship between SPA and reform outcome. This is particularly true in Japan, when several years can pass between the political initiation of a reform and the actual passage in the Diet (the ultimate moment captured in the reform index). This can explain the relatively low points reached by Japan in 1997 and 1998. Conversely, in faster systems, such as France and Korea, there may be a huge honeymoon effect in the first one to two years of a new government. By the second to third year, the effect disappears and reform fatigue sets in (e.g. France in 1999).

Once we also factor in the role played by strategic bureaucratic delegation, how do reform outcomes fit with the predictions contained in figure 2.3? As a case of technocratic reforms (high SBD, low SPA), France fits well in 2000 and 2001. By 2002, however, reforms slow down before the expected time, probably due to reform fatigue. Likewise, Japan in 1994 and 1995 falls before predicted. This is due to the delayed entry of the incentives from the golden bargain and to a degree of SPA so low that it prevents any outcome. Under the category of top-down autonomy (high SPA, high SBD), France in 1997–98 and Korea in 1997–2000 fit the predictions well. On the other hand, France falls below expectations in 1999 and especially in 1995–97. This latter case is due to an external factor, an extremely crowded political agenda dominated by fiscal reforms in the march toward the Maastricht deadline of 1997 (so that France could qualify for entry into the European monetary union). Most cases in the third quadrant (status-quo conforming, with low SPA and low SBD) fit the prediction (Japan 2001–02, Korea 2000–01). Finally, the fourth category (political bargains) combining high SPA and low SBD fits Japan in 1998 and 1999 well. However, Japan in 2000 falls below expectations, probably due to leadership chaos and other external factors.

These findings present a first cut at the relations between sources of political space for political entrepreneurs and reform outcomes. The following chapters use process tracing to explore the relationship in more depth and identify the source of variations with predicted outcomes.

The aggregate and comparative analysis of the three countries presented in this chapter presents the contours of three divergent reform pathways. Owing to a permissive political and party system, French political entrepreneurs have been able to push top-down corporate reforms that have served as catalysts for large-scale firm level change. This happened within a ruling coalition in 1997–2002 that was openly opposed to structural reform and steeped in an anti-globalization rhetoric. Political entrepreneurs used their political space to craft political bargains with their party majorities. They also relied on the highly unified elite bureaucracy to set the agenda through technocratic means.

In contrast, Japanese political reformists have faced a more constrained political space. Throughout the late 1990s and early 2000s, the elite bureaucracy has been weakened and fragmented, providing few opportunities for technocratic delegation. Political autonomy has ebbed and flowed according to the factional and coalition make-up of various cabinets. Periods of relative leadership autonomy have been followed by more constrained periods during which opponents have successfully rolled back some reforms. As a result, Japanese reformers have relied mainly on framework regulatory reforms that enlarged the realm of possibilities for firms without providing mandatory constraints for unified change. State-led change has been all but invisible and reforms have involved bargains, side payments, and selective implementation. Institutional change is taking place but in a selective and gradual way.

Korea is the most atypical case given the booster provided by the 1997 financial crisis and the IMF agreement. However, the process of systemic and mandatory change—particularly in 1998, 1999, and 2000—is one that can be traced to the high degree of political autonomy and concurrent bureaucratic delegation available to President Kim Dae-Jung within the Korean presidential system, at least until legislative reforms returned an opposite majority in spring 2000.

Thus, political entrepreneurs are in charge and make choices that shape reform paths. Their ability to carry these choices through, however, depends on key structural conditions: the degree of political autonomy and opportunity for bureaucratic delegation available to them.

3

France: Effective but "Shameful" Reforms

France is the kingdom of invisible reforms. It has the ability to generate low-visibility yet fast-flowing structural change ahead of its societal alignments. France acts first and justifies second. There is a great French paradox: despite a majority anti-globalization discourse and strong popular support for the social contract, French governments (of all political colors) have been actively engaged in reforming the French economic structure, facilitating its global economic performance, and modernizing its corporate regulatory framework. Despite its success at adapting to globalization, France remains opposed to it at the gut level. On this deep French contradiction, former finance minister Dominique Strauss-Kahn once said: "France is accepting globalization while at the same time refusing that globalization implies the diminishing power of the local country."[1]

Thus the coalition of Socialists and Communists who were in power from 1997 to 2002 not only reversed their electoral promise to force Renault, the state-controlled automobile company, to cancel its restructuring program (factory closure at Vilvoorde), they also privatized more companies than all previous conservative governments combined (since 1986; measured by value) and passed legislation to encourage stock options and increase the power of minority and foreign shareholders in corporations. Since the mid-1990s, French capitalism has continued its transformation and the state has been an important actor in the process. All these post-1997 reforms were not included in the election platform of the Jospin coalition during the campaign.

1. Dominique Strauss-Kahn. Public presentation at Stanford University, CA. 1 November 2000.

How could the French government go so far and so fast in transforming the economic structure from a nationalized and *dirigiste* (statist) system in 1982 to a quasi Anglo-Saxon model in 2000, all the while without a clear popular mandate to do so? Why could France go further than Japan, despite a discourse that remains dominated by anti-globalization and anti-Americanization arguments?[2] According to Michel Albert's evaluation, France has known a deeper and faster transformation than Germany and Japan and is becoming increasingly close to the U.S. model.[3] The comparison with Japan is striking, even if current discourses (pro-globalization in Japan, anti-globalization in France) disguise the actual processes of change on the ground. Former French finance minister and leading Japan scholar Christian Sautter jokingly says that while "in Japan, discourse changes quickly but things do not change," and "in France, things move quickly, but the discourse is slow."[4] The reality is that the French government has been able to orchestrate a more fundamental and more rapid change of the industrial structure than the Japanese government. Cross-shareholding data, corporate governance reports, capital markets data, and reform records are all evidence of this reforming gap between two systems that were formerly seen as similar (state-led economies with credit control).

At the same time, this image of a French transformation constitutes only one side of the story. The capitalist system has been modernized, but the pathway reveals zigzags and reversals. The state passed reforms of banking regulation, corporate takeovers, and public management that had a definite impact on firm level change. The state in turn acquiesced to the leadership of the market in the transformative cases of the takeover battle between France's major banks in the summer of 1999 and when Canada's Alcan took over Pechiney, a pillar of French capitalism. Yet, the state backtracked in its promotion of market-led restructuring when it bailed out Alstom in 2003 and blocked merger talks between Novartis and Aventis in 2004. In this latter case, the French finance minister (Nicolas Sarkozy) personally intervened to ensure that Sanofi, a formerly state-owned company,

2. See Gordon and Sophie (2001).

3. Michel Albert's interview on Japanese TV in the Banque de France and related discussion attended by author on 14 September 2000. It is worth contrasting this assessment with Schmidt's. In her comparative study of change in France, Germany, and the United Kingdom, Schmidt (2002) argues that all three have been moving in the direction of liberalization and have faced a more restricted range of policy choices (310). At the same time, their national varieties remain distinct. With respect to France, she argues that France has embraced change more significantly than Germany. It is not possible to speak of a "state-led" model, but rather of a "state-enhanced model" (111–12). As for the French welfare state, it has proved as resilient as most other European systems, even under new competitive pressures (Scharpf and Schmidt 2000), including the pressures from negative integration at the EU level (the removal of regulations and protections) (Scharpf 1999).

4. Discussion, September 2000.

would take over Aventis, a company born of the merger between France's Rhone Poulenc and Germany's Hoechst.

In addition, the French reform process has come at the price of considerable side payments to vested interest groups. Thus, the counterpart to industrial transformation and accrued corporate restructuring has been an expansion of labor rights (the thirty-five-hour week and increased obstacles to layoffs) and an increase in public employment and in the social commitments of the state. Furthermore, a tacit bargain was made with well-organized interest groups that structural reforms would not affect public sectors such as the national railways. Throughout the late 1990s and early 2000s, reforms in education, health care, and pensions were postponed, so as not to conflate industrial reforms and public sector reforms. France pursued modernization on one engine, transforming corporate governance and corporate management, while leaving untouched other components of the French system. Such a strategy may appear paradoxical and costly, given the complex interdependence between institutions of capitalist systems uncovered by scholars of the varieties of capitalism or regulation theory (Amable, Barré, and Boyer 1997; Boyer 2004; Hall and Gingerich 2004; Hall and Soskice 2001). In addition, the costs induced by the reforms relative to the benefits available in 2002 led to a voter backlash in 2002 and again in the 2005 referendum on the EU constitution.

This chapter offers an answer to the French paradox. It argues that the structural reform process has been a top-down process driven by political entrepreneurs with a large degree of bureaucratic delegation and some windows of high political autonomy. This process was not always openly acknowledged, hence the oft-used expression of "*réformes honteuses*" (shameful reforms, namely reforms that proponents do not dare to acknowledge, given the absence of public legitimacy).[5] One senior bureaucrat with a long history of insider experience in corporate restructuring in France presented the motivation of reformist politicians and supporting elite bureaucrats as follows: "The state is concerned with the following. What can be done to enable France to have the best possible position in the global economy of the twenty-first century? The solution lies in globalizing and opening the economy, but without upsetting the people, since they have not understood."[6]

5. Because corporate reforms were part of a gamble by reformist leaders, they were pursued below the radar screen. A top bureaucrat and former cabinet secretary of the finance minister put it very crudely: "Reforms are done discreetly. To reform is not very legitimate in France, a very conservative country. One does it without being proud of it. . . . Who is leading reforms? Yes, it is this elite that is working for the industrial interests of France: modernity, competitiveness" (interview at the Ministry of Finance and Economy, 7 September 2001).

6. Interview with a senior MINEFi bureaucrat with a long involvement with foreign investment policy, 12 September 2001.

Political leaders, such as Strauss-Kahn—in a troika with Prime Minister Lionel Jospin and Labor Minister Martine Aubry, and the support of key political advisers—led the transformation. They sought to adapt the French economy to the new world of global finance and enlarge their political coalition toward the center.

These reformers were able to push for corporate reforms that had little popular support (especially within the support base of the ruling Socialist Party) due to initially high levels of political autonomy within the Socialist Party, the ruling coalition, and the legislature—levels that shrank after the departure of one coalition party in July 2000 and local electoral defeats in March 2001. The key strategy to open political space consisted of anchoring the government in the majority through the thirty-five-hour week program. In the words of one of Jospin's key advisers, "once the symbol of the thirty-five-hour week was placed upfront, it was possible to act pragmatically on other issues. This allowed the government to overcome opposition on a case-by-case basis. But there never was an overall debate."[7] It is interesting to note that the thirty-five-hour week itself was an idea crafted by Strauss-Kahn. Later, he would find himself in the role of the reformer confronting Labor Minister Aubry on the thirty-five-hour week. However, this confrontation and the decision to set up two powerful ministries of equal size in the government (finance and labor) were the result of a political design by Strauss-Kahn and Jospin, not the result of ideological differences.[8]

To preserve their initial political space, reformers such as Strauss-Kahn and Jospin proceeded through several other bargains with their support coalition. Reforms would not affect public servants, the core support base of the Socialist Party, and would take second place in the public agenda to social policy. Through such precautions, reformists were able to "carry the cabinet coalition willy-nilly."[9] This being said, Strauss-Kahn pushed his reform agenda to the limits of political capacity and lost several battles. Finally, the reform process was facilitated by effective bureaucratic delegation, especially after the 1997 unification of the elite bureaucracy under Strauss-Kahn's leadership.

This chapter focuses on the key political entrepreneurs who led the reforms and explores the sources of their political autonomy. It follows their role in transforming the French political economy through three main battles: privatization, stock options and employee savings plans, and the reform

---

7. Interview with chief economic adviser to Prime Minister Jospin in 1997–2000, Jean-Pierre Jouyet, 4 April 2006.

8. Ibid. Similar points were made by the adviser to Martine Aubry and two high Treasury officials.

9. Interview with former finance minister, Christian Sautter, 6 December 2005. On the last quote, the French original citation was regarding the method of leftist reformism (*réformisme de gauche*): "on emmène la coalition de gauche bon gré, mal gré."

of corporate governance (New Economic Regulations). The chapter concludes by questioning the stability of the reform outcome in France. I argue that the process of political entrepreneurship in response to the golden bargain is increasingly meeting credible opposition from new civil society actors. The last section also analyzes the apparent schizophrenia of the French state, caught between a pro-market structural reform program and a social policy that is often seen as backward and costly.

Prior Framework Choices in the 1980s

French corporate reforms in the late 1990s did not appear out of nowhere. They built on an earlier great transformation in French political economy that took place in 1983 and ran its course until 1990. Even though this first batch of structural reforms—across-the-board reforms that covered macroeconomic policy, financial deregulation, and corporate reforms—took place before the global incentives of the golden bargain were in place, they nonetheless represented a response by political entrepreneurs to a changing global environment. Leaders such as Francois Mitterrand, Jacques Delors, Pierre Bérégovoy (and their political advisers, such as Jean-Charles Naouri, cabinet director for Finance Minister Bérégovoy in 1984–86) decided to implement far-reaching reforms that went against the position of their supporters in the hope of modernizing France and generating long-term public good that would offset short-term costs. The trigger was a financial crisis in 1982 caused by the exit of investors in the bond market in response to an unsustainable economic policy.

In 1981–82, France reached the high point of statism (or *dirigisme*). In the wake of a new wave of nationalization by the incoming Socialist president Mitterrand, the state directly controlled 74 percent of all top-fifty industrial corporations and almost all financial institutions in France.[10] The state was not only the regulator, it was also the main player in the industrial game, merging companies and directing funds to priority companies according to national goals (Cohen 1992). In finance, the state's presence was overbearing. In the words of Jacques Melitz (1990, 394), "Only as recently as 1983 the country was under tight capital controls, faced a wide range of administered and cartelized interest rates, possessed relatively few financial instruments, and had its banks strapped in a credit 'corset' or credit-ceiling arrangement, known as the '*encadrement du credit*.'" The new Socialist-Communist coalition that came to power in 1981 compounded the

---

10. See data presented in *Alternatives Economiques* of June 2000. In 1984, the state controlled management in 74 percent of the fifty largest industrial corporations, while families controlled 11 percent, foreigners controlled 10 percent, and management controlled 5 percent.

traditional role of the state in the micro-economic structure with a massive macro-economic policy of "redistributive Keynesianism" (Hall 1986, 193). This, eventually, led the government to an economic impasse. The subsequent turning point of 1982–83 marked not only the end of large-scale Keynesian policies in France and a decisive prioritization of European integration, it also initiated a major process of financial liberalization and deregulation that transformed the micro-economic role of the state as well.

In January 1984, the government first passed a far-reaching banking act (first major banking reform since 1945), which removed old divisions between investment and commercial banks and introduced new unified prudential rules for all financial institutions, under the leadership of an empowered independent commission, the Comission Bancaire.[11] The government abandoned credit control in November 1984, then created new financial instruments such as money markets, commercial markets, and financial futures. The crowning step in the process of financial deregulation came on 1 July 1990 with the abolition of capital controls, a decision that came as part of EU-wide liberalization, as contained in the Single European Act of 1986. Another related and very important reform was the liberalization of inward foreign direct investments (FDI), with the removal in the late 1980s of the requirement that the prime minister personally approve any foreign investment proposal in France (*autorisation préalable du Premier Ministre*).[12]

These financial reforms had a large impact on industry. They reduced the cost of corporate financing: it is estimated that interest rates paid by industrial corporations were reduced by 2 percent (two points) as a result of financial deregulation (Cerny 1989, 182). Beyond that, the program fully liberalized the market for corporate funding (and to some extent the market for corporate control). In that sense, it facilitated later corporate restructuring. Naturally, the financial deregulation program also made it possible for foreign investors to come and gradually take control of the French stock market, thus leading to the secondary effects that are the focus of this book.

Further, the government engaged in large-scale privatization of banks and corporations after 1986. The process was not initiated by the Socialist government, but by its successor, the conservative coalition under Prime Minister Chirac. Unlike post-1997 privatization, the offerings of the 1980s had a very specific feature that ensured the continuing role of the state: the constitution of stable shareholder cores (*noyaux durs*). The Ministry of Finance selected stable shareholders (institutional investors and large corporations

11. COB is *Commission des Opérations de Bourse*, created in 1967. Izraëlewicz 1999, 397; Melitz 1990, 397.
12. Interview with senior official at the Invest in France Network on 19 October 2000.

and banks) that should control the management of newly privatized companies. The whole process was highly regulated.

Finally, the government liberalized layoffs, a single major labor reform that had far-reaching consequences for corporate restructuring (*suppression de l'autorisation administrative de licenciement pour motif économique*). This law, passed in 1986 (July and December) by the conservative government, was fiercely opposed by the Socialists and partly reversed by them in 1989 (*Loi sur la prévention du licenciement économique du 2 Août*). Nonetheless, it had a lasting impact on corporate activities and stands in stark contrast to labor reforms in Japan. These waves of macro-economic and micro-economic reforms in the 1980s aimed to revamp the entire French economy and had important secondary effects on corporate restructuring, even if restructuring was not their primary target.

Strikingly, these early structural reforms of the 1980s were top-down reforms, led by a political elite that sought to solve a mismatch between the domestic political economy and the global economy by reorganizing national rules.[13] Socialist political leaders and top bureaucrats in the Ministry of Finance took a clear gamble in 1982–83 and drove reforms thereafter. Leaders such as Mitterrand, Delors, and Bérégovoy took the risk of accepting a short-term loss of support among traditional supporters in the hope of generating enough long-term public benefits and gaining new supporters in the center. The gamble was also party ideational, predicated on a vision of a competitive modern France. Political leaders did not plan to jettison the entire French model. Rather, they aimed at pursuing the traditional aim of French modernization with new tools that were both adapted to the changing environment and reinforced existing strengths and the role of the state.[14]

Throughout the process, the government pushed financial reforms against the resistance of organized interest groups such as the *agents de change* (brokers), big banks, and some industrial actors. Ironically, it was easier for a pro-labor government with no ties to corporate interest groups to push such far-reaching reforms than it would have been for a conservative coalition (Izraëlewicz 1999, 118).

The Socialist-Communist government later suffered dearly for pursuing an economic program that was the exact opposite to the one it had promised to pursue and had received a popular mandate for. It was also a program that tended to create costs (including layoffs) for the very constituency

---

13. Interviews with four top bureaucrats at MINEFI, with a top leader of a labor union, and with a member of parliament in September 2000. See also Philip Cerny's (1989, 183) argument of "state-led deregulation."

14. Interview with top political adviser to the finance minister at the Ministry of Finance and Economy on 5 September 2001. This point was repeated by at least two other top bureaucrats with different responsibilities, one senior labor union official, and a member of parliament.

of the Socialist and Communist parties. In 1984, when pro-reform Laurent Fabius became prime minister, the Communists quit the governing coalition. In 1986, President Mitterrand suffered a large setback in legislative elections and was forced to accept a prime minister from the opposition, opening the first chapter of *cohabitation* in the French Fifth Republic. The Communist Party suffered even more for condoning a shift toward market reforms and saw its share of the electoral vote halve from 20.6 percent in 1978 and 18.13 percent in 1981 to 9.7 percent in 1986 (Becker 1998, 377). But the conservative coalition that came to power in 1986 as well as the new Socialist government in 1988 never questioned the direction taken in 1983.

In sum, France engaged in far-reaching economic and structural reforms as early as 1983 and these early reforms had an indirect effect on corporate restructuring. Although these reforms were led from the top by political leaders and relied on the high degree of strategic political autonomy and bureaucratic delegation, they were pursued in response to a deep financial crisis and embedded in a commitment to European integration. This first wave of reforms was accomplished in 1990 with the full deregulation of capital flows. It was never questioned thereafter and the reforms of the 1980s were not undone in the subsequent decade. However, structural reforms did slow down beginning in 1988 (a slowdown ushered in by the Mitterrand policy to stop privatization, the so-called *ni-ni* policy). Between 1993 and 1997, two conservative governments with short electoral horizons re-launched the wave of privatization and accomplished some reforms such as the independence of the Bank of France (mandated by Maastricht). However, on the whole, the period between 1990 and 1997 can be seen as a transition or pause in the process of structural reforms. As of 1997, key companies had not yet been privatized, corporate governance remained untouched by the reform process, and stock options remained burdened by negative taxation.

Corporate Reform Outcome, 1997–2002

The period from 1997 to 2001 was marked by a flurry of mergers and a high degree of industrial reorganization. It even included the first hostile takeovers among major banks in summer 1999. Clearly the late 1990s marked a deep transformation of the structure of French capitalism.

As detailed in appendix table A1, this industrial transformation was accompanied and facilitated by a series of structural reforms through which the French state completed the reforms of the 1980s. These reforms included an acceleration in the privatization of industrial corporations after a lull between 1988 and 1993. Unlike the earlier wave of privatization in

1986–88, the post-1993 wave (and particularly the post-1997 wave) abandoned the concept of stable shareholder networks organized by the state (*noyaux durs*). In addition, the existing *noyaux durs* gradually unwound and in large part disappeared. Although this process was partly led by Axa's leader Bébéar and other firms beginning in 1997 (Culpepper 2005), the government also played an important role in jettisoning the concept of hard shareholder cores. Other reforms included stock option reforms, corporate governance reforms, and the creation of independent regulatory agencies.

Structural reforms particularly intensified after 1997 under the Socialist-Communist coalition of Prime Minister Jospin, as readily acknowledged by the OECD.[15] Some reforms, such as corporate governance reforms, directly affect the incentives of corporations and make them more likely to engage in efficiency-seeking restructuring. Others, such as privatization of symbolic groups, have a strong demonstration effect on the rest of the economy. Through an indicator of significance included in appendix table A1, I differentiate between more and less crucial reforms. The assessment of this indicator is based on interviews and press reviews. It shows that structural reforms underwent a long lull between 1990 and 1996 (after the first wave of reforms in the 1980s), a period during which Maastricht-induced fiscal reforms dominated the economic agenda. In 1997 and 1998, the reform indicator reaches very high numbers (+9) before tapering off at a robust level (+3 and +4) in 1999 and 2000.

The wave of post-1997 structural reforms is particularly puzzling because it runs against the positions of Socialist supporters and public opinion. It seems counter-intuitive that a Socialist-Communist coalition coming into power in 1997 on a wave of social uncertainties would go further in encouraging corporate restructuring than a conservative coalition that preceded it. Also, public opinion in France seems to be opposed to the concept of structural reforms and to globalization in general, particularly in more recent years and with the possible exception of privatization. In 1994, at the extreme low point of popularity of Socialist president Mitterrand, polls showed relative majority support for privatization. For example, 51 percent were in favor of privatizing Renault (with 37 percent opposed) although a majority of Socialist voters (51 percent to 40 percent) and Communist voters (66 percent to 26 percent) remained opposed (Duhamel and Jaffré 1995, 136). At the same time, French voters expressed fear that inequalities would rise as a result of privatization by a margin of 55 percent to 32 percent. A poll conducted in 1999 showed that 80 percent of French people

---

15. OECD Economic Survey of July 2000 (Chapter III: Structural Policies for Durable Growth). In the words of an OECD official: "Much has been done in France. The government strives to undo legal and administrative barriers." Interview, 13 June 2000.

wanted more state intervention to protect jobs and that 52 percent thought that corporate restructuring was the responsibility of the state (Duhamel and Jaffré 2000, 141).

A poll in July 2001 by SOFRES and *Le Monde* showed that 55 percent of the French saw globalization as a threat to jobs and companies (while 37 percent saw it as an opportunity). Seventy-six percent said that the economy was insufficiently regulated (60 percent in May 2000). In particular, 66 percent of French citizens wished for more rules restricting financial markets, 64 percent for more rules protecting the rights of employees, and 55 percent for more rules restricting world trade. Fifty-nine percent added that financial markets had too much influence on the world economy. The number for multinational corporations was 58 percent. On the other end, 39 percent thought that the state did not have enough influence (versus 21 percent who thought it had too much) and 48 percent thought that labor unions did not have enough influence.[16]

However, such polls provide an incomplete picture of attitudes toward structural reforms. At best, one may say that support for structural reforms is limited. French voters keep hoping for increased involvement of the state in the economy. They support a state that intervenes to protect jobs and social gains. They are leery of the power of financial markets and of multinational corporations. In addition, books that denounce globalization and neo-liberal reforms consistently dominate the list of bestsellers in France. Viviane Forrester's *l'Horreur économique* (1996), a scathing critique of the neo-liberal transformation of the French labor system in the 1990s, sold over 350,000 copies and became one of the most quoted books in France. The Association for the Taxation of Financial Transactions for the Aid of Citizens (ATTAC), the anti-globalization NGO created in France in early 1998, quickly grew into a 30,000–strong organization (at the end of 2001), and included one third of all French members of parliament in 1999–2000. ATTAC coalesced around the motto: "Another World Is Possible" and the proposal of a tax on all cross-national capital flows (the so-called Tobin Tax), but quickly became a force against corporate restructuring as well.

This gap between the dominant French discourse and the majority opinion displayed in polls on the one hand and the program of structural reform of the government on the other forms a key theme in a book published by Gordon and Meunier (2001, 4): "The apparent paradox at the heart of this book is that France is resisting globalization (sometimes loudly) and adapting to it (far more than most people realize) at the same time." How might we explain this puzzle? Given the enduring obstacles to the accomplishment of reform and the weak public support, what were the

16. *Le Monde*, "Les Français et la mondialisation" (article by Stéphane Marcel). 18 July 2001. Accessed online at www.lemonde.fr.

political mechanisms that made active structural reforms feasible during the post-1997 years?

A plausible explanation for post-1997 structural reforms is one that emphasizes the role of corporate interest groups and organizations, such as the organization of employers Mouvement des Entreprises de France (MEDEF).[17] Such an explanation expects producers to push for deregulation and other kinds of reforms that would maximize their competitiveness.[18] Hancke thus argues that in the late 1990s, "the state no longer directly intervenes in the economy but concentrates on offering a social policy framework" (2001, 334). He proposes a new interpretation of the French political economy in the late 1990s, according to which "the French adjustment trajectory [in the late 1990s] was a firm-led one" (333).[19]

Such a firm-centered explanation, however, is weakened by some key empirical facts. First, the firm-centered explanation tends to ignore the series of reforms listed in appendix table A1, reforms that have been considered very important by both international observers, such as the OECD, and by foreign investors.[20] Even the unwinding of cross-shareholdings after 1997 was not a purely firm-based process. Strauss-Kahn and Jospin encouraged it through signals and actions, given their views that such stable cores had been mainly a conservative agenda reinforcing a networked capitalist elite (*capitalisme de connivence*).[21] Second, when the firm-centered explanation is applied to the process of state-managed structural reforms, it ignores the weakness of organized corporate interest groups in France. As reported in interviews with think tanks, bureaucrats, and the OECD, MEDEF does not have much political power and is usually excluded from legislative processes. While its role since 1999 has grown in social areas (negotiations on the thirty-five-hour week or on the reform of employment insurances), its influence is largely absent in the field of industrial reforms. Finally, in the field of corporate governance, MEDEF and corporate management in general have been opposed to regulatory reforms. Corporate governance reforms such as the New Economic Regulations (limited regulatory reforms passed in 2001 and studied in depth below) tend to strengthen the power of shareholders relative to management and have thus been generally resisted by MEDEF. During the debates in parliament, it was reported that Ernest-Antoine Seillière, MEDEF president, declared his fierce opposition to the

17. Until 1998, the organization was called the Conseil National du Patronat Français (CNPF).

18. See for example Frieden and Rogowski (1996).

19. See also Hancke (2002).

20. See comments by Morgan Stanley Dean Witter and evidence on the NRE project examined hereafter.

21. Interview with chief economic adviser to Prime Minister Jospin in 1997–2000, Jean-Pierre Jouyet, 4 April 2006.

law and said that it "organized the pauperization of the economic sphere."[22] Interviews with the bureaucrats who drafted corporate governance reforms also confirm the general opposition of management to these reforms. Management was particularly opposed to increases in transparency and to reforms that decreased the uncontested power of French PDGs (combined CEO and chairman position).

A second plausible explanation emphasizes partisan politics. It can be argued that privatization and labor reforms only began in 1986 when a neo-liberal conservative coalition came to power. However, the correlation stops there. Reform outcomes in the 1990s have consistently been the opposite of those that could be predicted by partisan politics. The conservative coalition in power between 1993 and 1997 did restart privatizing but were slow on most other structural reforms. Instead, a Socialist-Communist coalition not only accelerated privatization (selling more state assets in two years than all previous conservative governments since 1986 combined) but also passed stock option reforms and corporate governance reforms.

How can one explain this puzzle? Part of the answer lies in the unusual characteristics of the Left and Right in France. On the left, the Socialist Party includes a "modernist" wing (led by the likes of Fabius, Delors, Pascal Lamy, and Strauss-Kahn) that preaches economic realism. On the right, the large French majority is not neo-liberal and continues to espouse strong state restrictions on the economy (in a Colbertist tradition).[23] The only true Thatcherite conservative leader is Alain Madelin, who does not garner more than 4 percent popular support. In addition, the Left is usually unable to govern effectively without giving guarantees to the Right. The reverse is true for the Right, who otherwise risk facing major public strikes and demonstrations (as the Juppé government experienced in December 1995). In fact, top bureaucrats report that the political elite as a whole has consistently supported structural reforms without major partisan differences.

Political Entrepreneurs in a New Environment

In the context of uncertainty and the absence of clear majority societal coalitions, political entrepreneurs drove the process of structural reforms. They accepted the risk of a short-term political backlash, but bet that long-term benefits would outweigh the costs of reform. Their reform outlook fit within

22. Full Report of Parliamentary Debates, 25 April 2000. Published by *Journaux Officiels*. Quoted by MP Eric Besson (p. 3253). The exact wording in French is: "organiser l'appauvrissement de l'espace économique."

23. Interviews with top bureaucrats at MINEFI in September 2000 and with one leftist member of parliament.

a long-term post-war vision regarding the responsibility of the state in steering the French people through modernization and adaptation to a changing world. The lineage of economic political entrepreneurs that leads to Strauss-Kahn goes through Socialist reformers of the 1980s, such as Delors (and Lamy), Beregovoy, and Michel Rocard. It also includes leaders of the right, such as Raymond Barre, Jacques Chirac (as prime minister in 1986–88), and Edouard Balladur.

The political entrepreneurs of the 1997–2002 period are principally Strauss-Kahn, finance minister from 1997 to November 1999, in cooperation with others such as Christian Pierret (minister of industry), Christian Sautter (minister of budget and then finance and economy), and Martine Aubry (minister of social affairs). Interestingly, the prime minister, Lionel Jospin, often acquiesced to key corporate reforms led by these leaders but only grudgingly and without claiming full ownership or responsibility. In other cases, the prime minister blocked his ministers and maintained the status quo. As for the president, Jacques Chirac, he was not a direct actor in most domestic economic reforms.

Equity Flows and the Golden Bargain in Post-1997 France

On the back of financial deregulation in France and portfolio diversification by global institutional investors, the share of foreign investors in the French market grew dramatically during the 1990s. The rise is particularly marked between 1996 and 1999. In 1990, foreign penetration was at 12 percent.[24] A first jump took place between 1990 and 1993 from 12 percent to 21.5 percent and is associated with an important wave of privatization. This first wave was not accompanied by much media or political attention. The level continued to rise gradually to 25 percent in 1996. A second rapid jump took place between 1996 and 1999 (from 25 percent to 35 percent). According to other calculations by *l'Expansion*, the figure in 1999 could be closer to 40 percent. The figure for the top forty corporations that make up the CAC-40 stock index is estimated at 45 percent (*Le Monde*). This second jump became much more visible in the French media and political scene. It attracted a flurry of newspaper analyses and several books.[25] Given that a portion of the capital of these corporations is not traded on the stock market (the so-called patient capital), the share of non-residents in the floating capital is even higher. Thus, the *Banque de France* evaluates

24. Banque de France (Enquêtes Titres) data for 1985, 1999, and 2000; Grandjean (2000) for the rates of growth in the years 1993 to 1999; author's estimate for 1985–93. The figures used in this section for the percentage of foreign ownership in the stock market are aggregate and rather conservative figures put together by the Banque de France.

25. Forrester 2000; Izraëlewicz 1999; Labarde and Maris 2000; Mauduit and Desportes 1999.

that in 2000 non-residents represent 82 percent of all stock transactions, giving them full control over price formation on the stock market (Banque de France, October 2000). The largest foreign investor funds in the French stock market are Fidelity, Templeton, Capital Research, TIAA, T. Rowe Price, and Merrill Lynch (Ponssard 2000).

While pension and mutual funds tend to be atomized and don't push for direct management change (except in the famous André case in 2000, where two foreign pension funds holding 41 percent of the shares of this shoe company attempted to force a change in top management by blocking the approval of annual accounts), they follow two key objectives: maximizing shareholder value, or return on equity (ROE), and demanding minority shareholder protection. The first objective is generally understood to mean a ROE of 15 percent, a target that has been blamed for the rapid increase in labor flexibility (Dumas 2001, 138–39). As emphasized in chapter 1, the second objective is not only proposed by individual funds such as CalPERS, but has been codified through the OECD principles of corporate governance.[26] These two objectives are increasingly achieved through the exit threat.

However, the influence of pension and mutual funds and non-resident investors in general go beyond the management of individual corporations. Gradually, the increasing level of foreign equity has provided an incentive for politicians and elite bureaucrats to facilitate corporate changes through state-led structural reforms. Although interviews with different bureaucrats confirm that foreign investors and pension funds have not engaged in political lobbying and have had minimum contact with the Ministry of Finance,[27] these interviews also reveal that some political leaders have been rapidly influenced by them. We now turn to the strategies and goals pursued by the key political entrepreneur in post-1997 France: Dominique Strauss-Kahn.

Intellectual and Political Architects: Dominique Strauss-Kahn and the Socialist Modernizers

Standing between a new global reality and enduring political resistance in his own camp, Finance Minister Dominique Strauss-Kahn was the prime

26. Interview with Michel Albert, who was involved in the drafting of the OECD principles of corporate governance. He admits that the principles primarily focus on shareholder interests and that proposals for larger definitions of corporate governance that would include stakeholders were rejected. Top union officials emphasize the fact that the OECD principles were drafted behind closed doors and did not include consultations with members of civil society (14 September 2000).

27. MINEFI has, however, been lobbied by two French associations of minority shareholders, particularly ADAM (led by Colette Neuville). Top bureaucrats report meeting leaders of these associations and discussing reforms with them. It is also reported that these associations have close links with U.S.-UK pension funds and in some cases receive support and funding from them.

intellectual and political architect of post-1997 corporate reforms (although Christian Sautter and Laurent Fabius followed the same overall direction after him).[28]. To be sure, he had the support of other key leaders such as Martine Aubry, but it was Strauss-Kahn who theorized the Socialist response to the golden bargain, a response that remained entrepreneurial in the sense that it never received the enthusiastic backing of either the Socialist grassroots militants or coalition partners.

Strauss-Kahn had long-term political ambitions and was building a reputation as an effective modernizer. In 1997, his ambitions were not yet presidential—that only came after 2002—but he was positioning himself to become prime minister should Jospin be elected president in 2002. Thus, Strauss-Kahn had two audiences: the middle class and Jospin. He understood that his reform advocacy might sometimes be away from the median position in the Socialist Party. However, as part of a governing portfolio (generation of public goods, competitiveness, long-term growth), his positioning might become indispensable for Jospin.[29]

In a speech in 1998, Strauss-Kahn lays out the case for a modern industrial policy that aims strictly at improving global competitiveness. The policy should focus on two main tools: horizontal regulatory policies to create a competitive and attractive economic environment (including solving market failures) and vertical policies in sectors where the state is a shareholder in key firms and should now behave primarily as a shareholder (Strauss-Kahn 1998). In a nutshell, Strauss-Kahn advocates a "socialism of production," according to which the state can play a key role not only in redistribution but also through investment-oriented policies, including privatization. The state can also encourage corporate competitiveness by acting as a "patient investor," allowing managers to take long-term risks aimed at creating value over time (as in the Renault alliance with Nissan).[30]

Strauss-Kahn (2002) presents an in-depth rationale for his reformist position in a book on the future of social democracy, *La flamme et la cendre*. This book, written in 2000–01 when Strauss-Kahn was out of power, provides the ex-post rationale for much of his actions as minister. The dominant theme of the book is the promotion of a "new-age socialism," one that that reoccupies the production field instead of focusing exclusively on redistribution. For Strauss-Kahn, modern socialism must pursue social justice in novel ways: not by resisting change, not by merely adapting to change, but by reinventing its approach to change (15). Redistribution, the traditional focus of Socialists, has reached its limits and the welfare state is no longer efficient (25). Mere

28. Interview with former finance minister Christian Sautter, 6 December 2005.

29. Interview with chief political adviser to Finance Minister Strauss-Kahn, 1997–99 (M. Villeroy de Galhau, directeur de cabinet), 4 April 2006.

30. Ibid.

social policy is likewise too limiting (55). Strauss-Kahn advocates a return to the origins of socialism and to thinkers such as St-Simon:

> We cannot be satisfied by the artificial survival of a socialism rooted in redistri-
> bution and public spending. We must find a new socialism, one that is favor-
> able to creation and innovation, one that is able to truly combat inequalities.
> For these reasons, we must reconsider a socialism of production. (29)

Strauss-Kahn's intellectual vision for a modern socialism is built on several pillars. First, he advocates a dose of realism. He is not interested by mere argumentation and "political abstention." In a very Downsian way, Strauss-Kahn writes that the only useful Socialist plan is one that can win elections (44) and therefore one that can address the needs of the "middle layers" (46) and "members of the intermediary group" (51): these groups form the foundations of society. Next, and this is Strauss-Kahn's key contribution, he urges Socialists to encourage "economic initiative" and a "taste for risk" (60). While it is legitimate for the Left to rise against a reductionist vision that only enshrines the market and negates the importance of social linkages and society (59–60), Socialists have usually gone too far in their total rejection of liberalism. What matters is not to eliminate risks and entrepreneurial attitudes, but rather to "mutualize risk" (62). With creative regulation, the state can facilitate a necessary industrial mutation and the "transformation of modes of production." (63). Instead of blocking industrial mutation, effective regulation can spread the related risks and encourage adaptation. Strauss-Kahn goes further by acknowledging the push from shareholders toward great profitability (67). He advocates an adaptive public policy that aims at correcting extreme behavior but also encourages risk-taking and rewards talents (71). In other words, rather than continuing old protective policies that are no longer efficient in a changed environment, Socialists should regain interest in the productive system and accompany innovation in production, while remaining committed to the correction of inequalities.

Last, Strauss-Kahn accompanies these two large principles with a renewed belief in the role of the state. Socialist political leaders should remain rooted to a voluntarist desire to control their destiny (33) and aim at "transforming reality by influencing economic processes" (304). Political leaders should set clear boundaries and then seize opportunities for action (306). Such an attitude is grounded in longstanding French traditions. Indeed, even for a modern economist like Strauss-Kahn, the French exception can be characterized as "the will to systematically organize society, to make it an object of reason and to do this from above, through the authority of the state" (266). Strauss-Kahn actually has a larger vision of the state and of the nation. For him, public action ought to take place gradually at the European level. In his industrial policy, he often acted with the aim of creating EU-wide "European champions." Key cases include the constitution of EADS, France Telecom, and the Framatome-Siemens alliance.[31]

Strauss-Kahn presents one of the clearest and most explicit political responses to the golden bargain. Instead of ignoring or rebelling against global finance, a Socialist political response consists of facilitating industrial restructuring and maximizing the positive effects of global capital so as to enlarge the economic pie for all. The state needs to intervene both to mutualize risks involved in the transformation process and to solve some induced market failures or social costs. Acting in this way should garner support from the middle of the political spectrum, even if Strauss-Kahn does not openly acknowledge the potential cost on the left side of his coalition.

In his book, Strauss-Kahn presents three clear types of actions for the state in pursuing this agenda: industrial policy, encouraging domestic savings in the stock market, and new regulations. Given the large public sector inherited from past governments, this public sector has become the primary tool for industrial action (289). Ironically, privatization of that large public sector became the primary tool of industrial policy in France in the late 1990s. Privatization offers a chance for the state to contribute to restructuring and strengthening France's industrial position (294). To balance and leverage foreign equity inflows into the stock market, Strauss-Kahn also supported measures that could induce higher levels of French domestic investment in stocks. In the past Strauss-Kahn wrote extensively about the need to move at least partially toward pension funds (instead of 100 percent reliance on the pay-as-you go system).[32] In addition to this long-term but politically infeasible idea, he advocates the generalization of a system of remuneration for employees that includes a contribution to corporate profits in the form of corporate equity (*épargne salariale*) (327). Last, Strauss-Kahn defends the need for new types of regulations that can facilitate necessary mutations and increase the benefits of globalization. This last component, partly reliant on delegation to independent agencies, led to fierce political debates and a pointed attack by Jean-Pierre Chevènement, a long-standing political actor on the Left and coalition leader in 1997–2000 (Chevènement 2004, 432–33).

Strauss-Kahn was not the only core political entrepreneur at the junction of the golden bargain and the domestic political process; he was rather a key intellectual organizer and the main power holder as minister of economy, finance, and trade in 1997–99. One should, however, also emphasize

31. Ibid.
32. See in particular the analysis of ideas presented in 1982 by Strauss-Kahn with Denis Kessler, the eventual vice president of MEDEF, the French employers' federation, in Izraëlewicz (1999, 185).

the roles played by Pierret, industry minister during the same period, and Sautter, budget minister under Strauss-Kahn and minister of finance and economy after him in 1999–2000. Sautter continued Strauss-Kahn's modern Socialist program through the pursuit of reforms initiated by Strauss-Kahn, including the new economic regulations. Finally, the role played by Martine Aubry, the minister of labor and social affairs responsible for the laws on the thirty-five-hour week, is an interesting one. While Aubry played the traditional Socialist role in government and often publicly fought against Strauss-Kahn's pragmatism,[33] her background and political action before and after her role in government pointed to a more modernist approach.[34] On certain key battles, such as the 2000–01 battle over new layoff regulations (*loi de modernisation sociale*), Aubry found herself more on the modernist side, opposing the regulations pushed by the Communists because of their lack of economic sense.[35]

A Pragmatic Prime Minister on the Fence: Lionel Jospin

Identifying Finance and Economy Minister Strauss-Kahn as the core political entrepreneur behind the state support of corporate restructuring raises the question of the role of the prime minister. As head of the cabinet, policy framer, and constitutional locus of political power, he is the central actor. Jospin, the prime minister from 1997 to 2002, was fundamentally a traditional Socialist ideologue who believed in the primacy of politics and felt allergic to market forces. In the words of former finance minister Sautter, Jospin accepted the necessity of liberal reforms to support long-term growth and employment, but the very process of it went against his own ideological convictions.[36] He was unwilling to confront the Socialist militants or his coalition partners in pushing for modernist policies. He was similarly unwilling to lead a revamped modernist Socialist movement a la Tony Blair and to betray his own view of socialism. In the end, he acquiesced to most of Strauss-Kahn's program out of pragmatism and a statist commitment to a French "industrial logic." In addition, Jospin did much to convince himself and others that the core focus of his Socialist action was not in its industrial action, but rather in the thirty-five-hour week, the law for political parity, or the new law for civil unions.

Jospin's core beliefs include a conviction that Socialists must be faithful to their leftist tradition and that the state has retained the capacity to transform

33. See, for example, Alexandre and L'Aulnoit (2002).
34. See, for example, Mital and Izraelewicz (2002, 47).
35. Interview with a top political adviser to Martine Aubry during the period, 21 December 2004.
36. Interview, 6 December 2005.

reality. In Strauss-Kahn's words, Jospin's view of the world is simple: "For him, market is disorder. The state is order and control" (Mital and Izraëlewicz 2002, 20). In a 1999 article, he publicly claimed: "We are not left liberals. We are socialists. And to be socialist is to state that politics have an absolute primacy over economics" (21). Jospin coined the sentence used by Mitterrand in his 1988 presidential campaign: "Neither nationalization, nor privatization." In 1997, Jospin campaigned on a promise to stop the privatization program and to return to a purer Socialist line. Jospin's (1991, 265) intellectual vision, aptly called "the invention of the possible," called for a true leftist economic policy that would prevent the rise of inequalities in the first place.

At the same time, Jospin (1991, 255) is a pragmatist who accepts the fact that necessary means may be at odds with political aims. He accepted Strauss-Kahn's urge to go back to the spirit of socialism, rather than the mere traditions adopted by the movement in the twentieth century. Thus, he adopted in his own treatise published in 2001 the same quote of Jean Jaures that forms Strauss-Kahn's book title: "To be faithful to a tradition means to be faithful to its flame and not its ashes" (5). He would stake out anti-privatization positions in discussions with Strauss-Kahn but would, in the end, yield to his finance minister on pragmatic grounds.

His pragmatism is doubled by a firm belief in "industrial logic," a French code word for the necessity of industrial policy to ensure the competitiveness of French industry. As early as 1991, Jospin (1991, 256) emphasized the role of incentives (*incitation*) in a "mixed economy" (as he calls the French economy). He argued that the state had to defend its automobile and electronics industries and should not shy away from an "active and voluntarist industrial policy" (259). He came to be convinced by Strauss-Kahn that the central tool available for an active industrial policy in the late 1990s was privatization (Mital and Izraëlewicz 2002, 213). He practiced privatization and industrial restructuring as the "heir to Colbertism," in an active demonstration that state action remained possible (173–74). In 2002, when asked why he ended up privatizing more companies (in value) than all his conservative predecessors combined and despite his electoral promises to not do so, he responded that his choices "corresponded to a modern and ambitious industrial policy" (Jospin and Duhamel 2002, 133). He made such decisions "in the name of the industrial imperative and for the benefit of related economic sectors in the French economy, thus for jobs and the interest of employees" (133). When pushed by his interviewer on the potential gap between such actions and his Socialist commitment, Jospin curtly replies that "means of action" must be adapted to realities in the "defense of industrial power" and jobs.

Jospin (2001, 12) accompanies this pragmatic commitment to industrial policy with a call for regulations to accompany and correct market processes: "To prevent private-sector interests from stifling the general interest, to prevent short-term profit-seeking from ignoring social justice and damaging the environment, 'rule of the games' must be defined." In late summer 1999, Jospin adopts Strauss-Kahn's new focus on regulation (as opposed to direct state action).

In the end, however, the tension between Jospin's commitment to traditional Socialist priorities and between his acquiescence to Strauss-Kahn's industrial pragmatism is not resolved. Regularly confronted by this tension through political conflicts over the privatization record or corporate restructuring (the battle over Michelin's restructuring plan in 1999, Danone in 2001), Jospin is ill at ease and opts for discretion. Because of this gap and because of the lack of direct political support from his party or coalition partners, Jospin ends up reforming secretly and without claiming credit for the outcome (Mital and Izraëlewicz 2002). Jospin lends political support to Strauss-Kahn's political entrepreneurship, but tries to do so while remaining faithful to his ideology and without provoking his political partners. This delicate act forces Jospin to make such reforms invisible, hiding them behind a screen of social reforms and an expansion of public expenses that are more palatable to his political supporters. This balancing act also relies on Strauss-Kahn's direct leadership and his delegation to the bureaucrats of the Ministry of Finance and Economy. Corporate reforms barely register on the radar screen of direct actions led by the prime minister. In his book reviewing the political agenda and key reforms of Jospin's cabinet, Olivier Schrameck (Jospin's right-hand man as *directeur de cabinet*) never refers even once to privatization or to corporate reforms (2001).

Enabling Tools: Sources of Strategic Political Autonomy

How do Jospin and Strauss-Kahn get away with reforms that deviate from the preferences of their support coalitions? What is the source of their political autonomy? French political parties tend to have hierarchical structures that bestow upon leaders a high degree of autonomy and control. This is true of the Socialist Party under Jospin. Between his selection as the presidential candidate in 1995 at a low point for the Socialist Party and his defeat in 2002, his leadership of the party was never in question. This was due to his credentials as a leader and his position as mediator between reformists and traditionalists in the party. His in-depth work in 1995–96 to reconstruct the party in the wake of defeat played an important role (Grunberg 1998). The only relevant question for the security of his leadership in the period from 1997 to 2002 was related to the threat of dissolution of the parliament, a dissolution that President Chirac could have brandished at any point, particularly toward the middle of the legislative term. Although Jospin and his cabinet considered this threat to be real (Schrameck 2001), it remained quite remote given the disaster of Chirac's first dissolution in 1997 and the stability of opinion polls.

The variable that defined the eventual level of political autonomy for Strauss-Kahn's and Jospin's political entrepreneurship was the stability of the five-party ruling coalition. In order to have a realistic chance of winning the 1997 legislative election, the Socialist Party had created an electoral alliance with other parties on the Left: the Communist Party (PCF), the Left radicals (RG), the Greens, and the *mouvement des citoyens* (MDC) led by Jean-Pierre Chevènement. Jospin named this coalition the Plural Left (*gauche plurielle*). The coalition of parties agreed principally on electoral cooperation (with automatic withdrawal of the least well-placed candidates in the second round and selection of safe seats for the Greens and the Communists in particular)[37] and a limited government program. The leftist victory was a limited one in terms of electoral vote; the plural coalition of the Left won only 44 percent of the popular vote in the first round and 48.3 percent in the second round. To a large extent, its victory was due to the role of the extreme right National Front, a party that took 15 percent of the vote in the first round and led to triangular situations and rightist defeats in the second.

When the dust settled, thanks to the first-past-the-post system, the plural majority secured a majority of 43 seats (out of a total of 577). The 318 total seats of the majority are made up of 250 Socialists or affiliated Socialists, 18 radicals, 6 MDC members, 8 Greens, and 36 Communists. In other words, the majority has a degree of safety but is also vulnerable. For example, Jospin could not afford to lose the support of the Communists *and* the Greens, or the Communists and MDC and one more member of parliament. Although the Socialist preeminence was clear and Jospin's personal leadership unquestioned, the zone of convergence between the five parties was limited.

Initially, however, Socialist reformers could rely on the weak positions of both the Communist Party and the Greens in pushing their agenda. The radical Left was in a weak position due to declining electoral fortunes. The Greens were a new party with a focus on selected issues. Strauss-Kahn's brilliance and power asymmetry were sufficient to carry the majority toward reforms until 2000. In the words of a former finance minister, there was "great liberty" for reform in the first two to three years.[38]

Smaller parties initially acquiesced to Jospin's leadership but gradually raised their voices as elections neared. Tensions came out in the open in September 1999 over Michelin's restructuring plan and Jospin's seeming acquiescence. This event signals the end of the easy ride with the coalition for

---

37. For excellent data, see Perrineau and Ysmal (1998).
38. Interview with former finance minister Christian Sautter, 6 December 2005.

Jospin and a growing cost in managing coalition partners.[39] Chevènement's MDC left the coalition first in July 2000[40] and the Communists rocked the boat after the local elections and the Danone restructuring plan in March–April 2001. The period 2000–01 marks the moment when the zones of political autonomy shrank. This was particularly true as two main leaders, Strauss-Kahn, and Aubry, left the government in November 1999 and December 2000 respectively, one because of a scandal and the other for personal reasons.

The conservative Juppé government (1995–May 1997) presents an interesting contrast. Despite high degrees of political autonomy and bureaucratic delegation, the output of corporate reforms remained extremely limited. This transitional and deviant period can be explained by two main factors. First, the political agenda was overwhelmingly dominated by the race to join the euro and the need to fulfill Maastricht criteria. Budgetary reforms and management crowded the agenda and led the government to use most of its political capital and time on that front. Second, the massive nationwide strikes and demonstrations that took place in December 1995 in response to budgetary reforms seem to have drastically reduced the security and autonomy of political leadership. The prime minister became unpopular and uncertain of the strength of his mandate, especially given the knowledge that legislative elections had to be called soon.

Throughout the period, however, the political autonomy enjoyed by key political entrepreneurs was boosted by a French institutional variable. In comparison to other democracies, particularly Japan and Germany, the structurally high executive control over the legislative agenda granted by the French constitution bestows great capacity upon government leaders. Even one of the prime beneficiaries of this situation, Strauss-Kahn himself, acknowledges that this executive control goes too far and limits the role of parliament to a greater extent than in any other modern democracy (Strauss-Kahn 2002, 371–73).

As in Japan, members of parliament have relatively few staff and most of the technical knowledge and bill-drafting power lies in the bureaucracy. However, in contrast to Japan, the French constitution directly empowers the prime minister and his cabinet to set the daily agenda of parliament, to declare that a bill is urgent and should be considered before all else, and to add important amendments to bills under review in parliament at almost any time. These prerogatives are set out clearly in the constitution of the Fifth Republic, making change difficult. In particular, Article 48 in the

39. See Mital and Izraelewicz (2002, 239–40) for the analysis of the costs of managing the "plural majority" for structural reforms. See also Schrameck (2001).

40. See Chevènement (2004) for a vivid depiction of the many conflicts with Jospin and Strauss-Kahn over industrial and economic management.

constitution stipulates that government bills have precedence on the parliamentary agenda and that the government also sets the order of precedence. Only when the government accepts them can bills proposed by MPs be receivable. The creation of a "parliamentary niche" of one day per month reserved for bills from members of parliament was only recently added through a constitutional amendment. De facto, it is estimated that 90 percent of laws passed by parliament are bills that originated in the government, a percentage that is even higher than in Japan (Gicquel 1998, 2).

Regarding legislative amendments, the constitution also greatly empowers the government (Arts. 40 and 44). The government is solely in charge of the process of amendments. In practice, this power is wielded by the minister in charge. For most corporate reforms, the minister was either the finance and economy minister (Strauss-Kahn, Sautter, then Fabius) or the secretary of state for industry (Pierret). While being able to add any amendment to the bill (sometimes unrelated amendments as well), the government must approve any parliamentary amendment submitted after the start of parliamentary debates. Furthermore, the government has the ability at any time to request a "blocked vote" (*vote bloqué*), through which parliament must vote on the bill proposed by the government including all government-sponsored amendments and only those amendments.

The power of the government to add new amendments at short notice has been used in at least two recent important reforms. First, the creation of advantageous stock options for entrepreneurs was discreetly added by the finance minister (with the acquiescence of the prime minister) as an amendment to the 1998 budget bill in December 1997. One top bureaucrat gloated in an interview that this ploy ensured maximum discretion and that parliamentarians had not understood the importance of this amendment. He added that when stock options entered the political debate in 2000–01, the administration was greatly hindered in its efficient management of the economy. A second recent case was the creation of the independent Agency for International Investments (Agence Française pour les Investissements Internationaux),[41] headed by a top bureaucrat with the rank of ambassador, through an amendment to the NRE bill in 2001. This agency was created through the consolidation of various agencies, with independent offices and a minimum of supervision by parliament. It aims at increasing FDI in France and lobbying the administration on behalf of foreign investors. The article in the NRE bill that created the agency (Article 144, the last one) was not present in the initial bill presented to parliament in March 2000, or even in the penultimate updated draft of January 2001.

Finally, the prime minister also has the opportunity to close parliamentary debates and force adoption of a bill through the so-called nuclear

41. Under the tutelage of MINEFI.

option. Article 49.3 allows the prime minister to give parliament twenty-four hours to either pass a non-confidence vote on the entire cabinet or to accept the bill under discussion.

The Bureaucratic Booster: Effective Tools for Delegation

The autonomy of a political entrepreneur like Strauss-Kahn is enhanced by the existence of a highly trained elite bureaucracy.[42] Any visitor to Bercy is struck by its size and by its atmosphere. The different aisles of the Bercy "fortress" carry names such as Vauban (the seventeenth-century master designer of fortified places) and Colbert (the seventeenth-century inventor of state capitalism). The contrast is particularly great with the crowded and run-down Ministry of Finance in Japan, one of the oldest remaining buildings in Tokyo and one that was completed in 1942 when building materials were strictly rationed. The construction of Bercy was part of the *Grands Travaux* launched by President Mitterrand in the early 1980s. It was completed in 1989 at the staggering cost of FF4 billion and the Ministry of Finance moved in in late December that year. The Ministry of Industry and Ministry of Finance were unified into a super economic ministry (MINEFI), beginning with Minister of Finance and Economy Balladur in 1986. The full integration of the ministry took place in 1997 under Strauss-Kahn. The Ministry of Industry completed its move to Bercy in 1998.[43] The unity of the whole economic bureaucracy is the first feature that stands in contrast to the Japanese situation. To be sure, there are some rivalries between the elites of the Trésor and those of the Ministry of Industry, but the clear hierarchical structure ensures that these rivalries are managed in-house, at least after 1997.[44] The MINEFI as a whole is able to propose one unified set of legislation.

How does political control of such a large bureaucracy take place? How can delegation be separated from abdication? In France, there are indeed cases of weak political ministers and high bureaucratic independence. Some ministers without a powerful political backing or with a too-short tenure found it hard to dominate the elite of the Trésor. This was partly true for Finance Ministers Edmond Alphandéry (1993–95), Jean Arthuis (1995–97), and Francis Mer (2002–03).

Such situations, however, are not the rule. Under political leaders that hold actual political power within their party and relative to the prime minister, such as Bérégovoy, Strauss-Kahn, Fabius, or Sarkozy, the political masters are clearly in control. This control relies on several tools including

---

42. See, for example, Dobbin (1994); Hall (1986); Shonfield (1965).

43. Interview with economic adviser to President Chirac, September 2000.

44. Confirmed in interviews with bureaucrats from both the Trésor and the Ministry of Industry, September 2000.

a large personal staff of about twenty (the *cabinet*, a staff that owes its position entirely to the minister), control of the legislative process, and a significant say in important appointments (Séréni and Villeneuve 2002). In addition, senior bureaucrats and political leaders emerge from the same fused elite class and share a similar vision (Baverez 2003, 42). This creates a common intellectual bedrock that has sustained the modernizing élan of political entrepreneurs and the tacit support of most mainstream politicians for this program.[45] Finally, the system of regular exchange between elite bureaucracy and the private sector allows political leaders to richly reward faithful bureaucrats through plum positions in the private sector. Many senior bureaucrats end up leading the very companies they privatized. The hierarchical and organized structure of the elite bureaucracy enables political leaders to control the entire bureaucracy just by coopting its top layer.

In addition to formal national tools, EU processes have also tended to increase the reform capacity of political entrepreneurs in France. Important reforms such as the abandonment of state subsidies to state-controlled groups and the privatization of groups such as Renault and Crédit Lyonnais occurred under pressure by the EU Commission (Directorate General in charge of the regulation of competition). The privatization of CIC and GAN (financial institutions), as well as the partial privatization of Air France were all consistent with commitments made to the EU (and to enforcement pressures from the EU).[46] On the national scene, the French government appears to have had no choice but to follow EU directives for the sake of European integration. In most cases, however, the French government agreed ex ante to key EU reforms or even initiated these reforms. The most recent case has been the deregulation of gas and electricity utilities. The issue came to the fore in early 2001 when the French government refused to privatize GDF, the state-owned gas utility, and was taken to court by the EU Commission. France likewise opposed the EU-led privatization of EDF, the electricity utility, and the full opening of the French electricity market. However, the record indicates that the French government initiated electricity deregulation in the mid-1990s to enable EDF to move into the Spanish and Italian markets. MINEFI officials admit that the EU is seen less as a threat to their power than as an opportunity for reform. In the words of a top bureaucrat,

> Although on many subjects EU directives go against our interests, France has always considered that it had a certain leverage over important EU decisions because of the Franco-German axis. . . . In addition, the commission

45. See the excellent analysis by thinkers of the Fondation Saint-Simon on the emergence of large reform consensus in the center (Furet, Julliard, and Rosanvallon 1988). For a larger historical context, see Rosanvallon (1995, 2004).

46. Interview with chief political adviser to Finance Minister Strauss-Kahn, 1997–99 (M. Villeroy de Galhau, directeur de cabinet), 4 April 2006.

represents a bureaucratic model that is close to the French model. French bureaucrats tend to do well in international institutions such as the EU Commission.[47]

Naturally, the instrumental use of the EU by French politicians for the sake of domestic reform may not be a durable option. Increasingly, the EU Commission is itself pushing change onto the French political system. Besides, as former finance minister Arthuis argued, the EU Commission is less impervious to corporate lobbying than the French bureaucracy, leading to the irony that French companies have increasingly lobbied the EU Commission to act against the French government (Arthuis 1998, 101).

Corporate Reforms through Privatization

The privatization program of the Jospin government came as one of the great surprises of its tenure, especially in light of Jospin's long-standing opposition to the process, and because the Right had led the two previous privatization waves. It came to be regarded as the paradox of Socialist privatization.[48] In the end, Jospin sold over €30 billion in public assets during the legislative time of his cabinet (Jakubyszyn 2002), while the overtly pro-privatization Right sold only €20 billion in assets from 1993 to 1997.[49] Furthermore, the Jospin government privatized some of the more sensitive and political firms. These included the continuation of the Renault privatization (state participation decreasing from 44 percent in 1996 to 25 percent in 2002), France Telecom (first 21 percent sold in October 1997 and 17 percent more sold in November 1998), Air France (first 45 percent sold in February 1999), and Credit Lyonnais (summer 1999). After initially opposing the sale of companies in the area of defense, the Jospin government ended up partially privatizing Thomson-CSF (1999), privatizing Aerospatiale while merging it with Matra (June 1999) and then organizing a mega-merger of the two with Germany's Dasa (Daimler-Benz group) and Spain's Casa to create a new European champion: EADS (October 1999). During the period from 1997 to 2002, the government also completed the privatization of France's banking and financial industry with the exception of the Banque Hervet (GAN-CIC, Credit Foncier de France, Credit Lyonnais). By

47. Labor union leaders also defend this point. One top leader said in an interview that the EU was used as a "battering ram" by the French government to break domestic deadlocks. Former finance minister Alphandéry (2000) likewise sees the euro and the EU as the best chances for pushing difficult reforms in France.

48. Interview with Michel Albert, September 2000.

49. The Chirac government of 1986–88 sold €11 billion, the Balladur government of 1993–95 €16 billion, and the Juppé government of 1995–97 €4 billion (Haby 1999, 151).

the end of the legislature, the weight of public companies in France fell back below the level of 1946, eclipsing both the postwar and the 1981 waves of nationalization.

Interestingly, post-1997 privatization marked the partial rejection of the concept of stable shareholder cores by the government. In both 1986–87 and 1993–95, the process of privatization was not an open one on the stock market. Rather, political leaders and the Trésor directly managed the privatization process through opaque transactions with large financial institutions and corporations often headed by ex-bureaucrats. It was the responsibility of the finance minister and his cabinet to handpick a core of stable shareholders who were willing to hold shares over the long term and to constitute the board of directors.[50] This last step created a hierarchy between insider-shareholders and others and strengthened cross-shareholding links. In its 1997 Economic Survey of France, the OECD criticized this pattern for merely reinforcing management relative to investors and for discriminating against foreign investors (1996–99, 121–22).

As readily acknowledged by top bureaucrats themselves, these early waves of privatization could be seen as the high point of state intervention and modern Colbertism. In 1993, the government lifted the ceiling on foreign ownership for EU corporations and in 1996 for non-EU corporations as well. The pattern changed dramatically after 1995. According to the 2000 OECD study on corporate governance quoted in chapter 2, core shareholdings declined by a third between 1989 and 1999, most of it after 1997. By 1999, the capital of most newly privatized corporations included over 50 percent foreign ownership. In fact, interviews reveal that the Trésor, under Strauss-Kahn's direction, abandoned the policy of core shareholdings in 1997 and instead moved to support principles of corporate governance and maximization of shareholder value. Chapter 6 presents details of this shift in the case of Renault.

Unlike in the 1986 and 1993 conservative governments, Jospin did not come with an ideological commitment to privatization (to the contrary) and a master plan. As a result, privatization came to be called "capital opening" (*ouverture de capital*) and had to be taken one step at a time, according to the industrial logic followed by Strauss-Kahn and Jospin. While the Chirac government focused on the creation of stable cores of cross-shareholding between French companies to control the newly created companies, Jospin was content to rely on capital from foreign institutional investors.

Yet, for Strauss-Kahn and Jospin, the privatization process became a master tool to shape the restructuring of French finance and industry and

50. Jean-Marie Messier, *chef de cabinet* for finance minister Balladur, played a key role in 1986–87.

increase its competitiveness.[51] An important example of this proactive government rule accompanying the process was the creation of a European champion in defense and space, EADS. An event to celebrate the birth of this new giant took place in Strasbourg on 14 October 1999, and brought together its five creators: Jean-Luc Lagardère (Lagardère Group), Jürgen Schrempp (Daimler-Chrysler), Gerhard Schröder (German chancellor), Dominique Strauss-Kahn, and Lionel Jospin. This event is depicted by both French leaders as a watershed moment (Jospin and Duhamel 2002, 133; Mital and Izraëlewicz 2002, 172; Strauss-Kahn 2002, 306). By privatizing and withdrawing, the state could end up shaping a new industrial structure, increase French competitiveness, and preserve jobs. Strauss-Kahn (2002, 307) writes:

> We are in the midst of the concrete application of the core principle of a modern industrial policy—let us say, of a leftist economic policy: namely, to intervene, for the sake of efficient mechanisms of the market economy, at the heart of the engine, where value is created, while inserting into it what no market actor can bring: a long term vision and a capacity to mutualize risks, in the service of job creation, of wealth generation, and common welfare. This is socialism of production.

Amazingly, Strauss-Kahn and Jospin turned a tool traditionally associated with the Right into a Socialist mechanism for intervening in the means of production. By responding to incentives from the golden bargain and eyeing long-term competitiveness and growth, Strauss-Kahn acts as the quintessential political entrepreneur. Strauss-Kahn adds that each privatization operation contributes to "restructuring and to reinforcing our industry" (294). While the Juppé government nearly sold Thomson Multi Media for a symbolic franc to soon-to-be-bankrupt Daewoo of Korea in the name of commitment to rapid privatization, Strauss-Kahn and Jospin point to their strategy of slowly nurturing Thomson and then privatizing from a position of strength. In this approach, the state acts first and foremost as a long-term shareholder seeking the highest value for its assets. In Renault's case, it was the backing of this long-term investor that allowed the company to take over Nissan in 1999, a huge financial risk that no financier would have accepted (302). At the same time, the state as shareholder accepted the need to bring private shareholders on board in an effort to transform governance and increase profitability. A company like EDF (the national electricity utility) is constrained by the shackles of national management, argues Strauss-Kahn.

51. The necessity of international alliances for industrial competitiveness is the key argument put forth by Jospin in his short review of privatization as part of a general book on his political vision (Jospin 2005, in particular p. 299).

This strategy was a political response to a new environment. Global equity flows changed incentives for political leaders such as Strauss-Kahn in comparison to leaders in the late 1980s. Interviews with officials at the Trésor reveal that the state had to incorporate the principles defended by pension funds into the management of state-controlled corporations such as Renault and France Telecom. Because of the scandal at Crédit Lyonnais and the bad reputation of state-owned enterprises in the early 1990s, the Trésor decided that it was "too risky for it to manage alone state-controlled corporations." The easiest solution, therefore, has been to adopt a principle of co-management with private sector partners. With the increasing influence of foreign investors on these private sector partners, the state has been inclined to follow corporate governance principles. Besides, once a corporation like Renault is partly listed in the stock market, the share price is set by dominant investors. Bureaucrats also explained that the "partial opening of capital" put a large share of the floating capital in the hands of foreign investors who threatened to leave if corporations did not adopt more transparent principles of corporate governance. Gradually, in the late 1990s, officials at the Trésor found out that the cost of resisting pension funds and principles of corporate governance was just too high, and they gradually converged. As the quality of state management is increasingly assessed through these stock prices, the state itself is led to adopt the principles demanded by key investors. Strauss-Kahn responded to these new incentives by organizing seminars on corporate governance for its public administrators at the Trésor.

Politically, privatization pushed the autonomy of political entrepreneurs to the limit. The case of France Telecom proved to be the most sensitive, given the public servant status of its employees and their close association with the Socialist Party. In response to a letter from the trade unions of France Telecom during the electoral campaign, Jospin had committed himself to not privatizing France Telecom. Consequently, he insisted on retaining a clear majority for the state.[52] In October 1997, Strauss-Kahn and the Trésor sold 20 percent of their shares, bringing the state's control to 66 percent.[53] Despite associated guarantees to retain the public servant status and to encourage employee shareholding (pushed by Jospin), this passage created a backlash in the Socialist Party. Jospin had an angry discussion with Strauss-Kahn over the issue, demanding a slower pace.[54] In the end, however, the government could partially privatize without trying to pass a law in

52. Interview with chief political adviser to Finance Minister Strauss-Kahn, 1997–99 (M. Villeroy de Galhau, directeur de cabinet), 4 April 2006.
53. A law on the books (*loi Fillon*, passed by a previous conservative government) authorized the government to open capital up to 49 percent.
54. Interview with chief economic adviser to Prime Minister Jospin in 1997–2000, Jean-Pierre Jouyet, 4 April 2006.

parliament (which would have been impossible), and was thus able to proceed in spite of its majority. A similar conflict took place over Air France. When the CEO of the state-owned company, Christian Blanc, demanded privatization, Jospin refused it. He knew that this symbolic move went beyond the possible political space he had with his ruling coalition. Christian Blanc resigned as a result.[55]

In the proactive pursuit of privatization and the introduction of modern management methods for public corporations, political leaders also delegated important components to the elite bureaucracy at the Trésor. For example, broad legislative bills (*lois cadre*) have authorized the process of privatization but have left the details up to bureaucrats. Thus, the Trésor discreetly proceeded to the privatization of Renault (a sensitive political issue) in May 1996 by reducing the state share from 53 to 47 percent. It did not enter the legislative agenda at the time. The same thing happened in 2001–02 with the next privatization move.

Stock Options

A second important case of structural reform relates to legislation on stock options and employee saving plans (*épargne salariale*). These two issues have been in the center of a lively political debate since 1998. The evolution of the legislation on stock options reveals once again a strong counter-partisan trend. In 1996, the Conservative Juppé government increased the taxation of stock options by imposing additional social charges on capital gains when options were exercised within five years. It seems that the move was primarily motivated by fiscal objectives (within the context of the Maastricht criteria). In 1998, the Socialist Jospin government took a big step by undoing some elements of the 1996 law and by creating a new kind of discreet stock option with an extremely advantageous fiscal regime for entrepreneurs, the "*bons de souscriptions de parts de créateurs d'entreprise.*" In doing so, the Left had to fight hard against the lock-in effect (*effet de cliquet*) involved in the initial move of the Juppé cabinet.[56] Politically, Strauss-Kahn prepared the bill, and carefully and skillfully evoked it in front of the prime minister. Jospin saw this as technical and relatively marginal.[57] Thus, he did not expect that the parliamentary majority would seize upon it and create a political crisis.

In 1999, Strauss-Kahn pushed for a general decrease in capital gains taxes, but the move ran into political counter-currents after the scandal of

55. Ibid.
56. Interview with high member of the political cabinet of former finance minister Strauss-Kahn, September 2000.
57. Interview with Jean-Pierre Jouyet, 4 April 2006.

the Elf-Total merger and the discovery of huge side payments in the form of stock options to the loser (M. Jaffré of Elf). Eventually, a compromise was reached in 2000 between the pro-stock option political reformers (Fabius having replaced Strauss-Kahn and Sautter) and the anti-stock option Socialist-Communist parliamentary majority and the tax decrease was included in the NRE project. It improved the fiscal treatment of stock options (with a rate of 26 percent) up to a certain ceiling and when stocks are kept at least for five years after the exercise of options. This compromise was seen as relatively pro-corporate and later regretted by Prime Minister Jospin. Interviews with bureaucrats at the Trésor indicate that the motivations of the minister of finance were simple: "improving the competitiveness of corporations," retaining top talent in France, and encouraging investments. One senior bureaucrat interviewed at the Trésor also indicated that foreign investors in France (both pension funds and providers of FDI) had exerted pressure on the government.

With hindsight, the battle over stock options was a strong clash point between political entrepreneurs and the governing party. Strauss-Kahn wanted to use this tool to attract a maximum of talent to France and to increase innovation and long-term growth. Yet he encountered harsh opposition from the Socialist Party.[58] His attempt to include a major step forward in the New Economic Regulations bill ended in failure. By 2000, the Socialist majority, led by First Secretary François Hollande, initiated a full battle against Strauss-Kahn's successor, Laurent Fabius. In this battle, Jospin sensed that his political window had closed and sided with the party (Hollande) over the finance minister, Fabius.[59] A compromise was reached, but the initial Strauss-Kahn idea was essentially watered down.

The New Economic Regulations

A key illustration of political mediation of the incentives of the golden bargain is the partial reform of corporate governance through the NRE bill, enacted in May 2001 after a nearly two-year long legislative process. It is a prime example of crab-walk reformism, led by political entrepreneurs despite the doubts of their own majority. In the words of former finance minister Sautter (in 1999–2000): "we pretend to target an objective, but actually move toward another one."[60] Officially, in its "political dressing" (*ha-*

58. Interview with chief political adviser to Finance Minister Strauss-Kahn, 1997–99 (M. Villeroy de Galhau, directeur de cabinet), 4 April 2006.

59. Interview with chief economic adviser to Prime Minister Jospin in 1997–2000, Jean-Pierre Jouyet, 4 April 2006.

60. I am indebted to former finance minister Christian Sautter for the term "*reformes en crabe.*" Interview, 6 December 2005.

billage politique), the law marked the renewed capacity of the state to regulate capitalism and to fix rules.[61] In its contents, however, the law included
elements that increased the voice and rights of minority shareholders and
simplified takeovers. At the same time, the political compromise over the
bill included the commitment by the government to follow up with a law
(*loi de modernisation sociale*) that would toughen conditions for layoffs.[62] One
finds here the classic compromise of corporate governance liberalization in
exchange for labor protection. One component of the NRE bill, the creation of an agency to promote inward investment (Agence Française pour
les Investissements Internationaux) was introduced as a last minute amendment by the minister, using the strategy of the "rider."

Minister of Finance and Economy Sautter presented the NRE bill to parliament on 15 March 2000. After a long legislative process and recurring
disagreements between the Socialist-controlled Assemblée Nationale and
the opposition-controlled Sénat, the law was finally enacted by the Assemblée Nationale on 2 May 2001. Between the beginning and the end of the
process the bill grew from 74 to 144 articles due to a large number of
amendments. The law introduces changes in three main areas: regulations
of mergers and takeovers, competition law, and corporate governance. The
first aims at increasing the transparency of mergers and keeping employees
informed. The second seeks to increase the regulations of competition in
order to protect consumers and thwart anti-competitive activities. Amendments dealing with fruit and vegetable markets and movie theater regulations were added to increase parliamentary support. In the third area, the
law aims at increasing the power of minority shareholders and the transparency of management. In particular, it provided the first important reform of the 1966 commercial code by creating the option to separate the
function of chairman and CEO. It requires directors of listed companies to
publish the full amount of their remuneration and stock options. It limits
the number of corporate offices held by directors and regulates the functions of the board of directors. It lowers the shareholding threshold required
for submitting written questions to the CEO and for suing management
from 10 percent to 5 percent. It also enables minority shareholders to participate in shareholder meetings through video conferencing and electronic
voting. These rules apply to state-controlled corporations as well. This third
area forms the main focus of the analysis here.

The NRE bill is marked by two great ironies. First, it allows senior bureaucrats of the Ministry of Economy and Finance to gloat that *dirigiste*
France is now way ahead of Germany and Switzerland in terms of corporate

61. Interview with chief economic adviser to Prime Minister Jospin in 1997–2000, Jean-
Pierre Jouyet, 4 April 2006.
62. Ibid.

reform and that France qualifies as a champion of corporate governance, courtesy of the state.[63] Second, and even more significantly, it illustrates the full control of the executive leadership over the legislative agenda even in a politically charged period. For the very NRE bill that ended up enhancing shareholder power and the responsiveness of management to shareholders was officially initiated by Prime Minister Jospin in September 1999 as a way to control the ability of shareholders to demand corporate restructuring resulting in large-scale layoffs. Indeed, the NRE bill was supposed to be a response to the *Affaire Michelin* and to restrict the push by shareholders for a higher ROE. Alain Madelin, a senior opposition leader, denounced this ultimate irony in a scathing attack on the first day of debate on the NRE in parliament (25 April 2000). Madelin underlined the huge gap between the promises made by Prime Minister Jospin in September 1999 and the poverty of the NRE bill. Amazingly, the ultraliberal Madelin said that he actually agreed with most of the NRE bill but would oppose it to force the government to face up to its inconsistency.[64]

The *Affaire Michelin* was a tragedy in six acts. The first act saw the CEO of Michelin announce in a meeting of financial analysts that its profits in the first six months of 1999 were up 17 percent from the year before and that it would lay off 7,500 people to continue the improvement of its margin. In response, the Michelin share rose 10.56 percent on that day and another 12.53 percent two days later (Forrester 2000, 113–14). In act 2, unfortunately for Michelin, Prime Minister Jospin was interviewed on a primetime news program on September 13. The news anchor had picked up on the Michelin profits-cum-layoffs announcement and asked the prime minister for his position on the matter. A visibly surprised prime minister, fresh from his minister of finance's seminars on the new role of the state, replied that the state was not omnipotent: "L'Etat ne peut pas tout." He added: "it is not through the law and legal texts that we can regulate the economy" (Alphandéry 2000, 108). This meek response had the effect of a bombshell on the political microcosm. The next day, the response of the prime minister made the front page of *Le Monde* and other mainstream newspapers. The prime minister came under fierce attack not only from his coalition partners, the Communist and Green parties, but also from within his own Socialist Party. Commentators indicated that this marked the gravest crisis since the inauguration of the Jospin government in 1997. Under fire from all sides, the prime minister prepared his rebuttal. In act 3, Prime Minister Jospin made a speech to a congress of the Socialist MPs in Strasbourg on 27 September. In that speech, the prime minister promised a drastic change of

---

63. Interview with bureaucrats of the Trésor, October 2000.
64. Report of detailed parliamentary debates. "Compte-Rendu Integral des Séances du Mardi 25 Avril 2000." Published by *Journaux Officiels*.

direction in his government and committed himself to the "erection of new tools of regulation." In particular, he declared: "we will fight against abusive economic layoffs. . . . It is unacceptable to announce substantial benefits and at the same time to ask the state to pay for part of the restructuring plan [through early retirement plans and other social plans]." Borrowing from Strauss-Kahn, he further declared that the state remained powerful and had countless tools at its disposal. It would from now on "invent new regulations" to control the market.[65] This speech formed the genesis of the NRE bill. The Ministry of Finance was hastily instructed to find ways to put together a bill that would meet Prime Minister Jospin's goals.

Act 4 of the tragedy came with the inclusion of the Michelin amendment (by the government) in the second thirty-five-hour-week bill in December 1999. This amendment made the approval of state support for layoffs conditional on successful negotiations of agreements on the thirty-five-hour week. However, the Conseil Constitutionnel (France's constitutional court) struck down the amendment in January 2000. Act 5 was the NRE bill (introduced in March 2000), which far from regulating restructuring motivated by shareholder demands, ended up empowering shareholders. Finally, act 6 revealed the bill of social modernization (*loi de modernisation sociale*), passed in the fall of 2001. The bill restricts the legality of economic layoffs to four strict cases. However, the Conseil Constitutionnel once again struck down the section of the law related to the Michelin Affair in January 2002 because it arguably infringed upon the freedom of enterprise enshrined in the Human Rights Declaration of 1789. So, in the end, the Michelin Affair marked the inability of political parties and coalitions to go against the modernizing trend supported by party leaders and senior bureaucrats.

The first key feature of the NRE bill, therefore, is the full degree of control throughout the legislative process exhibited by reformers such as Strauss-Kahn and Sautter and, by delegation, senior bureaucrats of the Ministry of Finance. Interviews with a wide range of actors, both within MINEFI and outside, confirm that Strauss-Kahn made the decision to turn the NRE bill into a vehicle for structural reform. The Trésor seized on the chance to implement some corporate governance ideas that had long been sitting inside its drawers (*les fonds de tiroir*). In the words of one of the bureaucrats, "the NRE bill was used by the government as a means to pass useful reforms, such as merger regulations [which, incidentally, increase the power of the ministry] and corporate governance changes."[66] Under guidelines set by Strauss-Kahn, senior bureaucrats drafted the bill. The finance minister

65. "Intervention du Premier ministre aux Journees Parlementaires du Groupe Socialiste." Strasbourg, 27 September 1999. Website of the Socialist Party: www.psinfo.net/entretiens/jospin/parlement99.html.
66. Interview at the Ministry of Finance and Economy on 7 September 2000.

directed the process in parliament by repeatedly declaring its official urgency and by controlling the amendment process. True, the ministry had in fact planned to also include drastic reforms of the fiscal treatment of stock options, pension reforms, and deeper reforms of the commercial code but was forced to back down by the parliamentary majority.[67] These reforms were just too important to be passed through the vehicle of the NRE. This instance shows the limits of political autonomy.

The Political Analysis of the NRE Bill

What were the goals pursued by Strauss-Kahn, Sautter, Pierret (the secretary of state for industry who often stood in for the finance minister to defend the bill in parliament) through the NRE bill? Interestingly, the law did meet some of the requests formulated by important foreign investors, such as CalPERS. Political leadership met the interests of capital. For example, CalPERS had requested in 1997 that France introduce a board with independent directors that would have the ability to control the CEO. The NRE bill did introduce the option of having a chairman for that purpose. CalPERS requested the mandatory publication of board members' remunerations. This is included in the NRE bill. CalPERS had also requested more protection for minority shareholders and improved voting methods. Both of these demands were met in the NRE (including a lower threshold for shareholder suits).

Another telltale sign was the extremely positive review of NRE by Andersen Legal Consulting. Andersen wrote that the NRE represented a translation into law of the 1999 Viénot *Report on Corporate Governance* (a report meekly sponsored by MEDEF but drafted by ex-bureaucrat Viénot). Although Andersen deplored the fact that it had taken almost two years to translate those principles into law, it welcomed the fact that all but the last of the Viénot recommendations had been incorporated. "The net effect has been increased regulation of all Sociétés Anonymes, making them much less attractive vehicles for any corporate enterprise other than listed companies."[68] Supporters also included a small lobby group of old boys of the Caisse Des Depots, led by Minister of Industry Christian Pierret with links to some members of parliament, such as Jean-Pierre Balligand.[69]

Politically, the detailed review of parliamentary debates reveals the reluctance of the Leftist majority to go along with the project, with some MPs denouncing it as a clearly liberal project that went in the wrong direction.

---

67. Interview at the Presidency of the Republic (Elysée) on 4 September 2000.
68. Redding, Blake. 2002. "Hot Issue. Corporate Governance in France: The NRE Act." Andersen Legal, 2002, www.iflr.com/?Page=17&ISS=16392&SID=514713
69. Interview with former finance minister Christian Sautter, 5 December 2006.

The parliamentary majority introduced many amendments, including an amendment to introduce a Tobin tax. But the government expressed its opposition to most of them and stuck to its guns, revealing the clear spectacle of a government in opposition to its own parliamentary majority. The government couched its defense in terms of support for democratic principles against the dominance of corporate management and for small individual shareholders. In its defense, the government also argued that the demands of foreign pension funds in terms of increased transparency were legitimate (see parliamentary debates, 25 April 2000). The following day, the minister of industry, Christian Pierret, declared to the conservative opposition: "I do believe that transparency, in particular toward employees and minority shareholders is a key condition for corporate performance." (parliamentary debate, 26 April 2000: 3335).

The minister added that the goal of this text was to promote globalization, but to also to regulate it. In fact, a large portion of the parliamentary debate focused on globalization and pension funds and what the appropriate response of the state should be.

The official report put together by Eric Besson, the chair of the parliamentary commission on the NRE bill and a close ally of the government on the bill, made a clear connection between the NRE bill and the requirements of global finance.

> The objectives of the present bill are ambitious. They relate to the competitiveness of French corporations. The archaism of some of the provisions [contained in the law before NRE] is indeed hardly compatible with the internationalization of capital movements, the development of large French industrial groups on the basis of equity financing, the increase in the number of shareholders, and the legitimate demands of minority shareholders. . . .
>
> The shareholding of corporations tends to become international: the share of non-residents in the French stock market has reached 40 percent, in comparison to less than 20 percent in the UK, and less than 10 percent in the US and Japan. These trends favor the harmonization of corporate management and French corporations cannot durably stand apart. [The current situation of the commercial law] is characterized by a lack of transparency on key elements of corporate management. . . . It also risks in the long-term being a brake to [foreign] investment into French corporations, whose modalities management can provoke the reluctance of international investors. Transparency has indeed become an investment criterion for many fund managers. (Besson 2000)

This important excerpt demonstrates the logic pursued by the state in the NRE bill. It is an attempt to increase the competitiveness of French corporations in their financing operations by forcing them to match more closely the requests of foreign investors in terms of corporate governance.

This reflects Strauss-Kahn's vision of a socialism that makes use of productive forces rather than resists them.

The national secretary of the Confédération Générale du Travail (CGT), Christophe le Duigou, was deeply involved in the NRE battle. He argues that the NRE was initially presented as a regulatory tool to control globalization. Yet it became clear to him that the law contained a deep bias toward "an anglo-saxon and financial conception of corporate governance." Strauss-Kahn and the Trésor successfully pushed forward a "clear logic of attraction of capital flows." Le Duigou attempted to mobilize leftist party supporters against it, but in vain. He argues that Jospin and Strauss-Kahn followed a "logic of arbitrage (optimization)," instead of following a grand vision.[70]

Jospin's role in the NRE bill remains limited. He was not much involved and left an open political space for his finance ministers. The bill is not mentioned in either his post-government (Jospin and Duhamel 2002) or his main lieutenant's memoirs (Schrameck 2001). Jospin had to face the defection of Chevènement's MDC[71] and serious opposition from his Communist partners. Clearly, neither labor unions nor leftist parties lobbied for the NRE bill;[72] grassroots support on the Left was extremely thin. Jospin chose to let the Ministry of Finance have a free hand in drafting the law (with limits on stock options and a few sensitive points), while effecting necessary bargains with his coalition. Clearly, the anti-layoff law (*loi de modernisation sociale*) that followed the NRE was a partial concession to the Communist Party. The two bills were the result of a grand bargain within the Left: corporate governance reforms in exchange for guarantees on the labor side.[73] It is important to note, however, that the 2001 social modernization bill only added mild restrictions on layoffs and that Jospin and Strauss-Kahn had successfully closed the debate on strict layoff regulations at the beginning of their mandate (Mauduit and Desportes 1999, 143–45). In the end, Jospin acquiesced to the NRE bill because, in the big picture, it fit his vision of the state as the prime mover of economic realities, a state that was still relevant and in charge. Jospin abhorred auto-regulation and corporate leadership more than the thought of using the state to push forward changes demanded by global markets.

Therefore, the NRE law was drafted in response to demands by foreign investors in the French stock market although it was presented to the

70. Interview, 30 May 2002.

71. See Chevènement (2004, 434).

72. Only the most moderate union, the Confédération française démocratique du travail (CFDT) expressed a degree of lukewarm support when the bill was passed. Pointing out failures to regulate international capital or takeovers and very limited relevance for workers, the CFDT pointed out that the bill played a useful rule in increasing transparency (Peillon 2000).

73. Interview with senior adviser to the prime minister, Jean-Pierre Jouyet, 4 April 2006.

French public as the opposite: an official attempt by the state to regain control over the global economy. In any account, it demonstrates the process of state mediation of global capital flows and emphasizes the role of the state and political leaders in corporate reforms.

Political Implications: Side Payments, Discontent, and the 2002 Election

Reformist political entrepreneurs such as finance minister Strauss-Kahn led corporate reforms after 1997. One of their aims was to adapt French corporations to the new reality of foreign dominance in the capital of major French corporations. In pushing for these reforms, the state took the necessary measures to lessen the mismatch between existing regulations and the new global reality, marking the continual relevance of the state in economic affairs. To be sure, the state took an increasingly indirect and regulatory role, but remained central nonetheless. Such a proactive political leadership in the French economic transition ensured that France continued to follow a mixed path, partly converging toward U.S. principles and partly developing its own regulatory features. In fact, this trend of continued state involvement in the economy continued in an even more direct way after 2002. Strauss-Kahn's successor Sarkozy seems to have returned to a more traditional interventionist approach. As a minister of finance and economy in 2004, Sarkozy directly intervened in mergers to change the outcome (Sanofi-Aventis merger) or engaged in muscled bailouts and restructuring operations (Alstom). In early 2005, President Chirac followed with a direct return to industrial policy through the creation of a new agency for industrial innovation. This agency, the Agence de l'Innovation Industrielle, empowered with a budget of several billion euros, contributes to research and innovation in selected corporations (Beffa 2005). Reports of the death of the state may have been premature.

Politically, Socialist Party leaders such as Strauss-Kahn (and by acquiescence, Jospin) gambled that they could engage in reforms that went beyond the preferences of their political support base and thus gain new supporters at the center that more than offset those they would lose on the Left. The exercise relied on the high degree of strategic political autonomy available to these leaders in 1997–2000 and on the high degree of bureaucratic delegation they had.

Such a top-down political entrepreneurial pathway involved three kinds of costs. First, at critical junctures, Jospin had to engage in important compromises with his coalition to ensure the political space necessary for structural reforms. He initially hid corporate reforms behind the more visible Socialist program of the state-led imposition of a thirty-five-hour work week (down from thirty-nine hours) with no loss of pay, a process that he led in a confrontational manner with business leaders (Alexandre and L'Aulnoit 2002). When politically exposed, Jospin did not hesitate to abandon other important reforms, such as the tax overhaul led by Strauss-Kahn and Sautter and education reforms in 2000 (Séréni and Villeneuve 2002; Villeroy de Galhau 2004). As analyzed by Baverez, Jospin enshrined a great quid pro quo between the transformation of the private sector and the "sanctuarization of the public sector kept out of any constraint of productivity or competitivity" (Baverez 2003, 16). This absence of reform of the public sector led to a rise in public expenditures and deficits and the reduced effectiveness of the welfare state. Baverez further depicts the "schizophrenic situation" between modern and agile corporations on one side and a frozen and bloated public sector on the other (44–45). In another analysis, Marseille (2004) describes a growing war between two Frances, one competitive and modern, and the other protected and inefficient. Others have looked at the rise in corporatist rebellions and the inability of the state to act effectively in response (Beau, Dequay, and Fressoz 2004; Charette and Tabet 2004; Duhamel 2003; Zimmern 2003). The window of political autonomy for political entrepreneurs has been maintained at a high economic cost.

In addition, top-down statist reformism leads to an imbalance in the reform mix: because political leaders focus on concepts of power and global economic competitiveness, they prioritize larger firms in the policy mix and do not pay enough attention to small businesses. During the reform period covered in this chapter, there was remarkably little reform output on that front (no small business act).[74]

The second cost is that a model of institutional change of political entrepreneurs bypassing or going beyond classic parties adds to the crisis of representation through political parties analyzed by Berger (2006). Because of the divisions within interest group coalitions and within parties due to uncertainty and external change, parties are less able to aggregate social preferences into a clear action plan. Political entrepreneurs solve the problem by moving ahead of the party, yet by the same token also lose a broad base of open support.

Third, the pursuit of discreet or invisible reforms through a high degree of delegation to the elite bureaucracy has eroded the political legitimacy of such reforms. It reveals an increasing gap between the reforming elite who is realistically acting for the sake of industrial competitiveness and the French people who do not fully understand and do not fully accept this process. The gap between reality and opinion has tended to widen in recent years. In stunning opinion polls in 2001, 65 percent of the people expressed their resistance to globalization and their support for

---

74. Interview with former finance minister Christian Sautter, 6 December 2005.

anti-globalization NGOs. This has been further demonstrated by the large-scale boycott of Danone products in 2001 in response to a major restructuring plan—a boycott led by ATTAC, the rising NGO start-up of the anti-globalization constellation (Aguiton 2001). ATTAC has openly criticized the discreet structural reform process in its 2002 platform and hopes to educate the people to see through it. Jospin faced this lack of comprehension from his Leftist union supporters in an emblematic encounter with laid-off workers of a LU-Danone factory during the presidential campaign (Attal 2002; Pingaud 2002, 94–95). Suddenly, years of discreet reform in favor of corporate restructuring carried a high political cost. This new reality came most strikingly to the fore in the 2002 presidential elections. On 21 April, Jospin—the leader of a government that had brought growth back to France and reduced unemployment from 12 percent to 8 percent—earned the lowest percentage of the vote for a Socialist leader since the 1970s: 16.18 percent. Beaten by both Jacques Chirac (19.88 percent) and the leader of the extreme Right (16.86 percent), Jospin was not able to compete for the second round. On the Left side, Jospin lost more supporters than expected, although they might have rallied behind him in a second round. Trotskyist candidates took an astonishing 10.4 percent of the vote, while Chevènement took 5.33 percent of the vote. These candidates all opposed the "liberal" drift of the Jospin government and privatization and corporate reforms in particular. One labor leader, le Duigou of CGT argues that the vote translated a deep frustration with the loss of the postwar social contract and the demise of social democracy in general. Referring to Polanyi, he adds that the election was a popular backlash against years of unavowed structural reforms that amounted to a fundamental revision of the French economic model.[75] Interestingly, the May 2005 referendum on the EU constitution in France also stunned the political class and transmitted a similar message. Reform entrepreneurship can be effective during key windows of political autonomy, but it also induces a political disequilibrium and a strong vulnerability to backlash.

75. Interview, 30 May 2002.

4

Japan: Of Change and Resistance

Since the mid-1990s, under new global incentives, Japan has responded with a transformed political discourse focused on the necessity of structural reform and with some significant institutional change. However, the actual change has remained selective and has kept the major pillars of Japan's system in place: What explains this relative endurance of the core institutional structure in Japan, despite a sweeping change of discourse? Why has Japan taken a more partial and limited course than France and Korea, as it faced the new incentives of the golden bargain?

By the late 1990s, it was common knowledge that Japan was stuck in the post-miracle doldrums and could not change easily. The forces of inertia, complementary linkages, and an unstable political system repeatedly thwarted reform attempts. Yet just as the idea of a paralyzed Japan was taking hold, a wave of corporate reform began to sweep Japan. Since 1999, reformers and advocates, with the support of a growing cohort of foreign investors, have actively pushed corporate reform forward and succeeded in bringing it to the top of the policy and corporate agenda (Dore 1999, 2000). They argued that Japan's economic structure was ill suited to a post catch-up period marked by quickly evolving technology, financial globalization, and intensified global competition.[1] Japanese firms needed to join the global restructuring wave[2] and reorganize their corporate structure, labor management systems, and *keiretsu* networks. The government had to step in to facilitate the process of creative destruction.

---

1. Bouissou 2003; Katz 1998, 2003; Lincoln 2001; Morishima 2000; Mulgan 2002; Schoppa 2001.
2. Roach 1998.

Years later, despite deep linkages and opposition to change, it is clear that significant reform has taken place in Japan. Firms across the board unveiled large restructuring plans, closing some factories and reorganizing supply chains. Some traditional firms, such as Nissan and Sony, took more drastic steps, including severing ties with long-term *keiretsu* suppliers (Nissan). Although large firms avoided direct layoffs, they reduced their labor force through attrition, and a relative increase in part-time and temporary staff. They also induced layoffs in subsidiaries and suppliers through the removal of financial support and ensuing bankruptcies. As a whole, the total manufacturing workforce reached its postwar peak in April–June 1999 with 11,855,000 workers (up from 9,764,000 in January–March 1990 at the time of the bubble collapse). By April–June 2005, the manufacturing workforce was down to 9,593,000, although it came back up to 9,916,000 in January–March 2006.[3] From the 1999 peak to the 2005 bottom, the manufacturing workforce dropped by 18 percent. Other indicators of active restructuring included new corporate structures, new shareholding structures in large firms, a budding market for corporate control (with active mergers and acquisitions), and an active use of new bankruptcy laws. Total stable shareholding among firms declined from 45 percent in 1994 to 24 percent in 2003.[4] Yet core elements such as lifetime employment, main bank and *keiretsu* linkages, and the signaling and coordinating role of the government remained in place. Politically sensitive small firms in local areas (except in some areas such as Hokkaidō) have also avoided drastic restructuring.

Accompanying and facilitating these partial changes at the firm level, significant institutional change took place in the regulatory framework across the board. The government played a crucial role in enabling change by removing obstacles and by transforming the incentives of firms and other economic actors through a cumulative process of structural reform. The significance of these structural reforms is considerable because they aim at undoing the very features of the Japanese political economy that were once recognized as the foundations of the three-decade long economic miracle.

However, in contrast to countries like Korea, the process was slow and gradual. Enabling measures were chosen over mandatory change, allowing for partial change in only parts of the economic system, while preserving some of the strategic institutional linkages. As a result, the Japan Inc. model fragmented into several components headed in different directions. On the whole, large manufacturing firms restructured more than small and medium companies, financial institutions, and some domestic service

3. Ministry of Finance, "Financial Statements Statistics of Corporations by Industry Quarterly," www.mof.go.jp/english/ssc/historical.htm.

4. Schaede (forthcoming) uses data from Nihon Life Institute's annual survey.

companies. Firms with foreign ownership restructured more than those with stable domestic ownership structures (Ahmadjian and Robbins 2002; Vogel 2006). The main bank system survived for some stronger well-linked companies, but not for some weaker ones (such as Nissan). Large city banks by and large significantly reduced their bad debts and improved their lending portfolios. Regional banks, however, did not and continued to provide beneficial lending to insolvent local companies (which avoided restructuring).[5] In other words, the Japanese system effected *selective restructuring*. Parts of the system that could be overhauled without affecting core institutional linkages were changed.

I argue that it is the political entrepreneurship of leaders such as Hashimoto Ryūtarō, Katō Kōichi, Yamasaki Taku, Yosano Kaoru, Obuchi Keizō, and Koizumi Junichirō that tipped the scale toward some of the most significant regulatory reforms. At the same time, their ability to act has been more constrained than in France and Korea due to lower political autonomy within the dominant party, coalition, and legislature. The high degree of flux in all three relationships opened up some windows for entrepreneurship, but these windows were limited and imposed constraints on entrepreneurship.

This chapter rejects classic models of Japanese political economy that emphasize bureaucratic, interest group, or even party dominance. In the realm of corporate restructuring, the bureaucracy is divided between elite ministries led by the Ministry for Economy, Trade, and Industry (METI) that develop blueprints for reform, and other sectoral ministries opposed to reforms. Yet even METI cannot go beyond the formulation of reform blueprints. The transformation of these blueprints into a political agenda and actual legislation requires *political entrepreneurship*. In the context of the golden bargain and deep uncertainty about the sources of long-term competitiveness, organized interest groups and parties are divided. If anything, the anti-reform coalition has a numeric advantage. The key mechanism to break such deadlocks over uncertainty and tip the system toward institutional change is political leadership.

Post-1996 political leadership comes in two forms. The Hashimoto and Obuchi pathway until 1999 is one of traditional factional control over the main Liberal Democratic Party (LDP) and intra-LDP grand bargains. Under demanding conditions, this pattern produced significant change but with great constraints and limits. The post-2001 Koizumi pathway is a more institutionalized prime ministerial leadership in the wake of significant administrative reforms and changes in party leadership rules.

This chapter tracks the ebbs and flows in the sources of political entrepreneurship in Japan through the analysis of three key battles: accounting

---

5. Financial Services Agency, July 2005. "The Status of Non-Performing Loans as of End-March 2005."

and transparency reforms, the Industrial Revitalization Law (IRL) of 1999, and corporate governance reforms. These three cases offer an interesting degree of variation. Accounting reforms constitute the strongest impact of global investors and more limited political leadership. The IRL, which gave tax breaks to corporations engaging in labor reductions and other restructuring activities, represents high political entrepreneurship during a period of good political autonomy. Finally, corporate governance reforms are a protracted process whereby political entrepreneurship goes up against strong interest group and party opposition. It offers a more limited constrained political entrepreneurship.

Structural Reforms in the Context of the "Lost Decade"

Equity inflows and structural reforms in Japan are not taking place in a vacuum. The financial crisis after the crash of the stock and real estate bubble in 1990 and the ensuing liquidity trap after 1997 constitute major intervening variables. How should we account for these contextual variables? Is the presence of a crisis a major factor in reforms? Certainly, the debate over reforms in Japan after 1996 is dominated by considerations about nonperforming loans (NPL), deflation, a drop in consumption, and occasionally negative economic growth. More broadly, Williamson (1994, 25) hypothesizes that "public perception of a crisis is needed to create the conditions under which it is politically possible to undertake extensive policy reforms." Williamson and Haggard (1994, 564) further argue that "crises have the effect of shocking countries out of traditional policy patterns, disorganizing the interest groups that typically veto policy reform, and generating pressure for politicians to change policies that can be seen to have failed."[6]

Although the financial crisis provides the general context for structural reforms, it is insufficient as a dominant explanation for at least three reasons. First, there is a growing consensus among economists that the fundamental causes of Japan's malaise predated the bubble and its collapse. Many argue that the Japanese system was embedded with a dual economy structure that was not sustainable once Japan finished catching up with the West (Boyer and Yamada 2000; Katz 1998, 2003). Prime Minister Koizumi's economic advisor, Tanaka Naoki, argues that the key problem of the Japanese economy is inefficient allocation of capital and that this problem became clear during the early 1980s. The bubble hid the problems and prevented the government from tackling this inefficiency problem head on.[7]

---

6. On the role of crisis in triggering political change, see also Calder's (1987) landmark work.

7. Discussion with Naoki Tanaka, University of British Columbia, 5 August 2002.

Second, the progress of structural reforms has moved rather independently of the phases of the Japanese crisis since 1990. When a sense of crisis first hit Japan in 1993, no reform took place. The Hashimoto reforms (including the financial deregulation reforms that came to be known as Japan's Big Bang) occurred when Japan thought it was out of the crisis. When the banking crisis hit its worst point in November 1997, reforms seemed to slow down, only to accelerate in 1999 when the economy was recovering.

Finally, it is important to note that the Japanese crisis since 1990 is an unusual type of crisis. It is slow and protracted. It is visible on certain indicators (NPLs, deflation, economic growth), but not on others (huge current account surplus, very low long-term bond interest rate, limited unemployment). The intensity of the crisis and the perception of crisis among ordinary citizens are low on average and variable from year to year. Because of Japan's huge financial surpluses, Japan is in no danger of a currency or liquidity crisis. There has been a lingering concern about the sustainability of the low interest rate in the bond market. Yet, so far, every forecast of an impending bond market crisis has proven to be a false alarm. These features mean that the government has had the luxury of time in its reform progress.

A Checkered Reform Outcome: Institutional Transition since 1997

The output of corporate reforms since 1997 has been uneven, gradual, and non-linear. The government has taken steps forward and backward in succession. In addition, many of these reforms are technical and fragmented. This is why observers have such a hard time agreeing on the degree of actual institutional change that is occurring.[8]

Appendix table A2 provides an assessment of important reforms of the corporate regulatory framework in Japan in the period 1990–2002. The table includes both direct corporate reforms that affect corporate governance or the course of corporate restructuring and indirect reforms that affect the financial system with secondary effects on the course of corporate restructuring. A positive sign on the farthest right column indicates a positive reform from the status quo whereas a negative sign signifies a counter-reform that strengthens the status quo. The relative significance of each reform is equally indicated (1 or 2). One observes a growing trend toward

---

8. The first group is one holding skeptical views (Katz 1998, 2003; Lincoln 2001; Schoppa 2001, 2006). Others present more optimistic evaluations (International Monetary Fund 1999; Milhaupt and West 2004; Vogel 2006).

reforms between 1996 and 1998 with a dramatic peak in 1999. This is followed by a near absence of reforms in 2000.

As can be seen in the table, reforms since 1997 have marked a definite break with the past. However, reforms share two interesting features. First, reforms are clustered in time. The main push for reform came during the Hashimoto prime ministership (1997), and above all, during the Obuchi government (both fall 1998 and summer–fall 1999). The Mori government and the early Koizumi government did not produce as much change until 2002. The year 2002 indicated a second reform peak (continuing in 2003–04). Second, reforms are fragmented, occurring in some areas (especially indirect regulatory area) and not in others (especially labor and proactive financial change). The years 2000–02 (and beyond) reveal intense disputes over the reform process, with a large concurrent output of positive and negative reforms. This assessment reveals the presence of both a significant push for change and a strong opposition, a political tug-of-war.

The strategy of the Japanese state in its pursuit of structural reforms has been three pronged. First, the government accelerated the deregulation process (begun by the Hosokawa Morihiro administration in 1993). The acceleration is particularly clear during the Hashimoto administration (1996–98). Second, the government pushed for accounting reforms and other reforms that increased the transparency of the economy. Most of these measures were drafted in 1996 and 1997, even if their implementation has been staggered over many years (until 2002). Third, after 1999, the government passed a series of legal changes and direct measures in support of restructuring. These regulatory measures also included measures to encourage the creation of small and medium enterprises (Sénat de France 2000). This third group of reforms is the main focus of this chapter.

The IMF asserted that five reforms passed by the Japanese government in 1999 were particularly significant and put them in the following order: the Industrial Revitalization Law, the revisions of the commercial code, the Bankruptcy Reform (Civil Rehabilitation) Law, the reform of accounting standards, and the reform of labor laws (temporary work and labor dispatching) (Kanaya and Woo 2000). In particular, the role of the government in the Renault-Nissan tie-up of 1999 and in the headline-making Nissan restructuring plan that began in the fall of 1999 stand in sharp contrast to its opposition to earlier Nissan restructuring moves in 1993. These measures are analyzed in chapter 6 and compared to actions taken by the French and Korean governments in the field of automobile manufacturing.

Are structural reforms significant? Preliminary private and public economic analyses suggest that government reforms have had a significant impact on the process of corporate restructuring. By removing legal impediments and bestowing national legitimacy on the process, they have accelerated restructuring. For example, the IMF found that the reforms had been accompanied by an increasing number of announcements of restructuring plans and by changes in the structure of corporations.[9] It further reported in December 2001 that "progress in corporate restructuring over the past year had been facilitated by a number of regulatory changes and other policy measures taken by previous administrations."

A direct yardstick of the role of government in restructuring is the tally of restructuring plans that are directly supported by the government under the Industrial Revitalization Law. By 28 September 2001, a mere two years after the law was passed, 112 large corporations had applied for government support in the context of this law and had their restructuring plans approved by the government. The list includes some of the most famous names in Japanese industry, including Nissan, Toyota, Suzuki, Japan Railways, and Asahi Kōgyō. Given its success, the Industrial Revitalization Law was extended in 2002. Also apparent is the acceleration of corporate restructuring and the change in corporate behavior in reaction to institutional change (Dore 2005; Milhaupt 2003a; Patrick 2004). In 1999 alone, important Japanese corporations announced major restructuring plans that went a long way toward undoing the warm-hearted and socially responsible capitalist system in place since the late Meiji era.[10] Nissan announced a revival plan that included a 14.2 percent workforce reduction (21,000); NTT announced a 16 percent cut (20,000); major banks IBK, DKB, and Fuji Bank announced a 17 percent cut as part of their merger, and Sumitomo-Sakura followed with a 30 percent cut (9,000). Other major headline-making restructuring plans in 1999 alone included Mitsubishi Motors (10,000), Nippon Express (3,500), and Sony (17,000) (*Nihon Keizai Shinbun* 2000).

The IMF has documented an explosion of mergers and acquisitions (M&A) activity from an average of 600 cases per year between 1993 and 1996 to 1,200 in 1999, and almost 1,800 in 2000. A further indicator of ongoing restructuring is the increase in the number of bankruptcies in 2000 in the wake of the bankruptcy reforms. The number of bankruptcies increased by 23 percent in 2000 alone and the total value of liabilities involved by 77 percent (International Monetary Fund 2001, 87).

In sum, the Japanese government clearly accelerated the structural reform process after 1996—particularly in 1999—and has had a significant impact on economic processes through these reforms. At the same time, the reform process remained constrained, partially incoherent, and prone to retreat. What has driven the government's reform push and halted its hand at the same time?

9. The IMF asserts that "the corporate sector has begun to respond to these reform initiatives." (International Monetary Fund 2000, 95). Similar assessments are made in other IMF publications, such as the 2000 *International Capital Markets* report.

10. Much work exists on the sources of community-minded capitalism (Dore 1983; Berger and Dore 1996; Dore 1973; Samuels 2003b).

Changed Capital Flow Environment

At first glance, Japan is a tough case for the study of the impact of foreign capital on domestic reforms. Owing to its robust capital account surplus (on average, 2.6 percent of GDP[11] or $109 billion[12] per year over the last four years 1999–2002), Japan is a capital exporting country. Its net international assets of ¥175 trillion[13] ($1.48 trillion)[14] at the end of 2002 make Japan the world's largest creditor, a position it has upheld since the late 1980s. Furthermore, the high household savings rate in Japan has led to the accumulation of ¥1420 trillion ($10.7 trillion, as of March 2002) of personal financial assets, 54 percent of which are composed of cash and bank or postal deposits.[15]

As a country long closed to foreign corporate investment, Japan still has the lowest amount of foreign direct investment (FDI) as a proportion of GDP among OECD countries. As of 2001, the stock of inward FDI in Japan represented a mere $50 billion or 1.1 percent of GDP (versus $300 billion or 6 percent of GDP for the stock of Japanese outward FDI)[16]. This level stands in contrast to FDI stocks of $480 billion (24 percent of GDP) for Germany, $310 billion (20 percent of GDP) for France, $500 billion (30 percent of GDP) for the United Kingdom, and a 17 percent average for all OECD countries. The Japanese level is also in contrast to FDI stocks of $63 billion (14 percent of GDP) in Korea at the end of 2000. At the end of 2005, the stock of inward investments to Japan had merely inched up to $101 billion or 2.2 percent of GDP.[17] Here again, such low levels of inward investment should not lead to a strong foreign voice in the Japanese political economy.

The picture changes dramatically when we turn to equity portfolio inflows. These flows reached levels of $50 billion a year of net inflows (¥6 trillion)[18] for the years 1996–99, before oscillating between negative and positive levels in the years 2000–03. Thanks to such inflows, the net stocks

11. Organisation for Economic Co-operation and Development 2002, 22.

12. OECD, "Balance of Payment: Current Balance," www.oecd.org (OECD statistics online, balance of payment data for Japan).

13. Ministry of Finance's "International Investment Position of Japan" report, www.mof .go.jp/english/houkoku/e2002.htm.

14. Using the yen/dollar closing rate for 2002 of $1=¥118, www.nni.nikkei.co.jp/FR/ MKJ/yen/.

15. Nakakita 2002, 191 (based on BOJ data).

16. United Nations Conference on Trade and Development (UNCTAD), *World Investment Report 2002*, www.unctad.org.

17. UNCTAD, World Investment Report 2006. Obtained from FDI Statistics online. www.unctad.org/Templates/Page.asp?intItemID=3198&lang=1.

18. Ministry of Finance, Inward Investment Report (various years). For the most recent years, see www.mof.go.jp/english/shoutou/monthstt3.htm#3-2_3b.

Table 4.1. Shareownership by type of investor (percent share of total stock market value)

	Rising actors		Weakening actors	
Year	Foreigners	Individuals	Financial institutions	Corporations
1990	4.7%	20.4%	43.0%	30.1%
1991	6.0	20.3	42.8	29.0
1992	6.3	20.7	42.9	28.5
1993	7.7	20.0	42.3	28.3
1994	8.1	19.9	42.8	27.7
1995	10.5	19.5	41.1	27.2
1996	11.9	19.4	41.9	25.6
1997	13.4	19.0	42.1	24.6
1998	14.1	18.9	41.0	25.2
1999	18.6	18.0	36.5	26.0
2000	18.8	19.4	39.1	21.8
2001	18.3	19.7	39.4	21.8
2002	17.7	20.6	39.1	21.5
2003	21.8	20.5	34.5	21.8
2004	23.7	20.3	32.7	21.9
2005	26.7	19.1	31.6	21.1

Source: Tokyo Stock Exchange. 2003 Shareownership Survey. Available on www.tse.or.jp.
Includes data from all domestic stock exchanges (Tokyo, Osaka, Nagoya, Fukuoka, and Sapporo).

of foreign equity investments in Japan at the end of 2002 reached ¥40 trillion ($340 billion), representing 18.8 percent at the end of 2000, before jumping to 21.8 percent at the end of 2003.[19] This presence is a major new force in the Japanese political economic game, one that has never been acknowledged by political scientists. As argued by Andrew Rose, the head of Japanese equities at Schroeders, "Just the sheer presence of foreign shareholders is having an effect on policy."[20]

Table 4.1 presents comprehensive data on shareholder ownership by type of investor from 1990 to 2005. It emphasizes the growing presence of foreign shareholders on the Tokyo stock market and the decrease in stock ownership by corporations and financial institutions. As shown by table 4.1, financial institutions have declined from 43 percent in 1990 to 34.5 percent in 2005 overall. There are actually significant differences in the category of financial institutions itself (not shown in the table). City banks show the biggest decrease from 15.7 percent to 4.7 percent; life insurance companies follow the same trend, with a drop from 12.0 percent to 5.3 percent. These losses are partly offset by the rise of trust banks from 9.8 percent to 18.4 percent. The large trend on the stock market since about 1998 has been

19. Tokyo Stock Exchange's annual Shareownership Survey, 2005 (published in July 2006).
20. Stafford 2005.

large sales by traditional actors (banks and corporations) and large purchases by foreign investors. Foreign investors have seen their share leap from 4.7 percent in 1990 to 18.6 percent in 1999 and 26.7 percent in 2005. They have been sustaining the stock market since 1998. Naturally, foreign ownership varies across companies. It is particularly high in companies in internationally competitive industries such as telecommunications, electronics, and automobiles. For example, as early as September 2000, the foreign share reached 57 percent in Nissan, 40 percent in Sony, 29 percent in Hitachi, and 31 percent in Kyocera (Shirota 2002, 54–55).

The presence of foreign financial firms goes beyond the mere ownership of shares. Foreign-affiliated brokers went from total absence on the Tokyo market up to 1986 to handling over 50 percent of all selling and buying on the market today (Katz 2003, 180). Analysis of brokerage trading by the Tokyo Stock Exchange reveals that the share of foreigners in all stock brokerage trading further increased from 41.4 percent in 1999 to 53.5 percent in September 2001 and then to 56 percent in November 2001. Foreign firms, such as Morgan Stanley Dean Witter, Goldman Sachs, and GE Capital, have entered Japan en force since 1997. Their huge branches (with a staff of 2,000 for Morgan Stanley alone) have developed leading positions in activities such as M&A and restructuring operations (Harner 2000).

This new reality in the stock market has been compounded by the presence of two mitigating factors: the banking crisis and the implementation of capital adequacy ratios since 1993 (the international banking regulations of the Bank for International Settlement (BIS) which require a minimum capital to asset ratio of 8 percent). The credit crunch induced by the large amount of nonperforming loans has made corporations more dependent on financial markets for financing. Increasingly, bank credits are dependent on credit ratings, and credit ratings are linked to share prices. Meanwhile, because banks own large portfolios of corporate stocks and the latent profits on these investments are included in their capital valuation, a drop in the stock market automatically translates into a decrease in lending (a mechanism of the BIS ratio). So, all mitigating factors analyzed in chapter 2 are present in Japan.

The crucial role of foreign investors on the Tokyo stock market becomes clearer when actual transactions are analyzed. In his book on the role of foreign investors in the Japanese stock market, Shirota (2002) provides in-depth analysis of these trends, pointing to the growing impact of foreign investors on stock price movements and on the management style of large corporations (pressures on the inclusive Japanese-style of management or *fukumi keiei*). Shirota points to the differences in transaction turnover rates (*baibai kaiten ritsu*) between foreign and domestic investors: 224 percent versus 65 percent, resulting in a 50 percent share of brokerage trading from an 18 percent shareownership base (5). Shirota further emphasizes that foreign investors hold large amounts of derivatives that contribute to abrupt changes in the stock index.

The link between equity inflows and stock price was particularly strong in 1999 when net equity inflows reached ¥11.2 trillion (about $110 billion), sustaining a major rebound in the stock price level (a 40 percent increase). In turn, as Prime Minister Mori took over in spring 2000 and slowed down structural reforms, a significant foreign outflow corresponded to a major drop in the stock market.

The impact of this new financial situation on large firms in Japan has been significant. A shareholder culture and a return-on-equity culture have been spreading among management since the late 1990s. Such a focus on the return given to shareholders may seem self-evident to foreign observers but was non-existent in Japan until the late 1990s.[21] Likewise, using data on 1,638 publicly listed companies in Japan in 1990–97, Ahmadjian and Robinson (2001, 645) have demonstrated the impact of the degree of foreign ownership of a given corporation on downsizing (as one measure of restructuring). Since 1999, there has also been a growing link between the announcement of a credible restructuring plan by a corporation and the rise of the level of its stock (Levy 2000, 182–83).

Interviews at the Bank of Japan (BOJ), Ministry of Finance (MOF), Nissan, and Nomura Research have confirmed this trend, although some analysts point to a possible decoupling between an enduring "old Japan" (focused on sales and employees) and the emergence of a "new Japan" (focused on return on equity, ROE). Shirota (2002) also found a link between high foreign shares in particular corporations and high ROE and Western-style restructuring.

To a lesser extent, change in the Japanese economy has come from a second source: large inflows of FDI, particularly in landmark cases such as the takeover of Nissan Motors by Renault or the purchase of the Long-Term Credit Bank by Ripplewood. Japan banned FDI inflows until 1964 and heavily restricted it until the early 1980s. Until 1995, Japan not only had the smallest level of FDI inflows among developed countries, the level was nearly zero as a percentage of GDP (an average of $0.7 billion between

---

21. Interview data from early 1999 on all major corporations in Japan by the Economic Planning Agency reveals that such a trend is indeed taking place across Japan. For example, 31 percent of all corporations interviewed say that ROE will be their dominant goal from now on, while only 3 percent say that it was such an important goal up to now. While only 20.1 percent of corporations believed that shareholders played a positive role in management up to now, 45 percent say that they expect shareholders to play such a role from now on. Forty-two percent also say that rating companies will be having a similar positive role from now on (versus 32 percent up to now) (Economic Planning Agency 1999, 39–55). Regarding cross-shareholding (*mochiai*), 47 percent of companies indicate that they expect it to decrease from now on, while only 27 percent say that it has decreased so far.

1985 and 1995, or less than 0.5 percent of GDP). This situation changed dramatically in 1999, with a sudden inflow of $13 billion, a level that was maintained in 2000–01. While these amounts still only represent 0.3 percent of GDP, compared to a 2.7 percent OECD average, they represent a sea change. All of the newly foreign-owned corporations have played major leadership roles, spearheading management, labor, and corporate governance reforms. The most famous case has been that of Nissan Motors. Led by Carlos Ghosn of Renault since 1999, Nissan has made headlines by launching a very ambitious restructuring plan, closing four factories and slashing the labor force by over 20,000. To the surprise of many, Ghosn succeeded in turning the loss-making Nissan around within a mere two years. In so doing, he has been hailed as a new General MacArthur leading Japan toward its future. Similarly, Long-Term Credit Bank, reborn as Shinsei Bank, has led the way in cutting non-performing loans and shaking up banking methods. The most famous battle came with the case of Sogo in June 2000, when Shinsei's refusal to go along with business-as-usual methods precipitated Sogo's bankruptcy (Amyx 2003).

The effect of corporate FDI inflows, however, remains lower than that of equity inflows. In fact, beyond the flagship Nissan-Renault and Shinsei stories, the effect has remained more limited.

Political Entrepreneurship during Limited Windows of Autonomy

Studying political entrepreneurship in the land of bureaucratic dominance, iron triangles, interest group networks, one-party dominance, consensus, and harmony, seems to be a tall order. It is well known that the nail that stands out in Japan is hammered down and that individual leadership is ground down to nothing as it runs through the gauntlets of bureaucratic councils, the LDP's policy structure, and the Diet's lengthy legislative process. Yet, even before the introduction of the golden bargain and new incentives for change into Japan, several political leaders stood up and shaped institutions. Even in a postwar system well-known for its weak prime ministers, Yoshida Shigeru played a crucial role in reorganizing this system, while Kishi Nobusuke proved indispensable in the party merger of 1955 that created the LDP. The lineage of political leadership runs through Tanaka Kakuei, a canny streetwise politician who enlarged the political profile of the LDP, reversed the budget dominance of the Ministry of Finance, and organized the massive construction state in Japan (Calder 1982, 1987; Murano 2002; Schlesinger 1997; Tanaka 1973). As for Nakasone Yasuhiro (1982–87), he played a major role in privatizing the national railways and destroying the power of labor, initiating administrative reforms, education reforms, and tax reforms, even if many of these reforms only came to fruition after his departure.[22] He and Takeshita Noboru played a crucial role during the negotiations that led to the 1985 Plaza Accord and greatly influenced the ensuing rise of the yen (*endaka*).[23] One may also single out the role of Ozawa Ichirō in shaping LDP dominance on the ground in the 1980s before turning against the LDP and precipitating its temporary fragmentation in 1993 (Baerwald 1986; Curtis 1999, 2002; Samuels 2003b). Ozawa nearly succeeded in reorganizing the Japanese party system, although he proved unable to complete his task. Ozawa also pushed forward the process of deregulation[24] and a more vigorous foreign policy under the banner of a "normal nation."

Political entrepreneurs in 1995–2002 continued this lineage, seizing the new opportunities presented by global capital flows to push for corporate reforms and facilitate the system restructuring of the Japanese system.

Political Entrepreneurs in Post-1993 Japan: Hashimoto Ryūtarō, Obuchi Keizō, Yosano Kaoru, and Koizumi Junichirō

A string of new leaders came to power in the late 1990s. Following a period when Nagatachō was fixated on electoral reforms and political change, the focus of political entrepreneurship turned to the economy. Hashimoto Ryūtarō came to power in early 1996 as a maverick and lone wolf, better known for his slick hair and his tough kendo skills than for his ability to build consensus within the LDP. Coming from a safe rural seat in Okayama prefecture (first won in 1963), he rose through the ranks of the LDP and of the mainstream Tanaka faction as a traditional politician. He served as minister of health and welfare (1978–79), transport (1986–87), finance (1989–91), and in the Ministry of International Trade and Industry (MITI) (1994–96). He had a combative style and was surrounded by reformist politicians (Katō Kōichi and Yamasaki Taku in particular) and ambitious political secretaries from MITI (Eda Kenji, Isayama Takeshi). As a result, he proved willing to undertake important reforms in 1997–98, although this first wave focused primarily on administrative reorganization and financial revival (with partial failure)[25] rather than on corporate restructuring.[26] Interestingly, Hashimoto made abundant use of institutional innovations designed to leverage the

22. See Baerwald (1986), Hayao (1993), Otake (1994, 1996), and Samuels (2003a).

23. See Fukui and Weatherford (1995, 246–47) for an excellent analysis. They remark that "Political leadership, however, can be exercised and a degree of policy coherence achieved if and when the prime minister, the chief cabinet secretary, and the minister or ministers in charge of the policy at issue are united in and committed to pushing a well-defined policy line" (235).

24. See his own vision in Ozawa (1994).

25. On the delays of vital financial reforms under Hashimoto, see Amyx (2004), Ihori (2002), Kume (2002), and Mabuchi (2002).

26. For great discussions on Hashimoto's government, see Eda (1999), Eda and Nishino (2002), Kusano (1999), Laurence (2001), Otake (1997, 1999), and Shinoda (2000).

power of the prime minister's office relative to traditional opponents. In the case of the budgetary reform, Hashimoto (supported by Yosano Kaoru, a key adviser) invited former prime ministers (Miyazawa Kiichi, Takeshita Noboru, and Nakasone Yasuhiro) to a special advisory meeting with coalition leaders, a meeting specifically designed to give more weight and credibility to prime ministerial leadership (Shimizu 2005).

Prime Minister Obuchi Keizō (1998–2000) emerges as an unlikely, yet effective, political entrepreneur. A quintessential LDP cadre from Gunma prefecture (a rural area) and a protégé of Tanaka Kakuei and Takeshita Noboru, he rose through the ranks and captured the presidency of the LDP through party connections in spite of a total absence of public support. Little by little, however, he presented an impressive array of reforms, even if he more likely acquiesced to them than led them from above. He led through his control of the biggest faction and his great ability to persuade opponents inside the party. Obuchi had a secure electoral seat, but was motivated by a long-term sense of history. Having reached the pinnacle of policymaking, he wanted to leave a transformative mark on Japan. He also thought of enlarging the support base for the LDP.[27] When it came to policy, however, Obuchi had precious little economic background. Unlike most other prime ministers, he had never occupied an economic ministry before. His main position had been that of foreign minister. That made Obuchi more reliant on his key lieutenant when it came to structural reforms. At the same time, Obuchi was very receptive and willing to be convinced.[28]

Under Obuchi, a new policy-focused politician came to a position of high power. As MITI minister, Yosano Kaoru set the agenda for industrial policy and the promotion of corporate restructuring with the tacit approval of Prime Minister Obuchi. In a departure from the usual pedigree of LDP power brokers, Yosano's constituency is urban (Tokyo-1). He is the grandson of the famous feminist and political activist, Yosano Akiko, herself the daughter of a rich merchant from Osaka. A graduate of Tokyo's law school, Yosano Kaoru was first elected to the House of Representatives in 1976 and won his seventh term in 1996, before being beaten by the Democratic Party's (DPJ) Kaieda Banri in 2000 and again in 2003 (but was saved by a good ranking on the proportional representation list). His defeats in 2000 and 2003 are part of a weakening trend for the LDP in large cities, where unaffiliated voters desert a party associated with old-time politics and rural favoritism. In 2003, before the election, Yosano left the conservative Kamei faction and tried to create a new image as a reformer. Against all odds, this allowed him to return to prominence in 2004 as chairman of the LDP's Policy Research Council and a rising star and potential successor to Prime Minister Koizumi. Between 1976 and 2003, Yosano served as parliamentary

27. Interview with METI official directly involved in managing the ICC, 10 April 2006.
28. Interview with key strategic assistant to Yosano at METI, 10 April 2006.

vice minister at MITI (1984–85) and MITI minister (1998–99), but also as chairman of Diet committees on Commerce and Industry (1989–90), Science and Technology (1990–91), and rules and administration (1993). He was minister of education in 1994–95 and deputy Chief Cabinet secretary under Prime Minister Hashimoto (1996–97).

Yosano Kaoru's urban base and strong knowledge of economic and industrial policy make him a quintessential political entrepreneur, ready to gamble on the golden bargain and promote corporate restructuring. As a MITI minister under Obuchi, Yosano became known as one of the main advocates of supply-side reforms and structural reforms. At MITI, he encouraged the design of forward-looking trade and industrial policy and tried to control the more protective branch of MITI that dealt with small and medium companies and rural issues. Yosano also believed in the necessity of pain (*itami*). In front of his staff, he referred to the analogy of "necessary surgery" to remove broken parts, even if this was an unpleasant process.[29]

His approach, repeated in multiple speeches abroad and at home, is succinctly summarized in his interview with *AsiaWeek* on 8 January 1999 (Yosano 1999a):

> In addition to promoting [stimulus] measures for eliminating the supply-demand gap, Japan also needs to take on the challenge of structural reform from the supply side. I believe that we are currently presented with the last window of opportunity in terms of responding to this challenge. . . . For example, industries and companies which feel that they are carrying too much weight in terms of employment, supply capacity and capital and financial structure must work to cut back on white-collar over-employment, streamline their supply structure in line with market needs and improve profitability.

In a long speech at the Council on Foreign Relations on 11 January 1999, Yosano emphasized the need for strong (political) governance and identified a "fundamental restructuring of the economic system" as the priority for Japan. In a context of global changes and with a stated goal of attracting foreign investment across the board, he argued for an infusion of speed and flexibility into the Japanese system. He sought increased efficiency and higher long-term growth. He concluded with a reference to the role of the state in accompanying this transition: "the Japanese government will play its part and throw its full weight behind efforts to restructure its domestic economic systems."[30] During the Obuchi cabinet, Yosano

29. Interview with METI official directly involved in managing the ICC, 10 April 2006.
30. Yosano 1999b. See also Yosano Kaoru's website and his long treatise on economic policy, beginning with a first chapter on supply-side reforms, www.yosano.gr.jp/policy/keizai_seisaku.html.

put these ideas into action and played a large role in the Industrial Revitalization Law and in the government support for Nissan's alliance with Renault and subsequent industrial restructuring (see chapter 6). Interestingly, Yosano has often confided to his staff that he saw the necessity for reforms as a condition to retain urban voters, and thus to be reelected.[31] This was particularly relevant for him, a Tokyo-based MP with an insecure political seat. Yosano was aware that unemployment would go up in the short run and that he would be criticized for it. Yet he expected that the curve would soon reverse in the medium-term and that he could ride the interim successfully.[32]

By the early 2000s, the most well-known political entrepreneur was Koizumi Junichirō, prime minister from April 2001 to September 2006. To a greater extent even than Yosano, Koizumi was a maverick who made his name by presenting a new look (including his famous lion-style hairdo) (as a *henjin*, or "strange man," in Tanaka Makiko's famous description) and by standing for the unpopular idea of postal savings privatization as early as 1996. Unlike Yosano, Koizumi was a second generation politician in a safe seat (Kanagawa-11), although from a semi-urban area. Koizumi has reaped the benefits of past administrative reforms and inherited a stronger cabinet, while making his mark on government through his refusal to follow past norms on cabinet appointments and management style. He is most well known for his effort to weaken the LDP's old guard, pushing for change like postal reforms that hit at the core of the LDP's traditional power base. Early in his mandate, he brandished the mantra of "structural reforms" as the absolute priority for Japan, launching several reform projects. However, unlike Yosano, his lack of a policy background meant that his knowledge of specific corporate reforms was thinner and a sustained debate on his real reform impact and significance has raged for years. On the whole, Koizumi was a clear political entrepreneur who prioritized structural reform over the maintenance of traditional support networks and who was ready to seize the golden bargain presented by foreign investors. In fact, he even agreed to be a poster boy in TV and newspaper ads created by the Japanese government to entice foreign investors.

What are the pathways to political entrepreneurship in Japan and what is the role of the prime minister? Given the Westminster-style parliamentary system in Japan, the prime minister stands out in the process of political entrepreneurship. Recent scholarship has rediscovered the central role of this actor and his chief cabinet secretary in the political process, particularly in the wake of administrative reforms and the new avenues for the cabinet to

31. Interview with METI official directly involved in managing the ICC, 10 April 2006.
32. Ibid.

directly introduce bills in parliament.[33] When passed, this reform was discounted as minor. With hindsight, it is clear that the Koizumi government has used this new power to great effectiveness in foreign policy: in launching the special economic zone bill or in the case of postal reforms. For corporate reforms, three patterns of political entrepreneurship stand out. The prime minister can lead reforms from his office, as with Hashimoto or Koizumi (and Nakasone before them). The prime minister can acquiesce to the program of an active economic minister, as with Obuchi and Yosano. Or the prime minister can delegate to ambitious young Turks within the party the job of drafting a new bill and pushing a reform agenda, as with the 1998 financial bills (Amyx 2004; Curtis 2002). This last case most famously occurred at the onset of Obuchi's cabinet, in the fall of 1998.

When do political entrepreneurs, however, get away with corporate reforms in a system that is well-known for its entrenched political inertia and multiple veto points? Their success depends on two sets of structural variables.

Strategic Political Autonomy

The strategic political autonomy of political entrepreneurs in Japan is structurally constrained by several key factors in comparison to France or Korea. As shown in chapter 3, the short electoral cycle and mismatching duality of this cycle (lower house and upper house) reduce the security and autonomy of leadership. Within the LDP, the dominant party in power from 1955 to the present day except for ten months in 1993–94, a highly bureaucratic structure and sticky norms and rules impose many constraints on the party leader. Coalition government since 1994 (with the partial exception of the Hashimoto period from 1996 to 1998) has imposed more constraints on government.[34] Finally, executive control over the legislative agenda is structurally limited in comparison to the French or British system. Indeed, party elders within the LDP, coalition partners, and even opposition parties, are in charge of setting the day-to-day agenda of the Diet, not the cabinet.

However, even within this constrained structure, the degree of strategic political autonomy has shown significant fluctuations between 1993 and 2005 based on several key factors: the type of selection process chosen within the LDP (from a backdoor decision made by four faction leaders in 2000 for Mori Yoshirō to an election among LDP militants within prefectural chapters in 2001 for Koizumi Junichirō), the control of the upper house by the LDP (high in 1995–98, low in 1998–2001), coalitional dynamics, and the factional

33. For analyses of the role of the prime minister in Japan and in comparative context, see Baerwald (1986), Hayao (1993), Rose (1991), Shinoda (2000, 2003, 2004), Weller (1985). For analyses of administrative reforms, also see Shinoda (2003) and Takenaka (2001).

34. However, Kusano (1999) makes an interesting argument that coalition government has allowed smaller parties to put novel issues on the political agenda. For the role of the Socialist Party in gender and human rights issues, see Chan-Tiberghien (2004).

power base of the LDP leader (low for Mori and Koizumi, high for Obuchi and Hashimoto). Also important was the ability to appeal to public support in fighting LDP resistance (in the case of Koizumi). As a background for these fluctuations was the fundamental transition in Japan's party politics and ruling coalitions summarized in table 4.2. This table lists each cabinet in power during the 1990s. For each cabinet, it analyzes the strength of the prime minister relative to the governing party, the type of governing coalition, and contemporary changes in the party system. The table emphasizes the great amount of change and fluctuation in the party system, ruling coalitions, and relations between party leader and party within the LDP that took place in the 1990s.

In addition, the period from 1995 to 2005 is dominated by two great political battles that affected the political space for entrepreneurs: while politicians (both LDP and DPJ) were out to wrest dominance from the legendary bureaucracy, the prime minister's office was trying to wrest leadership from the LDP party machinery.

In sum, as summarized in table 4.3, strategic political autonomy was highest under Hashimoto Ryūtarō (2.5 on a scale of 4) given a high level of security, relative autonomy within the LDP on the basis of solid factional support, a high level of control over the mostly disbanded coalition, and relative control over legislative leaders in the Diet. The Obuchi cabinet stood at an equivalent level (2.5 overall) with an even stronger autonomy within the party (factional control), but less security (low popular support) and less autonomy within the coalition (due to an upper house election in summer 1998). The Mori government in 2000–01 scores the lowest (0.5) with low legitimacy, low party control, and low coalition autonomy. Finally, the Koizumi government scores a medium level (2), given a very high level of security (indispensable to LDP, high popular support) and relative autonomy within the coalition, but difficultly controlling the LDP and poor control over the legislative agenda. The score rises to nearly 4 in September 2005, after the stunning electoral victory that destroyed Koizumi's LDP opponents.

A key variable that reduced the political autonomy available to political entrepreneurs in Japan in the 1990s was the low level of executive control over the legislative agenda. Mulgan argues that the weak ability of the cabinet to lead the Diet process and the weak party discipline in the Diet are key differences that set apart Japan and the United Kingdom and lower the ability of a reformist prime minister to push his agenda, even Koizumi Junichirō.[35] Indeed, a similar conclusion was reached by Baerwald in the early 1980s, when he observed that party factions within the LDP, coupled with the management of the Diet agenda through a broad committee reduced executive control over the legislative agenda (1986, 91–96).

---

35. Mulgan (2002). See the related discussion of the Japan-British comparison in Cerny (2004) and Holliday and Shinoda (2002).

Table 4.2. Governing coalitions and transformation of the party system in the 1990s

Time (years and months)	Prime minister (events at beginning and end of tenure)	Ruling coalition	New parties and party mergers
08/1989–11/1991	Kaifu Toshiki • elected by LDP party vote, following Uno scandal • forced out by LDP faction leaders	LDP (but minority in upper house)	
11/1991–07/1993	Miyazawa Kiichi • elected by LDP party vote, factional compromise • resigns after no-confidence vote on 6/18/1993	LDP (minority in upper house)	• 05/1992: JNP (Japan New Party) created by Hosokawa Morihiro) • 06/1993: New Party Sakigake formed by Takemura Masayoshi (splinter from LDP) • 06/1993: JRP (Japan Renewal Party) formed by Ozwa Ichiro and Hata Tsutomu (LDP splinter)
08/1993–04/1994	Hosokawa Morihiro (JNP) • comes as a result of Diet election (lower house) and coalition bargaining among parties • resigns in response to financial scandal and fatigue	NO LDP 7-party coalition (JNP, Sakigake, JRP, Kōmeitō, JSP, DSP, Shaminren, Independents)	
04/1994–06/1994	Hata Tsutomu (JRP) • elected by coalition • quits to preempt vote of non-confidence	NO LDP, minority coalition of 5 parties (JNP, JRP, Kōmeitō, DSP, Shaminren, Independents)	• 04/94: Creation of Kaishin Parliamentary group (5 coalition parties)

Date	Prime Minister	Coalition	Party developments
06/1994–01/1996	Murayama Tomiichi (JSP) • results from surprise agreement among old foes, LDP and JSP • surprise resignation	LDP-JSP-Sakigake	• 12/94: Creation of New Frontier Party under Ozawa Ichiro and Kaifu Toshiki. Mega-Merger of 6 parties and two political groups (JNP, JRP, Kōmeitō, DSP, Liberal Party, New Vision Party, Reform Association, Koshikai)
01/1996–11/1996	Hashimoto Ryūtarō • Result of coalition bargaining (Hashimoto is LDP president since 1995)	LDP-JSP-Sakigake	• 09/96: Creation of DPJ (Democratic Party of Japan) out of parts of Sakigake (split) and ex-JSP, renamed DSPJ (split). Led by Kan Naoto and Hatoyama Yukio.
11/1996–07/1998	Hashimoto Ryūtarō • Resigns due to scathing LDP loss in upper house election	LDP only (but continued cooperation in Diet with Sakigake and SDP until 05–1998)	• 12/1996: Creation of Sun Party by Hata (NFP split) • Dec 1997: NFP breaks up in 6 groups. 6 Diet members also join LDP. Kōmeitō regains independence. LP (Liberal Party) is created (Ozawa). • 01/1998: Creation of Minseito ouf ot 3 subgroups. • 03/1998: Minseito, DRP, and Shinto Yuai (NFP pieces) merge with DPJ. Creation of New DPJ (04/98).
07/1998–01/1999	Obuchi Keizō • Result of LDP factional compromise	LDP only (compromise in upper house with opposition DPJ)	• 11/1998: New Kōmeitō is created.
01/1999–10/1999	Obuchi Keizō • Result of coalition agreement Obuchi-Ozawa	LDP-LP	
10/1999–04/2000	Obuchi Keizō • Result of coalition agreement LDP-Kōmeitō • End: sudden coma and death of prime minister	LDP-LP- New Kōmeitō	• 04/2000: LP splits over coalition disagreement. NCC (New Conservative Party) created

(*Table 4.2*—cont.)

Time (years and months)	Prime minister (events at beginning and end of tenure)	Ruling coalition	New parties and party mergers
04/2000–04/2001	Mori Yoshirō • Selected by 4 key LDP factional leaders, agreed by Kōmeitō and LP • Resigns under pressure of LDP faction leaders (election fears)	LDP-NCC- New Kōmeitō	
04/2001–2006	Koizumi Junichirō • Selected through LDP party election. Grassroots prefecture vote overwhelms Diet factional compromise. • Reelected through same process in September 2003 (large margin).	LDP-NCC- New Kōmeitō	• 09/2003: merger of DPJ and LP

Table 4.3. Strategic political autonomy and strategic bureaucratic delegation in Japan, 1993–2005

Cabinet	SPA	SBD	Net capacity of entrepreneurship
Hosokawa: 1993–94	LOW: Fractious 7-party coalition, short term (1)	HIGH: Bureau. tensions, MOF voice (2.5)	Weak on economic affairs
Hata: 1994	LOW: Minority government (0.5)	HIGH: Status Quo (2.5)	Very weak
Murayama: 1994–96	LOW: LDP-JSP-Sakigake coalition, weak PM (0.5)	MED: MOF under attack, MITI ascendant (2)	Weak-divided
Hashimoto 1: 1996–Summer 1998	MED: LDP domination, control of LDP by PM (2.5)	MED: Close links with MITI, MOF tensions (1.7)	Medium-strong
Obuchi 1: 1998–99	MED: Good control of LDP by PM, but minority in UH (2)	MED: Close links MITI, reorganization MOF-FSA (1.7)	Medium
Obuchi 2: 1999–2000	HIGH: Control of LDP and stable coalition with Kōmeitō, LP (3)	MED: Close links MITI, reorganization, MOF-FSA (1.7)	Medium-strong
Mori: 2000–01	LOW: Legitimacy problems for PM, within LDP and with Kōmei (0.5)	LOW: Administrative reorganization. Jan 2001 (1.5)	Very weak
Koizumi: 2001–03	MED: Lack of control of LDP by prime minister, but strong personal leadership (2)	LOW-MED: Internal fragmentation (1.5)	Medium: Good initiation capacity but week actual reform capacity

The Japanese constitution is remarkably short on the legislative process. Article 72 does say that "the prime minister submits bills to the Diet" but does not give him or her power over the daily agenda of the Diet. In effect, the prime minister has very weak control over the legislative agenda, which is left to the discretion of each House. The Diet Law, a law that dates back to the Imperial Diet, even if it was revised in 1955, sets the workings of the Diet. In particular, the Diet Law sets the rigid timetable of the different sessions. For example, Articles 2 and 10 stipulate that the ordinary (budget) session must start in January and last 150 days. The Diet Law's crucial Article 68 strictly limits the carryover of bills from one session to the other.[36]

36. Article 68. A measure or matter on which no resolution has been made during a session shall not be carried over to the next session, except that when a measure or a disciplinary matter is being considered under the provision of paragraph 2 of Article 47 while the Diet is not in session, it shall be carried over to the next session.

The actual Diet timetable is not under government control. Rather, it is under the control of the majority parties (if they have a sufficient majority). This bottleneck provides ample opportunity for interest groups to lobby lawmakers and ensure that many law proposals die in the Diet, especially since parliamentary law stipulates that no project can be carried over from one Diet session to the next (Stockwin, 1999: 116). In that context, postponing a law proposal means killing it. At the core of the agenda-setting process are the house management committee (*un'ei iinkai*) and the counterpart within each party (*kokutai*) (91). The process in these committees is somewhat murky, but leaves much room for bargaining among faction leaders, coalition parties, and even opposition parties (a search for consensus) (Mochizuki 1982). This provides tremendous opportunities for factional leaders within the LDP and opposition members to shape the legislative program. The internal LDP tradition of thoroughly reviewing each bill within its own specialized committee before sending it on to the Diet has compounded the institutional weakness (see Shimizu 2005, 365–366).

The lack of direct cabinet control over the legislative agenda has often been underestimated in academic analyses of the Japanese political system, partly because of the long period of LDP dominance until 1993. Many analyses of Japan emphasize bureaucratic control over information and the large percentage of bills that originated in the bureaucracy. However, Muramatsu and Krauss pointed out in 1984 that it was "the LDP that decide[d] which bills [were] to be taken up, which [were] to be modified and how, and which [were] to be introduced into the Diet with what priority" (1984, 143). As a result, between 1952 and 1993, only 60 percent of government bills considered by the Diet have been passed without modifications and delay, while 23 percent were simply postponed or abandoned (130). These structural features have been further exacerbated by the fragmentation of the party system since 1993, the creation of ruling coalitions, and the decreasing power of bureaucrats.[37]

How can such constraints be measured? As shown by Masuyama (2000a, b), Japan actually scores in the middle of the index of institutional agenda-setting developed by Doering and used by Tsebelis (2002, 104). For example, committees cannot rewrite laws presented by the government (scoring a high 1 on a scale of 4), legislative debates are limited in advance by majority vote (1 on scale of 3) and bills lapse at the end of each session, arguably increasing the government's leverage (1 out of 4). These high scores, however, are offset by much lower scores on other dimensions, particularly the authority to determine the plenary agenda of the parliament (4 out of 7). Indeed, as shown by Masuyama, the legislative majority has significant tools at its disposal to force the opposition parties down

37. The latter is an older trend. See Inoguchi (1989, 185).

in most cases. However, the actual leverage of the cabinet over legislative agenda in case of disagreement between the cabinet and parliamentary leaders is nearly zero. This explains the legislative stalemate of the Koizumi cabinet in its early years.

Given the institutional constraints of agenda-setting in the Diet, a few conclusions can be drawn. First, structural reforms can only be passed during extraordinary sessions in the summer and in the fall. Second, a bill that is introduced mid-term or late in a Diet session is likely to be stalled by delaying tactics and die, given the obstacles involved in carrying it over to the next session. Third, the collective LDP leadership, as well as coalition parties and even opposition parties have a major say in setting the agenda priorities in the Diet, thus partly controlling the fate of particular structural reforms. Only a prime minister with clear control over party and coalition (either through force or through compensation) can expect to pass costly reform legislations.

Strategic Bureaucratic Delegation

Whether bureaucrats dominate politicians or politicians dominate bureaucrats has been a mainstay of debates within Japanese politics. This book sides with McCubbins's and Noble's argument that the appearance of bureaucratic power in Japan is deceiving. Institutionally, power rests in the cabinet and in the Diet. Politicians, especially as they gain policy knowledge, have ample opportunity and the power to guide the drafting of legislation and to block any disagreeable outcome. Bureaucrats are not able to shape the overall agenda.

This is particularly true in the context of a long-term trend through which power is flowing from bureaucrats to politicians.[38] Since 1991, the bureaucracy is increasingly seen as the culprit for the Japanese bubble and the poor response to its collapse. Its prestige collapsed and powerhouses such as the Ministry of Finance have become convenient targets for politicians. In response to separate scandals and crises, the Ministry of Finance has been hollowed out piece by piece. In particular, monetary policy was removed from the MOF's orbit with the independence of the Bank of Japan in 1998. Financial policy and financial control were gradually taken out of the MOF and consolidated into the Financial Services Agency (FSA). Even the MOF's stranglehold over the budget was eroded with the creation of the Council on Economic and Fiscal Policy in 2001. This process has given rise to a series of new actors within the elite economic bureaucracy, all of which have different interests and different views on the process of reform. Coordination is weak, particularly between the BOJ and MOF.

---

38. For example, see Baerwald (1986, 163).

In 1999–2001, a further round of administrative reforms took place. Under the influence of a junior government partner (Liberal Party) and the opposition, the governing coalition further limited the power of the bureaucracy by increasing the number of political appointments within ministries (vice ministers and state secretaries) and, more significantly, by prohibiting senior bureaucrats from directly answering questions in the Diet. These changes, together with the introduction of "question times" every Wednesday afternoon (as of 2000), have increased transparency in the Diet and forced politicians to become more policy-savvy.[39] At the end of 2000, the bureaucracy seemed clearly weakened in its influence over policymaking. Nevertheless, the net effect of the fragmentation of the bureaucracy is a multiplication in reform agendas and fewer opportunities for effective bureaucratic delegation. Political opponents and interest groups have multiple access points in the bureaucracy.

How and when do corporate reforms take place in the context of global capital flows and constrained opportunities for political entrepreneurship? We now turn to the process-tracing analysis of a few key cases.

Accounting and Transparency Reforms

At first glance, accounting is an utterly technical realm of codes, boring rules, and tedious reporting. It is left to accountants and bureaucrats, far from the hustle and bustle of policymaking and politics. Yet, in the late 1990s, accounting became a central battleground of globalization as global investors and international institutions pushed for common and transparent rules that would allow investors to make sound judgments about firms. It also became clear that accounting standards were not neutral technicalities, but actual policy tools with far-reaching consequences.[40] In Japan's case, accounting constitutes one of the few areas where significant mandatory change took place. Reforms were sometimes delayed or postponed, but never cancelled. The key political input came from Hashimoto as part of a grand plan named the Big Bang.

Accounting's critical function as the link between investors, managers, and financial markets became politically salient. As shown by Véron et al, loopholes and small allowances buried within accounting standards can drastically transform the results and image of a company. Because investors

---

39. See Takenaka (2001) for an analysis of the battle over junior ministers and Diet reforms.

40. For an account of the huge impact of accounting rules on investment processes, see Véron, Autret, and Galichon (2006).

and financial analysts operate under conditions of imperfect information, limited competence, and very short timeframes, accounts are often the only source of information used in investment decisions.[41] Yet the production of these accounts is highly contingent on accounting rules, the setting of which is a political process. In fact, accounting standards can be seen as industrial policy, as with the rules of stock options in the United States between 1994 and 2002.[42]

Accounting rules settle some critical tradeoffs between actors and changing the rules can have a major impact on the assessment of firms by financial markets, on the capital cost of firms, and ultimately on firm management. For example, sensitive issues with different treatments across national systems include the treatment of investment and acquisitions (rules for depreciation), the evaluation of bank loans (provisions for bad loans, stock options counted as expense or kept off the balance sheet), the assessment of the value of land and financial assets (book value or market value) and issues of consolidation (mandatory rules to include information on subsidiaries in the accounts of the main company).[43] Another sensitive issue relates to who should manage accounting codes and rules. Should it be delegated to a truly independent agency or even to the private sector? Should it be managed by the government as one policy tool?

Historically, key countries took different positions on these issues. Broadly speaking, the two poles on the spectrum are the continental European tradition (state-centered rule-setting) and the U.S./UK tradition of self-regulation by the business and financial communities.[44] Japan falls close to the European tradition, although the section setting accounting rules was managed within the Ministry of Finance and independently from possible political pressures. The Japanese status quo included less stringent reporting rules than in the United States or even in France. In particular, consolidation of subsidiaries (even majority subsidiaries) was not required and companies were not forced to reevaluate their financial holdings regularly according to market levels, nor to provision aggressively about bad loans (in the case of banks).

In the mid-1990s, a global trend of convergence toward a private governance pattern became visible. In 1973, eying a future integration of international markets, international accountants created the International Accounting Standards Committee (IASC) in London with private funds (Crouzet and Véron 2004, 19). In 2001, this organization was rejuvenated

41. Ibid., 60.
42. Ibid., 75.
43. See good discussions of the issues involved in Crouzet and Véron (2004), and Mistral, de Boissieu, and Lorenzi (2003).
44. See details in Crouzet and Véron (2004).

as the International Accounting Standards Board (IASB), incorporated and based in Delaware in London.[45] Since then, the movement toward adopting these global standards has accelerated. The United Kingdom, Germany, and Australia immediately allowed listed companies to publish their accounts in accordance with IAS/IFRS instead of national accounting standards (21). The European Union and Canada followed suit in 2005, in essence endowing the IASB with a sudden large responsibility and critical mass (Véron et al. 2006, chap. 7). For both, the transfer of economic sovereignty to the IASB is seen as a preemptive move against forced convergence with the U.S. GAAP. At least the IASB can be seen as genuinely independent and it is based in London. Meanwhile, discussions over the gradual convergence of accounting standards are ongoing with the Accounting Standards Board of Japan (ASBJ) and with the Chinese authorities (162).

Accounting standards became a key issue in corporate reform in Japan in the late 1990s. The Hashimoto government passed accounting reforms in 1996 with gradual implementation up to 2001 that increased accountability in corporate governance and partially removed the ban on holding companies in 1997. Still, in January 1998, accounting rules were used one last time to slow down financial reforms. MOF allowed banks to value land and stock shareholdings at book value to improve accounts. The reform process between 1996 and 2003 included both a change in governance structure and a change in the content of accounting rules. After a long simmering debate over administrative change, the authority was given to remove accounting standards from MOF's purview and to transfer them to the ASBJ, a private body under the control of the accounting profession and the Federation of Economic Organizations (Keidanren) (decision in March 2000, implemented in July 2000). In February 2001, the ASBJ was placed under the umbrella of the Financial Accounting Standards Foundation (FASF), a private-sector organization led by ten professional associations.[46] Officially, the FASF is expected to

---

45. Its structure ends up being very similar to the U.S. Financial Accounting Standards Board (FASB). On top of the governance structure is a board of nineteen trustees, at least six of which must be from Europe, six from North America, and four from the Asia-Pacific region. As of 2006, the board is led by Paul Volcker, the former governor of the U.S. Federal Reserve. Trustees appoint the fourteen–member board, chiefly according to technical expertise (and not nationality). This new global IASB produces international standards under the appellation International Financial Reporting Standards (IFRS) since 2001 and International Accounting Standards (IAS) before 2001.

46. Keidanren, the Japanese Institute of Certified Public Accountants, the Tokyo Stock Exchange, the Japan Securities Dealers Association, the Japanese Bankers Association, the Life Insurance Association of Japan, the Marine & Fire Insurance Association of Japan, Inc., the Japan Chamber of Commerce & Industry, the Security Analysts Association of Japan, and the Corporation Finance Research Institute, Japan.

assume an oversight role regarding ASBJ activities. The mission of the FASF is defined as follows:

> The objectives of the FASF are to promote progress of corporate finance disclosure and soundness of the capital markets in Japan by developing generally accepted accounting standards. The FASF will also contribute to the development of a high quality set of internationally accepted accounting standards.[47]

A discussion with the MOF bureaucrat in charge of the accounting standard-setting unit until 2000 revealed enduring bureaucratic opposition to the change, but also a recognition that a twin push from global investors and political leaders left no choice for the MOF.[48]

This, however, did not settle the debate over accounting governance, as the authority to set tax reporting requirements remains with MOF's tax bureau. This bureau has repeatedly opposed the spread of consolidated accounting; managing with the help of political allies within the LDP to block it several times (1999, January 2000, November 2001).[49] The law mandating consolidated accounting for tax purposes was finally passed in June 2002.

Accounting reforms present a fascinating political laboratory for the study of political entrepreneurship under reduced autonomy. The initial move in 1996–97 was clearly related to concerns about foreign investors and global standards (the golden bargain). This concern grew in importance over time. But the actual pathway of accounting reforms shows tremendous zigzagging and flip-flopping. The decision was made in 1996–97 under Hashimoto's leadership, but not fully implemented. The Obuchi-Yosano period led to an important change in governance (March 2000), as part of the large program favoring supply-side reforms. Yosano Kaoru and reformist politicians such as Shiozaki Yasuhisa were clearly involved in the process. The Mori period (2000–01) was dominated by delay and stalling in working out the details and implementing accounting reforms for tax purposes. This issue, along with the loose treatment of banks' bad loans and a generous deposit insurance scheme set the stage for a major confrontation with international bond rating agencies (Moody's, Standard & Poor's, and Fitch).[50] A series of banking downgrades took place, beginning in 1997 with Yamaichi Shoken. In the fall of 2001, Fitch identified the evaluation of bad loans as a major weakness,

---

47. Website of the ASBJ, in particular "Establishment of the Financial Accounting Standards Foundation," www.asb.or.jp/index_e.php.

48. Interview with senior MOF bureaucrat, 17 April 2000 (in the tiny and decrepit office area reserved for the unit until 2000).

49. The tax bureau was principally concerned about a reduction in tax revenues as large firms consolidated loss-making subsidiaries with their own profitable businesses. Interview at the tax bureau, April 2000.

50. See the excellent analysis by Sinclair (2005).

part of which was due to weak rules. Moody's and S&P made downgrades of bank bonds in 2002.[51] In 2000–02, the major rating agencies also downgraded the government's debt because of its purported lack of political willingness to tackle structural reforms and high deficit.[52] Part of the argument also related to problematic accounting rules. Ironically, the downgrading of government bonds also increased the cost of the then-ongoing shift to mark-to-market accounting (the annual reevaluation, up or down, of shares and other securities according to their current value in the market), given the higher probability of a domestic sell-off of government bonds. In any case, the active role of bond rating agencies in this period increased the global signals and the salience of the golden bargain to domestic political entrepreneurs.

In 2002–03, LDP stalwarts associated with corporate interest groups tried to stall the process of accounting reforms, leading to a major battle in May–June 2003 with Koizumi. On 24 April 2003, Ota Seiichi, head of the LDP's Administrative Reform Council, organized a meeting with LDP politicians and officials from the FSA. Participants decided to sponsor legislation to put a temporary freeze on the use of mark-to-market accounting. They were concerned that the drop in stock prices was forcing banks to report lower capital amounts (because latent stock profits are included in capital computations). In turn, this would lead banks to further cut lending, given the regulations on capital adequacy ratios for banks. Politicians feared that small and medium companies in rural areas would be hit hardest. They also feared the direct impact of stock price falls on firms holding share portfolios.[53] These, of course, are the principal support groups for the LDP. Ota was supported by other LDP stalwarts, principally Horiuchi Mitsuo (LDP general council chairman and faction leader) and Aso Taro (LDP policy council chairman), and Aizawa Hideyuki (former chairman of the financial committee, chairman of an anti-deflation task force).

That such high-ranking party officials would take positions opposed to those of the LDP leader and government speaks volumes about the lack of party discipline and constrained executive autonomy. Ota, Horiuchi, and Aso gained support from coalition partners, another Achilles' heel for political entrepreneurs like Koizumi. Fuyushiba Tetsuzō, secretary general of Kōmeitō, hinted that he would support the legislation proposed. The leaders of the anti-accounting rebellion argued that the Accounting Standards Board "did not have a real-world understanding of business" (Indo and

---

51. Ibid. 90–91.

52. Ibid., 142–44.

53. See for example, the analysis in the Nihon Keizai Shinbun (2003b): "Politicians in the ruling coalition are concerned about the impact recent steep falls in stock prices will have on firms with large share portfolios that will be forced to book heavy stock valuation losses under mark-to-market accounting rules."

Shikata 2003). They saw a freeze in mark-to-market accounting as a counter-solution to the cut in public spending pushed by Koizumi and his team. Arguments included the need to resist the "propaganda" of global standards (*Nihon Keizai Shinbun*, 2003). In June 2003, while the ASBJ was speaking strongly against the idea of stopping accounting reforms, the coalition of anti-reformers from the LDP, the Kōmeitō, and then the New Conservative Party as well announced that they had drafted their bill and planned to introduce it in the legislative agenda during the Diet session ending in July. On the pro-reform side stood Prime Minister Koizumi, Financial Services Minister Takenaka Heizō and LDP Young Turks such as Shiozaki Yasuhisa and Watanabe Yoshimi. They argued that freezing accounting reforms would cost Japan greatly in terms of global investment. Financial investors and analysts watched the battle closely.

In the end, the political entrepreneurs won the battle and kept accounting reforms on track, although with probable side payments to the LDP elders and relaxation of the strict control of public expenses. Reformers successfully convinced the party that the only way to bring the stock market back up was to push forward with the reform agenda and attract foreign investors. The battle revealed that the political world cared enormously about the level of the stock market and confirmed the relative political autonomy enjoyed by Koizumi, at least by 2003. Foreign investors and bond rating agencies played a role in raising the costs of non-reform to the political class.

The Industrial Revitalization Law and Bankruptcy Reforms

For many analysts of Japanese industry, 1999 was a crucial year when a major wave of corporate restructuring swept through the economy. As many corporations sought to outdo each other with major plans of capital reorganization and labor reduction, investors no longer doubted that the ground had shifted. In fact, the stock market reacted extremely positively and increased by 41 percent over the course of the year,[54] the best performance since the burst of the bubble in 1990.

What made the restructuring story so credible in Japan in 1999 was not only the gradual erosion of the main bank system and ensuing focus of corporations on the price of money after the 1997 financial crisis, but also the government's active support of corporate restructuring.[55] In 1999, the

54. The Nikkei 225 average opened the year on 4 January at ¥13,391.81 and closed the year on 30 December at ¥18,934.34. Nikkei Net, Markets Japan, historical data: www.nni.nikkei.co.jp/CF/AC/MKJ/mkjhistorical_d.cfm.
55. See Morgan Stanley's *Global Economic Forum (1999)*. Confirmed in interviews at BOJ, Nissan, and Nomura Securities.

Obuchi government clearly announced its support of supply-side reforms and took direct action, such as the Industrial Revitalization Law (August 1999), to induce corporate restructuring. Most of the corporate-related reforms passed in 1999 and 2000 emerged out of the Industrial Competitiveness Council (ICC), an advisory council set up by Prime Minister Obuchi to deal with industrial revitalization.

The reforms coming out of the ICC process were examples of political entrepreneurship in response to the golden bargain. Yosano Kaoru and MITI ministers designed the ICC framework, a strategic institution set up to enable a direct confrontation between prime ministerial power and usually diffuse (yet paralyzing) anti-reform interests. Prime Minister Obuchi was heavily involved every step of the way, making key decisions on the membership and structure of the council in long meetings with Yosano and others.[56] The ICC met at the *Kantei*, the prime ministerial residence, and was chaired by the prime minister.

Political leaders supported key reforms such as the IRL because of direct concerns about the stock market in general and the actions of foreign investors in particular. Obuchi also embraced the ICC as a response to the leadership threat posed by Katō Kōichi, a reformist positioning himself as an entrepreneurial leader able to break the hold of interest groups. The 1999 batch of reforms depended on the high degree of political autonomy enjoyed by the Obuchi-Yosano team, slowed as soon as Yosano was removed from his post that year, and stopped entirely when Obuchi passed away in April 2000.

What was the significance of the ICC in the larger Japanese reform pathway? The ICC was an advisory panel of business and government leaders set up on 19 March 1999 by Prime Minister Obuchi. It was meant to mirror the Competitiveness Council set up by President Ronald Reagan in the 1980s.[57] Just like the Maekawa panel of 1985–86 which produced the famous Maekawa report and suggested significant structural reforms to transform Japan for Prime Minister Nakasone, the ICC existed only through the power and will of the prime minister and had no legal standing. The members of the council were personally chosen and appointed by the prime minister, although in effect they were most likely selected by MITI after consultations with Keidanren. On the business side, the prime minister appointed seventeen top business executives, including Idei Nobuyuki, president of Sony Corp; Imai Takashi, chairman of Keidanren; and Okuda Hiroshi, president of Toyota Motor Corp. and chairman of Japan's Federation of Employers

---

56. Interviews with key adviser to Yosano on the ICC and with two METI bureaucrats involved in the process, April 2006. See also Shimizu (2005).

57. See JETRO *Focus Newsletter* of 30 April 1999. "Japan Moves to Adopt New Business Practices," www.jetro.org/newyork/focusnewsletter/focus5.html.

Association (Nikkeiren). This lineup thus grouped both traditional Keidanren stalwarts such as Imai and Higuchi Hirotarō (Asahi Breweries), and new industry renegades such as Ushio Jirō (Ushio), and Idei (Sony). To MOF's disappointment, the meetings included no representative from the financial industry. Interestingly, three new members were later added to the ICC during its fifth meeting to counter public criticism that the ICC privileged industrial firms over others: Son Masayoshi (Softbank), Suzuki Toshifumi (Ito-Yokado), and Fukutake Soichirō (Benesse Corp). On the government side, the ICC brought together all government ministers except the director general of the Defense Agency. The chief cabinet secretary (Nonaka Hiromu) was also present and held a key coordination role. The meetings were officially chaired by the prime minister, but the MITI minister (Yosano Kaoru) was in charge of running the proceedings (*giji shinkō*).[58]

The ICC met eight times between March 1999 and January 2000 at the residence of the prime minister. The official format of the meetings consisted of presentations and requests by industry leaders, requests that led to instructions by the prime minister to the relevant ministries to draft appropriate laws. These instructions were followed up by concrete proposals from cabinet ministers in subsequent meetings. On the surface, therefore, the ICC was constructed as a forum for business leaders to directly express their needs to the prime minister and other government ministers. It was also a public forum where the prime minister would make personal commitments that reforms would proceed and give direct instructions to the relevant ministries.

The ICC met for the last time on 18 January 2000 after a four-month interruption and its planned ninth meeting never took place. At least four elements contributed to the group's demise. To some extent, it can be said that it died of its own success. The series of reforms passed in August 1999 removed the sense of urgency and fulfilled its primary mission. On 5 October 1999, the formation of a new governing coalition and the associated government reshuffle heavily affected the ICC. It not only broke the dynamic of the ICC but also replaced one of its key leaders: Yosano Kaoru, MITI minister. The new MITI leader, Fukaya Takashi, showed more interest in small and medium enterprises than the revival of large corporations. Next, the period between November 1999 and March 2000 was almost entirely dominated by the requirements of drafting the budget, the usual priority of the annual Diet cycle. Finally, in April 2000, Prime Minister Obuchi fell in to a coma, and with him, the ICC came to a formal end, since it only existed through Prime Minister Obuchi's will.[59]

58. Official minutes of the ICC, as published on the prime minister's web page. "Sangyō katsuryoku kaigi no kaisai ni tsuite—naikaku sori daijin kessai," obtained from www.kantei.go.jp/jp in 2000.
59. Interviews with Keidanren point person, 17 April 2000.

Why did the ICC matter? Its importance can first of all be ascertained through the series of reforms passed in 1999 following the ICC meetings. These reforms included the Emergency Employment and Industrial Competitiveness Measures (11 June), the revised Employment Security Law and Manpower Dispatching Business Law (30 June), the initiation of the revision process of the commercial code concerning the division of companies (7 July), the IRL (6 August), the amendment to the commercial code concerning the swapping and transfers of shares (9 August), and the bankruptcy reforms (civil corporate rehabilitation procedures, 14 December).

In particular, the IRL (*sangyō katsuryoku saisei tokubetsu sochi hō*) aimed specifically at facilitating corporate restructuring and included measures such as:

- Exemptions of commercial law requirements regarding administrative procedures associated with divestiture and goodwill transferring.
- A rise in the upper limit of the amount of preferred stocks in case of a debt equity swap.
- Support for management buy-out and employee buy-out by facilitating stock purchases by managers or employees.
- Financial measures such as low interest loans and guarantees.
- Tax incentives such as a longer period of loss carry forward (from five to seven years), reduction of the registration license tax, and an acceleration of depreciation allowances (from 18 to 30 percent).

The measures provided to corporations, however, required approval by the government (mostly MITI) of their business restructuring plans. The IMF praised the law in various reports in 2000 as an important step forward. The Industrial Revitalization Law has also proved useful in the restructuring of many corporations in 2000 and 2001, including the path-breaking Nissan Revival Plan. As of 28 September 2001, 112 large corporations had seen their restructuring plans approved by the government (seventy-three of which were approved by MITI) and were relying on government support for their restructuring operations.[60] The law also gives legitimacy and political coverage to restructuring operations, a great contrast to the earlier restructuring wave (1993) when factory closures (such as the Zama closure by Nissan) led to political and mass media condemnations. At the same time, it is a relatively milder tool than the direct restructuring tools used by Korea and France.

Since its passage in August 1999, the IRL has shown increasing significance. Administering the law has become the key function of an important

---

60. METI's web page, "Sangyō katsuryoku saisei tokubetsu sochi hō no nintei ichiran hyō," www.meti.go.jp.

MITI (now METI) section, the Industrial Structure section. METI has thoroughly advertised the achievements of the law both nationally and internationally (repeatedly in newsletters by JETRO in the United States). In March 2001, MITI minister Hiranuma proposed that the IRL be applied to banks that forgive debts of companies already approved for support under the law.[61] In April 2001, the Fair Trade Commission indicated that it would be flexible with the 5 percent rule (limitation of the stake that a bank can have in non-financial firms) in the case of corporations that have been approved by METI under the IRL.[62] This measure would make debt-for-equity-swaps easier. Both developments signal that the law is increasingly seen as a benchmark for categorizing companies and as a foundation for further reform moves.

The success of the ICC is all the more surprising in light of the disappointing experience of other economic councils that operated around the same time. For example, Prime Minister Obuchi established an Economic Strategy Council (ESC, *keizai senryaku kaigi*) on 24 August 1998 to propose "visions for reviving the Japanese economy and for building a prosperous economic society in the 21st century." The ESC included ten members, four academics and six business leaders. It was chaired by Higuchi Hirotarō (Asahi Breweries). Three of the ten members would later be members of the ICC as well (Higuchi, Okuda Hiroshi, and Suzuki Toshifumi). The ESC met fourteen times and brought in dozens of senior academic and business leaders for discussions. It also exchanged opinions with all economic organizations in Japan. On 26 February 1999, the ESC produced a high-profile report titled "Strategies for Reviving the Japanese Economy: A Report to Prime Minister Obuchi."[63] The report presented a broad analysis of Japan's economic problems and proposed 234 precise measures to remedy these problems. The measures ranged from advocating an end to the Japanese system of corporate governance and further deregulation to the support of nonprofit organizations (NPOs) and measures to deal with the aging population. In particular, the chapter on industrial revitalization advocated measures to eliminate excess capacity, such as the special tax treatment that was eventually be adopted as part of the IRL. However, the immediate reaction to the report from both the Japanese press and foreign investors was pessimism. Some emphasized that measures such as the privatization of the postal saving system had been initially considered by the ESC but censored by politicians. It was also pointed out that there was no mechanism in place to bring these ideas to the political machinery and

---

61. *Japan Times*, 31 March 2001.

62. *Nikkei Weekly*, 16 April 2001.

63. Report obtained from the prime minister's website, www.kantei.go.jp (accessed in March 2000).

ensure that corresponding reforms could be passed by the Diet. In a report titled "Muffled Trumpet, Hesitant Generals," Robert Feldman, chief economist at Morgan Stanley Japan and one of the business leaders called in by the ESC (on 1 December 1998), wrote that the report would probably suffer the same fate as the 1986 Maekawa Report. While the report included many worthwhile and even "radical" reform ideas, "the politics of adoption of the recommendations in the report remain[ed] problematical." Feldman argued that there was no political actor to "carry the ball" and that it was doubtful whether the ESC could be an agent of "regime-changing legislation."[64] Indeed, the government took no immediate action. This negative assessment of the ESC was confirmed in interviews conducted with MOF bureaucrats and at Keidanren (March–April 2000). The failure of the ESC is strong evidence for the significance of the direct Yosano-Obuchi political input into the ICC process.

What the ICC Is Not About: Employment Support, U.S. Pressures, and Organized Interest Groups

What is clear is that the reforms emerging from the ICC were not driven by labor unions. In fact, labor was neither participating in the ICC, nor informed of its workings. Not surprisingly, the IRL drew fire from labor and mass media such as the *Asahi Shinbun* (the main center-left newspaper)[65] which saw in it an effort by the state to encourage restructuring (and thus layoffs). It even led to demonstrations by Communist-Party affiliated labor unions (Zenrōren), including one in front of the Diet in March 2000. That demonstration of thousands of union members included slogans that specifically criticized the IRL as a measure that encouraged layoffs (*kubi kiri sokushin hō*). Meanwhile, the mainstream labor federation (Rengō) opposed the law in the Diet through the DPJ. The DPJ is the main opposition party and is supported by most of the labor unions federated by Rengō.

Throughout the month of July 1999, the DPJ strongly criticized the IRL and pressured Yosano in the Diet's committees.[66] The criticism focused on two main issues. First, the DPJ disliked that the law would encourage restructuring and layoffs and would thus have a negative impact on the already gloomy employment front. In the Diet Committee meetings, a

64. Robert Feldman, 1 March 1999. "Japan: Muffled Trumpet, Hesitant Generals," in Morgan Stanley's *Global Economic Forum.*
65. See in particular the editorial published in *Asahi Shinbun* on 24 May 1999. "*Tsuke mawashi ha yurusenai. Sangyō saisei saku (shasetsu).*" The editorial argued that the government was about to act irresponsibly again by using public money to rescue private companies, just as it had done with private banks.
66. Interview with METI official directly involved in managing the ICC, 10 April 2006.

DPJ Diet member, Watanabe, declared: "in essence, this law is a law to support restructuring and to cut the necks of [lay off] employees. It will increase the unease of workers."[67] In particular, the DPJ wanted to amend the law to include a mandatory agreement between labor and management (*rōshi kyōgi no gōi*). The text of the law as proposed in July (and passed in August) only required management to obtain "understanding and cooperation" (*rikai to kyōryoku wo eru*).[68] MITI actually confirmed during the Diet deliberations that a restructuring plan could be approved under the law even in the absence of an agreement between labor and management, as long as management had shown enough consideration toward labor. The second line of attack used by the DPJ was the argument that the law would oppose the principle of competition and increase "administrative discretion."[69] This would go against the trend of deregulation and smaller government. On 13 July, Diet member Nakano, chairman of the DPJ policy research council, declared: "by increasing the authority of the government, [the law] runs counter to the formation of an impartial society."[70] The fierce exchanges were carried over to the question and answer sessions devoted to the supplementary budget (*hosei yosan no daihyō shitsumon*).

In the end, however, the LDP succeeded in building intra-party support (formally confirmed on 2 July) and getting the support of the Liberal Party (confirmed on 3 July,[71] as well as the support of its soon-to-be coalition partner Kōmeitō (confirmed on 13 July). In the face of the overwhelming votes of the coalition, the DPJ (and Rengō) settled for the inclusion of a "supplementary resolution" (*futai ketsugi*) titled "Employment Stability" (*koyō antei*).[72] This resolution set up a research group, led by Professor Sugano from Tokyo University, that was instructed to research ways to protect employment. The research group eventually had an impact on the next round of reforms in May 2000: the revision of the commercial code, this time accompanied by a "Labor Contract Succession Law."[73] In exchange for the supplementary resolution, the DPJ agreed to vote along with the coalition parties for the IRL, another typical example of Japanese consensus democracy. The vote was taken in the lower house on 29 July 1999. But the vote in May 2000 on corporate splits (*kaisha bunkatsu*) was a much more contentious one. Due to fierce labor and DPJ opposition and some cracks

67. *Asahi Shinbun*, 28 July.
68. Ibid. "*Koyō ni fuan—yatō hanpatsu. Sangyō Saisei hōan, honkaku shingi.*" See also *Mainichi Shinbun*, 27 July. "*Shūin shōkō iinkai ga tokubetsu sochi hō wo honkaku shingi.*"
69. *Asahi Shinbun*, 23 July.
70. *Mainichi Shinbun*, 13 July.
71. *Asahi Shinbun*, 3 July 1999.
72. *Ibid.*, 29 July 1999.
73. Interview with leading editorialist from *Asahi Shinbun* (21 April 2000).

within the LDP, the law nearly died. Interestingly, Yosano again saved the day in his new incarnation as head of the committee on legal affairs in the Diet.[74]

Another possible interpretation for the structural reforms of 1999 and the IRL in particular is international pressure from the United States. It is true that the IMF had urged Japan to move ahead with some of the structural reforms included in the 1999 package. It is also true that the project of the IRL was presented to visiting Deputy Secretary of the Treasury Larry Summers on 15 May. The Japanese government made this presentation (reported in the press as a public commitment to the United States) as a way to indicate that it was seriously committed to dealing with the problem of excess capacity and structural reforms in general.[75] The press reported a general interest and tacit support on the part of Summers. However, this point of view has serious flaws. When the IRL was passed in early August, it was immediately denounced by a delegation from the U.S. Trade Representative as an unfair subsidy. In a stroke of bad luck, the law was passed just as high-level U.S.-Japan trade negotiations were taking place in Tokyo regarding the ongoing steel dispute. On 28 July, the U.S. delegation charged that "the Japanese government [was granting] preferential treatment to its steel industry under proposed legislation to revive industrial competitiveness."[76] On 5 August, President Clinton himself seized on the issue as he condemned both Korea's and Japan's "unfair trade practices" in the steel sector. President Clinton invoked the IRL as one source of unfair industrial "subsidies" and denounced it.[77] Clearly the use of public money to encourage industrial restructuring was not to the liking of the U.S. government and did not find its inspiration there.

The last and most common explanation of the ICC and IRL suggests that Keidanren, as an interest group, drove them. This explanation, advanced by both labor activists and politicians[78] is also the official line of Keidanren.[79] The ICC seems to have originally been a Keidanren idea. According to Keidanren documents (confirmed by MITI), Keidanren formally submitted "a proposal for the enhancement of industrial competitiveness" and urged both the government and the LDP to establish the Industrial Competitiveness Council (name proposed by Keidanren chairman Imai).[80]

74. Interview with METI official directly involved in managing the ICC, 10 April 2006.
75. *Asahi Shinbun*, 16 May 1998.
76. *Japan Times*, 28 July 1999.
77. *Mainichi Shinbun*, 6 August 1999.
78. Interviews with labor union officials (Rengo and Zenroren) and with one senior Diet member.
79. Interview with ICC point person at Keidanren.
80. Keidanren. 10 November 1999. "Activities of the Industrial Competitiveness Council and other Keidanren Initiatives."

Imai played an important role in the ICC. At the first meeting of the ICC on 29 March, he made an official welcome speech (*aisatsu*) right after the introduction by MITI Minister Yosano and the introduction speech by Prime Minister Obuchi. Most ICC meetings devoted the bulk of their time to official presentations by business leaders, most of them Keidanren members. During the second meeting, on 28 April, Imai made a precise presentation that listed the problems encountered by Japanese corporations in global competition (with U.S. corporations). He argued that the government needed to set the right economic environment by reforming the commercial code, the tax system, the bankruptcy law, and the employment system.[81] Most important, at the beginning of the third ICC meeting (20 May), Chairman Imai issued a precise list of measures and reforms that represented Keidanren's requests to the government in the name of "international equal footing." The presentation, titled "First Proposal for Enhancing the Competitiveness of Japanese Industries," was made public. Reports in the press emphasized the leading role of Keidanren and of the business circles in general in pushing the government to pass reforms. The press also pointed out that the ICC represented a tool for corporate management to reduce labor's bargaining power.[82]

This depiction looks like a perfect case for interest-group-led reforms. However, this argument reveals several important flaws. The business leaders in the ICC sat as individuals, rather than as a Keidanren delegation. In fact, the group included well-known dissenters such as Ushio Jirō and Son Masayoshi (and even Sony's Idei Nobuyuki), who tended to take anti-establishment positions. In addition, a careful analysis of the minutes of the ICC meetings reveals that it was Yosano Kaoru who was really running the show (formally assisting the chair of the meeting, Prime Minister Obuchi). All meetings began with an introduction by Yosano (who sat directly to the left of the prime minister). A telltale sign of the strong METI leadership in the council can be seen in the reaction of MOF officials across the street. Many tended to see in the IRL a revival of the failed "*tokushin hō*" of 1966. In this old conflict,[83] MITI (and its most famous vice minister, Sahashi Shigeru) tried to directly organize corporate mergers in response to the capital liberalization required by the OECD. At the end of a protracted battle,[84] however, MITI failed to obtain the necessary legislative tools from a Diet and an LDP that had been heavily lobbied by Keidanren. In this 1999 version, however, politicians are clearly in charge.

81. Prime minister's office, "Dai 2 kai sangyō kyōsōryoku kaigi giji yōshi" (Summary of Minutes of the 2d Meeting of the ICC), www.kantei.go.jp/jp/sangyo/990518dai2.html.

82. *Asahi Shinbun*, 16 May, 24 May, 1 June, 1999.

83. Recounted in famous novels such as *Shiroyama* (1975).

84. Recounted in chapter 7 of Johnson (1982).

Even more revealing is Keidanren's reaction to the prime achievement of the ICC, the IRL. Despite the awkwardness of having to denounce a law officially passed in its name, Keidanren found serious flaws with the law. The *Nihon Keizai Shinbun*, an economic newspaper with views that are traditionally closed to those of Keidanren, summarized the problem in a late July editorial in which it denounced the increase in government control over corporate decisions. The *Nikkei Weekly* ran a similar article on 2 August, entitled "Bills Raise Fears of Bureaucratic Control." The article argues that the bills would increase the power of government officials and allow for arbitrary bureaucratic action, and concludes that "success in revitalizing Japanese industry will depend on deregulation and the extent to which the government can support the private sector without getting in the way."

Discussions at MITI also confirmed that, on the whole, Keidanren has been a slow mover on issues such as deregulation and financial reforms. Within Keidanren, however, a subgroup has been proactively pushing for reforms. This is the voluntary group of manufacturers that came together in 1995 under the name of Second Cooperation Group for the Facilitation of Corporate Financing (*shikin chōtatsu no enkatsuka ni kan suru kyōgikai 2 dantai*). Thus, it is highly probable that on issues as sensitive as supply-side structural reforms, Keidanren members are at odds with each other. Some, such as Chairman Imai, may have been willing to countenance a growing MITI role in exchange for legal reforms, while other reforms may be opposed by both.

A final element underscores the limits of any possible Keidanren dominance over the ICC. In September 1999, Obuchi was reelected to the LDP presidency by beating Katō Kōichi, his reform-focused opponent. With this threat gone, Obuchi removed Yosano from METI and lost interest in the ICC. The record indeed shows that the ICC became moribund as early as October 1999 with Yosano's removal and that it entirely died in April 2000 when Obuchi fell into coma (Shimizu 2005, 213). If the Keidanren had been the prime moving force behind the ICC, wouldn't the committee have continued its work?

To sum up, the ICC was much more a tool for Yosano to overcome resistance from MOF[85] and other ministries than an ad hoc forum where Keidanren could lobby the government for reform. There was certainly a high level of cooperation between Yosano and Keidanren (at least until the passage of the IRL in August 1999) but Yosano was clearly in the driver's seat. After the law was passed, implementation relied on delegation to MITI bureaucrats. They maintained the pressure applied by Yosano in the reform process.

---

85. Interviews with Keidanren officials, MOF officials, and MITI officials.

Political Genesis: Golden Bargain and Political Leadership

What was Yosano's and Obuchi's economic motivation in pushing for the IRL? The specific blueprints and ideas contained in the law arose out of a five-year long process of reflection on structural reforms within MITI. Yosano and Obuchi seized on these ideas and implemented them at a time of strong political autonomy. As argued by some MITI officials, the IRL and other reforms that emerged out of the ICC were part of a larger total plan for the transformation and revival of Japan's industrial structure.[86] Interestingly, Yosano served as deputy chief cabinet secretary under Hashimoto and was in charge of these issues of structural reform. He had good knowledge of METI's work and was politically involved in it from the beginning.[87]

The IRL design process also reveals key concerns about capital flows and cost of financing. The golden bargain was an important component in the motivations of political leaders. According to a key bureaucrat involved in the ICC process, private equity funds had been actively threatening to not invest further in Japan if it did not change its corporate structure. Both Yosano and METI were well aware of this voice.[88] In fact, a fascinating element of the IRL and other reforms flowing out of the ICC (such as the revision of the commercial code) is the extent to which arguments about the stock market were used to convince opponents and how successful they were. The document prepared by MITI (under Yosano's guidance) for lawmakers and others to explain the rationale for the IRL and its key objectives also included direct references to the stock market. The first paragraph of the first page described the international wave of corporate restructuring and the growth of a global market. The second paragraph presented return-on-asset (ROA) data that emphasized how low Japan's overall ROA had fallen (2.5 percent). The fourth paragraph then presented the key argument for the government's need to encourage restructuring in Japan:

Promoting Corporate Restructuring: as the world's capital markets have become one, a harsh situation has arisen whereby the world's money ends up flowing to the stocks or bonds that have even a little better capacity to generate

---

86. MITI has turned its attention to the necessity of structural reforms at least since 1993, partly in response to the "high-cost industrial structure" and the fear of hollowing out, and partly out of comparative analysis with other advanced industrial countries. This process was part of a larger ideational shift within MITI. The first related commission established by MITI was the 1993 deliberative Council on Industrial Structure (*sangyō kōzō shingikai*) (interviews with top MITI officials on 28 March and 13 April 2000). This council led to a whole program on structural reforms initially focusing on market deregulation, but gradually moving to other legal reforms.

87. Interview with key strategic assistant to Yosano at METI, 10 April 2006.

88. Interview with METI official directly involved in managing the ICC, 10 April 2006.

profits [than others]. . . . It is necessary to promote the process of 'selection and concentration' of the corporations in our country.[89]

Clearly, the records of the ICC and the IRL reveal that arguments about financial globalization and the stock market pervaded the debates. They seem to have been crucial in helping Prime Minister Obuchi convince LDP lawmakers to act quickly. The reaction of the stock market to the law and the ICC was exceedingly positive (as noted in various IMF reports); the graph of the Nikkei 225 index in 1999 shows particularly big jumps in June when the precise measures for industrial revitalization and the decision to extend the legislative session were announced by the government and in early August when the IRL was passed.

The political story of the ICC is one of both political entrepreneurs and a novel institutional creation, the ICC. Yosano acted as a shadow coordinator throughout the tenure of the ICC and as the clear leader during the legislative process in the Diet (although he was prudent enough to let Miyazawa Kiichi, the MOF minister, make many of the key political announcements). What made the ICC more successful than other councils such as the ESC is that Yosano, with the support of Obuchi, could seize the reform momentum and bring it to fruition in the Diet.

Yosano was the right man at the right time. He was a rare policy-oriented politician stemming from an urban constituency and with the vision of pushing structural reform forward. At the same time, many other individuals have ideas regarding the necessity of reform, but the fragmentation of responsibilities among ministries completely blocks the process (fiscal responsibility with MOF, commercial code responsibility with the Ministry of Justice, employment responsibility with the Ministry of Labor, pension responsibility with Ministry of Health and Welfare, and competitiveness with METI).[90] Supply-side reforms are thus particularly hard to move forward. Bureaucratic actors are divided between anti-reformers and pro-reformers. METI has great ideas, but cannot overcome the combination of bureaucratic opposition and underlying vested interest networks, networks that act both through other ministries and through the LDP.[91] Politicians rarely step above the mere management of interest group relations (*rigai kankei no chōsei*).[92] By nature, the Japanese policy system is risk averse and gives vested interests many chances to protect themselves. Only the prime minister could break the deadlock,[93] but is institutionally not involved in

---

89. MITI document, "*Sangyō katsuryoku saisei tokubetsu sochi hō no Ranyō*," final version, November 1999.

90. Interview with key strategic assistant to Yosano at METI, 10 April 2006, and interview with Shimizu Masato (Nikkei shinbun), April 11, 2006.

91. Interview with senior political assistant to Yosano Kaoru, 10 April 2006.

92. Ibid.

93. Interview with METI official directly involved in managing the ICC, 10 April 2006.

such arbitrage situations. There is no constituency for the collective good. By stepping in the void and creating the ICC framework,[94] Yosano solved this collective action problem and introduced an institution where the prime minister would be in a position to arbitrate and tilt the balance toward reform.[95] In the words of a key METI bureaucrat, what was unusual about the ICC was that it incorporated "a mechanism to appeal to politicians who normally never get involved in such policy decisions."[96] The fact that an elite bureaucrat emphasizes the key role of political leaders makes it especially credible.

The ICC framework was particularly innovative, as it created a forum where prime ministerial leadership could be expressed directly in support of Yosano's plan. Yosano prepared for each meeting thoroughly with his METI team and with Obuchi, drafting reform blueprints and gaining the prime minister's support. At the meetings of the ICC, Obuchi made decisions on the spot and in the presence of all cabinet ministers. For example, the decision to reform the commercial code to enable share swapping was made in such a fashion. The ICC collapsed the usual policymaking timeframe and prevented opponents from mounting a successful resistance (*hanron dekinai*).[97] Also crucial was that the ICC was a pure government body attached to the prime minister and without any involvement of the LDP. It short-circuited usual resistance pathways through LDP MPs. Another innovation of the ICC was the incorporation of the concept of the "TV drama series." Instead of having eight meetings leading to an elegant report that was not implemented (the ESC pattern), decisions were made and conclusions drawn at each meeting. Yosano would summarize the meeting and Obuchi would arbitrate and make a public political decision. The ICC was a council for decisionmaking (*jikkō kaigi*). Again, this concept was the brainchild of a key METI strategist, but it only saw the light of day because Yosano enthusiastically embraced it.[98] Gaining the support of all key ministers and enlisting key business leaders took some fancy footwork that Yosano delegated to his METI strategists. Nonaka Hiromu, a powerful LDP power broker and the chief cabinet secretary benefited from this delegation.[99]

The ICC framework stands in contrast to the laborious process of structural reform under Hashimoto Ryutaro in 1996–98. Hashimoto created an overall plan but left each ministry in charge of its own area. This led to

94. It is worth noting that the actual design of the ICC was the brainchild of the METI bureaucrat in charge of overall economic policy planning, Niihara Hiroaki, using a name proposed by a forward-looking team of junior Keidanren officials. The implementation of the idea, however, was the result of Yosano's enthusiasm for it. Without Yosano, the idea would have died like many others before it. Interview with Niihara Hiroaki, 10 April 2006.

95. Ibid.

96. Ibid.

97. Interview with METI official directly involved in managing the ICC, 10 April 2006.

98. Interview with key strategic assistant to Yosano at METI, 10 April 2006.

99. Ibid.

myriad low-level conflicts between METI and other ministries and an incredibly poor policy efficiency. In fact, the METI team in charge of structural reforms and deregulation measures never left the ministry and slept at their desks. They tried harassing other ministries, often in vain. After several weeks, a nauseating smell filled the METI office and the work atmosphere was terrible.[100] Even after all that, the final list of structural promises produced and updated each year could not be easily implemented (*jikkōsei ga nai*).

Obuchi's motivations were closely related to the upcoming leadership race within the LDP (September 1999), in which his main opponent was reform advocate Kato Koichi. Kato had criticized Obuchi for relying too heavily on fiscal stimulus and not resorting to micro-economic structural reforms.[101] By backing Yosano on supply-side reforms, Obuchi could seize on the advantages of the golden bargain, stimulate a rise in the stock market, and expand his coalition toward the center. The strategy worked and Obuchi easily beat Kato in the leadership race. In a way, the ICC process was a preemptive strike against Kato. It can even be said that Yosano played a key role in Obuchi's leadership victory.

The big lesson of the ICC was that, given the strength and divisions of interest group coalitions, reform could only move forward on the back on strong political leadership (*seiji shudō*). A key political entrepreneur needed to be ready to go to into battle against opponents.

The Conditions for Reforms through Political Entrepreneurship

Despite the period of high political autonomy for leaders like Obuchi and Yosano, the reform process revealed limitations arising from bureaucratic rivalry and fragmentation. In particular, the MITI-MOF rivalry was clearly felt during the ICC process. It is reported that MOF opposed the formation of the ICC in the first place and the MITI-MOF clash led all other ministries to watch in silence until this was settled.[102] MOF apparently opposed the likely use of public money and resented the leadership role that MITI was taking in shaping economic policy. At the first meeting of the ICC, the MITI-MOF clash erupted in the open as MOF minister Miyazawa deplored the exclusion of financial institutions from the meeting. He urged MITI to find a way to involve them. A decision was made to call a closed-door meeting between MOF minister Miyazawa, MITI minister Yosano, FRC

100. Interview with key strategic assistant to Yosano at METI, 10 April 2006. He was previously in charge of structural reforms under Hashimoto.
101. Interview with Shimizu Masato (*Nikkei shinbun*, author of *Kantei shudō* (2005) quoted above), 11 April 2006.
102. Interviews with Keidanren officials and MITI officials.

minister Yanagisawa, Chief Cabinet Secretary Nonaka, Keidanren chair Imai, and Prime Minister Obuchi. The meeting took place on 6 April and some arrangement was made. However, this arrangement seems to have left the MOF minister dissatisfied enough to skip the second meeting of the ICC, on 28 April. Repeatedly during the process that led up to the passage of the IRL on 6 August, MOF tried to pour cold water on expectations that the law would have great impact. This clash of visions on the effectiveness of the law between MITI and MOF was reported in the press on 25 July 1999.[103] MITI estimated that ¥30 trillion would be "returned to society" as a result of the law (tangible benefits), while MOF announced an estimate of only ¥7.5 trillion in likely "lost tax revenues." The press commented that these opposite estimates were rooted in "differences of philosophies" (*tetsugaku no chigai*) between the two elite bureaucracies.

At the same time, the need to resort to such a complex mechanism reveals the extent of political obstacles to structural reforms and the constraints under which political entrepreneurs operate in Japan. Yosano and Obuchi lost many other battles to MOF, in particular the battle over tax consolidation (until 2002). The Industrial Revitalization Law has enjoyed a second life since it was renewed in April 2002 under the leadership of Prime Minister Koizumi. Interestingly, the concepts of the IRL were used to shape the Industrial Revitalization Corporation of Japan (IRCJ) in the fall of 2002. The IRCJ was an attempt by the government to fill the gap in equity funds to deal with the restructuring of troubled bank borrowers.

Interestingly, the ICC institutional framework of setting the stage for a political leader to arbitrate among competing interests and to set a reform direction against party resistance became institutionalized after 2001 in the shape of the Council for Economic and Fiscal Policy.[104] In particular, Takenaka Heizō has been able to effectively use this council to push for new structural reforms. In 2005, Yosano Kaoru returned to the policy forefront when he took that position.

Reforms of the Commercial Code: Corporate Governance

The protracted process of commercial code reform from 1993 to 2005 was both a core area of institutional change in Japan and another laboratory for the enduring, yet fluctuating, constraints of political entrepreneurship in Japan. Reforms of the commercial code touch the core regulations of corporate governance and lead to profound changes in corporate behavior on the ground. As shown by Pauly and Reich, enduring differences in corpo-

103. *Mainichi Shinbun*, 25 July 1999.
104. Interview with key strategic assistant to Yosano at METI, 10 April 2006.

rate behavior between firms of different countries rely on deep differences in home country regulations (Pauly and Reich 1997). Commercial laws are rules of the game that affect the incentives of private actors (Milhaupt and West 2004).

Table 4.4 summarizes all the steps taken in commercial code reform, as well as the political pathway used in the reform and its key supporters. It lists all instances of commercial code reform since 1993, as well as the key political supporters behind each revision of the law.

The table demonstrates that corporate governance reforms followed an ebb-and-flow pathway. On one side, when supported by a powerful political entrepreneur, the METI-investor coalition pushed for investor-friendly reforms. On the other side, when the political autonomy of political reformers was weaker, an alternative coalition led by Keidanren and key backers within the LDP pushed for its own manager-friendly reforms through bills introduced by LDP MPs. Several LDP MPs thus became alternative commercial code entrepreneurs: Ota Seiichi and Yasuoka Okiharu in particular.

The opening shot of commercial code reform took place in 1993, when the Diet lowered filing fees in shareholder derivative suits from a percentage of requested damages to a flat ¥8,200 ($80).[105] The law was changed partly because of pressure from the United States in the Structural Impediment Initiative (SII) talks and partly following a legal judgment by the Tokyo High Court in the Nikkō Securities case. It is a case of institutional change happening without political leadership and with a court as the first mover. Few knew that this minor and technical change would lead to a drastic increase in shareholder suits and shareholder rights. Milhaupt and West (2004, 9) report that there were fewer than twenty derivative suits between 1950 and 1990 and only eighty-four pending suits in the legal system at the end of 1993. The high fees proved too high a transaction cost. By 1996, however, there were 174 pending suits and the number jumped to 286 suits in 1999. The impact of small institutional change became most visible in September 2000, when the Osaka District Court ruled against eleven managing directors of Daiwa Bank and ordered them to pay the unprecedented amount of $775 million to the company.

Despite this snowball effect, the 1993 reform was minor and significant commercial code reform only really began in 1997 under a different kind of political entrepreneurship. The main political actor in 1997 was Yamasaki Taku, head of the policy research council of the LDP (PARC), and a close ally to Prime Minister Hashimoto. Yamasaki provided support to Yasuoka Okiharu, a member of his faction. It is Yasuoka who introduced the

---

105. See the excellent analysis by Milhaupt and West (2004, 5–22).

Table 4.4. Revisions of the commercial code in Japan since 1993

Date (year–month)	Item	Significance	Legal process (government bill, MP bill)	Supporters (origin of amendment)
1993–05	• Easier shareholder derivative lawsuits and inspections • Introduction of board of statutory auditors (*kansayaku*)	++	Government (MOJ)	U.S. (SII talks) court system (1992 ruling)
1993–05	• Removal of limits on the issuance of corporate bonds	+	Government (MOJ)	Keidanren
1994–06	• Easier acquisition (*kisei no kanwa*) of Treasury stock (*jiko kabushiki no shutoku*)˙	+	Government (MOJ)	Keidanren
1997–5–16 (2 bills)	• Introduction of stock options • Introduction of possibility of cancellation of shares (*kabushiki shōkyaku*)	++	**MP Bill (Yasuoka Okiharu)**	Keidanren, LDP
1997–5–30	• Simplification of merger procedures	++	Government (MOJ)	MITI—Keidanren
1997–11	• Stiffening penalties on *sōkaiya*	++	Government (MOJ)	(related to scandal of Sagawa Kyubin)
1998–06	• Simplification of cancellation of shares	+	**MP Bill (Yasuoka Okiharu)**	Keidanren, LDP
1999–08	• Share transfer (*kabushiki iten*), stock-for-stock exchange (*kabushiki kōkan*) systems • Real value financial evaluation	++	Government Bills (fast track, linked to Industrial Competitiveness Council—ICC)	MITI, Prime Minister, Keidanren

(*Table 4.4*—*cont.*)

Date (year–month)	Item	Significance	Legal process (government bill, MP bill)	Supporters (origin of amendment)
2000–05	• Company spinoff system (*kaisha bunkatsu seido*) • Extension of authorization of cancellation of shares	++	Government (linked to ICC)	MITI Keidanren
2001–06	• Removal of ban on Treasury stocks (*jiko kabushiki no shutoku, kinko kabu*)—liberalization in principle • Elimination of stocks with set face value (*gakumen kabushiki*), easier use of stock splits (*kabushiki bunkatsu*) (allocation of voting rights)	++	**MP bill (Aizawa Hideyuki)**	Keidanren, LDP
2001–11	• Electronic shareholder meetings (electronic documents and voting), paperless commercial papers • Liberalization of stock options • Introduction of new types of stocks: tracking stocks, new stock acquisition rights (*shin kabu yoyaku ken seido*)	++	Government (linked to ICC)	METI, MOJ
2001–12	• Strengthening of statutory auditors, limitation of executive liability	+++	**MP Bill (*giin rippō*)—Ota Seiichi**	Keidanren, LDP (Ota, Yasuoka)
2001–2002–05	(Failure of attempt to introduce mandatory executive director, *shagai torishimariyaku no kyōsei*)	+++	Government (MOJ, METI)	METI (opposed by Keidanren)
2002–05	• Introduction of new option for corporate organization: U.S.-style board of directors okayed instead of statutory auditory system • Requirement of consolidated financial accounts	+++	Government	MOJ, METI Inclusion of Keidanren interests in compromise

			MP Bill (Shiozaki Yasuhisa)	
2003	• Liberalization of Treasury stock acquisition rules, change in mid-term dividend rules			Keidanren, LDP
2004	• Coercive paperless-stock system for public corporations, • Web-disclosure system	+	Government (MOJ)	
2005–05	• New Company Law (*Kaisha Hō*): modernization of language, introduction of limited liability corporations: - easier M&A (cash and bond OK, easier shareholder approval) - easier company creation - reduced director requirements - easier fundraising - internal controls required	++++	Government	METI, MOJ (role of former minister Yasuoka), LDP's Amari Akira on M&A issues; voice given to variety of actors in process (Keidanren, Rengo unions, legal scholars, SMEs.)

Sources: Chuo University 2006; Masaki 2007 (forthcoming); Nakamura 2005; Yokowo and Masaki 2002, 2004; and personal interviews (METI, MOJ, Keidanren). The author is also grateful for the comments received from Masaki Yoshihisa (Nippon Keidanren) and Matsui Tomoyo (Tohoku University).
The evaluation of the significance (from + to +++) is based on the emerging consensus within these interviews.

first MP-led bill as a means to force the Ministry of Justice to move toward reform. METI was not particularly opposed to reform but saw it as a lower priority compared to revisions on merger procedures or share swaps. METI feared that this amendment would slow the agenda on mergers. For Yasuoka and Yamazaki the reform process led to a good political outcome: it gave them policy traction, changed the view that choosing a specialization in legal affairs for a MP (*hōmu zoku*) was useless, and made the issue of legal change into a tool for gaining power. This issue does not require a budget (*okane iranai keizai seisaku*), only legal change.[106]

Interestingly, the Yamasaki link to commercial code reform remained intact under Koizumi, thanks to the close relationship between Yamasaki and Koizumi. However, the latest entrepreneurial LDP MP trying to ride the issue of commercial code reform is Amari Akira from the Yamasaki faction. He managed to create a new Diet committee in charge of commercial code reform (*Kigyō tōchi ni kan suru iinkai*). As a result, Amari tends to claim leadership of the commercial reform process but also defends a pro-management position due to his links to small and medium enterprises and to Keidanren.[107]

In 1999, under Yosano's and Obuchi's leadership, commercial reforms came to be seen as a way to boost the economy without using fiscal stimulus (win-win).[108] The amendments passed between 1999 and 2004 included the liberalization of stock options and stock swaps, partial liberalization of mergers and acquisitions, changes in the board structure (introducing the option of a U.S.-style board) and changes in the role of statutory auditors.[109] Although Dore (2005) questions whether all these changes are real or just cosmetic and Milhaupt (2003b) acknowledges that the Japanese pathway is one of *enabling* reforms, rather than making reforms mandatory (as in Korea), most current observers acknowledge that the combined effect of institutional change on firm behavior is considerable (Milhaupt and West 2004; Patrick 2004). Legal change has introduced a new set of incentives for private actors.

Politically, the reform of the commercial code is a protracted and checkered process with bursts of reforms, periods of low visibility, and periods of counter-reforms under high political visibility. In 1999 and early 2000, the reforms benefited from the strong involvement of Yosano and Obuchi. The preparation of subsequent change continued under MITI and the Ministry

---

106. Interview with senior Keidanren official in charge of commercial code reforms, 12 May 2006.

107. Ibid.

108. Ibid.

109. See Dore (2005); Jackson (2003); Milhaupt (2003a, 2004); Patrick (2004) for reviews of the sequence of legal reforms. See Gourevitch and Shinn (2005) for an analysis of change in Japanese corporate governance.

of Justice. At the same time, Keidanren was successful in developing its own alternative reform agenda, relying on bills introduced by MPs in the LDP.

The mother of all battles on the commercial code took place in 2001 over the METI-inspired idea to introduce two mandatory external directors in all corporations (*shagai torishimariyaku no kyōsei*). This was a pro-investor move. METI argued that corporate structures had to be improved for the sake of efficiency and transparency. Without such change, long-term competitiveness of Japanese firms would suffer. METI also argued that it was necessary to build a system "where the stock market could put pressure on corporations." The mandatory executive director plan was such a system. As a Ministry of Justice official said, "You cannot improve Japanese corporations without an external push."[110]

Due to the lack of political coverage, the METI plan ended in defeat. Instead, Keidanren and its LDP allies succeeded in strengthening the Japanese-style auditor's system through a competing MP-led bill. In 2002, a compromise bill introduced a French New Economic Regulations–style voluntary system.[111] In 2001, it was Ota Seiichi who introduced the strategic pro-Keidanren bill, outlining an alternative type of political entrepreneurship.[112] A member of the Horiuchi faction from Fukuoka prefecture, Ota had to make up for a weaker position within the LDP, because he defected in 1994 to join the new Liberal Party (*Jiyūtō*) and then the New Frontier Party (*Shinshintō*). Although Ota returned to the LDP in May 1995, he has been marked as a past betrayer (*ikkai uragiri*). As a result, he is motivated to prove his party commitment by entrepreneurially defending some of the key LDP supporters.[113] Ironically, Ota was a reformer in the late 1980s. Ohta had to resign from his Diet seat in November 2003 because of a scandal arising from sexist remarks.

The great battle over mandatory directors outlined a direct rift between post-Yosano METI and Keidanren over the interest of investors and the golden bargain. "METI was thinking of investors and also of its own interests," argued a Keidanren official.[114] Keidanren was suspicious of METI because of its international openness agenda, an agenda pursued since the 1960s and because of the close personal links between METI and foreign investors (or the U.S. Chamber of Commerce). An argument put forth by Keidanren to METI went along these lines: "Once you do all this, you will lose control of these companies and lose your job as well. They will be

110. Interview with key official at the Ministry of Justice involved in commercial code reforms. 10 April 2006.
111. Interview with Matsui Tomoyo, 27 March 2006.
112. Interview with key official at the Ministry of Justice involved in commercial code reforms, 10 April 2006.
113. Various interviews.
114. Interview, 12 May 2006.

foreign-controlled." LDP politicians side with Keidanren and are national-ist. Without the input of strong political entrepreneurs such as Yosano and Obuchi, the pro-reform agenda cannot win. The crux of the fight between Keidanren and METI revolved around one point: using the law to create in-centives and force change. Keidanren fought bitterly against this.[115]

The next big burst of change took place after 2002, under Koizumi's ac-quiescent leadership. By 2004–05, however, a political countercurrent rose, particularly in response to a high profile merger battle over the future of NBS broadcasting and Fuji television in spring 2005. The political scene in 2005 involved efforts by LDP leaders to reduce the impact of past reforms and make mergers and acquisitions by foreign firms more difficult, particu-larly through the postponement of M&A through share exchange.

In sum, the protracted battle over the commercial code is a wonderful experimental arena to test the politics of corporate reform. The process shows that significant pro-investor reforms took place when powerful politi-cal entrepreneurs had a high degree of political autonomy and the ability to outdo opponents or to effect grand bargains. When this capacity declined in 2000–02, this provided a crucial opening for interest groups and party mem-bers opposed to such reforms to strike a preemptive move through compet-ing regulation. Ironically, this countermove took place through another kind of political entrepreneurship in the Diet.

Institutional Change and Incomplete Reforms

In this chapter I have made several important contributions to the study of Japanese political economy. First, I have shown that significant structural reforms targeting corporate restructuring have been occurring in Japan over the past ten years. The trigger for such reforms has been provided by financial globalization, particularly the growing presence of foreign in-vestors in the domestic stock market. Once equity inflows reach a level high enough to have a significant impact on the stock market level, they become the vector of transmission for global corporate norms and clash with the traditional Japanese model. They carry the reality of the golden bargain into Japanese political economy.

Next, I have shown how political entrepreneurs, such as Yosano Kaoru, Obuchi Keizō, and Koizumi Junichirō have played a key role in pushing reforms forward. At the same time, Japan's structural reforms are slower than those in France and Korea because of greater constraints on the political au-tonomy of political leaders and fewer opportunities for effective bureaucratic

---

115. Interview with senior Keidanren official in charge of commercial code reforms, 12 May 2006.

delegation. In order to defeat entrenched domestic coalitions that oppose structural reforms, reforms require the personal involvement of a prime minister who controls his or her governing coalition and a relatively coherent bureaucratic support. Even then, structural reforms are slowed down in the Japanese case by legislative institutions that limit the cabinet's control of the legislative agenda. To break this last deadlock, the cabinet must have the ability to sway most key governing party leaders and cooperate successfully with opposition parties. Such conditions were fulfilled to some extent under Prime Ministers Hashimoto and Obuchi, but less so under their two successors. Furthermore, the Japanese state cannot rely on the Trojan horse of an international institution like the IMF or the EU to implement the structural reform agenda. Ironically, the Japanese state turns out to be weaker than is usually assumed, especially in comparison to France and Korea.

The structural reforms of 1999 were certainly quite an achievement for a Japanese political system that is well known for its aversion to reform. At the same time, the reform process revealed some important limits and vulnerabilities. These limits explain why such reforms have been rare and were not produced under the subsequent Mori government. In certain cases, counter-reforms have taken place. For example, in December 1999, the LDP decided in a closed-room meeting to postpone the imposition of a ceiling on government guarantees of certain bank deposits (payoff). This delay has been seen as a step backward for the spread of corporate governance and for corporate restructuring. Foreign investors have booed it. More crucially, the processing of bad bank loans and the imposition of strict criteria (ROE, ROA) for bank lending has been repeatedly delayed.

The successful experience of the ICC depended on a prime minister who was able to convince the majority party (LDP) and the coalition parties (LP, Kōmeitō) to extend the Diet and urgently consider the reform projects. This required an unusual combination of favorable political factors. During the Koizumi years, however, a combination of micro-level institutional reforms seemed to open more space for future political entrepreneurs. Legislative changes and changes in LDP custom have opened a new legislative pathway whereby the cabinet could directly introduce legislation in the Diet independent of party and bureaucracy. At the same time, changes in leadership selection rules in the LDP in 2001 and weaker factional cohesion resulting from electoral reforms have transformed the relationship between party leader and party. While Koizumi found himself limited by the opposition of his own party throughout most of his rule, it is likely that his successors will have more strategic political autonomy. Japan may be entering a phase of faster change through more Westminster-like cabinet leadership.

5

Korea: Systemic Transformation

It is no secret that the Korean miracle crashed in December 1997, and that Korea had to accept stringent conditions in exchange for an IMF bailout. Likewise, the relative speed and depth of structural reforms in Korea in the wake of the financial crisis are now well known and analyzed.[1] The resumption of rapid economic growth in the years 1999–2003, after the deep recession of 1998, has proven the effectiveness of Korean structural reforms. The centrality of corporate restructuring, or "*chaebol* reforms," to the process of post-1997 reforms is also well understood.[2] Most analysts of the Korean financial crisis concur that the uncontrolled dominance of large *chaebols* (conglomerates) in the Korean economy was an essential component of the crisis. In a typical analysis, Korean analyst You Jong-Keun (1999, 19) closes a review of the Korean reform process with the following words: "The success or failure of *chaebol* restructuring will determine the direction of Korea's paradigm shift." And indeed, despite some slowing in the reform process after 2000 and especially after 2002, the Korean reform path has been sweeping and has changed power relations within the Korean political economy. They have simultaneously strengthened market relations and the voice of the state. Naturally, these reforms took place in the context of an

1. Chow and Gill 2000; Drysdale 2000; Goldstein 1998; Graham 2003; Haggard 2000; Haggard, Lim, and Kim 2003; International Labor Office 1998; Kihl 2005; Korean Economic Institute of America 2000; Lamfalussy 2000; Noble and Ravenhill 2000; Park 2000; Pempel 1999b; Woo, Sachs, and Schwab 2000; Yoo 1999b; You 1999; Zhang 1998.

2. This is true both in the policy analyses (IMF, OECD, Korean government) and in the theoretical literature quoted above.

IMF bailout, but, as this chapter demonstrates, corporate restructuring reforms were not determined by the IMF agreement.

Why was the Korean government willing and able to engage in systemic reforms and to go much further than countries such as France or Japan? What explains the capacity of Korean leaders to do so and to act on the new incentives from the outside?

In response to these questions, this chapter argues that Korean corporate reforms were an extreme case of political entrepreneurship under conditions of high political autonomy and high capacity for bureaucratic delegation. The reform path cannot be understood without reference to President Kim Dae-Jung's personal involvement and leadership, together with key political advisers who developed a strong entrepreneurial vision of change in Korea. Kim happened to be elected in December 1997, just at the height of the Korean financial crisis. Yet it may have been the tipping point that shaped a large part of the corporate reform drive. His personal vision of a more democratic and less oligopolistic Korea played a large role in his reform plan. The fact that he came from a region long left behind by past pro-*chaebol* authoritarian governments also shaped his vision of a more liberalized Korea. In addition, Kim sought to enlarge his regional Cholla-based (Jeolla-based) support coalition into the greater Seoul area by taking the mantle of a modern reformist.

While reforms were initially motivated by the demands of the IMF, the U.S. Treasury, and foreign lenders (whose preferences were filtered through the U.S. Treasury and the IMF), the voice of global equity investors gradually became the dominant one after mid-1998. The government was particularly sensitive to the preferences of global equity investors because it supported a general shift from debt-financing to equity-and-bond financing. In order to make Korea attractive to foreign investors (and initially to meet IMF demands), the Korean government passed an amazing series of structural reforms in early 1998 and directly took on the very *chaebols* that it had nurtured for thirty years. As the reform process successfully unfolded, the share of foreign investors in the Korean stock market doubled from the limited level of 13.7 percent in 1997 to 30 percent in 2000 and 36 percent in 2002.[3]

Regarding the reform capacity of political entrepreneurs, Korea presents an interesting case of dualism. The period from 1997 to 2002 offers a shift from an extremely high level of presidential control of the legislative agenda to a very low level after the 2000 legislative elections. In the wake of a presidential election (such as that of December 1997, which brought Kim Dae-Jung to power), the president is usually able to obtain a ruling coalition

---

3. Data provided by Lim Wonhyuk (Korea Development Institute) based on data from the Korean Stock Exchange.

in parliament and to hold great power. He or she is able to rapidly push a reform agenda forward, especially in comparison to the Japanese case (and even the French case). The crisis situation in 1998 greatly enhanced the executive control of the legislative agenda by disarming the opposition.[4] However, both the single five-year term allowed to a president and the occurrence of mid-term legislative elections during the presidential term rapidly reduce the executive to lame-duck status and cripple the degree of executive control over the legislative agenda. Thus, the Kim Dae-Jung administration lost the ability to push important reforms after the legislative elections in April 2000. These institutional features have the side effect of shortening the political window of opportunity and enhancing the initial push for reforms in the wake of a presidential election. The same process occurred with the Kim Young Sam administration (1993–97).

Drawing on interviews with top bureaucrats and other insiders, I argue that the leeway of the Korean government in the process of corporate reforms was larger than is usually assumed. While the Korean government was forced to accept IMF conditions regarding monetary and fiscal policy and to accept U.S. conditions regarding financial liberalization and market opening reforms, it was the driving force in the area of *chaebol* reforms. In fact, the clauses relating to *chaebol* reforms were included in the December 1997 letters of intent at the request of the Korean side. President Kim Dae-Jung and his close advisers in the transition team saw the IMF agreement as a golden opportunity to push for corporate and financial reforms (micro-economic reforms) that had proven politically impossible in 1995–97. Thus, the Korean leadership pursued its own reform agenda, on top of reforms that were imposed by the IMF.

The Korean case supports the overall argument of this book and provides insight into the interactions between capital flows and domestic institutions because of the unusually high degree of executive control of the legislative agenda after presidential elections. At the same time, I acknowledge a few important limitations to the full comparability of Korea with Japan and France. First and foremost, the intensity of the financial crisis in December 1997 and the intrusion of the IMF agreement constitute an important difference. While the crisis provided the government with an unusual consensus for reform within the population and muted many of the fiercest opponents, the IMF agreement did force the hand of the Korean government in many respects, although not too significantly in the area of *chaebol* reforms. Furthermore, Korea found itself in a different initial situation from France and Japan in 1997. Having just joined the OECD in 1996, it was at an earlier stage of economic maturity. Having only begun financial liberalization in 1992–93, it was not yet fully exposed to free global portfolio flows. In fact,

---

4. See for example Haggard (2000, 101) on the cross-party cooperation in parliament in early 1998.

the post-1997 reforms include both the accomplishment of financial liberalization and the corporate structural reforms that are the focus of this book. Finally, the post-1997 reform process has proven extremely fluid and volatile and is still difficult to fully assess at the moment. Some analysts have taken an increasingly pessimistic view after the winter of 1999 and argue that *chaebol* reforms were insufficient and incomplete. The record of reform under President Roh Moo Hyun seem to partly confirm such assessments.

While these limitations are important and must be acknowledged, the Korean case remains a useful one in this comparative study. Not all post-1997 reforms were mechanically driven by the financial crisis and the IMF agreement. In fact, *chaebol* reforms are probably where the Korean government had the largest degree of autonomy. Financial liberalization had proceeded sufficiently far by 1997 to produce the financial crisis and thus to bring Korea into a post-financial deregulation stage. Even if the process of *chaebol* reforms is still ongoing and could yet lead to different outcomes, the sheer extent and speed of the transformation that occurred in 1997–99 are not disputed and warrant explanation.

The Great Financial Crisis and Degrees of Political Autonomy

The process of structural reform in Korea in 1998 clearly took place under unusual circumstances. First, Korea is unique with respect to the presence of massive conglomerates that have oligopolistic control over most major industries. In addition, in November 1997, Korea found itself close to a situation of national insolvency. Between June and December 1997, the won to dollar exchange rate decreased by 48 percent and the stock market collapsed by 50 percent (Goldstein 1998). With only a few days of foreign reserves left and a massive outstanding short-term debt denominated in dollars, Korea had no choice but to accept a massive $57 billion IMF rescue package, complete with a long list of tight conditions. The IMF-imposed high interest rates and budgetary restrictions led to a deep recession in 1998. During that grim year, Korea saw its GDP shrink by 5.8 percent (compared to positive growth of 9 percent in 1995, 7 percent in 1996, and 5 percent in 1997). Unemployment went from 2.6 percent in December 1997 to 9 percent by mid-1998. Given the weak nature of the safety net, the economic recession led to a huge increase in poverty, social despair, crimes, and suicides. The World Bank later criticized the IMF for creating unnecessary pain in Korea, as well as in other East Asian countries.[5] Both the depth of the economic crisis and the IMF program (on top of the feeling of

5. See chap. 5 in World Bank (1998). See also International Labor Office (1998).

national humiliation) certainly shaped the intense government reform program.

What matters most, however, is to analyze the forces that were at work in causing the crisis and in shaping the IMF program. A broad and intense intellectual debate on the origins of Asian and Korean financial crises has animated economists, political scientists, and policy analysts since 1997. The core of the debate can be summarized with one single phrase: Asian sins versus global speculators. Was the crisis precipitated by crony capitalism and structural weaknesses in the financial system or was it more the product of unprecedented contagion in the global financial system?

The broad consensus that emerges from the vast literature on the crisis is the probable interactive effects between an overly hasty financial deregulation (post-1992 in the Korean case), volatile capital flows, and an economic structure that was built upon a model of high-debt, high-investment, and weak corporate governance. *Chaebols* drove the Korean economic miracle (Clifford 1998, chap. 8; Kang 1996; Woo-Cumings 1999, 120) but were too risk-prone to be left free to roam on the global lending market. In addition, the principal-agent relationship between the state and *chaebols* was further eroded by post-1987 democratization and the decrease of direct influence by the state.[6] At its core, the Korean crisis was caused by unacknowledged socialization at the national level of the high risk incurred by expansive *chaebols*. They thrived on the moral hazard induced by the "too big to fail" perception. On the eve of the financial crisis, access to international finance allowed them to engage in a massive investment binge. In 1996 alone, Daewoo Motors began production in a new plant in Romania, took over a major corporation in Poland (establishing Daewoo-FSO), began production in new plants in Uzbekistan and Vietnam, launched a new car (the compact Lanos), and began production of passenger cars in the brand new domestic Kunsan (Gunsan) plant. This came on the heels of similar investments in China, Germany, and Korea in 1995. Investment on such a vast scale has rarely been witnessed anywhere.

The IMF agreement with Korea is particularly interesting for its breadth and variety of components. The agreement was contained in an initial letter of intent (3 December 1997). This letter was later complemented by four additional letters of intent (24 December 1997, 7 January 1998, 5 and

---

6. See an account of the *chaebol* debate in Yoo (1999a) and Yoo and Lim (1999). "Democratization since 1987 and the consequent instabilities put an end to the past patriarchal authoritarianism" (Yoo 1999a, 142). Yoo also argues that the "*chaebol* problem" includes six major failures: failure of corporate governance, failure of the financial market, failure of the exit market, political influence of *chaebol* economic power over government policy decisions, misconceptions on the nature of business corporations, and failure of law enforcement (146). See also Jung and Kim (1999, 350–51) for an argument that combines deregulation, globalization, and democratization.

7 February 1998). The most dramatic and high-stakes agreement was the one reached in the first letter of intent—the one that initiated the IMF bailout package. Blustein (2001) gives a vivid account of the ten intense days of negotiations between the IMF team, led by Hubert Neiss, the Korean team, led by newly appointed Finance Minister Lim Chang Yuel, and the secret U.S. Treasury team, led by undersecretary David Lipton (who had checked into the Hilton hotel on a different floor from the IMF team). The negotiations closed with the high-powered arrival of IMF Director Michel Camdessus on 3 December 1997 and the robust intervention of U.S. Treasury Secretary Robert Rubin through a lengthy phone call to Camdessus.

As Matthews (1998) argues, the core IMF agreements of 3 December and 24 December contained three distinct agendas. First, they included a classic IMF agenda that called for "monetary rectitude, financial austerity, and fiscal responsibility." This agenda was similar to that pursued by the IMF in previous stand-by agreements reached with Latin American countries. For example, the IMF demanded that Korea "play the confidence game."

The IMF stand-by agreements included a second component, "a conspicuous American agenda to open up the Korean economy to foreign investment" (Matthews 1998). This plan led to a series of clauses that called for liberalizing foreign investment (FDI as well as investment in the Korean stock and bond markets)[7] and allowing foreign banks to enter the domestic financial sector.[8] They required Korea to raise the ceiling on aggregate foreign investment in Korean equities from 26 to 50 percent immediately and to 55 percent by the end of 1998. This was changed in the second agreement of 24 December with the increased requirement that aggregate foreign investment in foreign equities be allowed up to 55 percent immediately and without restrictions by the end of 1998. They also included full access to domestic money market instruments and to the domestic corporate bond market. In fact, the 24 December agreement included an amazing eighteen separate clauses related to capital account liberalization (up from six in the 3 December agreement). Blustein (2001, 143) writes: "Lobbying by American financial service firms, which wanted to crack the Korean market, was the driving force behind the Treasury's pressure on Seoul."

This second agenda extended to trade as well, revealing an interesting facet of IMF politics. It is noteworthy that trade restrictions were not connected in

7. See clauses under the heading "Capital Account Liberalization" in the initial stand-by agreement. They require Korea to raise the ceiling on aggregate foreign investment in Korean equities from 26 percent to 50 percent immediately and to 55 percent by the end of 1998. They also include full access to domestic money market instruments, and to the domestic corporate bond market.

8. See for example the eleventh clause under the heading "Restructuring and Reform Measures" in the first agreement.

any way to the Korean financial crisis. The very extensive program of opening trade was included not only at the urging of the U.S. side, but also at Japan's urging. It became a rare case of Japan's readiness to use its financial muscle (and status as number 2 IMF shareholder) in international affairs. In fact, Japan managed to include in the IMF agreement the removal of the very trade restrictions that had targeted Japanese cultural products since 1945, a Korean response to Japanese colonialism. These restrictions fell under the so-called Import Diversification Program (IDP). According to a report from the Korean government, the IDP is "a system of restricting imports from a specific country from which Korea is experiencing a serious trade deficit. This system, which restricts importation by designating non-importable items from that country—but whose importation is allowed from other countries—is currently only applied towards Japan. The Korean government has agreed with the IMF to completely abolish the IDP by June 1999."[9] The abolition of the IDP program was included in the initial IMF agreement and confirmed in the more extensive 24 December agreement. The above definition underlines Japan's probable frustration with the IDP program and their likely satisfaction at its removal. The case further underlines the extent of the concessions Korea had to accept in this IMF agreement. Surprisingly, the suppression of the IDP regulation happened discreetly in both Korea and Japan, although the impact on Korean daily life was obvious. It led to a mild increase in the sales of Japanese videos and other cultural products.

The third component of the IMF agreement is a fascinating and unrecognized one. As already acknowledged by Matthews (1998), the long list of structural clauses relating to financial reforms, corporate governance, *chaebol* reforms, and bankruptcy reforms was a most unusual one for IMF agreements. The reason is simple: it was "Korean-instigated." In particular, under the "Financial Restructuring" clause, the initial agreement committed the Korean government to passing a bill to consolidate supervision of all banks as well as to the restructuring of troubled financial institutions. These features were clearly reminiscent of the failed financial reform bill of November 1997, a bill that had been championed by reformers such as Lee Suk-Chae (senior secretary to President Kim Young Sam) and voted down by parliament because of lobbying by financial institutions. The section on prudential regulation was nearly identical to a proposal made by the Korea Development Institute (KDI)—a Ministry of Finance and Economy (MOFE) think tank—in the preceding years.[10] In addition, the IMF agreement committed Korea to enforcing the BIS banking standards and principles and to

---

9. KIEP Policy Paper, 1998.
10. Interview with KDI official, May 2000.

a series of financial regulatory reforms. Such measures may have been part of the agenda of both the Korean government and the IMF/U.S. negotiators. In any case, they greatly empowered the Kim Dae-Jung government to unfold the thorough regulatory program that they had been drafting for years.

On the corporate front, the IMF agreement included clauses that committed Korea to consolidated accounting statements, the transparency of corporate balance sheets, and the end of government subsidies (in the initial IMF agreement). Moreover, the list of clauses included under the heading of "Corporate Governance and Corporate Structure" closed with two important stipulations that greatly empowered the state to act against *chaebols*:

> Measures will be worked out and implemented to reduce the high debt-to-equity ratio of corporations, and capital markets will be developed to reduce the share of bank financing by corporations.
>
> Measures will be worked out and implemented to change the system of mutual guarantees within conglomerates to reduce the risk it involves.

For good measure, these clauses were followed by a most unusual clause on the labor market that committed Korea to "improving labor market flexibility." This last clause appears counterintuitive in a time of deep social distress. Interestingly, nothing was added on *chaebol* reforms in the second and third letters of intent.

For this third component of the IMF agreement the Korean government negotiators (mostly from MOFE) put together some of the reform drafts that had been ready for months or years and passed them on to the IMF team. More precisely,

> The economic reformers believed that it was a good chance to impose measures on *chaebols* (a hidden agenda). . . . While the IMF agreement was bad with respect to the macro-economy, it provided a good opportunity to reform *chaebols* and formed the basis for the 200 percent ratio [later imposed on them]. . . . The Korean government just placed the draft on the table and gave it to the IMF. . . . It was not an official position of the Korean government. [It was done informally and made possible by the fact that] the Korean negotiators and the IMF negotiators were friends. The Korean negotiators were all former IMF people.[11]

Hence, the IMF became partly a tool for the Korean reformers in the Kim Dae-Jung team to push corporate reforms forward, similar to the way

---

11. Interview with top Korean bureaucrat, 8 June 2000.

French political leaders have sometimes used the EU as a Trojan horse to break domestic political deadlocks. The IMF agreement had the effect of increasing the degree of political control over the legislative agenda and the initial degree of political autonomy of the Kim Dae-Jung government. Corporate reforms had also been an enduring priority of MOFE and KDI in the few years preceding 1997. In fact, according to the high-level bureaucrat quoted above, the mid-1990s marked a shift in the attitudes of political leaders and MOFE bureaucrats from pro-*chaebol* to anti-*chaebol*. They became convinced that the future competitiveness of the Korean economy required them to break the nexus between *chaebols* and banks, and to push for corporate restructuring.

Chaebol reforms and corporate restructuring emerged as a reform priority for Korean political reformers in the mid-1990s, but their attempts hit the wall of *chaebol*-political networks. While the IMF agreement in the wake of the financial crisis of November 1997 imposed on Korea an amazing array of stringent conditions and market-opening measures, it also provided new Korean political entrepreneurs with a window of opportunity to initiate far-reaching *chaebol* reforms, while leaving them free to decide the precise process and content of these reforms.

The Korean Record: Rapid and Multi-Pronged Reforms after 1997

Two features mark the post-1997 process of *chaebol* reforms: their (initial) speed and depth, in contrast to earlier attempts in 1995–97, and their dual track nature. In the words of Yoon Youngmo, international secretary of the Korea Confederation of Trade Unions, "The Korean government's efforts—propelled by the prescription and close monitoring by the IMF and the World Bank—to bring about a 'reform' of the *chaebol* structure and system has been a mixed bag of classical liberal measures, neo-liberal measures, and measures typical of developmental dictatorships."[12] Likewise, Haggard argues that two lines (bank-led restructuring and command-and-control) "coexisted in an uneasy mix" (2000, 150).

Appendix table A3a presents the list of corporate reforms (Types I and II as defined in chapter 2), while appendix table A3b introduces the chronology of direct government interventions (Type III). In particular, seventeen major economic reforms were passed by the parliament on 14 February 1998 (eleven days before the inauguration of President Kim Dae-Jung). These laws included the Bank Act, the Corporate Reorganization Act, the Bankruptcy Act, and the Corporate Tax Law. All the measures detailed

12. Yoo 1999b.

below came at the same time as far-reaching reforms relating to labor, finance, public sector, trade, and foreign investment liberalization. Regarding investment, three key reforms took place in 1998: the opening of financial industries to foreign investment in March, the overhaul of foreign investment laws in April, and the Foreign Investment Inducement Act in September. As for trade, an important step took place in December 1998 when the government lifted the ban on imports of thirty-two Japanese products under the IDP. In June 1999, the ban on the last sixteen Japanese products was lifted as well.

The combination of these two tables reveals the extraordinary intensity and multi-pronged nature of corporate reforms, especially in 1998. Appendix table A3a shows, first of all, the dramatic speed and extent of corporate reforms in Korea in 1998, especially in contrast to Japan and France. The government deployed the full array of orthodox corporate reforms. In the first instance, it passed the full battery of corporate governance reforms recommended by the OECD and thus took concrete steps toward a flexible and market-led pattern of corporate restructuring. At the same time, the government created a fully independent regulatory agency, the Financial Supervisory Commission (FSC), with authority over both financial and corporate restructuring. As argued by Haggard (2000, 229), the FSC served "to reduce the problems caused by the existence of multiple veto gates and private-sector resistance." Through the FSC and through state control over banks (many of which were nationalized by the infusion of public funds after December 1997), the government pushed for orderly debt workout plans and bank-led corporate restructuring.

But the government went far beyond these twin orthodox engines in its drive for corporate restructuring. Appendix table A3b reveals the extent of direct state involvement in restructuring through Type III methods. The government relied on direct non-regulatory steps to force *chaebols* to accelerate restructuring. The two key planks of this direct action were the imposition of a debt-to-equity ratio of 200 percent on top *chaebols* (under the threat of removing their access to bank funding), and the Big Deal. The Big Deal was a direct attempt to force *chaebols* to rationalize and restructure by swapping and consolidating their different business sectors. The idea of the Big Deal originated in the Blue House (the president's office)[13] and was epitomized by a meeting at the Blue House between the president and the leaders of the top five *chaebols*. It is unparalleled in any other OECD country and probably any other Asian country affected by the East Asian crisis. Also important was the role of the government in letting Daewoo go

---

13. Information from interviews pointed to a group of key advisers around President Kim Dae-Jung as the masterminds behind the Big Deal. They include Kim Yong-Hwan (former bureaucrat during the 1971 management crisis), Kang Bong-Kyun, and Lee Hun-Jae.

bankrupt and in facilitating the takeover of Samsung Motors by Renault of France (itself controlled by the French state). The Daewoo decision was enormously sensitive because it was the fourth largest *chaebol* and had great impact on the job market: it is estimated that Daewoo employed 2.5 million people.

Tables A3a and A3b together underline key features about the Korean corporate reforms that have to be explained. The most immediate feature of these reforms is their intensity, speed, and reach. True, a vast debate about their actual effectiveness has arisen in Korea and beyond since 1999 (Graham 2000, 2003; Haggard, Lim, and Kim 2003; Noland 2000; Patrick 1999; Yoo 1999a, b). Most of the criticisms relate to the Big Deal and the 200 percent ratio, which are seen as returns to 1970s-era totalitarianism. Other criticisms relate to the slowness of restructuring in the Hyundai group (a long saga in 2000–01), the absence of further reforms after 1999, and the enduring weight of *chaebols* in the economy and the bond market. Concern has grown over *chaebol* domination of non-bank financial institutions (Noland 2000, 13). There was concern over the enduring high investments and debt of *chaebols*. While the full assessment of the effectiveness of corporate reforms is beyond the scope of this study, it is reasonable to say that these reforms have gone an amazingly long way in restructuring the Korean economy. Such recognition of the immensity of change wrought on the Korean economy is supported by OECD reviews (1999, 2000) as well as by interviews with OECD officials, bureaucrats in MOFE and KDI, labor officials at Daewoo, and a legal counsel to Daewoo. That *chaebols* did reduce their debt-to-equity ratio to 200 percent and that Daewoo went belly-up are testimonies to the intensity of change.

The contrast with earlier reform attempts under Kim Young-Sam also stands out. While Kim Young Sam marked his presidency with an ambitious program of "globalization reforms" (the so-called *segyehwa* reforms), most analysts agree that these reforms were a failure.[14] They did lead to a first round of financial liberalization (Organisation for Economic Co-operation and Development 1996, 40–82) but failed to bring significant change in the corporate governance of *chaebols* or to spur significant corporate restructuring (Yoo and Lim 1999, 143–46). Samuel Kim (2000, 30) argues that the *chaebols* succeeded in abusing the reform process. The main flaw of reforms lay in the incorrect sequencing of reforms: external opening and democratization before de-concentration. The reform process opened new avenues for *chaebols* without reforming their corporate governance, a classic recipe for moral jeopardy (31). The primary reason given for the failure of *chaebol* reforms under Kim Young Sam is the increased power gained by

14. Clifford 1998; Haggard, Lim, and Kim 2003; Jwa and Kim 1999; Kihl 2005; B.-K. Kim 2000; S. Kim 2000; Moon and Mo 1999; Oh 1999.

chaebols over the bureaucracy through post-1987 democratization and the collusion between *chaebols* and politicians (as well as some bureaucrats). As a final case in point, the package of financial supervision reforms that had been prepared since early 1997 died in the assembly in mid-November 1997. These reforms had been spearheaded by Lee Suk-Chae, a key advisor to President Kim Young Sam,[15] but in the end the president failed to give him the necessary political support, due to his own restricted political autonomy.

The last puzzling feature of post-1997 reforms relates to the odd mix of liberal and directive measures. In a typical analysis, Noland (2000, 13) writes: "The policies of the Korean government have been uneven. The government, through preference or lack of other means, has resorted to relatively illiberal means in its attempt to achieve a more liberal, efficient, and equitable South Korean economy." What are the possible explanations for the unusual reform path in Korea?

The usual explanation of interest-group led reforms is clearly untenable in the Korean case. Given their huge degree of control over the economy and rampant moral risk induced by economic institutions, *chaebols* could engage in one-way globalization: that is, their interest lies in both protecting their tight domestic structure and political voice while supporting financial liberalization. In fact, the saga of corporate reforms after December 1997 is dominated by a continuous fierce conflict between *chaebols* and the government. Throughout the reform process, the government has used all possible means of coercion (regulations, cutting funding, forcing some major bankruptcies) in order to break the opposition of *chaebol* managers. Korea offers the most clear-cut example of corporate reform against the will of corporations.

What about an explanation based on partisan politics? The financial crisis and the initiation of economic reforms did coincide with the election in December 1997 of Kim Dae-Jung, the first true change in ruling coalition since democratization in 1987. Kim Dae-Jung was known as the most enduring democratic opponent to military rule since 1960 and a defender of labor. He also received strong support from the increasingly thriving Korean civil society. Most important, he was known as a long-time opponent of *chaebols* and of *chaebol*-state collusion. However, despite the indubitable role of Kim Dae-Jung as a symbol of democracy and honesty, the partisan politics explanation has major weaknesses.

---

15. He was joined by Kang Kyung-Shik, MOFE minister in January 1997. Together Lee and Kang created the Kang-Lee Presidential Commission on Financial Reforms. After a lengthy process of consultation, Lee and Kang pushed forward the idea of an independent FSC. It is this eventual package that was voted down by the National Assembly in November 1997, the last straw before the full-blown crisis. I am grateful to Kim Byung-Kook for enlightening discussions on the topic.

First, Kim Dae-Jung received a very weak mandate on 18 December 1997 because he got barely 40 percent of the general vote (40.3 percent). His election was primarily due to a split in the opposition vote between the main candidate Lee Hoi Chang (38.7 percent) and Rhee In Je (19.2 percent). The weakness of his ruling coalition would be rapidly revealed when President Kim met with strong opposition in parliament, especially after April 2000. In addition, his predecessor Kim Young Sam had himself been a long-time democratic opponent with strong reform credentials and a strong electoral mandate. Yet, Kim Young Sam could not translate this political change into a capacity for reform.

Second, Korean parties are not split along ideological lines but along regional ones. Kim Dae-Jung came from the southwestern Cholla (Jeolla) region, a distant and historically under-represented region in Korean politics, while Korea's rulers, until 1997, had always come from the Kyongsang (Gyeong Sang) region. Kim Dae-Jung's party swept the vote in Cholla but did not have a single MP elected from Kyongsang. Kim Dae-Jung's primary political agenda lay in redressing the historical injustice between Cholla and Kyongsang, rather than in any ideological redress. Additionally, Kim Dae-Jung did have close connections with a few *chaebols*, particularly Hyundai (a *chaebol* that had fierce conflicts with the previous administration) and Daewoo. Hence the early favors given to Hyundai (the acquisition of Kia in 1998 and the authorization to start a costly and risky tourism enterprise with North Korea) and the fearless attitude of Daewoo in 1998. Kim Dae-Jung's government was a coalition with the most conservative and authoritarian party, the United Liberal Democrats led by Kim Jong-Pil, former director of the infamous Korean Central Intelligence Agency (KCIA) under dictator Park Chung Hee. Kim Jong-Pil was in fact Kim Dae-Jung's prime minister until early 2000. The key reform of the Big Deal did not originate with Kim Dae-Jung's party (the Millennium Democratic Party), but with Pak Tae-Joon, a seventy-year-old retired army general and legendary chairman emeritus of the Pohang Iron and Steel Company.[16] Reportedly, a senior bureaucrat at MOFE was also involved in the decision. This does not support an explanation rooted in partisan politics. Finally, all key reforms passed in 1998 passed under bipartisan leadership. So, the partisan politics explanation does not provide much leverage over the corporate reform process.

A final possible explanation for the intensity of corporate reforms emphasizes the role of public opinion. Given the depth of the financial crisis, the people accepted that reforms were inevitable and necessary. Admittedly, people were opposed to the level of dominance that *chaebols* exerted

---

16. Interviews with a former Korean minister, a political adviser to President Kim Dae-Jung at the Blue House, and a major opposition leader (May and October 2000). See Oh (1999, 228) for details on Pak Tae-Joon life.

over the Korean economy and abhorred the high level of corruption and collusion. This explanation cannot be dismissed outright. Opinion polls did indeed reflect generally strong support for *chaebol* reforms.[17] However, interview data reveals that this support is much more blurred than it appears. Many interviewees (from labor leaders to *chaebol* and political leaders) reported that people have in fact an ambivalent view of *chaebols*. They know that the *chaebols* spearheaded the economic miracle in which they take pride. Besides, given the huge weight of *chaebols* in the economy, it is often said that every voter either works for a *chaebol* directly or has a family member who does. Another top bureaucrat reported that, when forced to make a choice for or against *chaebols*, the people usually choose to support them. When the Daewoo bankruptcy occurred in late 1999 and when Samsung Motors was sold to Renault in mid-2000, there was general opposition by the public because of the negative impact on employment. The usual opposition between labor and management can commute into a common front when the lives of *chaebols* are endangered.[18] So policymakers always walk a thin line in respect to *chaebol* reforms. While public opinion provided an overall background for the process of reforms, it cannot explain the actual intensity and dual-track nature of *chaebol* reforms in post-1997 Korea.

The Impact of Global Equity Investors after 1997

It is well known that the financial crisis was triggered by the sudden reversal of foreign lending flows. Through their huge inflows of capital in the mid-1990s and their sudden mass exit in November 1997, foreign investors were the proximate cause of the crisis and of the ensuing IMF agreement. The crisis and the IMF agreement, in turn, gave the initial impetus for corporate reform. They have often been called a blessing in disguise, since they provided "an excuse for the government to act on policies that had been proposed but were not politically feasible before the crisis."[19] The focus of this study, however, is on the specific role of equity investors.

Equity investors were part of the initial crisis as they contributed to the 48 percent fall of the Korean stock market between June and December 1997. Following Kim Young Sam's liberalization efforts, foreign shareholders owned 13 percent of the stock market capitalization at the end

---

17. For example, the *Financial Times* of 20 October 1999 reported that 70 percent of Koreans "supported *chaebol* reforms."

18. This happened to some extent in the case of Daewoo Motors. An interview in May 2000 with both a senior manager and the top labor union official at one of Daewoo Motors' largest factories revealed the high degree of understanding and common interest between the two.

19. Interview at Merrill Lynch Korea, May 2000.

of 1996. This was already a significant level of ownership, but still below the tipping point. In 1997, as the ceiling on foreign ownership was further increased, the percentage rose steadily until the stampede out of Korean stocks at the end of 1997. At the end of 1997, foreigners still owned 13.7 percent of the Korean stock market capitalization. In fact, the increase of the ceiling for foreign ownership of stock in publicly traded companies, from 23 percent to 26 percent on 4 November 1997 (just before the crisis), was directly targeted toward foreign equity investors (Blustein 2001, 126).

A top Korean bureaucrat reported in an interview that stock market investors were important actors in the negotiations that led to the IMF agreements, although not as important as foreign lenders.[20] While foreign banks mostly cared about reestablishing confidence and bailing out Korean banks (so as to recuperate their loans), foreign equity investors were more interested in *chaebol* reforms and corporate governance reforms, reforms that would have a positive impact on the Korean stock market.[21] They were also interested in financial liberalization and the removal of ceilings on equity investments. These clauses were duly integrated into the IMF agreement.

Once the IMF bailout was agreed on and early financial liberalization reforms passed, foreign equity investors became a dominant force in pushing for *chaebol* reforms in particular. In the words of a top bureaucrat: "There were a lot of good reasons to listen to foreign [equity] investors: we badly needed foreign capital" to inject funds into the Korean economy. Equity capital became particularly important for corporations (and for the government overseeing the aggregate process) because of the sky-high interest rates imposed by the IMF and the banking crisis.[22] Another government official who advised President Kim Dae-Jung likewise reported that the government has used the stock market index and data on foreign capital inflows as scorecards for its reforms: "If we cannot earn the trust of foreign investors, then a new crisis will occur."[23]

The process of Korean structural reform did earn the support of foreign investors and their share of the Korean stock market rapidly grew from 13.7 percent in 1997 to 21.7 percent in 1999, 30.1 percent in 2000, and 36.6 percent in 2001.[24] Their investment represented a show of faith for Korean structural reforms. They also targeted individual blue chip companies that

20. Interview at KDI, 10 May 2000.
21. Ibid.
22. Ibid.
23. Interview with a high official in the presidential office, 10 May 2000.
24. MOFE, data received in response to personal request, January 2002. Data confirmed with KDI's Lim Wonhyuk based on newly released data from the Korean Stock Exchange (KSE).

engaged in active restructuring.[25] For example, at the end of 1999, foreign investors owned 56 percent of Samsung Electronics, 30 percent of POSCO, 27 percent of SK Telecom, 24 percent of KEPCO, and 16 percent of Korea Telecom.[26] By the year 2001, they owned 60 percent of Samsung Electronics, 52.6 percent of Hyundai Motor, 49 percent of (recently privatized) POSCO, and 71 percent of Kookmin Bank.[27] But even if foreign control of Korean companies only reached very high levels after 1999, Korean policymakers knew in early 1998 that attracting foreign equity capital was central to their goal of Korean recovery. The government became all the more beholden to the preferences of equity investors because of its drive to force down the overall debt-equity ratio of the Korean economy. The government also used the so-called global standards of corporate governance as an excuse for key reforms, such as the 200 percent debt-equity ratio. The government systematically defended its policy toward this ratio on the grounds that it was required by global standards.[28] Financial analysts did applaud the imposition of this ratio.[29] Finally, the expression of the interests of global equity investors on the domestic political scene was given a lift by the rise of shareholder activists after 1997. The most well known of such civic groups is the People's Solidarity for Participatory Democracy (PSPD), led by Korea University professor Jang Ha-Sung. Jang has gained an extremely large audience in the Korean press and has participated in numerous surveys and lawsuits against *chaebols*. He has also become well-known among foreign investors. *Global Proxy Watch*, "the newsletter of international corporate governance and shareowner value," featured Jang Ha-Sung in its 9 March 2001 issue. Describing the escalating conflict between Jang's PSPD and the Federation of Korean Industries (the mouthpiece for *chaebols*), it said: "The group's shareowner activist committee has gained influence with its penetrating exposes of cronyism at *chaebol* companies."

The increasing voice of foreign equity investors and the great consideration given to them by the Korean government after 1997 provide an essential motivation for rapid *chaebol* reforms. This goes a long way toward explaining the contrast with meek pre-1997 *chaebol* reforms. But equity flows alone cannot explain the peculiar path taken by *chaebol* reforms and their illiberal aspects, such as the Big Deal. The actual reform path is a result of

---

25. A very interesting example is Hyundai. In the words of a Korean financial analyst in May 2000, "Hyundai stock has been vastly underperforming because of big discounts given by foreign investors for Hyundai's corporate governance problems. Thus, it is less easy for Hyundai to raise cash to finance expansion. They are forced to converge to the corporate governance issue" (interview, May 2000).

26. Interview at Merrill Lynch Korea, 10 May 2000.

27. *Korea Herald*, 28 December 2001.

28. Interview with senior MP in the Hannara party (opposition), 12 May 2000.

29. Interview at Merrill Lynch Korea, 10 May 2000.

intense political entrepreneurship by President Kim Dae-Jung and his close advisers.

Political Entrepreneurship and *Chaebol* Reforms

Only the strategic calculations of President Kim Dae-Jung combined with a high level of executive control of the legislative agenda in the first three years of his presidency and a high level of bureaucratic delegation can explain the speed and illiberal nature of corporate reforms. This control was initially further enhanced by the IMF agreement, as analyzed above.

President Kim Dae-Jung is a survivor, an extraordinary man who braved persecution and death several times, and emerged with an enormous sense of mission (B.-K. Kim 2000). The Park Chung Hee regime abducted him in Tokyo in 1973 and nearly drowned him in the East Sea (Sea of Japan). He was saved by an urgent American intervention, but was then exiled and treated as a criminal. Furthermore, as noted earlier, he comes from a southwestern region that is far from the hallways of power and has been systematically disadvantaged under all previous regimes. He has a personal distrust of *chaebols* and a plan to embolden civil society and weaken the grip of large conglomerates and traditional networks. He has close links to labor, although he is not beholden to it. More than anything, Kim came to power after thirty years in the wilderness, impatient to leave a major mark in history.

In fighting the *chaebols* and entrenched interest groups, he sees global investors as potential allies and is willing to listen to them. Through his reform process, Kim discredited the Korean establishment and empowered progressive actors.[30] In the Blue House, Kim can rely on a group of core political insiders and advisers, including Kim Yong-Hwan, Kang Bong-Kyun, and Lee Hun-Jae.

Strategic Political Autonomy: High Control over the Legislative Agenda

In the pursuit of his political agenda, Kim Dae-Jung has the usual limitations in his party and coalition partners. But his security and autonomy were extremely high in the first two-and-a-half years, owing to his being elected in the midst of crisis. The main variable in Korea is the high degree of executive control over the legislative agenda when the assembly is in the hands of friendly parties. When the control switches, the executive control collapses (as it did after the legislative elections of April 2000).

30. I am grateful to Kim Byung-Kook for part of this analysis. Any misrepresentation is my responsibility.

Korea has a strong presidential system with a president elected by popular vote for a non-renewable five-year term. The constitution bestows great powers on the executive branch in its relations with the legislature. Several constitutional articles ground the control of the executive over the legislative agenda. As in France, most of the bills originate with the executive (ministries and presidency) and the presidency and the cabinet (under presidential control) have much control over the introduction of bills and amendments. A special feature further strengthens the role of the bureaucracy in parliament. While 253 out of 299 legislators are elected by popular vote for four years, the remaining forty-six seats are distributed proportionately among parties winning five seats or more in the direct election. As the website for the Korean government states, "this proportional representation system is aimed at encouraging legislative participation by leading technocrats through the political parties."[31] The president can usually use his or her leverage over budgetary tools and appointments to ensure that the assembly acts quickly on bills. But control over the legislative process breaks down when legislative elections produce a majority for the opposition or a very fragile majority (as happened in April 2000). The enduring tensions between parliamentary majority and presidential majority are a normal feature of presidential systems (Haggard and McCubbins 2001), but the fiercely divided party system in Korea aggravates the problem. When the parliamentary majority supports the president in the early years of his term, the process is wide open for rapid legislative action.

Strategic Bureaucratic Delegation

It is at this point that the elite bureaucracy comes into play. Interview data reveals that the bureaucracy is firmly under presidential control given the great power of the president over senior-level appointments. In a recent book challenging the bureaucratic dominance paradigm in Korea, Kang (2002) convincingly shows that the Korean bureaucracy has "been distinctly subordinate to political regime interests" (63) throughout the decades of the Korean miracle. Kang demonstrates that the president has full control over bureaucratic appointments and key decisions. The bureaucracy is unable to operate independently of its political masters. Kang also shows that Park Chung Hee created a "bifurcated bureaucracy," allowing him to pursue both a degree of patronage and efficient economic policy. That meant setting up different organizations in the pursuit of different goals.

31. "Korea: A New Economy for a New Age," central website of the Korean government, english.mofe.go.kr/.

Within the bureaucracy, a particularly interesting actor is KDI, described by Woo-Cumings as a "transnational elite" empowered with PhDs in economics from the United States (all thirty-five elite bureaucrats at KDI) and professing "allegiance to the goal of liberalization" (1997, 79). Interviews with KDI and Korea Institute for International Economic Policy (KIEP) officials reveal that indeed many corporate governance and financial supervisory reforms of 1998 originated in KDI. However, the Big Deal and the imposition of a strict 200 percent ratio did not stem from KDI. Rather, the Big Deal was fiercely opposed by KDI, leading to a high-stakes conflict with the Blue House. In the end, the main opponent of the Big Deal (Yoo Seong Min) was forced to resign in 2000 and ended up as head of the opposition party's policy think tank.[32]

Korean institutions provide for a very high degree of presidential control of the legislative agenda during periods of congruent legislative and presidential majorities. This level of control over a unified bureaucracy further allowed President Kim Dae-Jung and his entourage to lead the post-1997 economic reforms. It also explains the extreme nature of corporate reform in Korea, offering a great contrast with the Japanese case.

The 200 Percent Ratio and the Big Deal

Two cases—the 200 percent debt-to-equity ratio and the Big Deal—show full government autonomy and the absence of international convergence in the pathways of corporate reforms across countries. They also underline the duality in the motivation of the state in leading corporate reforms. At stake is not only the necessary response to the demands of foreign equity investors, but also the continuation of the power of the state in economic management.

As detailed in table 6.2, the government rapidly identified the debt-to-equity ratio as a critical variable in the process of corporate restructuring. The earlier section on the IMF agreement also argued that the clause requiring the government to take action on this ratio (without specifying the precise target) was included at the instigation of the Korean (MOFE) negotiators themselves. In early 1998, the government converged to the 200 percent ratio as a useful benchmark. Beginning in April 1998, the FSC urged *chaebols* to move toward this target and urged banks to put pressure on *chaebols* accordingly. The goals were twofold, reducing *chaebol* debt levels and automatically forcing *chaebols* to reduce their assets (overcapacity). But there was no legal means of enforcing the ratio. Ultimately, President Kim

---

32. Interviews with two senior opposition MPs and one KDI official (May 9–12, 2000 and November 14, 2000).

Dae-Jung forced the top five *chaebol* leaders to commit to reaching the 200 percent ratio by the end of 1999 in a high-stakes meeting at the Blue House on 7 December 1998. The government apparently used an array of direct and indirect threats to force *chaebols* to agree. This situation stands in amazing contrast to the Japanese process of corporate and financial reforms and is even far from the robust French reform process. The case first and foremost demonstrates the level of power of the president and of the bureaucracy under his control in Korea. In the end, the effort was rather successful and it was announced that most top thirty *chaebols* had achieved the target at the end of 1999.

Interestingly, the 200 percent ratio met with severe criticism from *chaebols* and from the opposition party (Hannara). A senior opposition leader explained in an interview that the ratio "promoted a sell-out of many companies" and forced *chaebols* to sell too quickly to get a good price. He stated that the argument that the 200 percent ratio was a global standard was nonsense, because each country had a different debt structure and the ratio could be rationally equalized among different industries.[33] Another senior opposition MP (and ex-KDI bureaucrat) argued that enforcing a debt-equity ratio was a good idea but that its implementation had had some inefficient consequences. For example, a lot of the *chaebol* efforts concentrated on reevaluating their assets rather than reducing their actual debt levels. In addition, the government arguably failed to enforce the ratio as strongly on Daewoo and Hyundai, the two *chaebols* that had political connections to President Kim Dae-Jung.[34]

On the other hand, foreign investors reacted positively to the 200 percent ratio, revealing the congruence of interests. A senior executive at Merrill Lynch Korea argued that the ratio was necessary in the Korean context, "you cannot handle corporate governance and other downstream economic reforms without tackling the fundamental financing problem first." Forcing *chaebols* to reduce their dependency on direct debt was a necessary step for subsequent changes. The OECD gave a relatively positive assessment of the amount of progress that has been stimulated by the ratio. In its 1999 report on Korea, the OECD documented the large ensuing decrease in the ratio among top *chaebols* as a result of large increases in equity levels. But it also underlined that the 200 percent ratio was challenging and possibly a hasty decision (Pauly 1999, 126).

For Kim Dae-Jung and for the bureaucracy under his rule (the FSC), the imposition of the ratio on *chaebols* meant a large increase in power. The FSC became the official monitor of progress and gained great discretionary power over the process of *chaebol* restructuring. On the whole, therefore,

---

33. Interview at the Hannara party office in the National Assembly, 12 May 2000.
34. Interview, 14 November 2000.

the saga of the 200 percent ratio can be seen as an extreme case of state mediation of global equity flows. The president used the policy to accelerate a process that met the preferences of foreign equity investors while enhancing his own power.

As for the Big Deal, it was a direct attempt by the president to restructure Korean industry through an agreement between the state and the leaders of top conglomerates. It constitutes the most extreme case of state-led corporate restructuring. As detailed in appendix table A3b, the Big Deal was initiated by the president as early as February 1998, co-opted behind the scenes in September 1998, and formalized through the high level meeting between President Kim Dae-Jung and the leaders of the top five *chaebols* on 7 December 1998. With the Big Deal, the government hoped to induce a consolidation of all key industrial sectors and thus enable an efficient process of internal restructuring. The traditional collective action problem encountered by *chaebols* in downsizing their overgrown assets could be solved rationally. The government wanted to complement the market where it felt that the market was not strong enough to induce structural change.[35] Yoo (1999a, 48) writes "Through business swaps or other types of consolidations, the 'excessive and duplicative investments' made by *chaebols* can be streamlined and the consequent consolidation of production will gain significant economies of scale."

Specifically, the Big Deal involved eight major industrial sectors. The most important deal was the planned merger of LG Semiconductor with Hyundai Electronics, under Hyundai's control, thus splitting the market 50–50 between Samsung Semiconductor and Hyundai-LG. This acrimonious merger took place in April 1999 and has had a significant impact. Next, Samsung Motor was slated for merger with Daewoo Motors, a deal that eventually fell through in mid-1999 when Daewoo collapsed. In railway vehicles, the Big Deal aimed at creating a monopoly by merging Daewoo, Hyundai, and Hanjin. Likewise in electric power generation, the merger of KHIS, Samsung, and Hyundai aimed at constituting a monopoly. Much has been written about the process of the Big Deal (Haggard 2000, 152; Joh 1999; Ministry of Finance and Economy 1998; Organisation for Economic Co-operation and Development 1999; Yoo 1999a, among others). In the end, the Big Deals were consumed in six industries and collapsed in two others (automobile and petrochemical) (Haggard 2000, 152). Their impact is partial, at best.

The politics of the Big Deal are clear. *Chaebols* and the opposition party (Hannara) were fiercely opposed. Two senior opposition leaders interviewed for this study emphasized that the Big Deals were the wrong method and were certainly driven by the search for political benefit. They argue

---

35. Interview with KIEP official, 10 May 2000.

that the Big Deals offered Kim Dae Jung a chance to influence *chaebols* and to obtain contributions from them in exchange for special treatment. More specifically, they blame Pak Tae-Joon, a former associate of Dictator Park Chung Hee. Other key officials were also deeply involved (Kim Yong-Hwan, Kang Bong-Kyun, and Lee Hun-Jae).

Interestingly, the subject of the Big Deal opened a rift within the executive and within the bureaucracy. KDI denounced it in clear terms. Yoo (1999a) blasts the project in February 1999 under the subtitle: "A New Industrial Policy Named the 'Big Deal.'" He writes that "Big Deals among *chaebols* are regarded as an out-of-market solution which may undermine foreign investors' trust in corporate restructuring in Korea and invite trade disputes from foreign governments" (48). Yoo also denounced the Big Deal as an exercise in government coercion and argued that it would undermine national competitiveness rather than enhance it (48–49). Joh (also from KDI) wrote that the Big Deal would probably be ineffective and would facilitate collusive behavior that hurts consumers" (1999, 28).[36] The Big Deal was even denounced by the minister of information, Pae Soon-Hoon. In the end, both the dissenting minister and Yoo at KDI were forced to resign. The argument presented by Yoo raises an important question: Did the Big Deal go against the preferences of foreign investors?

To a large extent, foreign observers severely denounced the Big Deal (Graham 2000; Noland 2000; Patrick 1999). The OECD gave a rather cold assessment in its 1999 survey of Korea, but did not directly criticize the Big Deal (127–29). An interview with an OECD analyst revealed that the page on the Big Deal had been the most contentious part of the whole report. Some within the OECD defended the Big Deal, rationalizing that *chaebols* were unique and that traditional economic measures could not deal with them effectively. In the end, the drafting committee decided to merely provide facts and to argue that, in the long term, the market approach should dominate.[37] But foreign investors did not react by dumping Korean stocks. A senior financial analyst at Merrill Lynch Korea actually presented the argument that Big Deals could be seen as "a necessary transitional initiative." Once merger and acquisitions flows were in full swing, such things would not be necessary anymore. But as of 1998, "the market was not conducive to such types of corporate restructuring with heavy swaps. Under the circumstances, it was the necessary move. It was a symbolic gesture to the public and to the corporate sector that reforms would go ahead one way or another."[38]

36. The fierce opposition of KDI to the Big Deal was confirmed in a interview with a senior KDI official on 10 May 2000. The argument was again that the Big Deal was "politically motivated" and useless in the 1990s.

37. Interview at the OECD, 8 June 2000.

38. Interview, 10 May 2000.

What were the true origins of the Big Deal? Many interviewees point toward Pak Tae-Jung and one senior ex-MOFE bureaucrat working in the Blue House for Kim Dae-Jung (Kim Yong-Hwan) as the brains behind the Big Deal. MOFE minister Lee Hun-Jae was also involved. At a deeper level, the government remained committed to free market principles but faced the situation of dominant *chaebol* power and the obdurate opposition of *chaebols* to reforms. In this situation, the Kim Dae-Jung administration decided to intervene as "a quick way to get to market principles."[39] Senior officials argue that the Big Deal was purely economically rather than politically motivated. What is also clear is that despite the high-visibility row between KDI and the Blue House over the Big Deal, MOFE was directly involved as the facilitator and implementer. In an interview with a senior MOFE official, the Big Deal was actually presented as "an agreement between business leaders" that was only "facilitated by the government." Granted, the official admitted that the government monitored the Big Deal and "backed up its implementation with tax incentives and the removal of tax obstacles."[40]

The Big Deal marks the most extreme example anywhere of government intervention in corporate restructuring. It was directed by the president, with the cooperation of a portion of the elite bureaucracy. It was essentially a quick fix to jumpstart the overall process of corporate restructuring, a process that was strongly motivated by the need to attract foreign equity investors. Even if many foreign investors did not support the extreme coercion involved in the Big Deal, they did not denounce it. Rather, it was seen as an odd detour through direct interventionism for the sake of breaking an old-style oligopolistic industrial structure and promoting modern corporate governance.

Implications and Legacy

This chapter has shown that corporate reforms in post-1997 Korea constitute a radical version of political entrepreneurship in response to the golden bargain. Corporate reforms moved at a brisk pace and followed a dual liberal-illiberal track, guided by a strong president. The Korean case underlines the capacity of foreign equity investors to offer new incentives to political entrepreneurs such as Kim Dae-Jung and to motivate rapid corporate reforms. But more important, the Korean case underlines the crucial roles of President Kim Dae-Jung and permissive domestic institutions in shaping the process and outcome of corporate reform. The unusually powerful

---

39. Interview with senior official with close links to President Kim Dae-Jung, 10 May 2000.
40. Interview with senior MOFE official, 9 May 2000.

executive in Korea and its ability to delegate reforms to a highly capable and controllable elite bureaucracy enabled Kim to engage in much more direct types of corporate reforms than in Japan and France. This systemic propensity for top-down political leadership also had a lasting impact on the post-reform industrial structure.

6

Political Entrepreneurs and the Great Transformation of the Automobile Industry

This chapter brings the analysis to the level of the firms and focuses on the implications on the ground of the variety of national responses to the golden bargain. It focuses on one major industry that is both economically significant and politically salient in all three countries: the automobile industry. The size and stakes involved in this industry are so high that all governments (including the U.S. and UK governments) have intervened in the process of automobile restructuring at one point or another. However, the French, Japanese, and Korean governments ended up intervening very differently and using different tools.

The Korean government directly affected all dimensions of restructuring (labor, finance, corporate governance, even mergers and acquisitions) in at least two major automobile corporations: Daewoo and Samsung Motor. The French government under Strauss-Kahn and Jospin only affected Renault because it was a state company in the process of restructuring. Political decisions allowed Renault to engage in the takeover of Nissan's management, using the state's patient capital. However, the government had less impact on the labor side of the equation. By contrast, the Japanese government had no direct role in the restructuring of automobile corporations. Toyota remained entirely autonomous, following its own Japanese management methods without major transformation. In the case of Nissan, political leaders did not have the ability to get involved directly in restructuring the company. They chose instead to facilitate the process of foreign-led restructuring through signals and framework legislation, while retaining some constraints on labor and corporate governance.

What explains the variation in national responses to the golden bargain at the firm level, even among relatively similar economies and within a similar industry? All three governments were responsive to global signals from financial investors and to global competitive pressures. First, the three respective governments have recently come to understand the importance of global credit ratings and stock market investors and this has changed their behavior. Second, the three governments' behavior has also been driven by a growing awareness of the importance of crossnational mergers and acquisitions in transforming the automobile industry. The cost of acting against these two developments has become prohibitively high and this reality has changed the political logic behind structural reforms.

In response to these incentives, the political entrepreneurs studied in the previous chapters took automobile restructuring on directly. However, their capacity to act decisively in such a politically sensitive industry was shaped by their degree of political autonomy within parties and relative to support groups, particularly industry and labor. The ability to delegate part of the process to national or even international institutions (such as the EU) also proved to be an important differentiating factor.

Through the comparison of the actions of governments over time and across the three countries, I demonstrate the relevance of the variation in national underpinnings of political entrepreneurship for issues of industrial restructuring and national competitiveness.

Political Significance of the Automobile Industry

> Manufacturers, it is widely believed, set the tone for Japanese corporate change. Not only are they closest to cyclical changes in demand, but they are often headed by trend-setting managers. If Sony, Toyota, and Honda are doing it, somewhere down the line other companies and industries will probably be singing the same tune.
>
> *Financial Times*, 13 July 1999

In Japan there remains a deep understanding that the manufacturing industry is the core of the economy and the source of Japanese economic strength.[1] Similar statements could be made about France and Korea. Within the manufacturing sector, the automobile industry can be seen as a crucial industry in each of the three countries. The most noticeable characteristic is its sheer size in the economy. It is usually estimated that the automobile industry (including the network of subcontractors) employs

1. Interview with former MITI vice minister, 1 December 1999.

directly or indirectly 10 percent of the entire workforce in Japan and France.[2] This reality is further amplified in local areas surrounding large automobile factories. Because of the hundreds of suppliers and related companies that are usually clustered around each factory, the local economy and employment situation in a city such as Nagoya (Toyota), Pusan (Samsung Motors), or Le Mans (Renault) are entirely dependent on the health of one automobile company. As a result, national and local politicians in each country care a great deal about the auto industry.

Furthermore, the automobile industry has historically been at the core of development strategies in each of the three countries and the ups and downs of major auto manufacturers have often been considered to be good proxies for the general economic health of the country. "When Renault sneezes, France catches a cold," goes a famous French proverb.[3] Similarly, major analyses of the Japanese miracle written in the 1980s relied heavily on examples drawn from the automobile industry. Johnson (1982, 131–32) emphasizes the pivotal role of Nissan in the development of Manchuria in the 1930s. Ayukawa Yoshisuke, Nissan's leader, was part of the five-person power structure in Manchuria (see also Samuels 2003b, 146–48; Iguchi 2003). Likewise, a large part of Johnson's analysis of the Japanese Ministry of International Trade and Industry's (MITI) industrial policy in the 1960s focuses on the automobile industry (Okimoto 1989; Prestowitz 1988). The move of large Korean conglomerates into the automobile business represents a crucial part of the Korean development story from the 1970s on. Finally, a focus on the automobile industry has one additional analytical advantage. It has become a highly globalized industry and is therefore a good testing ground for the interaction between globalization and national political settings.

I focus on four corporations in particular: Nissan (in Japan), Renault (in France), Samsung Motors, and Daewoo Motors (in Korea). This selection provides good control over numerous factors. The sample consists of companies that are all large and influential. They have historically been pillars of the national industrial structure and have always commanded a high level of respect (with the exception of Samsung Motors, which only began production in 1995). However Nissan, Daewoo, and Renault have usually been in second place in their national setting (even Renault was long seen as the

---

2. See Sautter 1996, 169. Sautter, former French finance minister, devotes an entire chapter to the analysis of the automobile industry in his landmark comparative study of the French and Japanese economies. Todd (1998) in the oft-quoted book *L'Illusion Economique*, gives the same estimate: "In France, 2.6 million people directly or indirectly work for the automobile industry, which represents 10 percent of the total national workforce. The sector also represents 12 percent of all R&D expenditures. Over the short or medium term, the automobile sector contributes massively to determining the general level of economic activity" (284).

3. Quoted in an interview with a French Member of Parliament, 13 September 2000.

laggard behind the more dynamic Peugeot-Citroen group). They also all had historically close government links.[4] Finally, all four companies have run into difficulties in the 1990s and have faced a crisis of profitability. As a result, I am focusing on large troubled automobile corporations in each of the countries and relying on two comparisons: cross-temporal for each company and cross-country to extract differences.

Broken Taboos and Contrasting Restructuring Stories in the Late 1990s

In the late 1990s, the drastic restructuring that occurred in Renault, Nissan, Daewoo, and Samsung caused great surprise and shock. The respective restructuring plans made front page headlines in newspapers in all three countries. In two cases (the French parliamentary elections in May 1997[5] and the Korean parliamentary elections in April 2000),[6] these restructuring plans became top electoral issues. In Japan, while Nissan's restructuring under Renault's leadership did not turn into an electoral theme during the June 2000 parliamentary elections, it became a top issue in the public and bureaucratic[7] debate. The new top Nissan executive, Renault's Carlos Ghosn, forced drastic change in Japan. Nezu Risaburō (2000), OECD's director for Science, Technology, and Industry (and an official from MITI) writes:

> In 1853 Admiral Perry forced the Japanese shogun to open their doors to foreign vessels with four gunboats. In 1945 General MacArthur stood on the outskirts of Tokyo after it had been completely destroyed by air raids. Each event marked the end of one era and the beginning of a new one. At the start of the

4. Renault was 100 percent state-owned from 1947 to 1994 and has been 44 percent state-owned since 1996, albeit still under effective government control. Nissan has always had extremely close ties with MITI and is often referred as the "company that listens to MITI." These ties have included numerous top-level MITI bureaucrats retiring to become auditors or board members in Nissan (*amakudari*). Similarly, Daewoo's chairman Kim Wu Chung has enjoyed extremely close ties with the Park, Chun, and Roh administrations (1960 to 1992). Daewoo was known as the favored *chaebol* of the Park regime.

5. Renault announced in early 1997 that it would close the recently renovated Vilvoorde factory in Belgium. Following the national uproar in both Belgium and France, Socialist candidate and future prime minister Jospin promised to force Renault to reconsider the closure should he be elected.

6. During the electoral campaigns, the opposition Hannara party used the sale of Samsung Motors to Renault to attack the government. They accused Kim Dae-Jung's government of selling out to foreigners (*Korea Herald*, 12 April 2000).

7. The author observed this countless times when the Nissan issue popped up in discussions with bureaucrats in Tokyo. All expressed amazement that such a quintessential Japanese company could have been taken over by a second-tier foreign company and that a restructuring that challenged the core of Japanese management methods could occur.

millennium, Mr. Ghosn may have his name inscribed in the history of Japanese business in very much the same way.

There are also important differences between the different restructuring processes in the three countries. Arguably, Renault, Daewoo, and Samsung have undergone deeper transformative change than Nissan. In Japan, the impact of Nissan's restructuring is also cushioned by Toyota's and Honda's continuing robust health without resorting to drastic restructuring. Toyota in particular, the established market leader (with over 40 percent of market share), is a central actor on the business and political scene,[8] one that can project a strong countermessage to the one uttered by Carlos Ghosn. By contrast, Hyundai in Korea and PSA in France are in relatively weaker positions and cannot present a strong alternative vision.

Renault's restructuring goes back further in history than Nissan's or Daewoo's. It actually began in 1985, although a clear acceleration and new approach did not start until 1994. Renault, one of the nineteenth-century pioneers of the automobile industry, was nationalized in 1945 by the French state as a punishment for its collaboration with the German occupation. Louis Renault, the founder and leader of the company, was arrested and died in prison in 1944. For over twenty-five years, from 1955 to the late 1970s, Renault was run by a tacit alliance between the state-appointed management and the Communist-affiliated labor union (CGT).[9] For decades, Renault was famous as a social laboratory and a mass-producer of affordable and popular cars. Renault is still remembered for being the first company to grant a third week of annual paid leave to its workers (right after the war).[10] This social reform, just like countless subsequent ones, spread from Renault to the rest of the industry. "Renault has played a major role as a social engine in France. . . . Renault was always at the forefront of social progress. . . . Hence the enormous politicization of each conflict in Renault."[11] Consequently, the rivalry between private Peugeot-Citroen and

---

8. For example, Okuda Hiroshi, Toyota's president, is the president of Nikkeiren, the association of Japanese employers, but also a close adviser to various prime ministers. In particular, as a member of all economic councils set up by the late prime minister Obuchi (the Economic Strategy Council, the Economic Council, and the Industrial Competitiveness Council), he has had much influence over economic policy. Finally, Okuda has projected a strong message in countless interviews with the press and on various TV shows, in which he emphasized his continuing commitment to Japanese-style management and lifetime employment (see in particular, the long and famous interview in *Bungei Shunjū* in October 1999: "Keieisha yo, kubi kiri suru nara seppuku seyo," which can be translated as: "Listen, Managers, if you decide to fire people, you must commit harakiri yourself as well!").

9. Freyssenet et al. 2000, 409.

10. This fact was quoted to the author in a few interviews, including an interview with the national secretary of the CGT labor union (14 September 2000).

11. Ibid.

Renault, as well as the rivalry between the unions of the two groups, was fierce.[12] Meanwhile, the French government always considered Renault to have a crucial traction role for the rest of the economy (*rôle d'entrainement sur l'économie française*) (Freyssenet et al. 2000, 427). As a result, Renault flourished during the high-speed growth of the 1950s and 1960s, but was hit badly during the two oil shocks. In the early 1980s, Renault lost most of its competitiveness and suffered six consecutive years of very large losses between 1981 to 1986 (culminating with two losses of F11 billion in 1984 and 1985). Debt skyrocketed and taxpayer money was also used to keep Renault afloat. When Renault CEO Bernard Hanon announced a major layoff plan in December 1984, the French government fired him. Renault's future looked very bleak at the time.

At that time, a first major turning point occurred. In 1985, Renault's new CEO Georges Besse initiated a classic restructuring plan. He refocused the company on core businesses and emphasized the bottom line over market share. He also announced that 21,000 jobs would be cut over two years. In a dramatic event that revealed the significance of this change, Georges Besse was murdered by an extreme Left terrorist group in 1986. His successor, Raymond Lévy, continued the restructuring plan initiated by his predecessor, a process that eventually led to the closure of the most famous Renault factory in Billancourt near Paris, in 1992. This first wave of restructuring essentially involved cost cutting and layoffs and did not rely on any financial restructuring. Renault remained 100 percent state-owned. The state merely responded to a financial crisis and to commitments made to Europe.

The second turning point nearly took place in 1990 with the announcement of an equity tie-up with Volvo of Sweden, but this alliance eventually fell through in 1993 and real change only began in 1994. Prime Minister Cresson was opposed to the deal and shelved it, while her two successors (Pierre Bérégovoy and Edouard Balladur) hesitated and played for time. Eventually, after the alliance was publicly announced in late 1993, it was turned down by Volvo shareholders, who were suspicious of the deep involvement of the French state in the deal. Balladur's industry minister, Gérard Longuet, also played a role in the collapse of the deal.

The real turning point for Renault occurred in 1994 and Renault thereafter entered the most dramatic and surprising part of its history. Renault was partly privatized in 1994 when 47 percent of its capital was sold to stable corporations, to the general public, and to Renault employees. For the first time since 1945, Renault's stock was publicly quoted on the French stock market. This partial privatization again occurred in the face of

---

12. Labor unions in Renault always had a golden status and felt some superiority over unions in other companies.

fierce opposition by unions and by the Communist Party. Then minister of finance, Edmond Alphandéry (2000, 172), recalls how delicate and politically charged the process was. He refers to the Renault privatization as a "booby-trap issue" (*dossier piège*). The (conservative) government initially attempted an authentic privatization but backed down because of political opposition[13] and kept 53 percent of the capital. The Juppé government nonetheless discreetly completed the privatization in July 1996, a month when French people are enjoying long summer vacations and are less aware of political events. The share of the state in Renault decreased to 44.22 percent and remained at that level until the early 2000s. But given the existence of a stable core of associated institutional investors and the dispersed nature of public ownership, the state still had effective control over Renault. Nonetheless, Renault seems to have taken on a radically different identity and to have pursued financial restructuring and reorganization after 1994.[14]

Renault surged onto the political scene again when, on 27 February 1997, it announced the closure of its recently renovated factory in Vilvoorde, Belgium. This move was spearheaded by Ghosn, nicknamed "the cost killer," who had already orchestrated a major revamping of Renault's purchasing and links with suppliers. Renault then ran into much bad luck with four major simultaneous political events. First, it turned out that Belgium's prime minister lived in the city of Vilvoorde, hence the immediate politicization of the event in Belgium.[15] Second, the simultaneity of the Vilvoorde closure and of further layoffs in France by Renault led to the first Euro-strike in European history. Strikes occurred in French Renault factories in sympathy with Vilvoorde workers. By 16 March, up to 100,000 people, both French and Belgian, demonstrated in Brussels against the factory closure. Third, the proximity of Vilvoorde to Brussels also led to the immediate involvement of the EU commission and EU parliament. EU institutions began to fear for their legitimacy, as demonstrators demanded a more socially-minded Europe. On 11 March, both the EU Commission and the EU parliament made the unusual move of condemning the decision by Renault. Fourth, the Vilvoorde question also became embroiled in French politics, as the conservative Chirac-Juppé government was vulnerable to attacks by Socialists. President Chirac, surprisingly, declared himself "shocked by the method followed by Renault."[16] Louis Schweitzer, Renault's chairman, was called to testify in the French National Assembly (13 March).

13. Interview with top official at the Trésor (in charge of the management of public companies) in September 2000.

14. Interviews with former director of industry division in the Ministry of Economy and Finance and two top Treasury officials, September 2000.

15. Interview with national secretary of CGT union, September 2000.

16. *Le Monde*, 6 March 1997.

But Renault's bad luck increased when Chirac dissolved the assembly and called for new elections in April 1997. As both French and European courts ruled against Renault and as the French electoral campaign heated up, Socialist candidate Jospin declared that he would force Renault to reconsider the decision if he was elected.[17]

If this huge political fallout for a corporate decision is surprising, the eventual outcome is even more astonishing. On 3 July 1997, a mere thirty-three days after the Socialist-Communist government took power, Schweitzer announced the final details of the closure. It occurred as planned on 31 July and was highly secretive. The finance minister, Strauss-Kahn, was convinced that the state actually had to support Renault's restructuring because of larger industrial logic and he managed to convince Prime Minister Jospin of this (see chapter 3).

The most dramatic evidence of Renault's deep transformation, however, came in 1999 and 2000. Over the course of a year, Renault took effective control of Nissan Motors with a 36.8 percent share of its capital for an investment of $5.4 billion,[18] took control of Romania's Dacia (51 percent stake), purchased 70 percent of Samsung Motors for $564 million, and sold its truck division (RVI) to Volvo in exchange for 15 percent of Volvo's capital. *Le Monde* summarized this flurry of M&A activities on 25 April 2000 under the title: "Renault Is Building an Empire." The *Financial Times* greeted the Renault-Nissan tie-up with considerable suspicion and doubt.[19] Renault quickly dispatched Carlos Ghosn to take charge of Nissan and he initiated the now famous restructuring plan.

Renault's restructuring process presents a startling puzzle. How could a state-managed corporation under a mostly Socialist government transform itself from a Socialist paradise to an aggressive capitalistic enterprise, one that has taken upon itself to introduce modern U.S.-style management methods into Japan? In particular, how can one explain the aggressive restructuring methods followed by Renault since about 1994 and the state's support for such methods, despite their political cost?

The case of Nissan also presents a drastic restructuring story supported, albeit indirectly, by the government despite entrenched obstacles to such a restructuring. Like Renault in France, Nissan is one of the respected pillars

17. Ibid., 29 May 1997.

18. This is a staggering investment given the relatively small size of Renault. This amount is also higher than the total of all FDI inflows into Japan in 1998 or in any previous year.

19. An article titled "A Hasty Marriage," the *Financial Times* of 29 March 1999 stated: "Renault executives were ecstatic at their Nissan deal but they may be blinded by the brilliance of their vision. . . . The rewards may be tempting, but the risks will be shouldered by Renault's shareholders, and in particular the French state, which still owns 44 percent of the company. There is a real danger that Mr. Ghosn may fail—and that the French taxpayer will end up paying for his and Mr. Schweitzer's ambition."

of the national economy. Nezu Risaburō (2000), OECD's director for science, technology, and industry and a high-ranking official from MITI writes:

> Nissan was the most prestigious company in the strategically important Japanese industrial sector. Unlike the independently minded Toyota, Nissan had traditionally been closed off and more attentive to the Ministry of International Trade and Industry (MITI), the powerhouse of the Japanese economy, which regarded Nissan as the centerpiece of its post-war industrial policy.

That Nissan should become the first major Japanese company to fall into the hands of foreigners and become the pioneer in the restructuring of Japan's industrial structure, all this with MITI's blessing, is especially puzzling. All the more so because the foreign company that took control of Nissan is a second-rank state-managed company that was itself restructured to fend off the threat from Toyota and Nissan.

Nissan's story is closely linked to Japan's industrial development. Four milestones are particularly noteworthy. As described by Jansen (2000, 588) and Johnson (1982, 131–32), Nissan was involved in the development of Manchuria in the 1930s. It was one of the two favored companies (*kyoka kaisha*) in a priority industry. In 1953, Nissan again became famous as the locus of one of post-war Japan's bitterest strikes (Jansen 2000, 745; Kume 1998, 69–71). The conflict became violent as management took a hard line, dismissing top union leaders and locking out workers. Eventually, management engineered a split in the dominant union and gave its full support to the newly created and more moderate union. In this way, management won over the leftist union but at the cost of a growing dependence on the moderate union. In 1965, Nissan merged with Prince Motors in a deal arranged by MITI and was rewarded with a handsome government loan (Johnson 1982, 268). This MITI-sponsored merger was in fact one of MITI vice minister Sahashi's few successes in his famous campaign for increased MITI power over the economy. With the Prince merger, however, Nissan gained one major factory (the now famous Murayama factory, the very factory that Carlos Ghosn decided to close), but also a hardline labor union affiliated with the Japanese Communist Party. In fact, about forty of these union activists from Prince Motors remained in the Murayama factory as of 1999 and led the fight against Carlos Ghosn's restructuring plan. Nissan also gained worldwide notoriety as it became the most aggressive Japanese automobile company outside Japan. Nissan built the first major Japanese transplant factories in the United States (in Smyrna, Tennessee) and in the United Kingdom (Sunderland). Nissan's name was deeply associated with the seemingly unstoppable Japanese miracle, particularly in the late 1980s.

After the burst of the bubble, however, Nissan's profitability and market share in Japan went downhill. Nissan underwent a first restructuring process in 1993–95, when it closed its Zama factory, but the effort did not go far enough in improving the bottom line. Nissan was in the red every single year since 1993 except for 1997. Nissan attempted several other restructuring plans, including in May 1998,[20] but none of these plans were followed through in a decisive manner. Then, on 27 March 1999, with Nissan in a dire cash flow situation, the news of the alliance with Renault was announced. It soon became clear that Renault was gaining full management control of the company and Ghosn was eventually named Nissan's president in June 2000. Nissan unveiled the Nissan Revival Plan (NRP) on 18 October 1999 and this major restructuring plan was immediately hailed as a breakthrough in the history of Japanese business. It involved a reduction in the labor force by 21,000 people over three years, the closure of five factories (including three car assembly plants), the reduction of purchasing costs by 20 percent over three years and a drastic cut in the number of suppliers, and a cut in sales and administrative costs by 20 percent over three years. The plan included major sales of assets and the introduction of stock options to motivate personnel. Ghosn personally committed to a return to profits in the year 2000 and promised to resign if this goal was not achieved. Never before had anything like this happened in Japan. Ghosn was affecting in one stroke the lifetime employment system, the social commitment of corporations to their local communities, and the *keiretsu* links with suppliers and affiliated companies. Carlos Ghosn declared that he had established "One rule: no sacred cows, no taboos, no constraints" in the preparation of this plan.

The impact on Japan's economy, society, and public opinion was huge. Ghosn instantly became the most-interviewed and most-quoted businessman in Japan. His photo became ubiquitous in Tokyo subways. One mass publication for career planning[21] put Ghosn on its front page with the large print title: "Ghosn-Style New Business Rules—Ghosn's Management Magic." Japanese business magazines began to take opinion polls about the Ghosn reform plans. A 20 December 1999 poll by *Nikkei Business Weekly*, revealed that 40 percent of respondents believed that Nissan would recover under this plan, but over 60 percent said that the working environment for employees would become more difficult. General criticism was voiced over the use of forceful "un-Japanese" methods. Toyota's president, Okuda Hiroshi, railed against irresponsible economists and managers and against the incomprehensible ratings by Moody's (which go up when companies announce restructuring plans and layoffs). Meanwhile, the small but hardline Nissan union managed to organize a major demonstration in cooperation

---

20. *Yomiuri Shinbun*, 16 May 1998, p. 1.
21. *Taipu (Type) Magazine*, 4 January 2000.

with Renault's CGT union in front of Nissan's headquarters, in which over 10,000 people participated. The two unions wrote a joint appeal to Prime Minister Jospin. Criticisms against the Ghosn plan continued unabated throughout 2000. On 7 December 2000, a top official of Japan's autoparts industry "blasted Nissan Motor Co's cost-cutting plan for the negative effect it is having on member companies' profitability."[22] This echoed a highly visible article in *Nikkei Business* on 1 January 2001, written by a former president of Yokoyama Kōgyō, a second-tier subcontractor of Nissan Motor, and titled: "Regretful Bankruptcy Makes Me Indignant with Ghosn's Way of Reform." In another article in *Nikkei Business*, Niwa Uichirō, Itōchu's president, wrote: "Depending on foreign power to reshape our business is a national disgrace."[23]

By March 2001, Nissan had returned to profitability. In 2002, Nissan boasted operating profits of ¥737 billion ($6.04 billion) and a 10.8 percent operating margin, the highest in the industry. By March 2003, the huge debt accumulated by Nissan over twenty years (¥2.1 trillion, $21 billion as of March 1999) was entirely eliminated. By 2001 Nissan had cut its purchase costs by 20 percent and it cut them another 7 percent in 2002. Also in 2002, Nissan launched twelve new products, the largest number in Nissan history. The Nissan transformation by a foreign white knight, with the support of the French state and, to a limited extent, the Japanese state, is truly a staggering one.[24]

Why was Nissan unable to reform itself for so many years when it was clear since the early 1990s that change was necessary? Why did the Japanese government lend only mild support to both the Renault takeover in 1999 and the restructuring plan despite much initial criticism? Why did the government prefer to rely on a foreigner, rather than take direct action itself?

Daewoo's and Samsung Motors' stories are as dramatic as Renault's and Nissan's, although less puzzling. Their demise, bankruptcy, and foreign takeover are clearly part and parcel of the larger difficulties of Korean *chaebols* in the wake of the East Asian financial crisis of 1997–98. Daewoo (led by Chairman Kim Wu Chung) was one of the most recent Korean conglomerates and was only created in 1967. But because of its close connections to the Park regime, it was favored by the state and became the fourth largest *chaebol* by 1980 (and number two by 1998). Daewoo often grew by absorption of ailing companies (Kim 1997, 164) and entered the automobile

22. *Kyōdō News*, 7 December 2000.
23. *Nikkei Business*, 18 December 2000.
24. In yet another final historical irony, in October 2001, the renewed Nissan-Renault alliance was incorporated as a new Dutch corporation. Renault increased its share in Nissan to 44 percent, while Nissan took a 15 percent share in Renault (thanks to a further decrease in the share of the French state to 25 percent). The French state was now in the business of putting one of its traditional companies under Dutch law, far from its own legal reach.

business in 1977 when it took over Shinjin's automobile business.[25] In 1981, Daewoo Motor was ordered by the state to merge with Hyundai, the Korean auto leader. But Daewoo managed to resist state pressures because of its political connections with President Chun. It firmly established itself as the number two automobile manufacturer and the only competitor to Hyundai (until Kia entered the auto business in 1987). In the late 1980s and 1990s, Daewoo engaged in a mad expansion that was entirely funded by state-supported bank loans (a central part of the larger Korean story just before the 1997 financial crisis). In 1995 alone, Daewoo began production at two new factories (one in Korea, one in China) and opened a technical center in Germany. In 1996, it began production at five new plants (in Romania, Poland, Uzbekistan, Vietnam, and Korea). Daewoo still managed to launch two new cars in 1997; take over Ssanyong Motors, launch a new car, and enter the U.S. market in 1998; and launch another new car in 1999.

Daewoo's leader declared that he would run for president in the 1992 general election but soon withdrew. In any case, this brazen act did not endear him to President Kim Young Sam (elected in 1992) and pushed Daewoo closer to opposition leader Kim Dae-Jung. When Kim became president at the height of the financial crisis of December 1997, Daewoo then found itself in a favorable position. It was able to easily raise funds despite the crisis and to acquire the recently created Ssanyong Motors. President Kim Dae-Jung also lobbied for the absorption of Samsung Motors by Daewoo Motors in late 1998.

Because of this great success story and the strong political connections with Kim Dae-Jung, the August 1999 announcement that the Daewoo conglomerate would be dismembered and reorganized under the leadership of its creditors and the state was a surprising event. The truth was that the Daewoo group was virtually bankrupt. The myth that *chaebols* were too big to fail was broken. A search by creditors and the state for a buyer for Daewoo Motor began and eventually failed in late 2000 because of labor's strong opposition. On 9 November 2000, Daewoo was declared bankrupt and later sold to General Motors.

Samsung Motors' story is shorter and simpler. Samsung Motors began production of its one product (SM5) in its single factory in Pusan in 1995. This was a bold act by Samsung Group to enter the automobile business with a bang and Samsung had been preparing for it for over a decade.[26] Samsung built its factory in cooperation with Nissan and poured an estimated $4 billion into it, making it the most advanced car factory in Korea. After the 1997 crisis, however, President Kim Dae-Jung pressed Samsung to transfer its auto business to Daewoo. When these negotiations collapsed,

25. Shinjin itself was founded in 1972 as a joint venture with General Motors.
26. Interview with Samsung Motors' top executive in May 2000.

Samsung Motor found itself in a major crisis. Creditors forced it to declare bankruptcy in late 1999. In April 2000, Samsung's creditors signed an agreement with Renault whereby Renault took 70 percent of Samsung Motors for $564 million. This led to major criticism from opposition MPs and from the media that President Kim was selling out to foreigners. This dramatic event for the Korean industry meant that a foreign-owned company now had the potential to control 10 percent of the automobile market in Korea. This was heralded by the Korean press as a major restructuring of Korean industry and viewed with much skepticism by the population. Labor was fiercely opposed and strikes occurred in other automobile companies.

The Korean government was directly involved in the bankruptcy process and subsequent (or attempted) sale to foreign companies of two major corporations. Why did the government proceed with such a drastic restructuring of the Korean automobile industry despite general public opposition?

Past Political Obstacles to Change

The review of major restructuring processes in the cases of Renault, Nissan, Daewoo, and Samsung in the late 1990s raises several questions. Was there any attempt at restructuring before this period? And, if so, why did it fail? What obstacles existed at the time, which might have been removed at a later period?

Renault offers two possible examples for comparison. In 1984–85, the first restructuring attempt failed and ended in the government firing Renault's top manager, Bernard Hanon. The factors for this failure included fierce labor opposition and a delicate political situation—a Socialist government that had just broken its coalition with the Communists. But this early period is too different from the late 1990s to be meaningfully compared to it. The globalization of the automobile industry had barely begun and the competitive pressures on Renault were different. A possibly more interesting comparison may be in 1991–94, when the government considered an alliance with Volvo and the privatization of Renault, but backtracked and hesitated long enough for the deal to fall through. This relative slowness in restructuring can be explained by three factors: continuing labor and political opposition, the absence of direct financial or shareholder pressures on Renault and on the state (corporate governance), and the absence of political entrepreneurship.

The Nissan case offers one clear comparison: the first restructuring plan announced in February 1993 leading to the discontinuation of production in the Zama factory, located in the western suburbs of Tokyo, in 1995. This closure was motivated by the large losses suffered by Nissan and above all by the need to increase the rate of capacity utilization (which stood at 60 percent).[27] It is important to note that the factory closure did not involve any layoffs, as the management announced that all workers and the entire production line would be transferred to other Nissan factories around Tokyo and in Kyushu.[28]

By U.S. standards, it was very mild restructuring. Nevertheless, the Zama closure was major headline news in 1993 and endured sustained political opposition. There was discussion in the Diet on calling Nissan's president to testify, although this never happened.[29] The Socialist Party launched a full investigation of the matter with the aim of designing countermeasures.[30] This was not a trivial matter given that the Socialist Party would soon be part of the ruling coalition under Hosokawa Morihiro in August 1993 and that Socialist leader Murayama Tomiichi would become prime minister in June 1994. More critically, Labor Minister Murakami made a high-profile visit to the Zama factory on 5 April 1993, urging Nissan to protect workers' interests. He also met with the mayor of Zama city, listened to his grievances, and gave him national exposure. This was the first time that a national minister had visited a factory to show concern about a closure and this received much attention in the press.[31] The closure even had a direct political impact on the July 1993 elections. It was reported that the candidate of the Social Democratic Party (Shamintō) in Kanagawa prefecture, who was running a strong campaign on the basis of support from small and medium enterprises, gave up because of the Zama closure.[32]

The Zama closure made front page headlines on 24 February 1993[33] and was a recurring theme for several years. Arguably, it contributed in a major way to the sense of crisis felt by the population, a sentiment that has been blamed for the collapse of household consumption and for the resulting economic crisis (see IMF reports in 1998 and 1999). A review of articles about the Zama closure for *Asahi Shinbun* alone reveals that as many as 131 articles published between 1993 and 2000 dealt with the issue, the bulk of them in 1993 and 1994. Dozens of these articles focused on the personal anxiety (*fuan*) and sense of crisis felt by workers and their families, as well as by nearby restaurant owners and businesses that catered to Nissan employees.

---

27. It was estimated that the Zama closure would bring this rate back to 85 percent (interview with former top executive at Nissan, 18 April 2000).

28. The same policy was held for Renault's closure of the Billancourt plant—unlike Vilvoorde, of course.

29. Interview with former MITI official in December 1999. Confirmed in interview with one of Nissan's auditors in April 2000.

30. *Asahi Shinbun*, 27 March 1993.

31. Ibid., 6 April 1993.

32. Ibid., 15 July 1993.

33. Ibid., for example.

The public concern focused particularly on the impact of the closure on parts suppliers and other "weak" actors.

The Zama closure had a particularly big impact on public opinion in Japan for one additional reason. As a modern factory conveniently located near Tokyo, Zama had been one of the factories where foreign VIPs were taken in the late 1970s and 1980s to witness the marvel of Japanese production technology.[34] Zama embodied the Japanese miracle. Its closure became the prime example of the first restructuring wave in Japan (1993) when the term *risutora* (literally restructuring, but with a narrower emphasis on the layoff of workers than in English) was coined. With hindsight, however, it is clear that this first restructuring wave only targeted basic costcutting and natural labor reductions (as well as shifting production abroad). There was no change in management methods and no pressure for change from creditors (main banks) and shareholders.[35] Nor was there any encouragement by the government (bureaucracy and politicians alike). In addition, a general sense of public opposition to industrial restructuring was visible.

As for Nissan, Zama's closure did not have much impact on the bottom line or on the health of the company. The closure proved very costly and the large Zama property could not be sold because Zama's mayor refused to grant an authorization. Given the size of the property, any real estate development there would have required considerable investment by Zama city (road construction, public sewage, utilities). To this day, it remains on Nissan's balance sheet and Nissan eventually kept some industrial activities there, and also put in a brand new automobile shopping mall. With hindsight, it was an ill-conceived and partial measure at best. But the difficulty of the operation discouraged Nissan from pursuing deeper restructuring thereafter.

The puzzle arising from this case study concerns the obstacles to major restructuring back in 1993. What explains Nissan's position and the government's attitude? One obstacle that was not significant in this case was opposition by labor unions. Interviews with officials of the Federation of Nissan's union (the dominant Nissan union) and the Confederation of Japan Automobile Workers' union (the umbrella automobile union) revealed that Nissan's management held talks with union leaders and gained their approval in the Zama closure. Union leaders understood Nissan's dire situation, lobbied for the sanctity of employment, and supported the plan once this was secured. The union felt that workers' interests were guaranteed since the plan included no layoffs. In fact, Nissan's union was in the midst of its own reforms at that time. It changed its name (from Jidōsha Rōren Nissan to Nissan Rōren) and policies in 1990 as a partial recognition of its past excesses in the 1970s and 1980s under the leadership of the notorious

---

34. Interview with top Nissan executive in April 2000.
35. Interview with industry analyst at the Bank of Japan, April 2000.

Shioji Ichirō.[36] In addition, the automobile union showed its support for the Zama closure by taking an important political step: during the July 1993 parliamentary election, the union threw its support behind a newly created conservative party (Shinseitō or Japan Renewal Party) in the Kanagawa third district (where Zama is located). It stated publicly that it would not support the Socialist incumbent because of the Socialist Party's criticism of the Zama closure.[37]

Three reasons can be advanced for the tepid commitment to Nissan's restructuring in 1993. First, there was no sense of urgency and no real desire to restructure because of continuing financial support to Nissan by its two main banks, Fuji and IBJ.[38] These two banks also formed the core of Nissan's stable shareholders. Second, Nissan and the government felt the pressure of fierce local opposition. The mayor of Zama was active and successful in organizing opposition to the factory closure. He became the focus of constant press attention and managed to prevent Nissan from fully realizing its gains by refusing to grant the crucial land sale authorization. The mayor was often quoted as saying that the entire Zama community would fall part once its central feature (Nissan, being compared to an ancient castle with a town built around it) was gone. At least one Nissan official contacted the local Diet member to put pressure on the mayor,[39] but this was to no avail.

A third factor was the lack of legitimacy of restructuring. Restructuring was seen as going against Japanese management culture and norms. There was no popular support for it. Managers were still partly seen as community leaders and did not want to break their relationship of trust with their surrounding community.[40] Nissan executives felt that it was beyond their power to cut old relationships with suppliers or workers.[41] Nissan managers were

36. Interview with top Nissan union official on 23 April 2000. Under Shioji's leadership, the union gained a very high degree of control over Nissan's management and abused this power. Shioji was referred to as the "Emperor" within Nissan. Any overtime work or business trip abroad had to be approved by the union. Shioji also strongly opposed Nissan's plans to build a major factory in the United Kingdom in the mid-1980s and managed to put the project on hold for a long time. But this was a Pyrrhic victory that led to his own downfall. Shioji was forced to resign in 1986 and the Nissan union began a process of renovation.

37. *Asahi Shinbun*, 1 July 1993. Until that election, the automobile union had supported the Social Democratic Party (Shamintō).

38. This fact was stated to the author in three different interviews with Nissan executives and in an interview with an industry analyst at the Bank of Japan.

39. Interview with a top Nissan executive, April 2000.

40. Interview with industry analyst at Nomura Securities, March 2000. See also Dore 2000, chapter 2.

41. Okuda Hiroshi, the chairman of Toyota, in a later interview on the Ghosn method, expressed similar feelings. "Such drastic restructuring is difficult for Japanese managers. Laying off workers is difficult for us because we remember the faces and lives of those who would have to go, and remember the faces of parts makers who would be hard hit. I think Ghosn was able to do it (drastic restructuring) because he wasn't fettered by such worries" (*Asahi Evening News*, 22 November 1990).

further dissuaded from ending these relationships through numerous visits to the site by national and regional politicians.[42] The legitimacy of restructuring was also affected by the lack of political support. Restructuring was neither supported in words by high-level politicians nor supported in actions by the government (structural reforms).[43]

A relatively similar story can be told in Korea, although there is no previous example of unsuccessful restructuring. The bureaucracy did try to control investments by *chaebols* and to initiate financial and corporate reforms, particularly during the Kim Young Sam administration (1993–97).[44] But these efforts were thwarted by the connections of *chaebol* leaders with political leaders. A famous episode involved the Daewoo conglomerate in 1988. Daewoo shipbuilding was on the brink of bankruptcy and its chairman, Kim Wu-Chung, lobbied high-ranking officials in the economic ministries in vain. Kim Wu-Chung then went public with a threat to let Daewoo shipbuilding go bankrupt and trigger a chain reaction in the Korean economy. This defiant act was successful and President Roh ordered the ministries to put together a new financial package for Daewoo. President Roh then had the National Assembly pass a law to allow the Korean Development Bank to increase both its capital and its loans to Daewoo (Kim 1997, 196). During the maddening period of expansion of Daewoo Motor in the mid-1990s, Daewoo met no financial or political obstacles and had no incentive to restructure. What role did the government play in each restructuring process?

The Varying Role of the State in the Restructuring Process

In contrast to previous periods, the government of each of these three countries became involved in the restructuring of automobile corporations in the late 1990s (earlier in the case of Renault). Naturally, government action depended on its level of control over companies. For example, the French state had a high level of control over Renault due to its partial ownership of the company. Similarly, the Korean state gained effective control of Daewoo and Samsung after their bankruptcies through its direct ownership of the creditors of these companies. This stands in contrast to Nissan's relative autonomy. By and large, government actions fell in three

42. Interview with former Nissan executive, April 2000.

43. The lack of political support for restructuring was naturally affected by political weakness. In February–March 1993, the Miyazawa government was in the midst of a corruption scandal and unable to initiate any reforms. His government was followed by relatively weak coalitions that were focused on political reforms (Hosokawa government) and included the Socialist Party.

44. Interviews with researchers at KDI as well as with senior politicians in May 2000.

categories: involvement in major M&A decisions, involvement in restructuring the process, and actions taken to deal with the losers and opponents of restructuring. The roles of the French, Korean, and Japanese states can also be differentiated by the contents of reforms. While the Korean state reorganized all aspects of management (labor, finance, corporate governance) and affected the balance of power within the firm, the Japanese state merely provided regulatory options and removed potential obstacles. Labor was untouched and the hard work was delegated to a foreign investor. The French state lay in between, mixing a degree of direct support for a major offensive M&A with a mere supportive role on labor and management issues. The French state chose to act as a patient value-oriented shareholder, rather than a hands-on manager or regulator. It reinforced the power of ambitious managers, without directly touching upon the balance of power in the firm.

Renault's dramatic actions in terms of restructuring plans and M&As have been accompanied throughout by political and bureaucratic decisions. The government nominated all of Renault's CEOs, including long-time CEO Schweitzer (to be replaced by Ghosn in April 2005). Schweitzer is now seen as a consummate global manager and U.S.-style restructurer, but he also used to be former prime minister Fabius's chief of staff (directeur de cabinet). The most crucial decision by the French government was of course the decision to privatize Renault, as part of a larger commitment to the increased competitiveness of the French economy. For the sake of comparison with Nissan and the Korean companies, a focus on the behavior of the French state toward Renault after this privatization is most appropriate.

The most fundamental political reform with respect to Renault and other partially state-owned corporations took place in the mid-1990s. Particularly under Strauss-Kahn's leadership, the French Trésor (which manages the state's investments in private corporations) decided to prioritize its role as shareholder over its role as an agent of the public and political good.[45] The state began to act as a rational investor. As a result of this, the Trésor became a supporter of corporate governance reforms and put its weight behind a management strategy that would maximize returns for shareholders. There are two interesting indicators of this change. First, the Trésor (under Strauss-Kahn's direction) became involved in the debate on corporate governance and even organized training seminars for its administrators on the principles of good corporate governance. Second, Trésor officials who sit on the boards of major corporations such as Renault have gradually deferred to the private shareholders on the boards. Consensus between

---

45. Interviews with two Treasury officials and a former director of the industrial division, September 2000.

Trésor officials and private shareholders has been relatively easy to obtain on major decisions, including Renault's decision to invest in Nissan. The only key divergence of interests between these two actors has been one of time frame. While private shareholders seek to maximize short-term profits and dividends, treasury officials aim at maximizing the long-term value of the corporation.[46] In fact, some argue that Renault was able to get shareholder support for its daring and risky investment in Nissan precisely because the state was the major shareholder. One official argued that Renault would not have been able to purchase Nissan if it had been 100 percent publicly owned. Financial investors would have voted with their feet given the high level of risk taken by Renault. Renault's takeover of Nissan was an entrepreneurial bet that only a shareholder with a long-term vision could support.[47] The state had become a rational investor with a long time frame.

The quiet but crucial reform made by the Trésor has been allowed to stand politically because of strong direct leadership by Strauss-Kahn and acquiescence by Prime Minister Jospin. The process was facilitated by the extremely close links between the Trésor and most managers in formerly state-owned companies, often because these managers are former Trésor officials themselves. Clearly, the political decision to emphasize the role of the state as a shareholder and to pursue its interest as a shareholder above all other roles has been critical in Renault's restructuring.

Bureaucrats and politicians have supported Renault's restructuring since the mid-1990s at three additional levels. On the national political scene, the government has strongly signaled that it was not in a position to block Renault's restructuring. The Jospin government supported the Vilvoorde closure only one month after it was elected to office on an electoral promise to force Renault to reconsider. On the international scene, the French government has been involved in supporting Renault's alliances with both Nissan and Samsung. In the case of Nissan, the French government gave its agreement to the deal (as a shareholder of Renault) only after contacting the Japanese government and making sure that they supported the deal.[48] Both MITI and the Ministry of Foreign Affairs were involved in these contacts. French government officials carefully followed the reactions by the Japanese press and felt reassured when MITI and some ministers voiced their support. They believe that this support by the Japanese government helped turn around the initial public reaction to the deal in Japan, which was rather negative at first. In the case of Samsung, state-to-state relations were

46. Interview with a top Treasury official in September 2000.
47. Interview with the former assistant cabinet director of the French Finance Ministry, September 2000.
48. Interview with a top Finance Ministry official who was involved in the decision process, September 2000.

even more important. The agreement between Samsung and Renault was signed in April 2000 after a March meeting between President Kim Dae-Jung and Jacques Chirac in Paris. This meeting included some negotiations on the Samsung issue.

The third arena where the French government supported Renault's restructuring has been the European Union, where it consistently supported EU decisions on fair competition and automobile negotiations with Japan.

The example of the Korean government presents an even clearer and larger role for government in the restructuring of the automobile industry beginning in early 1998. Apart from the general reform program on issues such as foreign investment liberalization, corporate governance, financial management, and labor relations that had a strong indirect effect on Daewoo and Samsung, the government made two major political decisions. In 1998, the government engineered the Big Deal. The chairmen of the five biggest conglomerates were called into President Kim Dae-Jung's office and asked to swap major business activities to rationalize Korea's industry. Under this plan, Samsung was instructed to transfer Samsung Motors to Daewoo. Negotiations between the two corporations lasted about four months for ten hours a day but finally broke down, as Daewoo's financial condition deteriorated and they demanded too many concessions from Samsung.[49] The second political decision allowed both Samsung Motors and Daewoo Motors go bankrupt (1999–2000). This was followed by a government-led effort (albeit through creditors) to sell the two companies to foreign investors. Samsung Motors was sold to Renault in April 2000 after an agreement on the future of Samsung Motors that involved both the French and Korean governments. Talks on the sale of Daewoo Motors to Ford and then to GM-Fiat broke down in 2000, but resumed in 2001. In 2002, GM ended up purchasing Daewoo Motors and turning it around. By 2006, Daewoo had become of the most profitable units within the GM group. From the point of view of Daewoo Motors, where employees and managers continued to have pride in the technological level of their corporations, the decision to let Daewoo go bankrupt was essentially led by the Ministry of Finance and Economy.[50] It was made in spite of President Kim Dae-Jung's continued sympathy for Daewoo and in spite of the political cost.

France and Korea both reveal direct political and bureaucratic involvement in the restructuring of the automobile industry. Political decisions were quick and usually visible. They had a large impact on the restructuring process. The Japanese government's involvement with Nissan's restructuring

49. Interview with a top executive at Samsung Motors (in charge of negotiations with Daewoo) in May 2000.

50. Interviews with a Daewoo Motors executive and Daewoo labor union leader in May 2000.

is less clear, less consistent, and less direct, but is nonetheless important. As noted earlier, this involvement was not existent in the early and mid-1990s—it did not begin until late 1997.

Many Nissan executives, labor union leaders, and bureaucrats who were interviewed, name the Yamaichi shock as the starting point for the chain of events that led to Nissan's transformation. In November 1997, Yamaichi Shōken, the fourth of the Big Four securities companies, declared bankruptcy. It was only one of three important financial institutions (including Sanyō Securities and Hokkaidō Takushoku Bank) that went bankrupt in that now famous month. But its impact was the greatest, because Yamaichi had been one of the pillars of corporate Japan and a common household name. For other financial institutions and for Nissan, it meant that the era of going concern among large Japanese companies had come to an end. The exact process of Yamaichi's collapse is still debated and some analysts mainly see a market process.[51] After all, the collapse of Yamaichi was the result of a run on its stock. But a variety of political theories are also proposed in Japan. Some see Yamaichi's collapse as the result of a political process that began with the poor handling of the financial bubble, its aftermath, and above all the Jūsen (Housing Loan Corporations) in 1996. Others see it as the result of the Ministry of Finance's attempt to prevent the separation of its fiscal and financial responsibilities. Still others see Yamaichi as the outcome of the Big Bang, a financial reform process initiated by Prime Minister Hashimoto in 1996.[52]

Nissan's former executives and labor leaders tend to blame the Big Bang and bad policies by the Ministry of Finance for the collapse of Yamaichi.[53] While the collapse of Yamaichi itself had no impact on Nissan, the new reality that financial institutions were now at risk, coupled with the collapse of the Japanese stock market in 1998, had great impact on bank behavior toward their customers. Nissan came under direct pressure by its main banks (especially Fuji and DKB)[54] to improve its bottom line or face a lending freeze. This was a major turning point for Nissan. Nissan entered its final years and suddenly realized that it could become bankrupt. Nissan executives still recall this drastic change with astonishment and amazement.

The next involvement of the government with Nissan's restructuring was the alliance with Renault. The press and most analysts assume that this deal was a purely private one, without government involvement. Careful analysis of the record reveals that this is not the case. When the deal first surfaced in

51. Interview with a former top-level official at the Japanese Ministry of Finance, April 2000.

52. Interview with an official at Japan's Ministry of Finance in March 2000.

53. This argument was presented to the author in at least six different interviews.

54. It seems that Nissan's other major bank, IBJ, put less pressure on Nissan in 1998 (interview with MOF official in April 2000). This may be one of the usual countersignals in Japan.

the press in mid-March 1999, newspaper headlines included these words: "Both MITI and the French Government Welcome the Deal" and "Both Governments Adopt a Supportive Position" (*shien shisei*).[55] This support by MITI right from the start was crucial in obtaining the general support of the population and the support of political leaders. MITI sent a strong signal to the nation that even the collapse of Nissan was acceptable and that change was necessary.[56] OECD director and MITI official Nezu Risaburō wrote: "MITI even stated publicly that they welcome the move. The Japanese accepted this news with traditional calm and understanding."[57] If MITI had declared its doubts on the deal, it is certain that the Diet would have initiated an inquiry into it.[58] MITI's blessing preempted that. Nissan union leaders confirmed that the involvement in MITI and Japan's Ministry of Foreign Affairs was important for their acceptance of the alliance.[59] MITI also showed its support for the deal by putting together a $730 million loan to Nissan through the Japan Development Bank during the negotiations with Renault.[60] Throughout these actions, MITI minister Yosano's role (with acquiescence by Prime Minister Obuchi) was critical.

Political support for the deal was not entirely preordained. Nissan's president, Hanawa Yoshikazu went to MITI and to key politicians for reports on its negotiations with Renault before the deal with sealed. After the deal was announced, he was contacted by Kamei Shizuka, the third top official in the ruling LDP party, and Kamei voiced strong opposition to the deal, criticizing Hanawa for not seeking alternative solutions. Kamei also contacted Nissan union leaders and urged them to oppose the deal. Some official questions arose in the Diet on the Nissan-Renault deal. Diet members affiliated with the Communist Party raised most of these questions, but at least an LDP Diet member raised one of them. Both Hanawa and the union leaders believed that the government would have organized a rescue plan if they had requested one. There was some room for political maneuvering and a clear decision had been made by MITI to support the deal after thorough discussion.

Finally, the government has been directly involved in Nissan's Revival Plan since its announcement in October 1999. First, Prime Minister Obuchi himself indicated his support. On 19 October 1999, the day after the NRP was announced, Obuchi made a statement to reporters at his

---

55. *Asahi Shinbun*, 14 March 1999.

56. Interview with OECD director Nezu Risaburo in June 2000.

57. *OECD Observer*, April 2000.

58. Interview with OECD director Nezu Risaburo in June 2000.

59. Interview with Nissan union leaders, April 2000.

60. Report by the Paribas Banque, *Conjoncture*, December 1999. The title of the article was "Recent Restructuring Signals the Normalizing of the Japanese Model. The Quest for Economic Growth Comes at the Price of the Social Contract."

official residence: "The government can understand Nissan's efforts to strengthen competitiveness . . . by drawing up the revival plan, amid changes in the environment of the automobile industry."[61] At the same time, Obuchi also urged Nissan to ease the pain for workers and subcontractors. This statement was echoed in similar statements by MITI minister Yosano and by the minister of labor.

Beyond this signaling role on Nissan's restructuring, the government was also concretely involved in Nissan's Revival Plan through crucial accompanying measures. The minister of labor instructed his ministry to consider Nissan as a model for the ministry's new role in restructuring. The Ministry of Labor (MOL) has tried to develop a standard procedure with the Nissan case that could be applied elsewhere in the future. As a result, the employment policy division put one MOL official in charge of the Nissan question. This official attended many of the local meetings between Nissan managers, subcontractors, and local officials. The MOL decided that Nissan was eligible for all four employment packages approved by the Diet between April 1998 and November 1999. This included subsidies for education and training of laid-off workers, subsidies for new job creation, unemployment subsidies, and measures to attenuate the local impact of factory closures.[62] Likewise, MITI has supported Nissan's restructuring through at least two concrete measures. First, it approved Nissan's application for tax breaks under the Industrial Revitalization Law passed in August 1999.[63] Second, MITI's automobile section became directly involved in cushioning the impact of Nissan's restructuring on subcontractors. In particular, MITI provided new loans to subcontractors who faced difficulties and assisted them in finding new customers and markets.[64] Needless to say, these measures lessened the social and economic impact of Nissan's restructuring and made it easier for Ghosn to proceed. Finally, Nissan's restructuring program has greatly benefited from structural reforms such as the introduction of stock option changes in commercial law (easing mergers and company spin-offs).

Different Responses to a Common Global Force

The French, Korean, and Japanese governments have all been motivated in their actions by a concern for global competitiveness and by the new global financial incentives regarding competition over corporate financing. At the same time, political leaders have shown variation in their response to this

---

61. *Kyōdō News*, 19 October 1999.
62. Two interviews with officials at the Ministry of Labor in March 2000.
63. *Kyōdō News*, 28 October 2000, on the case of Nissan Diesel.
64. Interview with MITI official in the automobile division, March 2000.

common impetus, in relation to their capacity for political entrepreneurship.

The growing importance of financial investors has been the clearest in Korea where the drastic change in government behavior, with respect to industrial conglomerates, is directly traceable to the financial crisis of 1997. This crisis was triggered by the sudden loss of confidence of foreign investors (both creditors and equity investors) in the Korean economy. Since 1998, the voice of foreign financial investors in the Korean economy has been very strong (including their role in shaping the IMF agreement) and has been critical in the decision made about Daewoo in 1999.

Financial investors have also been very influential in the decisions of the French government regarding Renault since 1994. One high-ranking official said that everything changed with Renault once it became publicly quoted (albeit state-controlled). The presence of financial investors on the board of Renault after 1994 has given them the capacity to monitor management and pull the alarm when profitability goes off target (the so-called *pouvoir d'alerte*). If they disagree with management decisions, they can vote with their feet and provoke a collapse of Renault's stock. Increasingly, stock prices have become a core management criterion that have a major impact on all financing decisions.[65] As a result, French political leaders and the Trésor have increasingly deferred to financial investors on the board for major decisions on Renault's management. Given the conversion of leaders such as Strauss-Kahn to corporate governance principles, Renault is no longer able to obtain inexpensive financing if its stock price falls too much. In France, this reality has taken an additional twist with the support of employee stock ownership during the privatization of Renault. Shareholder employees do not have the ability to influence stock prices, but their wealth depends heavily on these prices. When stock prices fall, employees put pressure on management. Ironically, the CGT labor union initially opposed the deal with Nissan because of the projected halving of company profits in 2000 and the major impact on the value of stocks owned by workers.[66] Part of their salary is also indexed on company profits.

Likewise, a growing focus of Japanese government officials on credit ratings and stock prices has changed their behavior with respect to corporations such as Nissan. During his press conference on the Nissan-Renault alliance in March 1999, MITI minister Yosano repeatedly referred to Nissan's credit ratings and how unacceptable it was for such a central corporation of Japanese industry.[67] Yosano urged necessary management reforms. The conversion of the Japanese government to the need for structural

---

65. Interviews with top Treasury officials in September 2000.
66. Interview with the CGT's national secretary in September 2000.
67. *Asahi Shinbun*, 14 March 1999.

reform in the spring of 1999 was partly driven by a need to support the stock market.[68] At a broader level, the banking crisis in 1997–98 was triggered by the collapse of the Japanese stock market in 1998 and by the impact this had on banks, given their high stock investments. The collapse of the stock market itself was in large part due to foreign investors' loss of confidence in the Japanese economy.

The second major factor influencing government behavior was the transformation of the global automobile industry through the explosion of cross-border mergers and acquisitions. Cross-border investments (or foreign direct investment) had become common since the 1980s (a multiplication of transplant factories) but the M&A wave began in earnest in 1998 with the merger of Daimler and Chrysler. This one event acted as a trigger for many subsequent M&A activities and was repeatedly mentioned in interviews with officials in France, Japan, and Korea. The three governments clearly understood that the national auto industry could not remain competitive over time unless it was involved in this global wave of M&A links. The rule of thumb stated by Nissan, MITI, and Trésor officials alike is that an auto company needs to produce 4 million vehicles to amortize growing research and development expenses and survive over time. All automobile corporations are engaged in a race for global growth and global survival, and governments received that message.

However, what differentiated the responses of the three governments to these common pressures were the different degrees in political autonomy enjoyed by political leaders and the differences in the bureaucratic tools available to them, as shown in chapters 3–5.

Another major factor that differentiated the behavior of the French and Korean governments from that of the Japanese government was the existence of binding commitments to an international institution. In the Korean case, most obviously, many of the corporate reforms (but not all) were included in the IMF agreement following the financial crisis. Korea was committed to reform. In the French case, many of the Renault reforms were driven by EU regulations, especially on competition, deregulation, national subsidies, and trade relations with non-EU countries. The privatization of Renault occurred following a commitment to the EU by the French government and Trésor officials were deeply aware that the EU Commission would block any attempt by the French government to favor Renault in any way.

In contrast to these two cases, the Japanese government has had no such direct constraint and has not been driven toward structural reforms and corporate restructuring by an international institution. This explains the slower pace of reforms in Japan.

68. Interviews with high-ranking MITI and MOF officials, March–April 2000.

The Encounter of Political and Corporate Entrepreneurships

This chapter has brought the analysis of political entrepreneurship in response to global incentives to the level of interaction with industrial strategies. Political involvement in firm-level corporate restructuring has been redefined as an encounter between the two types of entrepreneurships: corporate and political. Political industrial strategy remains strong even in the age of globalization.

In a major industry such as the automobile industry, governments can go beyond shaping the institutional framework within which firms operate or beyond providing catalysts. Governments can directly mediate the relationship between investors, managers, and labor and shape the process of corporate restructuring.

Political actions and the outcome of these interventions have varied significantly between Korea, Japan, and France. The variation in the government's involvement in automobile restructuring mirrors the variation in legal frameworks emphasized in previous chapters. This variation is material because it ends up shaping firm strategies and the eventual market position of these mega-firms. Interestingly, this variation in political responses is not a function of partisan preferences and lobbying relationships with key interest groups. Rather, it is a function of the ability of political leaders to gain enough political space so as to nudge big national firms toward the creation of long-term industrial and financial value. When political autonomy is high and the tools of delegation are present, political leaders can directly shape the process and participate in the reorganization of power relations, as in Korea and to a lesser degree in France. When political space is more constrained, political leaders can end up acting as constraints (as in Japan in 1993–95). However, even under such conditions, political entrepreneurs can delegate the process to a foreign private actor, as in the case of Obuchi's acquiescence to Renault's controlling participation in Nissan. This weak type of delegation induces a loss of control, but this very loss guarantees a credible commitment on the part of reformist leaders who know the limits of their political autonomy.

Conclusion: From Social Contract to Golden Bargain?

In the late 1990s, many OECD countries engaged in far-reaching corporate structural reforms. While these reforms may appear to be mere technical measures or legal revisions, their cumulative effect amounts to a major transformation of the post-1945 industrial and social contract. Corporate structural reforms are measures instigated by the state to facilitate the process of corporate restructuring and to bring flexibility and reactivity into the industrial structure. They aim to increase the competitiveness of the economy and ensure long-term growth. In most cases, structural reforms have happened discreetly and have not been the object of electoral debates during important elections.

In this book, I have focused on the corporate structural reforms in three large state-led capitalist countries, namely, Japan, France, and Korea between 1995 and 2002. All three countries used to be seen as classic alternatives to the liberal capitalist model. In fact, France, in the 1960s, and Japan and Korea, in the 1980s, were considered a superior alternative and even a threat to the liberal capitalist model. Although their style of economic organization seemed to be more competitive, it was intrinsically a choice made for social reasons and as part of a post-war social contract. In return for hard work and strong regulations imposed by the state, workers were guaranteed stable employment and managers a secure financial environment.

During the 1990s, all three countries faced new global incentives in the form of an explosion of global financial flows. They responded to external changes by taking important steps to reform the postwar structure, although each very differently. One acted to transform power relations within firms and in the larger political economy (Korea), while another maintained key power relations and only reformed selectively (Japan). What explains such different national responses to similar external forces? I have shown that in situations of globally induced uncertainty, interest group coalitions fragment and neither parties nor bureaucrats are able to steer the reform path. Political entrepreneurs step in and act as tipping mechanisms, creating new bargains and reorganizing underlying coalitions. Their capacity to act depends on the degree of political autonomy available in their relationship with their party, coalitions, and legislation. It also depends on the opportunity for bureaucratic delegation.

Motivation for Change: The Golden Bargain and Political Entrepreneurship

In this book, I have argued that national political leaders now face a golden bargain whereby equity investors promise abundant capital inflows to countries who engage in corporate reforms. The trends of financial deregulation and technological change have greatly reduced transaction costs and led to a massive increase in global capital flows. The 1990s have seen the emergence of global norms of corporate governance, norms that serve as focal points for global investors.

Corporate structural reforms constitute the response of political entrepreneurs to these emerging global forces. In the face of a stalemate between coalitions of interest groups and a sticky status quo, the core proponents of reforms are political entrepreneurs in the executive branch. Political entrepreneurs identify the growing gap between the enduring national system and the global economic system and sense the potential long-term benefits involved in taking up the golden bargain. They are ready to discount the short-term costs of change and to gamble that structural reforms can create a new winning coalition in the long term. They also know that the costs of inaction are high and that adverse economic conditions may slowly reduce their existing coalition within party and interest groups. In addition, other political entrepreneurs are likely to rise up and seize the golden bargain for themselves.

A political entrepreneur may come to power with an open promise to take on the golden bargain and to engage in structural reform. More often, however, political leaders become active political entrepreneurs once in power, since the golden bargain is not popular with militants in large parties. The exercise of power offers the opportunity for political entrepreneurs to bypass opponents within their party base, although this opportunity varies greatly across countries.

I have argued that the success of political entrepreneurs in launching structural reforms that shift the status quo of their own support base depends on the degree of strategic political autonomy available within their party, their governing coalition, and the legislature. It also depends on the opportunities for bureaucratic delegation available within the political system. A strong and unified elite bureaucracy allows political leaders to delegate policymaking more effectively because of the higher degree of monitoring and control. A fragmented bureaucracy offers multiple access points and enables political opponents to gain a policy base in opposing reforms. Opportunities for strategic delegation may also exist within international institutions, such as the EU.

Distinct National Pathways

In this book, I have applied the framework of political entrepreneurship in response to the golden bargain in each of the three cases, contrasting the emergence of reforms in the post-1997 years with the relative absence of reforms in the early 1990s. I also analyzed the varying content mix of reforms in each country.

In Japan, significant corporate reforms took place from 1996 to 1999, and particularly in 1999. During that year, Japan not only passed reforms of its commercial code and Bankruptcy Law, it also passed a law, the Industrial Revitalization Law, that was specifically aimed at enhancing corporate restructuring with the use of taxpayers' money. The process-tracing analysis of the reform cases has shown that individual political leaders, such as Yosano Kaoru, Obuchi Keizō, and Koizumi Junichirō, were the central actors in deciding how a stalemate between opposite coalitions could be broken. All three responded to new incentives related to the surge of equity flows in Japan after 1998 and to accompanying global norms. But they also saw in the adoption of such norms a chance to revitalize Japan and lead the country out of its prolonged post-bubble crisis. They recreated themselves as reformists and used the new resources provided by global investors to enlarge their political coalition in the center.

At the same time, Japanese political entrepreneurs were hindered in their attempts to reform Japan's industrial structure because of its low level of control over the legislative agenda. Meanwhile, the Ministry of International Trade and Industry often found itself in competition with other elite ministries, such as the Ministry of Finance or the Ministry of Justice. This competition diluted the control of the elite bureaucracy over the legislative process. The inability of the Japanese cabinet to set the legislative agenda and the absence of unified party leadership greatly hindered the ability of political leaders to pass reforms. The slow pace of reform and the fragmentation of political leadership in the Diet left ample opportunity for interest groups to oppose reforms.

In 1999, Yosano and Obuchi proved able to circumvent these obstacles because of two factors. Like Prime Minister Hashimoto in 1996–97, Prime Minister Obuchi was able, for a brief period, to provide a reasonable degree of party control and leadership. This was due to his control of the dominant faction in the Liberal Democratic Party. In addition, Yosano created the Industrial Competitiveness Council, which allowed the prime minister to make credible reform commitments and to break the opposition of other ministries. These conditions, however, proved short-lived and ceased to exist during the rule of the subsequent prime minister, Mori Yoshrō. A more institutionalized version of the ICC (the Council on Economic and Fiscal Policy) was created in 2001 for economic management as a whole. This institution should lead to an increase in the capacity of political entrepreneurs over time. Even though the Abe Shinzō government has been less reliant on it than Koizumi, the council offers a permanent opportunity for future leaders.

In France, the years from 1997 to 2000 saw a series of important structural changes. These changes included a drastic acceleration of privatization, a transformation of the management of state-owned corporations by the Trésor, stock option reforms, and corporate governance reforms. Most of these changes occurred out of the political limelight and seemed to run counter to the ideological preferences of the Socialist-Communist coalition in power. They were given political coverage by the highly visible labor reform that reduced the workweek from thirty-nine to thirty-five hours for all companies without a reduction of pay.

The data presented in this book show that the burst in structural reforms in France between 1997 and 2000 corresponded to a large increase of foreign participation in the domestic stock market from 26 percent in 1996 to 35 percent in 1999. During these years U.S. and UK pension funds became important actors in the French stock market. Foreign investors collectively took control of two dozen large French corporations, particularly recently privatized corporations. French political entrepreneurs such as Dominique Strauss-Kahn followed these trends closely and espoused the cause of corporate governance as the best means to continue France's modernization. Socialist reformers like Strauss-Kahn often found themselves arguing against the dominant views of their parties.

Clearly, the unity of the elite bureaucracy under the leadership of the Trésor, the many direct levers in the hands of the bureaucracy, and the unusually high level of direct control over the daily parliamentary agenda by the cabinet all facilitated the French reform process. In some cases, the ability of reformist politicians to use the European Union as a Trojan horse to break through domestic strongholds further enhanced the reform process. These means allowed the state to rely on direct interventions and to keep a niche for itself through a novel reliance on regulatory tools.

Meanwhile, Korea provides an extreme case of systemic change led by presidential leadership. Korea started from an unusual position, given the dominance of a few large industrial conglomerates (*chaebols*) over the industrial structure. *Chaebols* were successful in thwarting most reform attempts during the period of financial deregulation in 1993–97. In contrast, in the wake of the December 1997 financial crisis, Korea embarked on one of the fastest and most comprehensive programs of structural reform in any OECD country. This program covered the entire gamut of structural reforms, including investment, corporate governance, banking, and regulatory. The program also included direct state intervention in the industrial structure through the financial system. At the same time, the Korean reform program relied on unusually direct state coercion. While adhering to principles of market-based changes, the Korean state imposed precise debt-equity ratios on *chaebols* and directed them to swap and merge entire industrial sectors. Some analysts have argued that the reform program did not go far enough and did not solve all the problems that had led to the financial crisis. I argue, however, that the breadth and depth of reforms that did pass were by themselves an unusually stark departure from the past and from the usual path of reform in most OECD countries.

The IMF bailout agreement of December 1997 figures centrally in the analysis of the Korean case. The IMF agreement with Korea contained a rare series of clauses that committed Korea to structural change and corporate reforms. The IMF agreement represented an intrusion of the interests of foreign investors into the Korean political scene, in a much more direct way than mere equity inflows and outflows. The IMF agreement also served the interests of a large set of investors, from bank creditors to portfolio and industrial investors, as well as their large supporters (the United States and Japan). But the Korean reform process was not a mechanical implementation of foreign preferences as filtered through the IMF agreement. The evidence presented in chapter 5 reveals that the Kim Dae-Jung government initiated many of the clauses pertaining to *chaebol* reforms, seeing in the IMF agreement a rare chance to push for the reforms it desired. A high degree of national autonomy remained in the reform process, and even at the level of the IMF agreement.

In pushing for *chaebol* reforms in 1998–2000, the government was not just implementing the IMF agreement; it was also trying to guide the Korean industry away from a high reliance on debt and toward more direct financing. Critical to this plan of national revival was the necessity to attract foreign equity investors. And as foreign equity investors came, the Korean stock market and access to plentiful direct financing became critically dependent on them. Their presence and their growing voice provided a continuing impetus for corporate structural reforms. This presented a striking contrast to the earlier period of 1992–97, when the presence of foreign investors was still limited. The reform process between 1997 and 2000 corresponded to a doubling in the level of foreign ownership of the domestic stock market from 14.6 to 30.1 percent.

The high degree of presidential control over the legislative agenda, however, determined the peculiar mix of Korean structural reforms (relying both on corporate governance principles and strong direct state interventions). Due to the circumstances of the crisis and the great institutional power of the president in the early period of his term, President Kim Dae-Jung and his close advisers had a relatively free hand and could use methods that served his interests as well as those of foreign investors. The executive leadership was able to try coercive tools to shortcut the usual process of market-led reforms. This capacity disappeared after 1999–2000 when the opposition controlled parliament and paralyzed the government's capacity to act.

I also provide a comparative analysis of restructuring in the automobile industry in each of the three countries, underlining the role of the state in the process. The automobile industry is a crucial one in all three countries, employing on average 10 percent of the workforce. Companies such as Nissan, Renault, and Hyundai were central players in the respective economic miracles of the three countries. All had very close ties to the state, either direct (Renault) or indirect (Nissan). Yet in all three cases the state accepted and encouraged a process of drastic restructuring that represented a significant departure from its traditional policies. In the case of Nissan, Samsung Motors, and Daewoo Motors, the Japanese and Korean states even supported the takeover of these national treasures by foreign rivals. Coincidentally, both Nissan and Samsung Motors were taken over by Renault, itself controlled by the French state (with 44 percent state ownership). Thus, in a historical turn of fate, a French national corporation, controlled by a Socialist-led state, and itself drastically reformed under the threat of Toyota and Nissan, became the agent of a U.S.-type restructuring in one of the key pillars of the Japanese economic miracle.

In all three cases, the state was motivated by the need to increase the return on equity and meet foreign investors' targets. Otherwise, the government knew that these corporations would lack the ability to compete for financing on the international financial markets and would quickly lose their competitiveness. The French state, however, relied on more direct tools and on the EU to rapidly reform Renault. In contrast, Japanese political leaders had the capacity to support and facilitate a takeover by Renault, but did not have the means to preempt such a takeover by earlier direct interventions.

Comparative Analysis

The comparative analysis of the three countries reveals that the starting industrial structure was markedly different in each case. State-owned companies dominated the industrial scene in France (at least until 1986, but even until 1997). Oligopolistic (but private) conglomerates controlled the industrial structure in Korea. Loosely linked *keiretsu* networks organized around main banks were the dominant feature of the Japanese industrial map. These structures called for different types of reforms. At the same time, these industrial structures contained similar concepts of stability, long-term employment, and bank-led financing.

Despite their different starting points in terms of industrial structure, all three countries have started to engage in reform and change. Japan proceeded with more reforms in 1996–99 than is commonly understood, even if they were not sufficient to jumpstart the Japanese economy. In all three cases, many of the reforms were technical and discreet. They have not yet been fully acknowledged by the general public and by political analysts.

In all three cases, the growing presence of foreign investors in the domestic stock market has provided the push for corporate reforms after 1996–97. In Japan, an important rise took place between 1996 (11.6 percent of domestic stock market capitalization) and 1999 (18.6 percent). In France, a jump occurred between 1995 (25.4 percent) and 1999 (35 percent). In Korea, the jump took place between 1997 (14.6 percent) and 2000 (30.1 percent). In each country, the years between 1996 and 2000 saw an increasing focus on ROE as a management objective and on shareholders' interests among corporations, plus an increase in equity financing. Corporate restructuring has accelerated. The government has accompanied the trend with a comparable conversion to the discourse of corporate governance, backing it up with concrete reforms. All three countries signed the OECD principles of corporate governance in 1999.

While all three countries have engaged in corporate structural reforms, they show great variation in the type of reforms they have adopted. Japan has moved slowly and has mostly relied on indirect corporate governance reforms. The state has been unable to engage in proactive corporate reforms through active financial reforms (cleaning up bad loans and forcing a change in bank behavior). It has not transformed the core of corporate governance. The state has also not been able to rely on direct interventions (except for limited tax incentives) or on labor reforms to stimulate corporate restructuring. In contrast, the French government has not only passed a series of regulatory reforms that affect corporate governance and facilitate restructuring, it has also given a major push to the process through its management of state-owned corporations and privatization. At the same time, the French leadership has not affected the balance of power within corporations and has not reformed labor. It merely reinforced the existing power structure. The Korean state has gone the furthest, relying on the entire spectrum of reform options, including a high degree of coercion.

The key variables that explain the variation in path and outcome among these three countries are the degree of strategic political autonomy and the opportunity for efficient bureaucratic delegation. In comparison to France and Korea, Japan appears strikingly weak in terms of executive control over parties and legislature. Contrary to what is often assumed about Japan, the elite bureaucracy in the late 1990s was, on average, highly constrained in its capacity to push reforms forward. Under rare circumstances in 1999, however, political reformers and MITI were able to bring about reforms thanks to the creation of a novel institution, the ICC, and thanks to a rare period of prime ministerial autonomy in the Diet. These circumstances did not present themselves again under Prime Minister Mori and only rarely under Prime Minister Koizumi.

France and Korea, however, stand out as cases of strong political leadership in the late 1990s. In both countries, political entrepreneurs have been able to rely on bureaucratic unity and direct powers. Both the French and Korean leaderships are strengthened by the constitutional prerogatives granted to the cabinet in its relations to parliament.

The role of international institutions as domestic Trojan horses is another variable presented in this book. When a country is committed to international institutions that require a significant transfer of sovereignty and when that country has significant leverage over the decision-making process in the international institution (due to its size and power), the hand of political reformers is strengthened. The presence of such commitments to international institutions increases the control of political leaders over the legislative agenda by giving them an extra-national route to determine the national legislative process. The European Union has provided such an avenue for French reformist politicians, although voters seemed in the mood to call off the game in the 2005 referendum over the European Constitution. The IMF agreement to some extent also provided an opportunity for Korean leaders to include some of their priorities in the domestic reform agenda. In contrast, the lack of such international commitments has narrowed the options of political entrepreneurs in Japan. With the possible exception of the agreement on the BIS banking ratios in the late 1980s, political reformers have not been able to bring their reform agenda to the international sphere. The oft-mentioned U.S. pressure (or *gaiatsu*) is at best a weak and erratic substitute because of the blatant loss of sovereignty relative to one particular country. Recent events show that MITI has been trying to remedy this situation by promoting bilateral free trade agreements that include a wide series of non-trade and regulatory issues (WTO-plus agenda). The first such agreement was signed with Singapore in 2002 and has been depicted by some MITI bureaucrats as a chance to bring about reforms in Japan.

In any case, the advantage of international institutions for political leaders appears to be a one-time effect on the reform process. The IMF agreement determined the 1998 reforms in Korea, but was not relevant after 1999. The EU has proven to be a key tool for French reformists in the 1980s and up to the mid-1990s, but may be gradually drifting from the control of French elites.

Finally, comparative analysis of the three state-led economies shows that the process of structural corporate reform has been losing steam after 2000 and has shown politicians sometimes willing to take hits from global investors. In France, the process of state mediation of global financial forces came under fire in 2001–02 and the government was willing to take an important step backward with an anti-layoff law in mid-2001. A similar slow-down happened in Korea in 2002 and again in 2005. What seems to be taking place is a backlash led by anti-globalization NGOs in France, organized interest groups in Japan, and labor, NGOs, and corporations in Korea.

Political Entrepreneurship and Restructuring in Other Settings

Though this book focuses on three stakeholder capitalist OECD countries, its argument can be extended to Germany, Italy, and beyond. The debate over corporate reform and corporate governance is at the core of a larger debate on the possible obsolescence of the German model in the early 2000s (the so-called German disease) and the loss of competitiveness and growth that has plagued Germany since the early 1990s.[1] On the whole, German reforms have been more limited than in France or Korea and, similar to Japan, mostly indirect (enabling reforms, without an effect on the balance of power within the firm). Since 1997, strong positive moves have been offset by countermoves or by last minute defeats in the Bundesrat. To be sure, a few key milestones were reached in 1998 (the Control and Transparency Law, or KonTrag) and in 1999 (tax reform to facilitate the dissolution of cross-shareholding ties) and these correlate with periods of high entrepreneurial capacity.

The German case confirms that the motivation provided by global investors is at work in countries beyond France, Japan, and Korea. Indeed, with foreign penetration of the domestic stock market at 31 percent in 2002,[2] Germany is quite similar to France and Korea. Political entrepreneurs,

1. For excellent reviews of the structural reform debate in Germany, see Beyer and Hoepner (2004), Cioffi (2002), Höpner (2003, 2004), Jackson (2003), Kitschelt and Streeck (2004).
2. For fascinating analyses of global investors in Germany, see Goyer (2006).

mainly Chancellor Gerhard Schröder, have picked up the golden bargain and developed a reform agenda that seeks to restore long-term competitiveness in Germany, while enlarging the electoral base of the Social Democratic Party (SPD) toward the center. A case in point has been the 1988 KonTraG law. Work by Cioffi (2002) reveals the importance of political entrepreneurship in this law. Political elites wanted to "promote modernization of the German economy," while facilitating improvement in the cost of capital and overall competitiveness (361). He singles out the role played by Gerhard Schröder and his centrist lieutenant, Hans Martin Bury (363). These political actors pushed for a centrist political program (*Neue Mitte*) as part of their effort to re-center the SPD.

However, the government has developed extensive reform programs that are often blocked in the parliament. The key constraint limiting the autonomy of political entrepreneurs is the strong voice of the second chamber, the Bundesrat. The Bundesrat must approve all legislation that affects the prerogatives of *Länder* (states), de facto, 60 percent of all legislation. The Bundesrat represents individual *Land* governments and these governments have non-coinciding election cycles. As a result, the SPD has been blocked by an opposition-controlled Bundesrat most of the time since taking control of the government in 1997. The net outcome of the reform process is shown in appendix table A4.

Another country failing to take advantage of the golden bargain's incentives and not engaging in active corporate reforms is Italy.[3] Slowness of reform is not due to an absence of political entrepreneurs, rather there is an extremely low level of strategic political autonomy available due to the fragmented nature of the party system and the succession of fractious coalitions.

At the level of the European Union, the actions of political entrepreneurs during political windows of opportunity are the engine behind the process of EU integration. Jean Monnet, regarded as the architect of European unity, exploited the chaos of the postwar period and the new incentives of the postwar order to initiate the European Steel and Coal Community in 1951. More recently, in the 1980s, the EU Commission under Jacques Delors played a crucial entrepreneurial role in the lead-up to the 1986 Single European Act, mediating new global market incentives into an agenda for EU integration (Jabko 1999, 2006; Sandholtz and Zysman 1989). The balance of power within the European Council and the support of France, Germany, and the United Kingdom gave Delors the necessary political space to act. With hindsight, these actions went beyond the preference of the average voter in many countries, particularly in Delors' France. Delors knew that only a free market agenda could carry the torch of EU

3. See, for example, "Addio, Dolce Vita: A Survey of Italy," *Economist*, 26 November 2005.

integration at that time. However, the consequences have been asymmetric integration with social policy lagging behind.

The recent conflict over the EU takeover directive has been the most direct agenda pursued by the EU in support of corporate restructuring. A fifteen-year battle raged over the directive until a watered-down version was passed in December 2003. The battle pitted an EU Commission led by the internal market commissioner (particularly Frits Bolkestein at the peak period of the battle, in 2000–2004) against organized industrial and labor interests acting through the European Parliament and through key states in the EU Council (particularly Germany). In the latter part of the conflict, Bolkestein was the quintessential political entrepreneur, acting in the name of capital efficiency and European competitiveness with the support of financial investors. However, his travails with the directive underscored the multiple veto points present within the ever-evolving structure of EU governance. His political autonomy remained limited. Recent EU institutional reforms have increased the power of the European Parliament and of the council, gradually limiting the political autonomy available to the leaders within the EU Commission.

Beyond industrialized countries, restructuring of state-owned enterprises (SOEs) has also become one of the major battlefronts in China since 1997. The Chinese government has engaged in a major process of state-led mergers, regrouping, factory closures, layoffs, and privatization that may yet seal the fate of the Communist leadership.[4] Interestingly, even in a totalitarian system such as China, the political autonomy of reformers was limited on the issue of restructuring until 1997. A coalition of local party leaders, managers, labor, and banks had a lock on effective SOE restructuring.[5] The fear of social unrest provided a further rationale against restructuring. The government pursued so-called urban reforms that modified the incentives for managers and decentralized SOEs. Yet these partial reforms did not remove guarantees over employment (the "iron rice bowl") and the soft-budget constraint of SOEs (Oi 2005, 2006).

Things changed after 1997 under a surge of strong political leadership. With the acquiescence of President Jiang Zemin, Prime Minister Zhu Rongji injected political capital into the process of SOE restructuring, breaking coalitional deadlocks. To circumvent opposition, he created high-level commissions that were insulated from interest groups and provided a venue to steer reforms from the top (similar to the ICC in Japan). He also encouraged reform experimentation.[6] Under his leadership, new framework rules

4. See also the debate on corporate restructuring in Latin America (Fajnzylber 1990).
5. See Oi (2005). This section Also relies on an unpublished manuscript by the author on SOE restructuring in China (1998).
6. On the issue of reform experimentation, I am grateful to Sebastian Heilmann for great insights (discussion during conference at Stanford University on Systemic Restructuring in East Asia, June 2006).

for SOE restructuring were established, many SOEs were liquidated or privatized and others were merged into roughly one thousand "national champions" (emulating Korean *chaebols*).[7] Between 1997 and 2002, nearly 30 million SOE workers were laid off.[8] In February 2006, China took a further big step toward corporate restructuring when it declared that it would adopt the global IFRS accounting rules, joining Canada, the EU, and others in the process—and moving ahead of Japan.[9]

Interestingly Zhu relied on delegation to local governments and specific commissions. He also used the WTO as a potential external deus ex machina. By accepting strict conditions on SOE restructuring in the WTO agreement for China's entry into the organization in 2002, he effectively delegated politically difficult reforms to the external level and enlarged his political space. Finally it is important to note that owing to a closed capital account in China, foreign equity investors are not present as of 2006. However the large merger and acquisition flows within foreign direct investment (FDI) act as an equivalent transmitter of global investor preferences. China may also be acting in anticipation of the actual future flows and thus already reacting to the incentives of the golden bargain.

India presents an interesting contrast. India is currently an attractive target for global portfolio investors and the sirens of the golden bargain are knocking at its door. Portfolio investors have brought more cash into the Indian stock market in 2004 and 2005 alone than in the previous eleven years combined.[10] This led to a boom in the stock market (up 50 percent in 2005). However to keep these levels of equity inflows, move India to the next level of growth (beyond the current 6 percent per annum), and rival China's speed, many foreign investors are calling for more liberalization, changes in labor laws, and changes in infrastructure.[11] India has not yet reached the tipping point in structural reform and recent analysts report a long list of interested foreign investors (both equity investors and FDI-types) waiting for that moment to occur.[12] In its February 2006 report, the

7. See Oi's (2005) excellent analysis of the different forms of corporate restructuring in China. Oi shows how fears of instability influenced the choices made by China's leaders over the type of restructuring.

8. Cai Yongshun, "Industrial Restructuring in China: The Distribution of Reform Cost," Presentation at Stanford University, Asia/Pacific Research Center, June 2006 (1). The exact figure is 27.2 million laid-off workers. For systematic data on laid-off workers and the associated protest movement, see Cai (2002, 2006).

9. Richard McGregor, "China to Adopt Global Accounting Code," *Financial Times*, 16 February 2006, p. 6.

10. "India and Globalization: Surging with Self-Confidence and Ambition," a special report of the *Financial Times*, 26 January 2006, p. 1.

11. See, for example, "Now for the Hard Part: A Survey of Business in India," *Economist*, 3 June 2006, p. 1.

12. "India and Globalization" *Financial Times*, 26 January 2006, p. 1.

IMF argued that only through structural reforms, such as labor reforms, privatization, and liberalization of foreign investment rules, could India attract large amounts of foreign investment and reach a 10 percent annual growth rate. It warned against complacency and policymaking paralysis.[13] However recent years have shown that India's political reformers, such as the Prime Minister Manmohan Singh, remain constrained by unwieldy parliamentary coalitions and the grip of interest groups over the main parties (and the Congress Party in particular). The fragmented party system may be the most significant constraint on political autonomy in India.

Implications for Democratic Legitimacy

Given that political entrepreneurs initiate reforms with the aim of responding to external signals and offering a long-term public good that is not yet clearly in demand, they do so without a clear public mandate. In fact, their reform programs have no explicit endorsement from either voters, party militants (in most cases), or from supporting interest groups. Such structural reforms are reforms from above for the sake of the long-term public good (and the private good of the political entrepreneur), rather than bottom-up reforms. The lack of explicit grassroots support exposes them to shifting winds.

There seems to be a significant trade-off between wealth and democracy. As countries mediate global financial constraints, political entrepreneurs serve the interests of national development and national modernization. They steer the country on a course that is more compatible with a new stage in the global economy, a course that should optimize national wealth and enlarge the national pie. At the same time, many of the structural reforms are neither understood nor supported by the public and the reforms are later presented as a *fait accompli*, which raises the issue of democratic accountability. Although the process of state mediation of global financial forces is a mere continuation of state-led capitalism, it may not fit the more advanced stage of democracy reached by countries such as Japan, France, and Korea. In the 1990s, citizens and voters expected a more deliberative type of democracy and expected that policy processes should include input from civil society actors. Citizens used to support state leadership in the 1960s because of a conviction that the country was under a national imperative to develop itself. But that consensus has disappeared in the 1990s. The situation is the clearest in the case of Korea, where democratization only began in 1987 and where structural reforms and continued democratization coexisted in the late 1990s.

13. Jo Johnson, "IMF Urges India to Speed up Reforms," *Financial Times*, 22 February 2006, p. 3.

As a result, structural reforms are never secure and may backtrack. Reforms may face a party or coalition backlash if the political entrepreneur loses autonomy in the midst of the process. They may also face voter backlash if elections take place before the fruits of reform are visible. Thus, even a country where political entrepreneurs are endowed with a high degree of political autonomy may backtrack on reforms in the wake of such an electoral response. Fast reformers may need to halt the process. A rapidly reforming Korea faced just such a backlash around the middle of 2000. On the one hand, labor organized massive strikes in the winter of 2000 in opposition to the continuation of *chaebol* reforms. They were joined in that opposition by some of the public and by opposition politicians. On the other hand, in the spring of 2001, the Federation of Korean Industry, the official mouthpiece for *chaebol* interests, organized a high-level convention, and submitted a formal request to the government to revise some of the *chaebol* reforms. They also promised non-compliance and opposition by all means possible if the government did not change course. Meanwhile, in France, the spring of 2001 saw the first appearance of nationwide boycotts, along with strikes and protests by a large portion of the public in response to major restructuring plans by Danone and Marks & Spencer. These groups, with the support of a majority of the French population, called on the state to pass counter-reforms that would make industrial restructuring more difficult. In turn, the growing opposition to corporate restructuring, privatization, and other corporate reforms played a role in the 2002 electoral defeat of Prime Minister Lionel Jospin.

The topic of corporate structural reforms in these three state-led capitalist countries points to a new type of conflict over public policy. In this new situation, a post-global "trilemma" is visible. Instead of a two-dimensional conflict between labor and management (or between Left and Right), the process of structural reforms in a globalized era can be seen as a three-dimensional conflict among global investors, domestic interest groups, and the average citizen. Global investors push for a narrow definition of corporate governance, one that focuses exclusively on shareholder value, investor rights, and economic flexibility. Domestic interest groups, including both labor and organized management, tend to fight for continuing stability in the domestic industrial structure. They try to protect the advantages they have enjoyed for decades. Finally, the average citizen is interested in an economic structure that ensures growth and opportunity (wealth), while also protecting a number of social and community rights. Therefore, the average citizen is interested in seeing the state take the lead in creating new types of regulations that are compatible with both growth and social equity. These regulations impose a degree of constraint on investors and lead to the abolition of some of the advantages enjoyed by particular interest groups. When the policy process leans too much toward the support of established interest groups (as in Japan and Germany in 2001–02), the country has to endure high costs in terms of lost growth. When the policy process leans too strongly toward the interests of global investors (as in Korea and France in 1998–99), a coalition between specific interest groups and the larger public may force a slowdown in reform.

A top-down reform process that sidelines mainstream political parties has a further consequence. It opens up political space for new mainstream organizations outside political parties, particularly for NGOs focusing on the effects of globalization. In France, a highly visible NGO has been the Association for the Taxation of Financial Transactions for the Aid of Citizens (ATTAC). Created in 1998, it boasted more than 20,000 members by the end of 2000 and over one third of all parliamentarians. By 2001, its national impact was so great that the finance minister, Laurent Fabius, had to organize official meetings with ATTAC representatives, notably about the issue of the Tobin tax. ATTAC has also developed branches in more than twenty countries and been a significant player in the World Social Forum. Around the same time, ATTAC opened a branch in Japan, linking with dozens of domestic NGOs there. In Japan, its rallying cry became opposition to the wave of financially induced restructuring, in particular—and quite ironically— the restructuring process in Nissan led by French state-controlled Renault.

The process of structural corporate reform in Japan, France, and Korea points toward the growing importance of interactions between global economic forces and domestic state actors. In the late 1990s, global financial actors intruded on the domestic chessboards of major countries and induced an impressive degree of transformation. At the same time, domestic political entrepreneurs mediated this process of change. The end result is a constellation of distinct outcomes and the appearance of new political dynamics.

Of Human Agency and Societal Change

Ultimately, this book brings human agency back to the center of political analysis. During periods of transition, empowered individuals who break free from existing structural constraints are the true drivers of societal change. In fact, most economic and political institutions result from the purposeful actions of political entrepreneurs. This was Machiavelli's key insight when he wrote *The Prince* in 1513. In his chapter on yearning for Italian reunification, Machiavelli intimated that only a Prince (a political entrepreneur) could create a state. The Prince, for Machiavelli, is the instrument of initial formation, the deus ex machina that can break initial constraints and bring about a new institutional structure. Likewise, for Max Weber, the actions of a Prince are at the origin of the organization of the state. And the charisma of the Prince is at the origin of key institutions (We-ber 2001, 82). Although Weber is remembered as a theorizer of structures and bureaucracies, he remained a believer in the necessity of political lead-ership in the initial formation or reorganization of these structures. Of course, both Machiavelli and Weber saw the Prince as a source of danger as well. The Prince must quickly be replaced by formalized institutions and rules, lest he wreak havoc in the country.

In the end, how should we evaluate the contribution of political entre-preneurs to systemic reform? At one level, they are a problem for democ-racy. They exploit loopholes in institutions, stretch their political mandate beyond its limit, and try to shift the status quo in society. They are hard to control. As a democratic agent of the people, they are particularly prob-lematic. Furthermore, they are ready to engage in Faustian bargains with external actors in the name of the public good. By this interpretation, it is surprising that political systems leave so much political space for such evident threats to operate.

At another level, however, as recognized by Machiavelli and Weber, there may be a good reason to condone the actions of political entrepreneurs. All political systems, and particularly democracies, get stuck in rigid and en-trenched suboptimal situations. As shown by Olson (1982), well-organized and well-motivated interest groups can paralyze democratic decision-making and prevent a system from promoting the public good.[14] Such blockages can lead a country to economic downfall, social unrest, and ultimately, political chaos. An entrenched status quo may be democratic and yet also lead to long-term economic or social decay. Only political entrepreneurs who man-age to find some political space and use it to transform coalition lines have the ability to stem such vicious cycles. Political entrepreneurs are the safety valve through which political systems can adjust to changed external cir-cumstances and internal pressures. At the source of all institutions lies an influx of purposeful human agency.

Appendix

Evaluation of Corporate Reform Intensity in France, Japan, Korea, and Germany

Table A1. Structural corporate reforms in France, 1990–2002

Year	Direct and indirect (through financial reforms) corporate reforms	Direction of change and significance	
1990	**Rocard government** (since 1988)		
	• Renault restructuring plan (−2,346 jobs) + merger agreement with Volvo. Renault transformed from *Régie* into *Société Anonyme* (normal PLC)	+1	
	• Partial privatization Roussel-Uclaf (35% to Rhone-Poulenc)	+0.5	
	• PTT reforms: scission in Post and France-Telecom	+0.5	**+2**
1991	**Cresson government** (May 1991)		
	• Large state subsidies to Air France (FF 2b), Thomson (1.8b), Bull (4.7b)	−1	
	• Renault-Volvo merger stalled by Cresson government	−0.5	
	• Partial privatization of Crédit Local de France (27%)	+0.5	**−1**
1992	**Beregovoy government** (Apr. 1992)		
	• Renault restructuring: end factory closure Boulogne		
	• End privatization total (−27% to 15% state control)	+0.5	**+0.5**
1993	• Loi Aubry (Jan.) tightens layoff law	−0.5	
	• Rhone Poulenc privatized (state 57% → 43%) (Jan.)	+0.5	
	Balladur government (Mar. 1993) after legislative election (Right = 57.9% of vote)	+0.5	
	• Credit Local de France privatized (Jun.)	+1	
	• New privatization law (Jul.), 21 companies planned → Privatization BNP, Rhone-Poulenc		
	• (Banque de France made independent (Aug.)		
	• Renault-Volvo merger deal collapses in Sweden	−0.5	
	• Air France restructuring abandoned (strikes)		**+1**

(*Table A1—cont.*)

Year	Direct and indirect (through financial reforms) corporate reforms	Direction of change and significance
1994	• Government opposes gas and electricity deregulation, EU Commission sues France at the ECJ (given 1991 agreement)	−0.5
	• First Rescue plan for Crédit Lyonnais (6.9b)	−0.5
	• Privatizations: Elf (state from 51% to 13%, keeps golden share), Renault (state keeps 53% due to labor opposition), UAP (50%)	+1
	• Capital injections to Air France (10b) and Bull (11.1b), after agreement with EU Commission (prep. to privatization)	−0.5
	• Telecom reforms initiated (rapports Lasserre + Roulet)	**−0.5**
1995	**Chirac presidency—Juppé government** (May)	+0.5
	• Privatization: Seita (10% kept) (Jan), Bull (36.4% kept), Société Marseillaise de Crédit, Usinor-Sacilor	−0.5
	• State rescue plan Crédit Lyonnais (FF 12 b) (Feb)	−0.5
	• Government steps in to discourage merger of 3 private financial groups: BNP, UAP, and Suez (Jun.)	−0.5
	• Government gives up reform of France Telecom	−0.5
	• Finance Minister Madelin fired over pension reform attempt–negative reaction by financial markets (Sep.)	+0.5
	• Privatization of Pechiney (state keeps 12%) (Dec.)	−1
	• France paralyzed by strikes, public pension reforms abandoned (Dec.)	**−1**
1996	• Privatization of Renault (state sells 6% down to 47%)	+0.5
	• Privatizations: AGF, CGM	+0.5
	• Government suspends privatization of Thomson-CSF (Dec), vetoing project to transfer defense activities to Matra and digital communications to Daewoo of South Korea.	0
		+1
1997	• Reform of SNCF (railway): infrastructure management transferred to new entity (RFF) (Jan.).	+1
	• Merger Air France-Air Inter (March).	+0.5
	• Government subsidies to GAN Insurance—FF 20b (Feb.)	−0.5
	• Bill creates retirement savings plan in private sector, the PER (*Plan d'Epargne Retraite*), after *proposition de loi* by Jean-Pierre Thomas (Jan.–Feb.)	+1
	• Mar. 1997: Updated law related to the Conseil des Bourses de Valeurs (CBV) on takeovers	+1
	Jospin government (PS) (Jun.)	
	• Telecom reform: government decree forces network interconnection in preparation for deregulation in 1998	+1
	• Privatization of Thomson-CSF halted (July) after government veto to offer by GEC of the UK (Apr.). But new plan to privatize as part of EU-wide restructuring.	+1
	• Partial Privatization–France Telecom (20%, inc.). Commitment with EU to restructure/privatize TMM; privatization Thomson CSF (state keeps 30%) (Oct.)	+1
	• Government validates Vilvoorde factory closure by Renault, despite contrary electoral pledge and outcry (Jun.).	+1
	• Government opposes Socialist Party proposal to reintroduce required government approval of layoff plans (PS has majority)	+1

(*Table A1*—cont.)

Year	Direct and indirect (through financial reforms) corporate reforms	Direction of change and significance	
	• Creation of stock options for creators of new companies, deferred taxation on capital gains, included in draft budget	+1	**+9**
1998	• Internet action plan by government (Jan.)		
	• Privatizations: Crédit Foncier (partial), AGF sold to German Allianz (Feb), Air France (partial, state from 87% to 60%), CIC bank sold to CM (state keeps 33%)(Apr.), Crédit Lyonnais (state from 82% to 10% by 1999, agreement with EU), Thomson-CSF (state from 58% to 43%)(Jun.), GAN insurance (12.9% kept)(Jul.), Thomson Multimedia (partial), France Telecom (+20%)	+3	
	• Package of measures to promote innovation, including overhaul of stock option rules (May)	+1	
	• Reform allows companies to buy back own shares (06)	+0.5	
	• Government announces merger of Aérospatiale and Matra		
	• Draft bill to end EDF's monopoly (Sep.)	+0.5	
	• French withdrawal from MAI negotiations (multilateral investment agreement) led by OECD (11)	−1	
	• Reform of commercial justice system outlined (Nov.)	+1	**+5**
1999	• Privatization: Air France partial (state to 55%–Jan.), Eramet (state at 30%), Aerospatiale, Credit Lyonnais, Matra-Aérospatiale merger (and privatization)	+2	
	• Measures to encourage the creation of high-tech companies (Apr.)—FF 0.2b	+0.5	
	• Charpin Report on pension reforms (Apr.)	+0.5	
	• Reform of Caisse d'Epargne (June)	+0.5	
	• Second law on 35-hour work week includes Michelin Amendment (restricting layoffs) (Dec.)	−0.5	**+3**
2000	• Michelin Amendment struck down by Supreme Court	+0.5	
	• Opening of electricity market to competition (up to 30% in 2000, 34% more in 2003) (Feb.)	+1	
	• Package of measures to support company creation (04)	+0.5	
	• Initiation in parliament of two reforms: New Economic Regulations and employee savings plan (*epargne salariale*)	+1	**+3**
2001	• Reform of employee savings plans passed (Feb.)	+2	
	• New Economic Regulations (NRE) adopted. Reforms competition law, corporate governance, and merger procedures. Also sets up independent agency for investments. Lowers taxation on stock options. Tobin tax proposal refused by government (May 2)	+3	
	• Adoption of social modernization law, including regulations to make layoffs more difficult (*Modernisation Sociale*) (Jun.–Oct.)	−1	**+4**
2002	• Important part of anti-layoff law struck down by Supreme Court.	+0.5	
	• March: further privatization (Thomson Multimedia, Autoroutes du Sud de France)	+1	
	• Jul.–Dec.: privatization plan for Air France decided	+1	
	• Sep.: limited labor deregulation (overtime)	+0.5	**+3**

Sources: OECD Economic Surveys for the years 1997 to 2001; Documentation Francaise, *Regards sur l'Actualité*, special issues; *Le Monde*'s annual chronologies (L'Année 1995–2001).

Table A2. Structural corporate reforms in Japan, 1990–2002

Year	Direct and indirect reforms of the corporate regulatory framework	Direction of change and significance	
1990	None		
1991	None		
1992	None		
1993	• Oct.: Commercial code revision (simplifies derivative lawsuits by shareholders)	+1	**+1**
1994	None		
1995	• Mar.: Ban on holding companies upheld	−1	
	• Sep.: Stock options rules simplified	+1	**0**
1996	• Mar.: Labor reforms blocked by LDP	−1	
	• May: MITI decision to facilitate job-changing (restructuring)	+1	
	• Sep.: Accounting changes drafting in MOF council	+2	**+2**
1997	• Jun.: Revised labor law (deregulation, women, overtime)	+1	
	• Jun.: Abolition of ban on holding companies.	+1	
	• Nov.: Revision of commercial code: fines on *sōkaiya*	+1	
	• Nov.: Privatization of postal savings blocked	−1	**+2**
1998	• Jan.: Accounting countermove (land, stock at book value)	−1	
	• Oct.: Twin financial revitalization laws, nationalization LTCB	+3	**+2**
1999	• Mar.–Oct.: Government support for Renault-Nissan alliance	+1	
	• Jun.: Liberalization of temporary work	+1	
	• Aug.: Industrial Revitalization Law	+1	
	• Aug.: Commercial code reforms (swaps)	+1	
	• Sep.: FRC sells LTCB to Ripplewood	+1	
	• Dec.: Revised Worker Dispatch Law	+1	
	• Dec.: Bankruptcy Law reforms	+1	
	• Dec.: Reform of deposit limits put off	−1	**+6**
2000	• Feb.: Independent Accounting Standard Board of Japan	+1	
	• Feb.: MOF postpones tax consolidation	−1	
	• Feb.: Weak FSA inspections (Ochi Michio)	−1	
	• May: Deposit protection extended to 2002	−1	
	• May: Commercial code reforms (spinoffs)	+1	
	• May: Law on continuation of contracts in case of spinoffs	−1	
	• Jul.: Collapse of Sogo, Civil Rehab. Law (no public bailout)	+1	**−1**
2001	• Feb.: LDP measures to prop up stock market	−1	
	• Sep.: No bailout for Mycal	+1	
	• Nov.: Commercial code reforms: liberalization of stock options, electronic voting, tracking stock	+1	
	• Nov.: Consolidated taxation postponed 1 more year	−1	**−1**
	• Dec.: Commercial code reform: limitation of exec. liability	−1	
2002	• Jan.–Feb.: Bailout package for Daiei (¥520 billion)	−1	
	• Feb.: FSA urges banks to accelerate disposal of bad loans	+1	
	• Feb.: FSA institutes tighter rules on stock short-selling	−1	
	• Mar.–Sep.: Special deregulation zones	+1	
	• Apr.: Establishment of Industrial Revitalization Corp (IRCJ), prolongation of Industrial Revitalization Law for 3 years	+1	

(**Table A2**—*cont.*)

Year	Direct and indirect reforms of the corporate regulatory framework	Direction of change and significance	
	• May: Commercial code reforms, option of U.S.-style board	+1	
	• Jun.: Law for consolidated tax payments	+1	
	• Sep.–Oct.: Takenaka Heizō appointed FSA minister, tougher	+1	
	• Dec.: New fast-track bankruptcy law	+1	
	• Dec.: Decision to codify layoffs through law (tighter)	−1	**+4**

Sources: Nikkei's annual almanac, *Nikkei Weekly*, Nikkei Net, IMF country reports, Japan Echo; Hoshi and Kashyap (2001), author's evaluations (last column).

Table A3a. Major "orthodox" corporate reforms in Korea, 1998–2002

Year	Type I reforms: Corporate governance framework	Direction of change and intensity	
1998	• Feb.: Transparency and corporate governance (consolidation, international accounting standards, mandatory external directors	+3	
	• Feb.: Accountability, derivative shareholder suits eased, cumulative voting rights, proxy voting	+1	
	• Feb.–Nov.: Improvement of capital structure: removal of restriction on capital infusion. Improvement of bank capital structure. Asset-backed securities, debt-to-equity swaps.	+2	
	• Feb.–Apr.: Corporate restructuring: adoption of corporate-split system, liberalization and simplification of M&A procedures	+1	
	• Feb.: Bankruptcy reform	+2	
	• Oct.: Prohibition of cross-debt guarantees among affiliates in unrelated industries by the end of 1998, others by 2000.	+2	**+11**
1999	None		
2000	• Apr.: Prohibition of cross-company investments over 25%	+1	
	• Jun.: Revised corporate governance reforms (lawsuit threshold, 25% external director requirement)	+2	**+3**
2001	• Mar.: Bankruptcy reform (pre-packaged bankruptcy)	+1	
	• Dec.: Transparency reforms (FSC): increase in disclosure	+1	**+2**
2002	None	0	

	Type II reforms: Bank-led restructuring		
1997	• Nov.: Financial reform legislation dies in parliament. Finance Minister Kang is dismissed (absence of reforms)		**−1**
1998	• Apr.: Establishment of Financial Supervisory Commission (FSC)	+1	
	• Apr.–Jun.: Prudential regulation: mark-to-market securities, banking disclosure, loan procedures, BIS capital ratio, etc.	+1	
	• May–Jun.: Exit of non-viable firms: creditor banks establish formal review committees to assess the viability of 313 client firms showing financial weaknesses. 55 firms classified as non-viable.	+2	
	• Jun.: Closure of 5 commercial banks	+1	
	• Oct.: The FSC imposes limits on financial institutions' holdings of bonds issued by the top 5 *chaebols*	+2	
	• Corporate workout programs: creditor-corporation negotiations	+2	**+9**
1999	• Intensification of corporate workout programs	+3	**+3**
2000	• Sep.: 2d stage of financial restructuring program, W40 trillion	+2	
	• Oct.: Tighter FSC criteria to select viable firms (bank lending)	+1	**+3**
2001	• Jan.: "Corporate restructuring vehicle" setup by banks and FSC		**+1**
2002	• Oct.: New Daewoo reorganization through creditors		**+1**

Sources: Joh 1999; Korea Institute for International Economic Policy 1998a, b; Ministry of Finance and Economy 1998; Organisation for Economic Co-operation and Development 1996.

Table A3b. Direct state interventions in corporate restructuring (Type III actions)

Year	Structural reform targeting corporate restructuring	Direction and intensity of change	
1997	• Jan.: Hanbo Steel (*chaebol*) goes bankrupt, no state bailout	+1	
	• Jul.: Kia Motors goes bankrupt, no state bailout	+1	+2
1998	• Jan.: Meeting between president-elect Kim Dae-Jung and the heads of the top four *chaebols* (Hyundai, Samsung, Daewoo, LG). Five-point agreement: improving corporate transparency, eliminating cross-debt guarantees, strengthening accountability of shareholders and managers, as well as reducing dependence on debt-financing and concentrating on core	+2	
	• Feb.: Agreement extended to top-30 *chaebols*, then okayed by FKI	+1	
	• Feb.–Apr.: Tax incentives for structural adjustments	+1	
	• Apr.: Newly created FSC urges top 30 *chaebols* to reduce their debt-to-equity ratio to 200%. Requires *chaebols* and banks to enter into "Financial Structure Improvement Agreements."	+2	
	• Apr.: MOFE announces proposals to accelerate restructuring. Establishes Corporate Restructuring Fund	+1	
	• Sep.–Oct.: Big Deals are announced: major swaps and consolidation between top *chaebols* in eight industrial sectors (e.g. swap of Samsung Motors for Daewoo Electronics)	+1	
	• Dec.: Blue House meeting between President Kim Dae-Jung and the heads of the top five *chaebols:* 20-point action plan (200% debt-equity ratio by end of 1999, FSC as regulator, Big Deals).	+2	+11
1999	• Privatization of public companies: POSCO, Korea Heavy Industries, KTCB, Korea Telecom, Korea Tobacco and Ginseng, KEPCO. Restructuring in all SOEs	+3	
	• Important Big Deal: merger of two large semiconductor companies (Hyundai and LG)	+1	
	• Hyundai Group restructuring plan, dissolution by 2003	+1	
	• Emergency plan for Daewoo (4th largest *chaebol*, employing 2.5 million employees). Tough restructuring plan, workout program	+2	+7
2000	• Apr.: Renault (of France) purchases Samsung Motors for W620 billion. Direct involvement of Korean (and French) governments	+3	
	• Nov.: Daewoo Motors declared bankrupt	+2	+3
2001	None	0	**0**
2002	None	0	**0**

Sources: Graham 2000; Joh 1999; Korea Institute for International Economic Policy 1998a, b; Ministry of Finance and Economy 1998; Organisation for Economic Co-operation and Development 1996; Yoo 1999a; Yoo and Lim 1999.

Table A4. Evaluation of German corporate reforms, 1990–2003

Year	Direct corporate reforms and indirect financial reforms	Direction of change and significance	
1990	35-hour work week agreed, reduction over five years	−2	
1991	NONE		0
1992	• Government of North Rhine-Westphalia offers West LB (state bank) a capital infusion in the form of publicly owned housing assets	−1	
	• Dec.: Reform of Credit Business Law (*Kreditwesensgesetz*, KWG) in line with EC directive passed; restrictions on banks holding shares in non-banks, postal savings to be treated as bank from 1996 on	+1	0
1993	• Jan.: Law on Securing the Industrial Location (*Standortsicherungsgesetz*, StandOG) passed;	+1	+1
1994	• Jan.: German Railway privatized	+1	
	• Jul.: Securities Trading Act (*Wertpapierhandelsgesetz*), Fifth Act Amending Banking Act; Second Law Promoting Financial Markets (*2. Finanzmarktförderungsgesetz*) passed; bans insider trading and legalizes various investment fund transactions	+1	+2
1995	• Jan.: Post/Telekom is privatized	+1	
1996	• Apr.: Government decides on "Action Programme for Investment and Employment," including corporate tax reform, support for SMEs, flexibilization of labour market	+1	
	• Sep.: "Action Programme for Investment and Employment" passed in Bundestag (*Arbeitsrechtliches Beschäftigungsförderungsgesetz*): easing of redundancy provisions	+0.5 +0.5	+2
1997	• Apr.: Act on Temporary Employment Businesses (*Arbeitnehmerüberlassungsgesetz*, AÜG) passed; relaxation of the legal regulation of work through temporary work agencies	+1	
	• Nov.: Control and Transparency Law (KonTraG) proposed	0	+1
1998	• Feb.: Bundestag rejects opposition proposal for takeover law	+1	
	• Mar.: Bundestag passes new law liberalizing energy markets; rejects SPD proposal for corporate governance reforms	−1	
	• Mar.: German accounting standards commission established to reform accounting laws in line with U.S. standards	+1	
	• Apr.: Law facilitating the raising of capital passed (*Kapitalaufnahmeerleichterungsgesetz*, KapAEG); companies may submit financial statements according to IAS or GAAP	+1	
	• Apr.: Control and Transparency Law (KonTraG) reduces bank control and strengthens shareholder rights, proxy voting restricted, allows maximum of 10% share repurchases, but leaves codetermination and anti-takeover VW law untouched	+1	
	• Mar.: Third Financial Market Promotion Act (*Finanzmarktförderungsgesetz*) deregulates the provision of venture capital to unlisted firms, extends admissible range of investment funds	+0.5	
	• Sep.: Labor Law Act on the Promotion of Employment repealed		

(*Table A4*—*cont.*)

Year	Direct corporate reforms and indirect financial reforms	Direction of change and significance
	• Dec.: "Alliance for Jobs, Training and Competitiveness" (*Bündnis für Arbeit, Ausbildung und Wettbewerbsfähigkeit*) established as a new permanent tripartite arrangement at national level, including regular top-level talks between the leading representatives of all three parties as well as various joint working groups	+0.5 **+5**
1999	• Aug.: Law implementing European Council decisions on transparency of annual reports and international accounting standards (*Kapitalgesellschaften- und Co-Richtlinie-Gesetz*, KapCoRiLiG) proposed	0 **0**
2000	• Jan.: Bündnis für Arbeit issues unprecedented tripartite recommendations for the collective bargaining round that result in minimal wage increases	+1
	• Feb.: Law implementing European Council decisions on transparency of annual reports and international accounting standards (KapCoRiLiG) passed; allows use of IAS and GAAP rules instead of German annual reports	+1
	• Mar.: Several German *Länder* threaten to block EU enlargement if EU Commission pursues Landesbanken reform further	+1
	• Oct.: Tax Reform Act abolishes capital gains tax, allows for unwinding of cross-shareholdings. Retained and distributed profits of corporations are taxed at a uniform 25 percent from 2001 onwards. The imputation system for taxation of distributed profits will be abolished.	+2 **+3**
2001	• Jan.: Repeal of the law restricting rebates and promotional offers; creation of an electricity division within the Federal Competition Authority; full opening of postal service markets is postponed to 2007	+1 −1
	• Feb.: Government enters an accord with the EC to phase out public guarantees to state banks.	+1
	• Jun.: Takeover directive defeated in EP	−2
	• Nov.: Securities Acquisition and Takeover Act passed	+1
	• Dec.: Fourth Financial Market Promotion Law proposed (*Viertes Finanzmarktförderungsgesetz*); Law on Offers in Takeovers (*Wertpapiererwerbs- und Übernahmegesetz*, WpÜG) passed; restricts "poison pills," grants greater rights to shareholder meetings.	+1 **+1**
2002	• Mar.: Commission for employment office reform under VW executive Peter Hartz installed	+1
	• Jun.: Fourth Financial Market Promotion Law (*Viertes Finanzmarktförderungsgesetz*) passed; legalizes range of brokerage transactions and expands shareholder protection	+1
	• Sep.: Reforms of unemployment benefits passed: welfare to work-legislation (Hartz I)	+1
	• Nov.: Bundesrat blocks Hartz I reforms	−1
	• Dec.: tax exemption of low-wage jobs (Hartz II) passed after mediation in committee (*Vermittlungsausschuss*)	+1 **+3**
2003	• Sep.: Bundestag passes Hartz III reforms (reorganization of federal labour office)	+1
	• Commission on reform of federalism installed	+1
	• Jun.: Law on Promotion of SMEs (*Kleinunternehmerförderungsgesetz*) passed; cuts red tape for SMEs and start-ups	

- Nov.: Major reforms of unemployment benefits (Hartz IV) fail to pass in   +1
  Bundesrat; Law on the Modernization of Investments
  (*Investmentmodernisierungsgesetz*) passed; allows hedge funds and
  expands derivatives trading; harmonizes according to EC directives
- Dec.: *Vermittlungsausschuss* agrees on compromise on Hartz IV,   +1
  passed in Bundestag and Bundesrat.   **+2**

Sources: OECD Economic Surveys 1997–2003; Bundesgesetzblatt; Database of the German Bundestag on Parliamentary Motions (http://dip.bundestag.de); IMF country reports.

Notes:
- The index captures all significant legal changes or government intervention with respect to corporate restructuring, from the point of view of foreign investors (based on tracking of evaluations in analyst reports, publications such as the *Financial Times* and the *Economist*, and the daily reports from Morgan Stanley Dean Witter.
- The changes are captured at the time of passage in parliament (for laws) or at the time of decion for non-parliamentary government actions.
- A government move that facilitates corporate restructuring takes a positive value, while a move that hinders restructuring and reinforces the status quo takes a negative value.
- The great majority of reforms are coded as 1 (+1 or −1). Under a few circumstances, legal changes with a very significant impact and significant trickle-down consequences are coded as +2, or even +3 in a few cases.

References

Abdelal, Rawi. 2007. *Capital Rules: The Construction of Global Finance.* Cambridge, MA: Harvard University Press.

Aberbach, Joel D., Bert A. Rockman, and Robert D. Putnam. 1981. *Bureaucrats and Politicians in Western Democracies.* Cambridge, MA: Harvard University Press.

Aguiton, Christophe. 2001. *Le Monde nous appartient.* Paris: Plon.

Ahmadjian, Christina, and Gregory Robbins. 2002. A Clash of Capitalisms: Foreign Shareholders and Corporate Restructuring in 1990s Japan. In *Working Paper Series,* no. 203. New York: Center on Japanese Economy and Business, Columbia Business School.

Ahmadjian, Christina, and Patricia Robinson. 2001. "Safety in the Numbers: Downsizing and the Deindustrialization of Permanent Employment in Japan." *Administrative Science Quarterly* 46:622–54.

Alexandre, Philippe, and Béatrix de L'Aulnoit. 2002. *La dame des 35 heures.* Paris: Laffont.

Alphandéry, Edmond. 2000. *La réforme obligée: sous le soleil de l'euro.* Paris: B. Grasset.

Amable, Bruno. 2003. *The Diversity of Modern Capitalism.* New York: Oxford University Press.

Amable, Bruno, Rémi Barré, and Robert Boyer. 1997. *Les systèmes d'innovation à l'ère de la globalisation.* Paris: Economica.

Amyx, Jennifer. 2003. "A New Face for Japanese Finance? Assessing the Impact of Recent Reforms." In *Challenges for Japan: Political Leadership, US-China-Japan Triangle, Financial Reform and Gender Issues,* edited by Gil Latz, 43–74. Tokyo: Tokyo International House of Japan.

——. 2004. *Japan's Financial Crisis: Institutional Rigidity and Reluctant Change.* Princeton, NJ: Princeton University Press.

Andrews, David. 1994. "Capital Mobility and State Autonomy: Toward a Structural Theory of International Monetary Relations." *International Studies Quarterly* 38, no. 2:193–218.

Aoki, Masahiko. 2001. *Toward a Comparative Institutional Analysis.* Cambridge, MA: MIT Press.

Arthuis, Jean. 1998. *Dans les coulisses de Bercy: le cinquième pouvoir.* Paris: Albin Michel.

Attal, Sylvain. 2002. "Quand Jospin a buté sur les 'LU.' " *Le Monde,* 28 November 2002.

Avril, Paul, Maurice Duverger, and Centre d'analyse comparative des systèmes politiques (France). 1986. *Les régimes semi-présidentiels.* Paris: Presses universitaires de France.

Avril, Pierre. 2001. "Le cadre institutionnel de la Ve République: la nature de la Ve République." *Cahiers Français (la documentation Française),* no. 300:3–6.

Baerwald, Hans H. 1986. *Party Politics in Japan.* Boston: Allen & Unwin.

Banque de France. 2000. "Les marchés des capitaux." *Bulletin de la Banque de France,* no. 82:31–48.

Bartels, Larry M. 1996. "Uninformed Votes: Information Effects in Presidential Elections." *American Journal of Political Science* 40, no. 1:194–230.

Baverez, Nicolas. 2003. *La France qui tombe.* Paris: Perrin.

Beau, Nicolas, Laurence Dequay, and Marc Fressoz. 2004. *SNCF, la machine infernale.* Paris: Cherche midi.

Becker, Jean-Jacques. 1998. *Crises et alternances: 1974–1995.* Paris: Editions du Seuil.

Beffa, Jean Louis. 2005. *Pour une nouvelle politique industrielle.* Paris: Documentation Francaise–Rapport au Président de la République.

Berger, Suzanne. 2006. "Representation in Trouble." In *Changing France: The Politics that Markets Make,* edited by Pepper Culpepper, Peter A. Hall, and Bruno Palier, 276–91. New York: Palgrave Macmillan.

Berger, Suzanne, and Ronald Philip Dore. 1996. *National Diversity and Global Capitalism.* Ithaca: Cornell University Press.

Besson, Eric. 2000. *Rapport: Nouvelles régulations économiques. Tome I: Examen des articles.* Paris: Assemblée Nationale.

Beyer, Juergen, and Martin Hoepner. 2004. "The Disintegration of Organised Capitalism: German Corporate Governance in the 1990s." In *Germany: Beyond the Stable State,* edited by Herbert Kitschelt and Wolfgang Streeck, 179–98. London and Portland, OR: Frank Cass.

Blustein, Paul. 2001. *The Chastening: Inside the Crisis that Rocked the Global Financial System and Humbled the IMF.* New York: Public Affairs.

Bouissou, Jean-Marie. 2003. *Quand les sumos apprennent à danser: la fin du modèle japonais.* Paris: Fayard.

Boyer, Robert. 2004. "How and Why Capitalisms Differ." *CEPREMAP Working Paper.*

Boyer, Robert, and Toshio Yamada. 2000. *Japanese Capitalism in Crisis: A Regulationist Interpretation.* London: Routledge.

Cai, Yongshun. 2002. "Resistance of Chinese Laid-off Workers in the Reform Period." *China Quarterly* 170: 327–44.

——. 2006. *State and Laid-Off Workers in Reform China : The Silence and Collective Action of the Retrenched.* London ; New York: Routledge.

Calder, Kent. 1982. "Kanryo vs. Shomin: Contrasting Dynamics of Conservative Leadership in Postwar Japan." In *Political Leadership in Contemporary Japan,* edited by Terry Edward MacDougall and University of Michigan. Center for Japanese Studies, 1–28. Ann Arbor: Center for Japanese Studies, University of Michigan.

——. 1987. *Crisis and Compensation.* Princeton, NJ: Princeton University Press.

Callon, Scott. 1995. *Divided Sun: MITI and the Breakdown of Japanese High-Tech Industrial Policy.* Stanford: Stanford University Press.

Carpenter, Daniel P. 2001. *The Forging of Bureaucratic Autonomy: Reputations, Networks, and Policy Innovation in Executive Agencies, 1862–1928.* Princeton, NJ: Princeton University Press.

Carr, Edward Hallett. 1939. *The Twenty Years' Crisis, 1919–1939.* New York: Harper and Row.

Cerny, Philip. 1989. "The Little Big-Bang in Paris: Financial Market Deregulation in a Dirigiste System." *European Journal of Political Research* 17:169–92.

———. 2004. "Political Economy and the Japanese Model in Flux: Phoenix or Quagmire?" *New Political Economy* 9, no. 1:101–11.

Chan-Tiberghien, Jennifer. 2004. *Gender and Human Rights Politics in Japan: Global Norms and Domestic Networks.* Stanford, CA: Stanford University Press.

Charette, Laurence de, and Marie-Christine Tabet. 2004. *EDF: un scandale français.* Paris: Laffont.

Chevènement, Jean-Pierre. 2004. *Défis républicains.* Paris: Fayard.

Chow, Peter C. Y., and Bates Gill, eds. 2000. *Weathering the Storm: Taiwan, Its Neighbors, and the Asian Financial Crisis.* Washington, DC: Brookings Institution Press.

Chuo University, Ikuokai Institute. 2006. Shouhou (kaishahou) kaisei no rekishi (document for bar exam preparation).

Cioffi, John. 2002. "Restructuring 'Germany Inc.': The Politics of Company and Takeover Law Reform in Germany and in the European Union." *Law and Policy* 24, no. 4:355–402.

Cioffi, John, and Martin Höpner. 2004. "The Political Paradox of Finance Capitalism: Interests, Preferences, and Center-Left Party Politics in Corporate Governance Reform." Paper presented at the APSA, September, Chicago.

Clifford, Mark L. 1998. *Troubled Tiger: Businessmen, Bureaucrats, and Generals in South Korea.* New York: M.E. Sharpe.

Cohen, Elie. 1989. *L'Etat brancardier: politiques du déclin industriel, 1974–1984.* Paris: Calmann-Lévy.

———. 1992. *Le colbertisme "high tech": économie des télécom et du grand projet.* Paris: Hachette.

Cowhey, Peter F., and Mathew D. McCubbins. 1995. *Structure and Policy in Japan and the United States.* New York: Cambridge University Press.

Cox, Gary. 1987. *The Efficient Secret: The Cabinet and the Development of Political Parties in Victorian England.* New York: Cambridge University Press.

Cox, Gary, Mikitaka Masuyama, and Mathew McCubbins. 2000. "Agenda Power in the Japanese House of Representatives." *Japanese Journal of Political Science* 1, no. 1:1–21.

Cox, Gary, and Mathew D. McCubbins. 1993. *Legislative Leviathan: Party Government in the House.* Berkeley: University of California Press.

———. 2005. *Setting the Agenda: Responsible Party Government in the U.S. House of Representatives.* New York: Cambridge University Press.

Crouch, Colin, and Wolfgang Streeck. 1997. *Political Economy of Modern Capitalism: Mapping Convergence and Diversity.* Thousand Oaks, CA: Sage.

Crouzet, Philippe, and Nicolas Véron. 2004. *Accounting for Globalisation: The Accounting Standards Battle.* Paris: En Temps Reel.

Culpepper, Pepper D. 2005. "Institutional Change in Contemporary Capitalism: Coordinated Financial Systems since 1990." *World Politics* 57, no. 2:173–99.

Curtis, Gerald. 1999. *The Logic of Japanese Politics: Leaders, Institutions, and the Limits of Change.* New York: Columbia University Press.

———, ed. 2002. *Policymaking in Japan: Defining the Role of Politicians.* Tokyo: Japan Center for International Exchange.

Dobbin, Frank. 1994. *Forging Industrial Policy: The United States, Britain, and France in the Railway Age.* New York: Cambridge University Press.

Dore, Ronald. 1973. *British Factory, Japanese Factory; The Origins of National Diversity in Industrial Relations.* Berkeley: University of California Press.

———. 1983. "Goodwill and the Spirit of Market Capitalism." *The British Journal of Sociology* 34, no. 4:459–82.

———. 1999. "The Reform Debate in Japan: Patriotic Concern or Class Interest? Or Both?" *Journal of Japanese Studies* 25, no. 1:65–89.

———. 2000. *Stock Market Capitalism: Welfare Capitalism.* Oxford: Oxford University Press.

———. 2007. "A Decade of Change: Cosmetic and Real." In *Corporate Governance in Japan,* edited by Masahiko Aoki, Hideaki Miyajima and Gregory Jackson. Oxford: Oxford University Press.

Downs, Anthony. 1957. *An Economic Theory of Democracy.* New York: Harper.

———. 1966. *Bureaucratic Structure and Decision-Making.* Santa Monica, CA: Rand Corporation.

Drysdale, Peter. 2000. *Reform and Recovery in East Asia: The Role of the State and Economic Enterprise.* London: Routledge.

Duhamel, Alain. 2003. *Le désarroi français.* Paris: Plon.

Duhamel, Olivier and Jérôme Jaffré. 1995. *L'Etat de l'opinion 1995.* Paris: Seuil.

———. 2000. *L'Etat de l'opinion 2000.* Paris: Seuil.

Dumas, Georges. 2001. *Le miracle socialiste: 1981–2000.* Paris: L'Harmattan.

Duverger, Maurice. 1968. *La cinquième république.* Paris: Presses universitaires de France.

———. 1978. *Echec au roi.* Paris: Albin Michel.

Economic Planning Agency. 1999. *Kitai seichōritsu teika no naka de no kigyō kōdō: Heisei 11-nen kigyō kōdō ni kan suru ankēto chōsa hōkokusho.* Tokyo: Economic Planning Agency.

Eda Kenji. 1999. *Dare no sei de kaikaku o ushinau no ka (Who Should we Blame for the Failure of Reforms?).* Tokyo: Shinchōsha.

Eda Kenji, and Tomohiko Nishino. 2002. *Kaikaku seiken ga kowareru toki (When the Reform Cabinet Falls Apart).* Tokyo: Nikkei BP sha.

Eichengreen, Barry J. 1996. *Globalizing Capital: A History of the International Monetary System.* Princeton, NJ: Princeton University Press.

Epstein, David, and Sharyn O'Halloran. 1999. *Delegating Powers: A Transaction Cost Politics Approach to Policy Making Under Separate Powers.* New York: Cambridge University Press.

Fajnzylber, Fernando. 1990. *Unavoidable Industrial Restructuring in Latin America.* Durham, NC: Duke University Press.

Forrester, Viviane. 1996. *L'horreur économique.* Paris: Fayard.

———. 2000. *Une étrange dictature.* Paris: Fayard.

Freyssenet, Michel, Andrew Mair, Koichi Shimizu, and Giuseppe Volpato, eds. 2000. *Quel modèle productif? Trajectoires et modèles industriels des constructeurs automobiles mondiaux.* Paris: Découverte.

Frieden, Jeffrey, and Ronald Rogowski. 1996. "The Impact of the International Economy on National Policy." In *Internationalization and Domestic Politics,* edited by Robert O. Keohane and Helen V. Milner, 25–47. Cambridge: Cambridge University Press.

Frieden, Jeffrey A. 1991. "Invested Interests: The Politics of National Economic Policies in a World of Global Finance." *International Organization* 45, no. 4:425–51.

Frohlich, Norman, Joe Oppenheimer, and Oran Young. 1971. *Political Leadership and Collective Goods.* Princeton, NJ: Princeton University Press.

Fukui, Haruhiro, and Stephen Weatherford. 1995. "Coordinating Economic Policies: A Schematic Model and Some Remarks on Japan-US Exchange-rate Politics." In *Structure and Policy in Japan and the United States,* edited by Peter F. Cowhey and Mathew D. McCubbins, 226–52. New York: Cambridge University Press.

Furet, François, Jacques Julliard, and Pierre Rosanvallon. 1988. *La République du centre: la fin de l'exception française.* Paris: Calmann-Lévy.

Garrett, Geoffrey. 1998a. "Global Markets and National Politics: Collision Course or Virtuous Cycle?" *International Organization* 52, no. 4:787–824.

———. 1998b. *Partisan Politics in the Global Economy.* Cambridge: Cambridge University Press.

Geddes, Barbara. 1994. *Politician's Dilemma: Building State Capacity in Latin America.* Berkeley: University of California Press.

Gicquel, Jean. 1998. "Question n° 9 : Les rapports entre le Parlement et le Gouvernement dans la Constitution de 1958." In *La Constitution de 1958 a quarante ans,* edited by Conseil Constitutionnel. Paris: Conseil Constitutionnel. Available at www.conseil-constitutionnel.fr/dossier/quarante/q09.htm.

Goldstein, Morris. 1998. *The Asian Financial Crisis: Causes, Cures, and Systemic Implications.* Washington, DC: Institute for International Economics.

Goodman, John, and Louis Pauly. 1993. "The Obsolescence of Capital Controls? Economic Management in an Age of Global Markets." *World Politics* 46, no. 1:50–82.

Gordon, Philip, and Sophie Meunier. 2001. *The French Challenge: Adapting to Globalization.* Washington, DC: Brookings Press.

Gourevitch, Peter Alexis. 1977. "International Trade, Domestic Coalitions, and Liberty: Comparative Responses to the Crisis of 1873–1896." *Journal of Interdisciplinary History* 8, no. 2:281–313.

———. 1986. *Politics in Hard Times: Comparative Responses to International Economic Crises.* Ithaca: Cornell University Press.

Gourevitch, Peter, and James Shinn. 2005. *Political Power and Corporate Control: The New Global Politics of Corporate Governance.* Princeton, NJ: Princeton University Press.

Goyer, Michel. 2006. "Varieties of Institutional Investors and National Models of Capitalism: The Transformation of Corporate Governance in France and Germany." *Politics & Society* 34, no. 3:399–430.

Graham, Edward. 2000. "The Reform of the Chaebol since the Onset of the Financial Crisis." Paper presented at the Joint US-Korea Academic Studies, The Korean Economy in an Era of Global Competition.

———. 2003. *Reforming Korea's Industrial Conglomerates.* Washington, DC: Institute for International Economics.

Grandjean, Hervé. 2000. *La détention des actions françaises cotées.* Paris: Banque de France.

Grunberg, Gérard. 1998. "la victoire logique du Parti socialiste." In *Le vote surprise: les élections législatives des 25 Mai et 1er Juin 1997,* edited by Pascal Perrineau and Colette Ysmal, 189–206. Paris: Presses de Sciences Po.

Guillén, Mauro F. 2001. *The Limits of Convergence: Globalization and Organizational Change in Argentina, South Korea, and Spain.* Princeton, NJ: Princeton University Press.

Haby, René. 1999. *Regards sur l'Actualité: la vie publique en France, Août 1998–Juillet 1999.* Paris: La Documentation Francaise.

Haggard, Stephen. 2000. *The Political Economy of the Asian Financial Crisis.* Washington, DC: Institute for International Economics.

Haggard, Stephan, Wonhyuk Lim, and Euysung Kim. 2003. *Economic Crisis and Corporate Restructuring in Korea: Reforming the Chaebol.* New York: Cambridge University Press.

Haggard, Stephan, and Mathew D. McCubbins. 2001. *Presidents, Parliaments, and Policy.* New York: Cambridge University Press.

Hall, Peter. 1986. *Governing the Economy.* New York: Oxford University Press.

Hall, Peter A., and Daniel W. Gingerich. 2004. "Varieties of Capitalism and Institutional Complementarities in the Macroeconomy: An Empirical Analysis." *MPIfG discussion paper—Max Planck Institute for the Study of Societies* 04, no. 5:1–44.

Hall, Peter A., and David W. Soskice. 2001. *Varieties of Capitalism: The Institutional Foundations of Comparative Advantage.* New York: Oxford University Press.

Hancke, Bob. 2001. "Revisiting the French Model: Coordination and Restructuring in French Industry." In *Varieties of Capitalism: The Institutional Foundations of Comparative Advantage,* 307–34, edited by Peter Hall and David Soskice. Oxford: Oxford University Press.

——. 2002. *Large Firms and Institutional Change.* Oxford: Oxford University Press.

Harner, Stephen M. 2000. *Japan's Financial Revolution and How American Firms are Profiting.* Armonk, NY: M.E. Sharpe.

Hayao, Kenji. 1993. *The Japanese Prime Minister and Public Policy.* Pittsburgh, PA: University of Pittsburgh Press.

Helleiner, Eric. 1994. *States and the Reemergence of Global Finance: From Bretton Woods to the 1990s.* Ithaca: Cornell University Press.

Holliday, Ian, and Tomohito Shinoda. 2002. "Governing from the Centre: Core Executive Capacity in Britain and Japan." *Japanese Journal of Political Science* 3, no. 1:91–111.

Höpner, Martin. 2003. "European Corporate Governance Reform and the German Party Paradox." *MPIfG discussion paper* 03, no. 4.

——. 2004. "Unternehmensmitbestimmung unter Beschuss: Die Mitbestimmungsdebatte im Licht der sozialwissenschaftlichen Forschung." *MPIfG discussion paper* 04, no. 8.

Hoshi, Takeo, and Anil Kashyap. 2001. *Corporate Financing and Governance in Japan: The Road to the Future.* London: MIT Press.

Howell, Chris. 2003. "Varieties of Capitalism: And Then There Was One?" *Comparative Politics* 36, no. 1:103–24.

Huber, John D. 1996. *Rationalizing Parliament: Legislative Institutions and Party Politics in France.* New York: Cambridge University Press.

Huber, John D., and Nolan McCarty. 2004. "Bureaucratic Capacity, Delegation, and Political Reform." *American Political Science Review* 98, no. 3:481–94.

Huber, John D. and Charles R. Shipan. 2002. *Deliberate discretion?: the institutional foundations of bureaucratic autonomy.* New York: Cambridge University Press.

Iguchi, Haruo. 2003. *Unfinished Business : Ayukawa Yoshisuke and U.S.-Japan Relations, 1937–1953.* Cambridge, MA: Harvard University Asia Center

Ihori Toshihiro. 2002. "Saki okuri genshō no bunseki (analysis of the postponing phenomenon)." In *Heisei baburu no kenkyū: hōkaigo no fukyō to furyōsaiken shori mondai. (The Study of the Heisei Bubble (Vol II): The Recession after the Collapse and Non-Performing Loan Problem),* edited by Michio Muramatsu and Masahiro Okuno, 51–82. Tokyo: Toyo Keizai Shinposha.

Indo, Bunryo, and Hiroshi Shikata. 2003. "Politicians Meddle in Accounting Rules: Lawmakers' Move Threaten Rule-Making Role of Private Sector Boards." *Nikkei Weekly,* 12 May.

Inoguchi, Takashi. 1989. "Bureaucrats and Politicians: Shifting Influence." In *Inside the Japanese System,* edited by Daniel Okimoto and Thomas Rohlen, 185–86. Stanford, CA: Stanford University Press.

International Labor Office. 1998. *The Asian Financial Crisis: The Challenge for Social Policy.* Geneva: ILO press.

International Monetary Fund. 1999. *World Economic Outlook.* International Monetary Fund.

——. 2000. *World Economic Outlook.* International Monetary Fund.

——. 2001. "Japan: Economic and Policy Developments," IMF Country Report #01/221. Washington, DC: IMF. Available at www.imf.org/external/pubs/ft/scr/2001/cr01221 .pdf.

——. 2005a. *International Financial Statistics*. International Monetary Fund.

——. 2005b. *Portfolio Investment: CPIS* (Coordinated Investment Portfolio Survey) Data.

Izraëlewicz, Erik. 1999. *Le capitalisme zinzin*. Paris: B. Grasset.

Jabko, Nicolas. 1999. "In the Name of the Market: How the European Commission Paved the Way for Monetary Union." *Journal of European Public Policy* 6, no. 3:475–95.

——. 2006. *Playing the Market: A Political Strategy for Uniting Europe, 1985–2005*. Ithaca: Cornell University Press.

Jackson, Gregory. 2003. "Corporate Governance in Germany and Japan: Liberalization Pressures and Responses during the 1990s." In *The End of Diversity? Prospects for German and Japanese Capitalism*, edited by Kozo Yamamura and Wolfgang Streeck, 261–305. Ithaca: Cornell University Press.

Jakubyszyn, Christophe. 2002. "Privatisations: la politique des petits pas." *Le Monde*, 05 September 2002.

Jansen, Marius B. 2000. *The Making of Modern Japan*. Cambridge, MA: The Belknap Press of Harvard University Press.

Joh, Sung-Wook. 1999. *The Korean Corporate Sector: Crisis and Reform*. Korean Development Institute Working Paper. Working Paper: Korean Development Institute.

Johnson, Chalmers A. 1982. *MITI and the Japanese Miracle: The Growth of Industrial Policy, 1925–1975*. Stanford, CA: Stanford University Press.

Jospin, Lionel. 1991. *L'invention du possible*. Paris: Flammarion.

——. 2001. *The Flame, Not the Ashes*. Nottingham, UK: Spokesman.

——. 2005. *Le monde comme je le vois*. Paris: Gallimard.

Jospin, Lionel, and Alain Duhamel. 2002. *Le temps de répondre*. Paris: Stock.

Jung, Ku-Hyun, and Dong-Jae Kim. 1999. "Globalization and International Competitiveness: The Case of Korea." In *Democratization and Globalization in Korea: Assessments and Prospects*, edited by Chung-In Moon and Jongryn Mo, 349–68. Seoul: Yonsei University Press.

Jwa, Sung-Hee, and Jun-Il Kim. 1999. "Korea's Economic Reform: Political Economy and Future Strategy." In *Democratization and Globalization in Korea: Assessments and Prospects*, edited by Chung-In Moon and Jongryn Mo, 247–72. Seoul: Yonsei University Press.

Kanaya, Akihiro, and Woo David. 2000. *The Japanese Banking Crisis of the 1990s: Sources and Lessons*. Washington, DC: International Monetary Fund.

Kang, David C. 2002. *Crony Capitalism: Corruption and Development in South Korea and the Philippines*. Cambridge: Cambridge University Press.

Kang, Myung Hun. 1996. *The Korean Business Conglomerate: Chaebol Then and Now*. Berkeley: University of California.

Kasza, Gregory James. 2006. *One World of Welfare: Japan in Comparative Perspective*. Ithaca: Cornell University Press.

Katz, Richard. 1998. *Japan: The System that Soured*. New York: M.E. Sharpe.

——. 2003. *Japanese Phoenix: The Long Road to Economic Revival*. Armonk, NY: ME Sharpe.

Katzenstein, Peter J. 1985. *Small States in World Markets: Industrial Policy in Europe*. Ithaca: Cornell University Press.

Keohane, Robert, and Helen Milner, eds. 1996. *Internationalization and Domestic Politics*. Cambridge: Cambridge University Press.

Kihl, Young Whan. 2005. *Transforming Korean Politics: Democracy, Reform, and Culture*. Armonk, NY: M.E Sharpe.

Kim, Byung-Kook. 2000. "The Politics of Crisis and a Crisis of Politics: The Presidency of Kim Dae-Jung." In *Korea Briefing 1997–1999: Challenges and Change at the Turn of the Century*, edited by Kongdan Oh, 35–74. New York: M.E. Sharpe.

Kim, Eun Mee. 1997. *Big Business, Strong State.* New York: State University of New York Press.

Kim, Samuel, ed. 2000. *Korea's Globalization.* Cambridge: Cambridge University Press.

Kindleberger, Charles Poor. 1986. *The World in Depression, 1929–1939.* Berkeley: University of California Press.

———. 2000. *Manias, Panics, and Crashes: A History of Financial Crises.* New York: Wiley.

Kingdon, John W. 1984. *Agendas, Alternatives, and Public Policies.* Boston: Little Brown.

Kitschelt, Herbert. 1994. *The Transformation of European Social Democracy.* Cambridge: Cambridge University Press.

———. 2003. "Competitive Party Democracy and Political-Economic Reform in Germany and Japan: Do Party Systems Make a Difference?" In *The End of Diversity? Prospects for German and Japanese Capitalism,* edited by Kozo Yamamura and Wolfgang Streeck, 334–63. Ithaca: Cornell University Press.

Kitschelt, Herbert, and Wolfgang Streeck, eds. 2004. *Germany: Beyond the Stable State.* London: Frank Cass.

Kogut, Bruce, and J. Muir Macpherson. 2003. "Direct Investment and Corporate Governance: Will Multinational Corporations "Tip" Countries Toward Institutional Change?" In *Corporate Governance and Capital Flows in a Global Economy,* edited by Peter Cornelius and Bruce Mitchel Kogut, 183–215. New York: Oxford University Press.

Korea Institute for International Economic Policy. 1998a. *Adjustment Reforms in Korea since the Financial Crisis: December 1997–June 1998.* KIEP Policy Paper. Korea: KIEP.

———. 1998b. *Korea's Economic Reform Measures under the IMF Program: Government Measures in the Critical First Six Months of the Korean Economic Crisis.* KIEP Policy Paper. Korea: KIEP.

Korean Economic Institute of America. 2000. Korean and the Asian Economic Crisis, One Year Later: Symposium sponsored by George Washington University, the Korean Economic Institute of America, and the Korean Institute for International Economic Policy.

Krasner, Stephen D. 1977. "US Commercial and Monetary Policy: Unravelling the Paradox of External Strength and Internal Weakness." *International Organization* 31, no. 4:635–71.

———. 1984. "Approaches to the State: Alternative Conceptions and Historical Dynamics." *Comparative Politics* 16, no. 2:223–46.

Kuklinkski, James H., Paul J. Quirk, Jennifer Jerit, and Robert F. Rich. 2001. "The Political Environment and Citizen Competence." *American Journal of Political Science* 45, no. 2:410–24.

Kume, Ikuo. 1998. *Disparaged Success: Labor Politics in Postwar Japan.* Ithaca: Cornell University Press.

———. 2002. "Kōteki shikin wo meguru yoron, seiji (The Public Opinion and the Politics of Public Investment)." In *Heisei baburu no kenkyū: hōkaigo no fukyō to furyōsaiken shori mondai. (The Study of the Heisei Bubble (Vol II): The Recession After the Collapse and Nonperforming Loan Problem),* edited by Michio Muramatsu and Masahiro Okuno, 109–56. Tokyo: Toyo Keizai Shinposha.

Kusano, Atsushi. 1999. *Renritsu seiken: Nihon no seiji 1993 (The Coalition Government: Japanese Politics since 1993).* Tokyo: Bungei Shunjū.

Labarde, Philippe, and Bernard Maris. 2000. *La bourse ou la vie: la grande manipulation des petits actionnaires.* Paris: A. Michel.

Lamfalussy, Alexander. 2000. *Financial Crises in Emerging Markets.* New Haven: Yale University Press.

La Porta, Rafael, Florencio Lopez-de-Silanes, Andrei Shleifer, and Robert W. Vishny. 1997. "Legal Determinants of External Finance." *Journal of Finance* 52, no. 3:1131–50.

———. 1998. "Law and Finance." *Journal of Political Economy* 106, no. 6:1113–55.

Lau, Richard R., and David P. Redlawsky. 2001. "Advantages and Disadvantages of Cognitive Heuristics in Political Decision Making." *American Journal of Political Science* 45, no. 4:951–71.

Laurence, Henry. 2001. *Money Rules: The New Politics of Finance in Britain and Japan.* Ithaca: Cornell University Press.

Lemasle, Thierry, and Pierre-Eric Tixier, eds. 2000. *Des restructurations et des hommes: accompagnement social et gestion du changement.* Paris: Dunod.

Levy, Joaquim. 2000. "Financial Reorganization and Corporate Restructuring in Japan." In *Post-Bubble Blues: How Japan Responded to Asset Price Collapse*, edited by Tamin Bayoumi and Charles Collynsm, 182–83. Washington DC: International Monetary Fund.

Lijphart, Arend. 1984. *Democracies: Patterns of Majoritarian and Consensus Government in Twenty-One Countries.* New Haven: Yale University Press.

———. 1999. *Patterns of Democracy: Government Forms and Performance in Thirty-Six Countries.* New Haven: Yale University Press.

Lincoln, Edward. 2001. *Arthritic Japan: The Slow Pace of Economic Reform.* Washington, DC: The Brookings Institution.

Lindblom, Charles Edward. 1977. *Politics and Markets: The World's Political Economic Systems.* New York: Basic Books.

Lodge, Milton, Marco R. Steenbergen, and Shawn Brau. 1995. "The Responsive Voter: Campaign Information and the Dynamics of Candidate Evaluation." *The American Political Science Review* 89, no. 2:309–26.

Loriaux, Michael, Meredith Woo-Cummings, Kent Calder, Sylvia Maxfield, and Sofia A. Perez. 1997. *Capital Ungoverned: Liberalizing Finance in Interventionist States.* Ithaca: Cornell University Press.

Lupia, Arthur, and Mathew D. McCubbins. 1998. *The Democratic Dilemma: Can Citizens Learn What They Need to Know?* Cambridge: Cambridge University Press.

Lupia, Arthur, Mathew D. McCubbins, and Samuel L. Popkin. 2000. *Elements of Reason: Cognition, Choice, and the Bounds of Rationality.* Cambridge: Cambridge University Press.

Mabuchi Masaru. 2002. "Zaisei seisaku no seikō to kin'yū seisaku no shippai: sakidori to sakiokuri no seijikeizaigaku (The Success of Financial Policy and the Failure of Monetary Policy: The Political Economy of Preempting and Postponing)." In *Heisei baburu no kenkyū: hōkaigo no fukyō to furyōsaiken shori mondai.(The Study of the Heisei Bubble (Vol II): The Recession After the Collapse and Non-performing Loan Problem)*, edited by Michio Muramatsu and Masahiro Okuno, 83–105. Tokyo: Toyo keizai shinpōsha.

Marseille, Jacques. 2004. *La guerre des deux France: celle qui avance et celle qui freine.* Paris: Plon.

Masaki, Yoshihisa. Forthcoming in 2007. *Finance Laws: From the Viewpoint of Financing Receivers.* USJP Occasional Papers. Cambridge, MA: Harvard University.

Masuyama, Mikitaka. 2000a. "Is the Japanese Diet Consensual?" *Journal of Legislative Studies* 6, no. 4:9–28.

———. 2000b. "Legislative Time and Agenda Power in the Japanese Diet." *Journal of Asian and Pacific Studies* 20:65–85.

Matthews, John. 1998. *Fashioning a New Korean Model Out of the Crisis.* JPRI Working Paper. Working Paper: Japan Policy Research Institute.

Mauduit, Laurent, and Gérard Desportes. 1999. *La gauche imaginaire et le nouveau capitalisme.* Paris: Grasset.

McCubbins, Mathew D., and Gregory Noble. 1995. "The Appearance of Power: Legislators, Bureaucrats, and the Budget Process in the United States and Japan." In *Structure and Policy in Japan and the United States*, edited by Peter F. Cowhey and Mathew D. McCubbins, 56–80. Cambridge: Cambridge University Press.

McCubbins, Mathew D., and Terry Sullivan. 1987. *Congress: Structure and Policy.* Cambridge: Cambridge University Press.

Melitz, Jacques. 1990. "Financial Deregulation in France." *European Economic Review* 34:390–402.

Meyer, Claude. 1996. *La puissance financière du Japon.* Paris: Economica.

Michels, Robert. 1962. *Political Parties: A Sociological Study of the Oligarchical Tendencies of Modern Democracy.* New York: Collier Books.

Milhaupt, Curtis J. 2001. "Creative Norm Destruction: The Evolution of Non-legal Rules in Japanese Corporate Governance." *University of Pennsylvania Law Review*, no. 149:2083–129.

———. 2003a. A Lost Decade for Japanese Corporate Governance Reform?: What's Changed, What Hasn't, and Why. In *Working Papers*, no. 254. New York: Columbia Law School, The Center for Law and Economic Studies.

———. 2003b. *Global Markets, Domestic Institutions: Corporate Law and Governance In a New Era of Cross-Border Deals.* New York: Columbia University Press.

———. 2004. "Choice as Regulatory Reform: The Case of Japanese Corporate Governance." Paper presented at the Brown Bag Lunch No. 250, 2004/05/12, Tokyo, Japan.

Milhaupt, Curtis J., and Mark D. West. 2004. *Economic Organizations and Corporate Governance in Japan: The Impact of Formal and Informal Rules.* Oxford: Oxford University Press.

Ministry of Finance and Economy, Republic of Korea. 1998. *Korea's Economic Reform: Progress Report.* Seoul: Government of Korea.

Mistral, Jacques, Christian de Boissieu, and Jean-Herve Lorenzi. 2003. *Les normes comptables et le monde post-Enron.* Paris: Rapports de la Documentation Francaise.

Mital, Christine, and Erik Izraëlewicz. 2002. *Monsieur ni-ni: l'économie selon Jospin.* Paris: Robert Laffont.

Miwa, Yoshirō, and J. Mark Ramseyer. 2001. *The Myth of the Main Bank: Japan and Comparative Corporate Governance.* Cambridge, MA: Harvard Law School.

———. 2002. *Capitalist Politicians, Socialist Bureaucrats?: Legends of Government Planning from Japan.* Cambridge, MA: Harvard Law School.

———. 2006. *The Fable of the Keiretsu: Urban Legends of the Japanese Political Economy.* Chicago, IL: University of Chicago Press.

Mochizuki, Mike. 1982. Managing and Influencing the Japanese Legislative Process: The Role of Parties and the National Diet. Ph.D. dissertation, Harvard University.

Moe, Terry M. 1980. *The Organization of Interests: Incentives and the Internal Dynamics of Political Interest Groups.* Chicago, IL: University of Chicago Press.

Moon, Chung-In, and Jongryn Mo. 1999. *Democratization and Globalization in Korea: Assessments and Prospects.* Seoul: Yonsei University Press.

Morishima, Michio. 2000. *Japan at a Deadlock.* Basingstoke and New York, NY: Macmillan and St. Martin's Press.

Mulgan, Aurelia George. 2002. *Japan's Failed Revolution: Koizumi and the Politics of Economic Reforms.* Canberra: Asia Pacific Press.

Muramatsu, Michio, and Ellis S. Krauss. 1984. "Bureaucrats and Politicians in Policymaking: The Case of Japan." *The American Political Science Review* 78, no. 1:126–46.

Murano Masayoshi. 2002. *Koizumi kaikaku vs. Tanaka Kakuei (Koizumi's Reforms vs. Tanaka Kakuei).* Tokyo: Shinchousha.

Nakakita, Tōru. 2002. "After the Big Bang: Financial Reform in Japan." *Japan Review of International Affairs* 14, no. 33:182–98.

Nakamura Yoshio. 2005. *Sokuhō shin kaishahō: [kaisha hōsei no gendaikai] yōkō no setsumei to jitsumu taiō* (*Quick Information on the New Company Law: Modernization of the Corporate Law System: Explanation of Key Points and Actual Implementation*). Tokyo: Seibunsha.

Nestor, Stilpon, and John Thompson. 2001. "Corporate Governance Patterns in OECD Economies: Is Convergence Under Way?" In *Corporate Governance in Asia: A Comparative Perspective,* edited by OECD (Organisation for Economic Co-operation and Development), 19–42. Paris: OECD.

Neustadt, Richard E. 1980. *Presidential Power: The Politics of Leadership from FDR to Carter.* New York: Wiley.

Nezu, Risaburō. 2000. Carlos Ghosn: Cost Controller or Keiretsu Killer? *OECD Observer,* April.

Nihon Keizai Shinbun. 2000. *Japan Economic Almanac.* Tokyo: Nihon Keizai Shinbunsha.

Nihon Keizai Shinbun (Nikkei Net). 2003a. "Disclosure: Global Race in Accounting Standards Under Way." June 11.

——. 2003b. "LDP Aso: Want a Bill for Choice in Mark-to-Market Accounting Soon." April 2.

Noble, Gregory, and John Ravenhill, eds. 2000. *The Asian Financial Crisis and the Architecture of Global Finance.* Cambridge: Cambridge University Press.

Noland, Marcus. 2000. *An Overview of South Korea Economic Reforms in Korean Economic Institute of America.* The Korean Economy in an Era of Global Competition: Symposium Sponsored by George Washington University, the Korean Economic Institute of America, and the Korean Institute for International Economic Policy: Korean Economic Institute of America: Joint US-Korea Academic Studies.

North, Douglass Cecil. 1990. *Institutions, Institutional Change and Economic Performance.* Cambridge: Cambridge University Press.

Oh, John Kie-Chiang. 1999. *Korean Politics.* Ithaca: Cornell University Press.

Oi, Jean. 2005. "Patterns of Corporate Restructuring in China: Political Constraints on Privatization." *China Journal* 53:115–36.

——. 2006. "Corporate Restructuring and Social Security in State Owned Enterprises: Lessons from China." In *India-China: Managing Globalization,* edited by David Kelly and Ramkishen Rajan, 147–66. London: World Scientific Publishing Co.

Okimoto, Daniel. 1989. *Between MITI and the Market.* Stanford, CA: Stanford University Press.

Olson, Mancur. 1965. *The Logic of Collective Action.* Boston, MA: Harvard University Press.

——. 1982. *The Rise and Fall of Nations.* New Haven, CT: Yale University Press.

Organisation for Economic Co-operation and Development. 1996–2000. *Economic Survey: Korea.* Paris: OECD.

——. 1996–99. *Economic Survey: France.* Paris: OECD.

——. 1998. *Corporate Governance: Improving Competitiveness and Access to Capital in Global Markets.* Paris: OECD.

——. 1999. *Principles of Corporate Governance.* Paris: OECD.

——. 2002. *OECD Economic Survey: Japan.* Paris: OECD.

——. 2004. *Corporate Governance: A Survey of OECD Countries.* Paris: OECD.

Otake Hideo. 1994. *Jiyūshugi teki kaikaku no jidai: 1980 nendai zenhan no Nihon seiji.* (*The Era of Liberal Reform: Japanese Politics in the Early 1980's*). Tokyo: Chūōkōronsha.

——. 1996. *Sengo Nihon no ideorogi tairitsu.* Tokyo: San'ichi Shobō.

——. 1997. *Gyōkaku no hassō* (*An Idea of Administrative Reform*). Tokyo: DBS Britannica press.

——. 1999. *Nihon seiji no tairitsujiku: 93–nen iko no seikai saihen no naka de* (*Pillars of Contention in Japanese Politics: In the Midst of Political Realignment since 1993*). Tokyo: Chūō Kōron Shinsha.

Otake Hideo, and Nonaka Naoto. 1999. *Seiji katei no hikaku bunseki: Furansu to Nihon.* Tokyo: Hoso Daigaku Kyozai.

Ottenheimer, Ghislaine. 2004. *Les intouchables: grandeur et décadence d'une caste: l'inspection des finances.* Paris: Albin Michel.

Ozawa, Ichiro. 1994. *Blueprint for a New Japan: The Rethinking of a Nation.* Tokyo: Kodansha International.

Pagano, Marco, and Paolo Volpin. 2004. "The Political Economy of Corporate Governance." *CSEF Working Papers,* no. 29:41.

Park, Yong-Shik. 2000. *The Asian Financial Crisis and Its Effects on Korean Banks.* The Korean Economy in an Era of Global Competition: Symposium sponsored by George Washington University, the Korean Economic Institute of America, and the Korean Institute for International Economic Policy: Korean Economic Institute of America: Joint US-Korea Academic Studies.

Patrick, Hugh. 1999. *A Summation of the Conference.* Korean and the Asian Economic Crisis, One Year Later: Symposium sponsored by George Washington University, the Korean Economic Institute of America, and the Korean Institute for International Economic Policy: Korean Economic Institute of America: Joint US-Korea Academic Studies.

———. 2004. *Evolving Corporate Governance in Japan.* Working Paper Series No. 220. New York: Center on Japanese Economy and Business, Columbia Business School.

Pauly, Louis. 1999. "Good Governance and Bad Policy: The Perils of International Organizational Overextension." *Review of International Political Economy* 6, no. 4:401–24.

Pauly, Louis, and Simon Reich. 1997. "National Structures and Multinational Corporate Behavior: Enduring Differences in the Age of Globalization." *International Organization* 51, no. 1:1–30.

Peillon, Luc. 2000. *Utile mais timide, la loi sur les nouvelles regulations economiques.* www.cfdt.fr/edito.htm.

Pempel, T. J. 1999a. "Structural Gaiatsu: International Finance and Political Change in Japan." *Comparative Political Studies* 32, no. 8:907–37.

———. 1999b. *The Politics of the Asian Economic Crisis.* Ithaca: Cornell University Press.

Pempel, T.J., and Keiichi Tsunekawa. 1979. "Corporatism without Labor? The Japanese Anomaly." In *Trends Toward Corporatist Intermediation,* edited by Phillippe Schmitter and Gerhard Lehmbruch, 231–70. Beverly Hills, CA: Sage Publications.

Perrineau, Pascal, and Colette Ysmal. 1998. *Le Vote Surprise: Les Elections Legislatives des 25 Mai et 1er Juin 1997.* Paris: Presses de Sciences Po.

Pingaud, Denis. 2002. *L'impossible défaite.* Paris: Seuil.

Polanyi, Karl. 1944. *The Great Transformation: The Political and Economy Origins of Our Time.* Boston, MA: Beacon Press.

Ponssard, Jean-Pierre. 2000. *Montee en puissance des fonds d'investissement étrangers et impact sur la gestion des entreprises industrielles.* Paris: DIGITIP (Ministry of Industry).

Popkin, Samuel L. 1991. *The Reasoning Voter: Communication and Persuasion in Presidential Campaigns.* Chicago, IL: University of Chicago Press.

Prestowitz, Clyde. 1988. *Trading Places.* New York: Basic Books Inc.

Rajan, Raghuram, and Luigi Zingales. 2004. *Saving Capitalism from the Capitalists: Unleashing the Power of Financial Markets to Create Wealth and Spread Opportunity.* Princeton, NJ: Princeton University Press.

Rhodes, Martin, and Yves Mény. 1998. *The Future of European Welfare: A New Social Contract?* New York: St. Martin's Press.

Riker, William H. 1982. *Liberalism against Populism: A Confrontation between the Theory of Democracy and the Theory of Social Choice.* San Francisco, A: W.H. Freeman.

——. 1986. *The Art of Political Manipulation.* New Haven, CT: Yale University Press.

Roach, Stephen S. 1998. *Special Economic Study: Global Restructuring: Lessons, Myths, and Challenges.* International Investment Research. New York: Morgan Stanley Dean Witter.

Roe, Mark J. 2002. *Political Determinants of Corporate Governance.* New York: Oxford University Press.

Rosanvallon, Pierre. 1995. *La nouvelle question sociale: repenser l'Etat-providence.* Paris: Éditions du Seuil.

——. 2004. *Le modèle politique français: la société civile contre le jacobinisme de 1789 à nos jours.* Paris: Seuil.

Rose, Richard. 1991. "Prime Ministers in Parliamentary Democracies." *West European Politics,* 14, no. 2:9–24.

Rousseau, Jean-Jacques. 1762. *Du contract social, ou Principes du droit politique.* Amsterdam: Chez Marc Michel Rey.

Ruggie, John Gerard. 1982. "International Regimes, Transactions, and Change: Embedded Liberalism in the Postwar Economic Order." *International Organization* 36, no. 2:379–415.

Sabel, Charles F. 1982. *Work and Politics: The Division of Labor in Industry.* Cambridge: Cambridge University Press.

——. 1997. "Constitutional Orders: Trust Building and Response to Change." In *Contemporary Capitalism: The Embeddedness of Institutions,* edited by Robert Boyer and Rogers Hollingsworth, 154–88. Cambridge: Cambridge University Press.

Sakakibara, Eisuke. 1993. *Beyond Capitalism: The Japanese Model of Market Economics.* Lanham, MD: University Press of America.

——. 1997. Change and Continuity in Modern Japan. *Japan Echo,* 24, special issue. Tokyo: Japan Echo, Inc.

Samuels, Richard. 2003a. "Leadership and Political Change in Japan: The Case of the Second Rincho." *Journal of Japanese Studies* 29, no. 1:1–31.

——. 2003b. *Machiavelli's Children: Leaders and Their Legacies in Italy and Japan.* Ithaca: Cornell University Press.

Sandholtz, Wayne, and John Zysman. 1989. "1992: Recasting the European Bargain." *World Politics* 42, no. 1:95–128.

Sautter, Christian. 1996. *La france au miroir du Japon.* Paris: Editions Odile Jacob.

Schaede, Ulrike. forthcoming. *Choose and Focus: Japan's New Business Strategies and Small Firms.*

Scharpf, Fritz. 1999. *Governing in Europe: Effective and Democratic?* Oxford: Oxford University Press.

Scharpf, Fritz, and Schmidt Vivien. 2000. *Welfare and Work in the Open Economy: From Vulnerability to Competitiveness.* Oxford: Oxford University Press.

Schlesinger, Jacob. 1997. *Shadow Shoguns: The Rise and Fall of Japan's Postwar Political Machine.* New York: Simon and Schuster.

Schmidt, Vivien Ann. 2002. *The Futures of European Capitalism.* Oxford: Oxford University Press.

Schoppa, Leonard. 2001. "Japan, the Reluctant Reformer." *Foreign Affairs* 80, no. 5:76–90.

——. 2006. *Race for the Exits: The Unraveling of Japan's System of Social Protection.* Ithaca: Cornell University Press.

Schumpeter, Joseph. 1942. *Capitalism, Socialism and Democracy.* New York: Harper.

Schrameck, Olivier. 2001. *Matignon Rive Gauche: 1997–2001.* Paris: Seuil.

Sénat de France. 2000. *Japon: Crise et douloureuses mutations.* Document de travail du Sénat no. GA 28. Paris: Sénat de France.

Séréni, Jean Pierre, and Claude Villeneuve. 2002. *Le suicide de Bercy: la réforme est-elle impossible en France?* Paris: Plon.

Shimizu Masato. 2005. *Kantei shudō (Leadership by the Prime Minister's Office): Koizumi Junichiro no Kakumei (Koizumi Junichirō's Revolution)*. Tokyo: Nihon Keizai Shinbunsha.

Shinoda, Tomohito. 2000. *Leading Japan: The Role of the Prime Minister*. Westport, CT: Praeger.

———. 2003. "Koizumi's Top-Down Leadership in the Anti-Terrorism Legislation: The Impact of Political Institutional Changes." *SAIS Review* 23, no. 1:19–34.

———. 2004. *Kantei gaikō*. Tokyo: Asahi Shinbunsha.

Shirota Jun. 2002. *Nihon no kabushiki shijō to gaikokujin tōshika (Foreign Investors in the Japanese Stock Market)*. Tokyo: Toyo Keizai Shinbusha.

Shiroyama Saburō. 1975. *kanryōtachi no natsu*. Tokyo: Shinchosha.

Shonfield, Andrew. 1965. *Modern Capitalism: The Changing Balance of Public and Private Power*. London: Oxford University Press.

Shugart, Matthew Sobert, and John M. Carey. 1992. *Presidents and Assemblies: Constitutional Design and Electoral Dynamics*. Cambridge: Cambridge University Press.

Simmons, Beth. 2001. "International Politics of Harmonization." *International Organization* 55, no. 3:589–620.

Sinclair, Timothy J. 2005. *The New Masters of Capital: American Bond Rating Agencies and the Politics of Creditworthiness*. Ithaca: Cornell University Press.

Sinclair, Timothy J., and Kenneth P. Thomas. 2001. *Structure and Agency in International Capital Mobility*. New York: Palgrave.

Smith, W. Rand. 1998. *The Left's Dirty Job: The Politics of Industrial Restructuring in France and Spain*. Pittsburgh, PA: University of Pittsburgh Press.

Sniderman, Paul M., Richard A. Brody, and Philip Tetlock. 1991. *Reasoning and Choice: Explorations in Political Psychology*. Cambridge: Cambridge University Press.

Stafford, Philip. 2005. "Shareholder Power Wins Support." *Financial Times*, 3.

Stiglitz, Joseph. 2002. *Globalization and Its Discontents*. New York: Norton Press.

Stockwin, J. A. A. 1999. *Governing Japan*. Third Edition. Oxford: Blackwell Publishers.

Strange, Susan. 1998. *Mad Money: When Markets Outgrow Government*. Ann Arbor: The University of Michigan Press.

Strauss-Kahn, Dominique. 1998. "La nouvelle politique industrielle: allocution introductive de Dominique Strauss-Kahn." Paper presented at the Les entretiens de l'industrie: "quelles strategies industrielles pour aborder le XXIeme siecle?" December 14, 1998.

———. 2002. *La flamme et la cendre*. Paris: Grasset.

Streeck, Wolfgang, and Kozo Yamamura. 2001. *The Origins of Nonliberal Capitalism*. Ithaca: Cornell University Press.

Suleiman, Ezra N. 1984. *Bureaucrats and Policy Making: A Comparative Overview*. New York: Holmes & Meier.

Takahashi Ryoko. 2000. *Kigyō risutora no genjō to tenbō ni tsuite (The Recent Developments and the Outlook for Corporate Restructuring in Japan)*. Working Paper (Kojin Mei Ronbun). Tokyo: Bank of Japan.

Takahashi Ryoko, and Oyama Tsuyoshi. 2000. *Insights into a Recent Increase in Foreign Direct Investment in Japan*. Working Paper. Tokyo: Bank of Japan.

Takenaka, Harukata. 2001. "Introducing Junior Ministers and Reforming the Diet in Japan." *Asian Survey* 42, no. 6:928–39.

Tanaka, Kakuei. 1973. *Building a New Japan: A Plan for Remodeling the Japanese Archipelago*. Tokyo: Simul Press.

Tiberghien, Yves. 2002a. Political Mediation of Global Economic Forces: The Politics of

Corporate Restructuring in Japan, France, and South Korea. Ph.D dissertation, Stanford University, Stanford, CA.

Todd, Emmanuel. 1998. *L'illusion économique: essai sur la stagnation des sociétés développées.* [Paris]: Gallimard.

Toya, Tetsuro, and Jennifer Amyx. 2006. *The Political Economy of the Japanese Financial Big Bang: Institutional Change in Finance and Public Policymaking.* New York: Oxford University Press.

Tsebelis, George. 1995. "Decision-Making in Political Systems: Veto Players in Presidentialism, Parliamentarism, Multicamerism and Multipartyism." *British Journal of Political Science* 25:289–325.

——. 2002. *Veto Players: How Political Institutions Work.* Princeton, NJ: Princeton University Press.

Uriu, Robert. 1996. *Troubled Industries: Confronting Economic Change in Japan.* Ithaca: Cornell University Press.

Véron, Nicolas, Matthieu Autret, and Alfred Galichon. 2006. *Smoke & Mirrors, Inc.: Accounting for Capitalism.* Ithaca: Cornell University Press.

Villeroy de Galhau, Francois. 2004. *Bercy: la reforme sans grand soir?* Paris: En Temps Reel—Cahier 13.

Vogel, Steven K. 1996. *Freer Markets, More Rules.* Ithaca: Cornell University Press.

——. 2006. *Japan Remodeled: How Government and Industry Are Reforming Japanese Capitalism.* Ithaca: Cornell University Press.

Wade, Robert. 1990. *Governing the Market.* Princeton, NJ: Princeton University Press.

Weber, Steven, ed. 2001. *Globalization and the European Political Economy.* New York: Columbia University Press.

Weller, Patrick Moray. 1985. *First Among Equals: Prime Ministers in Westminster Systems.* Boston: G. Allen & Unwin.

Williamson, John. 1994. "In Search of a Manual for Technopols." In *The Political Economy of Policy Reform,* edited by John Williamson, 11–28. Washington, D.C.: Institute of International Economy.

Williamson, John, and Haggard Stephan. 1994. "The Political Conditions for Economic Reform." In *The Political Economy of Policy Reform,* edited by John Williamson, 525–96. Washington, DC: Institute of International Economics.

Woo, Wing Thye, Jeffrey Sachs, and Klaus Schwab, eds. 2000. *The Asian Financial Crisis: Lessons for a Resilient Asia.* Cambridge: MIT Press.

Woo-Cumings, Meredith. 1997. "Slouching toward the Market: The Politics of Financial Liberalization in South Korea." In *Capital Ungoverned: Liberalizing Finance in Interventionist States,* edited by Michael Loriaux, Meredith Woo-Cumings, and Kent Calder, 57–91. Ithaca: Cornell University Press.

——. 1999. "The State, Democracy, and the Reform of the Corporate Sector in Korea." In *The Politics of the Asian Economic Crisis,* edited by T. J. Pempel, 116–42. Ithaca: Cornell University Press.

World Bank. 1993. *The East Asian Miracle.* Oxford: Oxford University Press.

——. 1998. *East Asia: The Road to Recovery.* Washington, DC: World Bank.

——. 2005. World Development Indicators. Available at web.worldbank.org/.

Yamamura, Kozo, and Wolfgang Streeck, eds. 2003. *The End of Diversity?: Prospects for German and Japanese Capitalism.* Ithaca: Cornell University Press.

Yokowo Kenichiro, and Yoshihisa Masaki. 2002. *Shouhou Kaisei ni yoru atarashii kabushiki seido Q&A (Q&A about the New Shareholding System Resulting from Amendments to the Commercial Code).* Tokyo: Keidanren.

———. 2004. *Saishin Kaisei Kaishaho Q&A* (*Q&A on the Newly Amended Company Law*). Tokyo: Nippon Keidanren Rengokai.

Yoo, Seong-Min. 1999a. *Corporate Restructuring in Korea: Policy Issues Before and During the Crisis.* Korean Development Institute Working Paper. Working Paper. Seoul: Korean Development Institute.

———. 1999b. *Corporate Restructuring in Korea: Policy Issues Before and During the Crisis.* Korean and the Asian Economic Crisis, One Year Later: Symposium sponsored by George Washington University, the Korean Economic Institute of America, and the Korean Institute for International Economic Policy. Joint US-Korea Academic Studies. Washington, DC: Korean Economic Institute of America.

Yoo, Seong Ming, and Youngjae Lim. 1999. *Big Business in Korea: New Learning and Policy Issues.* Korean Development Institute Working Paper. Working Paper. Seoul: Korean Development Institute.

Yosano, Kaoru. 1999a. *A Better View from the Top: Ministers Give Their Side of the Story.* www.asiaweek.com/asiaweek/99/0108/cs2.html.

———. 1999b The Japanese Economy and the Road Ahead for the US-Japan Partnership. Paper presented at a Speech at the Council on Foreign Relations, January 11, New York.

You, Jong-Keun. 1999. *Paradigm Shift in Korea.* Korean and the Asian Economic Crisis, One Year Later: Symposium Sponsored by George Washington University, the Korean Economic Institute of America, and the Korean Institute for International Economic Policy. Joint US-Korea Academic Studies. Washington, DC: Korean Economic Institute of America.

Zaller, John. 1991. "Information, Values, and Opinion." *American Political Science Review* 85, no. 4:1215–37.

———. 1992. *The Nature and Origins of Mass Opinion.* Cambridge: Cambridge University Press.

Zhang, Peter G., ed. 1998. *IMF and the Asian Financial Crisis.* London: World Scientific.

Zimmern, Bernard. 2003. *La dictature des syndicats.* Paris: A. Michel.

Zysman, John. 1983. *Governments, Markets, and Growth.* Ithaca: Cornell University Press.

Index

Page numbers with an *a*, *f*, or *t* refer to appendix, figure, or table